ALCOHOL AND EMERGING MARKETS

**INTERNATIONAL CENTER FOR ALCOHOL POLICIES
SERIES ON ALCOHOL IN SOCIETY**

Grant and Litvak—*Drinking Patterns and Their Consequences*
Grant—*Alcohol and Emerging Markets: Patterns, Problems, and Responses*

ALCOHOL AND EMERGING MARKETS: PATTERNS, PROBLEMS, AND RESPONSES

Edited by
Marcus Grant
International Center for Alcohol Policies
Washington, DC, USA

USA	Publishing Office:	BRUNNER/MAZEL
		A member of the Taylor & Francis Group
		325 Chestnut Street
		Philadelphia, PA 19106
		Tel: (215) 625-8900
		Fax: (215) 625-2940
	Distribution Center:	BRUNNER/MAZEL
		A member of the Taylor & Francis Group
		47 Runway Road, Suite G
		Levittown, PA 19057
		Tel: (215) 269-0400
		Fax: (215) 269-0363
UK		BRUNNER/MAZEL
		A member of the Taylor & Francis Group
		1 Gunpowder Square
		London EC4A 3DE
		Tel: +44 171 583 0490
		Fax: +44 171 583 0581

HD
9350.6
.A4
1998

ALCOHOL AND EMERGING MARKETS: Patterns, Problems, and Responses

1 2 3 4 5 6 7 8 9 0

Printed by Edwards Brothers, Ann Arbor, MI, 1998.

A CIP catalog record for this book is available from the British Library.
∞ The paper in this publication meets the requirements of the ANSI Standard Z39.48-1984 (Permanence of Paper).

Library of Congress Cataloging-in-Publication Data

Alcohol and emerging markets : patterns, problems, and responses / edited by Marcus Grant.
     p. cm. -- (Series on alcohol in society / International Center for Alcohol Policies)
   Includes bibliographical references and index.
   ISBN 0-87630-978-3 (case : alk. paper)
   1. Alcoholic beverage industry. 2. Alcoholic beverage industry--Government policy. 3. Drinking of alcoholic beverages--Social aspects. 4. Alcoholic beverages--Marketing. I. Grant, Marcus. II. Series: Series on alcohol in society.
HD9350.6.A48   1998
380.1'456631--dc21   98-29521
                                  CIP

ISBN 0-87630-978-3

Contents

PART 2—ENCOURAGING BETTER PRACTICE

Contributors

WILSON ACUDA
University of Zimbabwe
Harare, Zimbabwe

JEFFREY DAY
The Drug Addiction Research Unit
University of Hong Kong
Hong Kong, China

MARCUS GRANT
International Center for Alcohol Policies
Washington, D.C., USA

JUDITH HARWIN
School of Cultural and Community Studies
University of Sussex
Sussex, UK

ALAN HAWORTH
National Mental Health Resource Center
University of Zambia
Lusaka, Zambia

DWIGHT HEATH
Brown University
Providence, Rhode Island, USA

ELENI HOUGHTON
International Center for Alcohol Policies
Washington, D.C., USA

ATANAS IONTCHEV
National Center for Addictions
Sofia, Bulgaria

MOHAN ISAAC
National Institute of Mental Health &
  Neurosciences
Bangalore, India

DAYANATH JAYASURIYA
UNDCP Regional Office
New Delhi, India

SHANTI JAYASURIYA
Independent Attorney-at-Law
New Delhi, India

JENNIFER KAST
International Center for Alcohol Policies
Washington, D.C., USA

ENRIQUE MADRIGAL
World Health Organization/Pan American
Health Organization
Washington, D.C., USA

MARIA ELENA MEDINA-MORA
Mexican Institute of Psychiatry
San Lorenzo Huipilco, Mexico

GAYE PEDLOW
Diageo plc
(formerly Guinness plc)
London, UK

ANDREI VROUBLEVSKY
State Research Center on Addictions
Moscow, Russian Federation

BRENDAN WALSH
University College
Dublin, Ireland

SHEN YUCUN
Institute of Mental Health
Beijing Medical University
Beijing, China

WANG ZUXIN
Institute of Mental Health
Beijing Medical University
Beijing, China

Acknowledgments

The editor wishes to acknowledge the invaluable contribution of Eleni Houghton, who coordinated the editorial process, and of Jennifer Kast, who undertook the final editing of all the chapters. Both demonstrated endless sound judgement and patience in dealing with the many problems of a multi-authored book with contributions from around the world. In addition, David Thompson is to be thanked for his meticulous attention to detail in providing technical editorial commentary. Marjana Martinic, Linda Schmidt, Sally Carreiro, and Tatiana Metody all provided help at various stages in the process of bringing this book to completion.

Chapter 1

Introduction: Drinking Patterns and Policy Development

Marcus Grant, Eleni Houghton, and Jennifer Kast

THE IMPORTANCE OF DRINKING PATTERNS

This is the second volume in the International Center for Alcohol Policies (ICAP) series on alcohol in society.[1,2] The first volume—*Drinking Patterns and Their Consequences* (Grant & Litvak, 1997), advanced the proposition that people's pattern of drinking is what best predicts whether they will experience positive or negative consequences of their alcohol consumption. There is now widespread support for this position (Duffy, 1977; Duffy & Cohen, 1978; Parker & Harman, 1978; Pittman, 1980; Pittman & Strickland, 1981; Skog, 1982; Alanko, 1992), although most would agree that there is a pressing need for further empirical research to explore the relationship between patterns and consequences at the individual and population levels.

The term "drinking patterns" refers to how people drink and the circumstances in which they drink (Single & Leino, 1997). It, therefore, includes, but is not limited to, levels of drinking. Other components of drinking patterns include temporal variations in drinking, the number and characteristics of heavy drinking occasions, the settings where drinking takes place, the activities associated with drinking, the personal characteristics of the drinkers and their drinking confed-

---

[1] The opinions expressed in this book are those of the individual authors and do not necessarily reflect the views of the sponsors of the International Center for Alcohol Policies (ICAP).

[2] Sponsoring companies of ICAP are Allied Domecq Spirits and Wine, Bacardi-Martini, Brown-Forman, Coors Brewing Company, Diageo, Foster's Brewing Group Limited, Heineken NV, Miller Brewing Company, Joseph E. Seagram & Sons, and South African Breweries.

erates, the types of beverages consumed, and the clusters of drinking norms and behaviors often referred to as drinking cultures (Rehm et al., 1996).

For both individuals and populations, drinking patterns help to elucidate interaction effects between, for example, drinking levels and number of heavy drinking occasions (Single et al., 1994) and to explain how relatively low-level consumers who occasionally drink immoderately can nevertheless experience more acute alcohol problems. They also help to clarify the relationship between moderate consumption and associated health benefits. In this sense, it is both possible and useful to distinguish between beneficial drinking patterns, which can be promoted as contributing to quality of life, and negative patterns, which are more likely to be associated with health and social problems.

It is implicit in this approach that much drinking is either entirely or virtually harm-free (Grant & Single, 1997). This assertion is not intended in any way to diminish the seriousness of the harm that can be caused to individuals and communities by inappropriate or reckless drinking. Much of this book is devoted to presenting evidence on such harm, with a prospective view to identifying how best to avoid or reduce it. The value of an approach based upon drinking patterns is that it throws into sharp focus those negative aspects of drinking behavior most likely to lead to harm to self and others. It also emphasizes that it is not merely the quantity of alcohol consumed, either by an individual or a society, that determines the probability of harm, but all the components of drinking patterns referred to above.

Rehm and colleagues (1996) have called for the development of standardized measures of the various components of drinking patterns and for more sophisticated methodologies and methods of analysis. It is clear that the epidemiological community is beginning to rise to this challenge (Arria & Gossop, 1997; Saunders & de Burgh, 1997), although there is still a long way to go before a comprehensive typology of drinking patterns can be proposed with confidence. A crucial test of the value of this effort will be the extent to which it is relevant not just to those countries with long traditions of alcohol research, but also to those parts of the world which do not have well-established drinking patterns or where the drinking patterns are quite different from those commonly found in North America and Western Europe.

This book is intended to focus attention on the best available information from some other parts of the world, in order to highlight the importance of developing policies that are based on reality rather than ideology. To capture both discrete and common conditions among the selected regions, the book is divided into two parts. The first part attempts to describe contemporary trends in alcohol consumption and consequences in particular regions and countries, and is presented in nine case studies. The second part, taking a broader view, addresses the common issues and conditions among the areas discussed.

The authors of the case studies—all from renowned scientific institutions in the regions or countries about which they are writing—assess alcohol issues in four regions (Asia, Central and Eastern Europe, Latin America, and sub-Saharan

Africa) and four countries (China, India, Mexico, and Russia). Although the chapter formats are relatively consistent, differences in the availability of information and authors' fields of expertise create variations with regard to the depth and scope of the topics discussed. Issues such as past and current public policy developments, prevention programs, and treatment of alcohol-related disorders are addressed, as well as patterns of drinking and the health consequences of alcohol use and abuse. Limitations in the data as well as future areas for research are also considered. All the authors recognize that the available data are less detailed, extensive, and relevant than they would have preferred.

The remainder of this chapter, and the whole of the second part of the book, looks at some of these issues from a wider perspective. In this chapter we consider the importance of the patterns approach for understanding alcohol consumption and its consequences in the developing world. Chapter 11 provides an epidemiological and anthropological perspective on alcohol issues in developing regions. Chapter 13 considers the role of the alcohol beverage industry in emerging markets and suggests a set of guidelines developed by ICAP's sponsors to address alcohol misuse issues in the developing world and emerging markets.

PATTERNS AND EMERGING MARKETS

In this chapter and throughout the book, the terms "developing countries" and "emerging markets" are used more or less interchangeably to describe the regions and countries under discussion. These terms encompass a variety of countries and regions, some of which might be traditionally referred to as belonging to the "developing world," as well as countries that might be considered for geopolitical reasons to have moved from centrally planned to free market economies.[3] The countries and regions in this book can be considered together because, first, they are regions or countries which are currently undergoing or have recently undergone major socio-economic changes. Second, they are countries or regions where there has been a conspicuous lack of reliable information regarding alcohol issues. And third, they represent areas where the international beverage alcohol industry is becoming more active.

Although the world's developing countries represent a vast array of political, economic, and social configurations, they share many similar conditions: weak or limited state capacity; limited monetary resources; ethnic, racial, and/or religious diversity; and increased and growing social dislocation that often results in disorder and migration. Given the diversity among and within developing countries, there is a need to design social research programs that are capable of

---

[3]Generally, the book is concerned with those countries that fall within the low- and middle-income economy classifications of The World Bank. Low-income economies are characterized by a per capita GNP less than or equal to US $765. Middle-income economies are characterized by a per capita GNP between US $766 and US $9,385. Countries with a per capita GNP above US $9,385 are considered to be high-income countries (World Bank, 1997).

addressing and analyzing the effects of social and economic diversity on alcohol consumption. Not only will per capita consumption data be even less reliable than in countries with more highly developed information systems, but use of such data for policy purposes is likely to be unresponsive to the real needs and priorities of the countries. Examining this diversity, using the patterns approach, is the most appropriate first step in developing a comprehensive understanding of the consequences and benefits of alcohol consumption in developing countries.

The political and economic conditions of developing countries reveal a diversity and transformation of cultures, norms, and practices which suggests that a policy approach based on traditional country-specific control measures is likely to be less effective in mitigating the potential harms associated with abusive alcohol consumption than would an approach which has diversity as its defining characteristic. Although "large-scale recent international efforts tend to follow the general guidelines" of limiting the availability of alcohol (Heath, 1995, p. 341), many in the public health community have come to recognize the limitations of exclusive or even predominate reliance on supply-side control measures (for a review of recent literature, see Bondy, 1996). There is a growing recognition of the important role that social norms and structures play in forming drinking behavior (Rehm et al., 1996; Rosovsky & Romero, 1996).

The control measures approach is based largely on the assumption that mean consumption levels determine the prevalence of heavy drinking and the type of alcohol-related problems that are typical for a society. Once the mean consumption within a country is known, then one can "predict with reasonable accuracy the number of persons consuming at any level, including the number who might be deemed to be high-risk or alcoholic" (Single & Leino, 1997, p. 13). The control-of-consumption approach, in effect, excludes social dimensions by assuming homogeneity.

A closer look at traditions within emerging markets reveals both an embedded role for alcohol use in society and a diversity of traditions within the individual markets (Caetano & Carlini-Cotrim, 1993; Sharma, 1996). In other words, alcohol has played a central and *varied* role in the traditional social interaction of most communities within and among the emerging markets. Our contributors make reference to this phenomenon in most of their case studies, although it seems particularly relevant in the chapters on Africa, China, India, Latin America, and Mexico.

Prevalence studies and control measures establish the state as the unit of analysis and ignore the cultural diversity of those states that were created out of the successive phenomena of colonization and decolonization. Moreover, the very *emerging* nature of many of these economies means that large percentages of the population live under conditions of extreme poverty, rendering them difficult to account for in larger epidemiological surveys (Andrade, 1995). In terms of understanding consumption patterns and their consequences within developing countries, the state represents an inadequate unit for analysis, thus bringing any policy derived from this analysis into question as well.

If, as the patterns concept proposes, "drinking patterns are intrinsically linked to social variables" (Rehm et al., 1996, p. 1617), then establishing an understanding of those variables and their effects is likely to offer insight into how alcohol is used and what types of consequences and benefits may arise from its use. Apparent in the studies in this volume and many others in the field (Heath, 1995) is the correlation between the multiplicity of cultures and the multiplicity of patterns of alcohol consumption within developing countries.

One of the key stumbling blocks in the way of creating effective alcohol policies within developing countries is a dearth of consistent, meaningful, and reliable data. Adelekan, in his 1996 overview of substance abuse problems in the West African subregion, enumerated four difficulties related to central data collection endured by researchers in the developing world: most of the available data are derived from secondary sources (hospital records, arrests, etc.); where national coordinating bodies for research and statistical collection exist, their resources are limited and they are ill-equipped to handle basic data processing; research funding is limited in scope and coverage because of the nature of the donors; and most reported surveys "are of the 'snapshot' cross-sectional design, and are, therefore, limited in predicting trends" (Adelekan, 1996, p. 232). Such a lack of data hampers researchers' ability to create comprehensive pictures of the various consumption patterns within the developing world.

The inadequacy of sound data sources is a central theme of every chapter in this volume as well. The authors' observations do not refer solely to the absence of complex survey data related specifically to alcohol consumption (although these too are lacking). Rather, they relate to the absence of the most rudimentary data, those often associated with basic demographics, mortality, and other standard official information.

The problems articulated by Haworth and Acuda (Chapter 2) are common: "On the whole, mortality statistics from most countries in the region (sub-Saharan Africa) are not of great value. The small number of doctors and lack of medical facilities generally mean that reliable data (for example, from post-mortem examinations) are unlikely to be obtainable" (Chapter 2). Day (Chapter 4) takes this concern one step further, suggesting that the availability of statistics is related to the government's interpretation of the problem. Since governments interpret the problems associated with alcohol differently, they rely on different indicators (i.e., statistics) to formulate policies. Thus, the types of statistics tracked vary from country to country, rendering cross-country comparisons less meaningful. The paucity of data is not restricted to understanding morbidity and mortality; it is also a factor in understanding the economic impact of alcohol in developing countries. On the economic issues of the global alcohol market in Chapter 12, Walsh indicates that discrepancies in data regarding consumption levels, revenues, morbidity, mortality, and so forth, make it difficult to assess the costs and benefits of the alcohol market accurately.

From this, it is clear that there is at least one area of consensus among all those involved in studying alcohol policies in emerging markets, namely, the immediate and urgent need for better methods of data collection supported by increased resources.

Given the want of data, it becomes immediately obvious, upon reviewing the country and regional assessments in this volume, that none of the contributing authors build a complete picture of consumption patterns within their designated areas of investigation. Each author approaches the problem differently, using available resources to piece together a partial picture of local patterns. When reading the authors' analyses, one experiences a sense of both frustration and urgency regarding the limitations of the data available. Per capita consumption, deaths due to cirrhosis, and emergency room admittance statistics pervade the analysis, usually with the caveat that even these data are unreliable and may very well be misleading. Estimates of alcohol consumption generally fail to account for the substantial contribution of "home-brew" and other nonregulated, noncommercial alcohol beverages, despite the fact that these may actually represent the majority of the alcohol consumed in some countries and contribute disproportionately to health and social problems (Moskalewicz, 1981; Crush & Ambler, 1992; Rosovsky & Romero, 1996).

Although it can be argued that the patterns approach has yet to demonstrate its utility for policy and program planning purposes, it would be difficult to imagine that its impact could be less impressive than the current situation, in which policy measures are imported from the industrialized north and supported with profoundly flawed consumption data and unrepresentative snapshots of negative effects of alcohol abuse.

Trends in Drinking Patterns

The aim of this book is twofold: first, it offers an assessment of the current understanding of patterns of alcohol consumption and their attendant outcomes (both positive and negative) within developing countries; and second, it outlines possible responses that could help to reinforce the positive outcomes and reduce the negative ones. In considering the question, What do we know about patterns of alcohol consumption in emerging markets?, we are bound to conclude that we know much less than we would like to. This is acknowledged by all the authors as a significant impediment to the development of policies more closely geared to particular cultures. One important weakness in available data, which it is hoped this book highlights, is the need to move beyond per capita consumption figures to more sensitive measures of drinking patterns. It can be agreed—and this is stated explicitly by several authors—that information on drinking patterns is even more important in the developing world than in the industrialized one. Especially if alcohol policies are to address national priorities, more complete information on drinking patterns will become an urgent necessity.

For the time being, the country and regional chapters in this book strive to provide such information on drinking patterns as is available, even though its inadequacy is acknowledged. Indeed, curiously, and despite all the imperfections of the data, we know more about problems than we do about patterns. This imbalance is reflected in virtually every chapter in this volume. Since the problems described are certainly unlikely to be representative of the drinking outcomes for the majority of the population—or even the majority of drinkers within predominantly abstinent cultures—it is certainly not possible to infer the patterns of drinking from the patterns of problems.

The components of drinking patterns are set out at the beginning of this chapter. The question for which there is the most information is that of who is drinking. Many studies focus on understanding the relationship between age, gender, socioeconomics, religion, ethnicity, and alcohol use. Among the emerging markets, the most work seems to have been undertaken on gender and age. There are, for example, some generalizations one can make across many cultures regarding alcohol consumption by women and young people.

Nearly all the contributors to this volume highlight the difference in consumption between the genders. The women of Mexico, China, India, and sub-Saharan Africa consume less alcohol than the men in their societies. Data available from China suggest that the majority (51.3 percent) of women there are abstainers (Xiao Jiacheng, 1995). A recent assessment of alcohol consumption in India indicated that the "prevalence rate of alcohol consumption was eight times higher among males than females" (Mohan & Sharma, 1995, p. 136), while the rate of Mexican female abstainers is 63 percent in comparison with a male rate of 27 percent (Medina-Mora, Chapter 10). A cross-national drug prevalence analysis of Latin America and the Caribbean countries also indicated a higher alcohol consumption prevalence among men (Jutkowitz & Eu, 1994).

The difference is largely attributed to the power of cultural norms that suggest that women, if they consume alcohol at all, should consume only in moderation. Visible displays of intoxication in women are typically unacceptable. In Malaysia, for example, alcohol consumption by women is often considered an indication of a "lack of virtue" (Arokiasamy, 1995, p. 172). The drinking context for rural Mexican women is also culturally circumscribed, as they are discouraged from drinking outside the home, in the company of men, and before marriage (Natera-Rey, 1995). According to Oshodin, Nigerian women, although often participants in drinking occasions, are subject to cultural norms that prescribe that they drink less than men (Oshodin, 1995). Culturally imposed moderation is even a factor in those societies where alcohol production is a traditional role of women. This is particularly true in sub-Saharan Africa, where despite the fact that women were key producers of alcohol, males "both black and white, commonly portrayed drink and drinking establishments as the 'ruin' of black women and the source of unfettered immorality" (Crush & Ambler, 1992, p. 7).

Such broad assessments of available data do not constitute a comprehensive portrait of women's consumption in emerging markets. The pattern of women's drinking is difficult to establish because the very norms that discourage women from drinking also may discourage them from admitting to drinking. In his assessment of alcohol consumption in Honduras, Bustillo indicated that there are significant differences between the genders regarding consumption, but that " 'females imbibe covertly' and, hence, frequency is difficult to establish for them" (Bustillo, 1995, p. 113). So while we can probably rightly say that more men than women in emerging markets consume alcohol, our data regarding the number of women drinkers (to say nothing about data on how much they drink) does not tell the whole story.

The subject of alcohol consumption by young people is receiving much attention and is one that nearly all our contributors address. Much of the data used to understand youth alcohol consumption patterns (both in this volume and elsewhere) are the result of studies done in schools and universities. These institutional settings afford a controlled population, allowing for cross-cultural comparisons. For example, in piecing together their assessment of consumption patterns among sub-Saharan youth, Haworth and Acuda (Chapter 2) cite several studies of schools and college students, including one among Zambian secondary school children and college students in the 1980s, and one of Zimbabwean school children in 1990. While studies focusing on school and university students are a key to understanding certain populations, they exclude a vast number of youths in emerging markets.

Rates of school enrollment among children in many emerging markets are very low. According to The World Bank, enrolled male secondary students in Zambia in 1980 represented only 22 percent of their age cohort, and female students only 11 percent of theirs. In Zimbabwe in 1993, boys enrolled in secondary school represented 51 percent of their age cohort (World Bank, 1997). Data on overall youth consumption are difficult to obtain, thus limiting our ability to generalize about the broader youth populations. Often, children do not have access to schools and their families live in remote areas cut off from telephones and field survey takers. Moreover, many developing countries have large populations of street children and orphans, a youth population for whom traditional epidemiological survey methods may not be appropriate. Recent qualitative surveys in Latin America have sought to set the population parameters for future quantitative studies of such children (Andrade, 1995). It is this type of complementary use of quantitative and qualitative methods that Heath encourages in Chapter 11.

Part of describing patterns of alcohol consumption is understanding what people are drinking (Del Rio et al., 1995). Beverage preferences vary greatly across and within cultures, depending on such factors as cultural tradition, available choices, and the relationship between indigenously and commercially produced beverages. A common observation among the contributors to this book, and others in the same field, is that typically there is a significant difference between what rural and urban people consume and where they consume it. Rural inhabitants are more likely to consume noncommercially produced products associated with the natural raw materials of the area. Urban dwellers, on the other hand, will be more likely to consume commercially produced and nonindigenous beverages.

Beyond specific gender, age, socioeconomic, and ethnic differences, there have been studies suggesting that differences in beverage preferences may reveal differences in overall level and frequency of consumption among individuals. Such preference differences may influence the nature and severity of attendant consequences. (For a review of literature on beverage types and consequences see Smart, 1996.) In their recent study on school children in Zimbabwe, Eide and Acuda consider the relationship between students' choice of beverage—traditional and imported—and the regularity of consumption. Their study suggests that different patterns of drinking are associated with different types of alcohol and concludes that investigation into beverage preference should be included in prevention and harm-reduction strategies (Eide & Acuda, 1996, p. 32). This is an area of investigation that has received little attention in the developing world.

Political and economic conditions within a society also help to determine what is being consumed. If the infrastructure in a country is limited, as it is in the outer reaches of China, for example, then the distribution of nonindigenous beverages is limited, thus restricting the choices. Sometimes the infrastructure exists, but the political conditions within the country limit access to it. In his assessment of alcohol consumption in Guatemala, Adams (1995) attributed the increase in "moonshining" in the 1980s to the protracted civil war there. The war caused relative economic collapse and dangerous travel conditions, resulting in decreased availability and demand for legally produced beverages. In Chapter 8, Vroublevsky and Harwin paint a similar portrait of the conditions in Russia today. Central to their analysis are the negative consequences of the collapse of the Communist regime and the subsequent difficulties in building policy during a period of political, economic, and social instability. The result in Russia, as in Guatemala, has been a significant increase in the production and consumption of illicit alcohol, as well as an infiltration of the criminal underworld into the alcohol market.

Given the diversity of alcohol beverages produced in the world and the variety of ways they are categorized, it is difficult to make cross-cultural generalizations about the types of beverages being consumed. While a European or North American might stress distinctions based on the categories of beer, wine, and spirit, an African might draw distinctions according to the place of production. A government official might confine the categories to licit and illicit beverages or to taxation levels, while an enthusiastic consumer might distinguish only between what is and what is not available.

The range of typologies offered by the contributors to this volume is indicative of other possible classifications. In Chapter 2, Haworth and Acuda classify the alcohol beverages available in sub-Saharan Africa into five categories: factory produced, home-brewed, factory-brewed, homemade, and illicit. In this typology, the beverages that fall into the broad European category of beer could be represented in three categories. Isaac, in his assessment of the Indian market in Chapter 6, establishes three categories: country liquor, Indian-made foreign liquor, and illicitly distilled liquor. In this instance, production methods (i.e., fermented or distilled) are not distinguished and the prime variable seems to be origin. In their commentary on China, Shen and Wang (Chapter 5) differentiate according to processing method and percentage of pure alcohol, deriving three groups: distilled spirits; fermented wine, including beer, yellow wine, and fruit wine, with an alcohol content of 20 percent or less; and compound wine, including beer, yellow wine, and fruit wine, with an alcohol content between 20 and 40 percent.

Other questions central to establishing the pattern of alcohol consumption are those of the context of consumption. Where do people drink? Is consumption generally restricted to the home, pubs, restaurants, or the workplace? When do people drink? Is drinking restricted to celebrations or does it occur everyday with meals? With whom do people drink? Is drinking a segregated activity where only people of a like group consume together, or do people drink with a mixture of groups? Is drinking a solitary activity, or generally engaged in with other people? These are the types of contextual questions that help determine the pattern of drinking. At the moment, the data on the contemporary context of drinking within emerging markets are severely limited.

Given the shortage of current data regarding the drinking context, many of the contributors to this volume have supplemented the data available with reviews of the historical context of drinking. The contributors have attempted to sketch the historical context of alcohol and its use, offering insights into the cultural antecedents of alcohol norms today. All the contributors indicate a substantial role for alcohol in society, both throughout history and in the present day. Examples can be found in all regions: in China alcohol has been used for centuries as a central element in festivals and ceremonies as well as being a constant factor in daily life (Chapter 5); in Hungary, Bulgaria, and Romania alcohol features strongly in "family and group rituals" and where "religious practices and everyday life have adapted to drinking and its consequences" (Chapter 7); and in Mexico and throughout Latin America traditional-indigenous norms of alcohol consumption strongly influence the contemporary norms (Chapters 9 and 10).

There comes a point, however, when history no longer represents a sufficient lens for analysis. A central characteristic of today's emerging markets is change, both social and economic. Historical assessments of the context of consumption do not address the impact of earlier norms on contemporary society. All the countries discussed in this volume exist in a global environment that is changing through increases in free trade, interdependence, and communication capabilities due to technological advances. Encompassing these more specific changes are broader changes in the composition of the international order since the collapse of Soviet communism.

On an individual and regional basis, countries are dealing with separate but related transitions. There are the political and security changes taking place in Central and Eastern Europe, where new identities are being formed in accordance with democratic governance and Western European affiliation. In Africa, growing urbanization and political destabilization among many countries are causing mass migration and economic and political uncertainty. In Asia, many countries have experienced tremendous rates of economic growth, industrialization, and more recently, extreme monetary instability, while others are just emerging from or still languishing in long periods of violent political tumult. And in Latin America, after working their way through the economic difficulties of the 1980s (and 1990s for Mexico), countries are building new forms of regional cooperation as a means of sustaining economic growth and political stability.

One example of change that runs through virtually all the chapters in this book is increased urbanization.[4] Whether this migration to cities is a response to work availability, as is the case among many Mexican (Chapter 10) and Macedonian (Chapter 7) migrants, or a response to decreased availability of land because of agricultural consolidation or adverse climatic conditions, as is often the case in sub-Saharan Africa (Kortteinen, 1989), the resultant change in physical location yields a concomitant change in the norms of consumption. In rural areas, tradition often constrains and forms drinking behavior; in the urban areas of developing countries, however, drinking "seems to be a phenomenon without any clear traditional antecedents, and has developed more as a learnt behavior" (Saxena, 1997, p. 45). The migration of large numbers of the rural population towards the urban centers results in a diminished role for traditional norms, creating space for the adoption of new norms. One of the tasks ahead is to determine the origins of these new norms and how they interact with the older ones.

Under these conditions of social transition and reconfiguration, the old historical patterns of social interaction are being altered and new ones are being forged. Integral to the course of social interaction are patterns of alcohol consumption, and one can therefore conclude that these changes are bringing with them significant changes in the patterns of alcohol consumption.

Patterns and Problems

The previous section provides an impressionistic overview of some elements of drinking patterns, drawing mainly on information contained in the chapters that follow. If, as proposed above, understanding drinking patterns is the most useful basis for rational alcohol policies, and if, as seems highly probable, drinking patterns in all these regions and countries are undergoing significant transformations, then there is an urgent need to increase knowledge about these changing patterns in order to be able to develop alcohol policies which will be responsive

[4]The World Development Report 1997 gives the following comparative statistics regarding the average annual percentage growth rate of urban populations between the years 1985 and 1990: Haiti, 3.9; Honduras, 5.2; Indonesia, 4.8; Lithuania, 1.8; Madagascar, 5.7; Malaysia, 4.3; Mexico, 3.1; Mozambique, 8.5; Namibia, 6.2; Republic of Korea, 3.5; Sierra Leon, 4.9 (World Bank, 1997). The rate of urbanization is highest among the African countries, the Asian countries coming in slightly behind them. The Latin American countries seem to have somewhat lower rates of urbanization, while the Central and Eastern European countries have the lowest rates among the regions under discussion.

to the priorities of these regions and countries, rather than merely to replicate policies which have already shown themselves to be comparatively ineffective in the industrialized countries. Attempts to transport traditional alcohol control policies based on per capita consumption and to impose them upon developing countries are not only ill-conceived but arrogant. A country's alcohol policies, like so many other aspects of public policy, must respect and find their roots in the culture and tradition of the country.

Since we knew at the outset of planning this book, however, that data on drinking patterns would be extremely elusive in the regions and countries under consideration, we asked authors to provide an account of whatever alcohol-related social and health problems had been documented. Here, too, the data are incomplete and may sometimes be misleading because they are based on small samples which are unlikely to be representative of the whole population. But at least there are some studies in all of the countries and at least these studies serve to sketch in the outlines of those problems which alcohol policies, as they are developed and implemented, should be seeking to reduce.

Because of this apparent emphasis on problems, some readers may find that the book appears to be close to a catalogue of woes. Every chapter seems to concentrate on the physical and psychiatric diseases and on the family and social problems associated with alcohol abuse. Two points, therefore, need to be made in relation to all of these chapters so that they do not need to be repeated in each one of them. First, the health and social problems described are indeed the consequences of alcohol abuse and there is no reason to assume that any increase in responsible drinking will change that situation for the worse. And second, it is only by acknowledging the scale and severity of problems that one is likely to be able to respond to them adequately. It would do no one a service to appear to minimize the importance of alcohol problems in the developing world if the purpose of this book is help propose a better basis for dealing with them.

Thus, in reviewing each chapter, we ask readers to be sensitive to the virtual absence of data on drinking patterns and the disproportionate concentration on alcohol-related problems. This emphasis has one distinct advantage—it provides a kind of "worst case scenario" in which the benefits of responsible drinking tend to be minimized and the problems of alcohol abuse loom large. It, therefore, helps to focus attention on what needs to be changed and should encourage all those with a legitimate and long-term stake in the future to play their part in effecting change in directions that will be to the advantage of the society as a whole.

PROBLEMS AND RESPONSES

Following the chapters which focus on the situation in the regions and countries selected, there are three broader, overarching chapters—Chapters 11, 12 and 13—which discuss the way ahead. A controversial but essential feature of this book is that the last of those chapters represents the perspective of some of the major international companies producing and marketing beverage alcohol and seeking to expand their business in the emerging markets of the developing and post-Soviet world. In the past, this is a perspective which has generally been either ignored or rejected.

There are many reasons why those with a commitment to reducing alcohol-related problems might distrust the beverage alcohol industry. There is a genuine and legitimate concern that, in seeking to develop new markets, companies may find it seductively easy and commercially advantageous to adopt marketing practices that exploit vulnerable sections of the population in a desperate attempt to carve out market share. Even some of those observers who have been impressed by industry self-regulation in mature markets fear that double standards may emerge in which a company will behave one way in Europe and North America, but quite differently in the face of the huge potential profits that could be generated by getting it right in China or Latin America.

The inclusion of the industry perspective is, therefore, a challenge to such companies to demonstrate what it means to be good corporate citizens with a responsibility not only to their shareholders but also to the wider society in which they do business. No doubt there will be those who will object to the inclusion of the industry perspective on ideological grounds, but we hope there will be many more who see it as expression of willingness to engage in a common mission where nobody, finally, has a monopoly on best practices. It is for this reason that all the companies represented in the collective authorship of Chapter 13 have already pledged their support for the Dublin Principles (1997) of ethical cooperation among the beverage alcohol industry, governments, scientific researchers, and the public health community.[5]

Another reason for the inclusion of this perspective is the increasing emphasis within the United Nations system and the international community generally on the importance of public/private partnerships (Kickbusch et al., 1997). It is now more than 20 years since the World Health Assembly first drew attention to the need of addressing alcohol-related problems in the developing world.[6] Since that time, there have been various attempts by the World Health Organization (WHO) to confront this issue. There was a flurry of activity in the early 1980s, which led to a WHO publication on the public health implications of alcohol production and trade (Walsh & Grant, 1985) and an independent publication on the activities of multinational corporations (Cavanagh & Clairmonte, 1985).

The lack of the perspective of the beverage alcohol industry has limited the relevance of much subsequent international analysis. Readers of this volume will be able to judge for themselves the relative merits of an approach which

---

[5]The full text of the Dublin Principles can be obtained from Professor Joyce O'Connor, President, National College of Ireland, Sanford Road, Ranelagh, Dublin 6, Ireland or on her website: www.ncir.ie/links/pecop.html. The Principles also appear in full in *Drinking Patterns and their Consequences* (Grant & Litvak, 1997: Appendix).

[6]Resolution WHA28.81 (May 1975).

includes the perspective of the beverage alcohol industry and an approach which excludes it. At the very least, it is to be hoped that scientists and scholars will always feel free to publish where they wish.

CONCLUSION

As was noted at the outset, this is the second volume in the ICAP series on alcohol in society. It is a book which no one could accuse of seeking to minimize the importance of alcohol problems in the developing world or in the countries formerly connected to the Soviet Union. At the same time, it is a book which is based upon the premise that companies involved in the production and marketing of beverage alcohol are likely to become increasingly active in emerging markets over the next couple of decades. The book, therefore, explores how a balance may be achieved between public health and commerce. Its proposal might seem uncontroversial, even self-evident—namely, that all those with a legitimate interest in alcohol policies should be involved in their design, implementation, and evaluation.

What this means in practice is that governments, scientists and scholars, public health experts, nongovernmental groups, and the beverage alcohol industry all need to have a place at the table. All have relevant points-of-view, even if all of them may not be easy to reconcile. But the days are long gone when it was enough to mouth the words "less is better" as if they were some kind of religious mantra encapsulating divine truth. Alcohol policies are, happily, rather more closely rooted in the everyday experience of men and women all around the world. Many of these men and women choose to drink beverage alcohol; and of those who do, the vast majority experience considerable pleasure and little or no harm. For all those people, effective alcohol policies are those which reduce the adverse consequences of alcohol abuse without restricting unreasonably the freedom of choice of responsible drinkers. What that requires is a balance between government regulation, industry self-regulation, and individual responsibility. And, in turn, what that requires is that all should be open to points-of-view other than their own.

REFERENCES

Adams, W. R. (1995). Guatemala. In D. B. Heath (Ed.), *International Handbook on Alcohol and Culture* (99–109). Westport, CN: Greenwood.

Adelekan, M. L. (1996). West African Subregion: An overview of substance abuse and problems. *Drugs: Education, Prevention, and Policy, 3*, 231–237.

Alanko, T. (1992). Per capita consumption and rate of heavy use of alcohol: On evidence and inference in the single distribution debate. *18th Annual Alcohol Epidemiology Symposium of the Kettil Bruun Society.* Toronto, Ontario, CN, June 1–5.

Andrade, S. J. (1995). Researching "hidden populations" through qualitative research: Ethnographic lessons from street children in Bolivia. In H. Kirsch (Ed.), *Drug Lessons and Education Programs in Developing Countries* (61–79). New Brunswick, NJ: Transaction.

Arokiasamy, C. V. (1995). Malaysia. In D. B. Heath (Ed.), *International Handbook on Alcohol and Culture* (168–178). Westport, CN: Greenwood.

Arria, A. M. & Gossop, M. (1997). Health issues and drinking patterns. In M. Grant & J. Litvak (Eds.), *Drinking Patterns and Their Consequences* (63–87). Washington, DC: Taylor & Francis.

Bondy, S. J. (1996). Overview of studies on drinking patterns and consequences. *Addiction, 91,* 1663–1674.

Bustillo, K. W. V. (1995). Honduras. In D. B. Heath (Ed.), *International Handbook on Alcohol and Culture* (110–116). Westport, CN: Greenwood.

Caetano, R. & Carlini-Cotrim, B. (1993). Perspectives on alcohol epidemiology research in South America. *Alcohol Health and Research World, 17,* 244–251.

Cavanagh, J. & Clairmonte, F. F. (1985). *Alcoholic Beverages: Dimensions of Corporate Power.* New York: St. Martin's Press.

Crush, J. & Ambler, C., (Eds.) (1992). *Liquor and Labor in Southern Africa.* Athens, OH: Ohio University Press.

Del Rio, C., Prada, C., & Alvarez, F. J. (1995). Beverage effects on patterns of alcohol consumption. *Alcoholism: Clinical and Experimental Research, 19,* 1583–1586.

Dublin Principles: Principles of Cooperation Among the Beverage Alcohol Industry, Governments, Scientific Researchers, and the Public Health Community (1997). In M. Grant & J. Litvak (Eds.), *Drinking Patterns and Their Consequences* (299–301). Washington, DC: Taylor & Francis.

Duffy, J. C. (1977). Estimating the proportion of heavy drinkers. In *The Ledermann Curve: Report of a Symposium.* London: Alcohol Education Centre.

Duffy, J. C. & Cohen, G. R. (1978). Total alcohol consumption and excessive drinking. *British Journal of Addiction, 73,* 259–264.

Eide, A. H. & Acuda, S. W. (1996). Different alcohol types—different modes of drinking: The association between alcohol type preferences and indicators for regular drinking among adolescents in Zimbabwe. *Journal of Child & Adolescent Substance Use, 5,* 15–34.

Grant, M. & Litvak, J., (Eds.) (1997). *Drinking Patterns and Their Consequences.* Washington, DC: Taylor & Francis.

Grant, M. & Single, E. (1997). Shifting the paradigm: Reducing harm and promoting beneficial patterns. In M. Grant & J. Litvak (Eds.), *Drinking Patterns and Their Consequences* (287–298). Washington, DC: Taylor & Francis.

Heath, D. B. (1995). An anthropological view of alcohol and culture in international perspective. In D. B. Heath (Ed.), *International Handbook on Alcohol and Culture* (328–347). Westport, CT: Greenwood.

Jutkowitz, J. M. & Eu, H. (1994). Drug prevalence in Latin America and Caribbean countries: A cross-national analysis. *Drugs: Education, Prevention and Policy, 1,* 199–252.

Kickbusch, I., Mitchell, P., Lumsden-Dill, Y., Zunino, H., Litvak, J., & Israel, Y. (1997). Public and private partnerships in prevention and research. In M. Grant & J. Litvak (Eds.), *Drinking Patterns and Their Consequences* (267–286). Washington, DC: Taylor & Francis.

Kortteinen, T. (1989). *Agricultural Alcohol and Social Change in the Third World, Vol. 38.* Helsinki: Finnish Foundation for Alcohol Studies.

Mohan, D. & Sharma, H. K. (1995). India. In D. B. Heath (Ed.), *International Handbook on Alcohol and Culture* (128–141). Westport, CT: Greenwood.

Moskalewicz, J. (1981). Alcohol: Commodity and symbol in Polish society. In E. Single, P. Morgan, & J. de Lindt (Eds.), *Alcohol, Society and the State: Vol. 2. The Social History of Control Policy in Seven Countries* (9–30). Toronto: Addiction Research Foundation.

Natera-Rey, G. (1995). Mexico. In D. B. Heath (Ed.), *International Handbook on Alcohol and Culture* (179–189). Westport, CT: Greenwood.

Oshodin, O. G. (1995). Nigeria. In D. B. Heath (Ed.), *International Handbook on Alcohol and Culture* (213–223). Westport, CT: Greenwood.

Parker, D. A. & Harman, M. S. (1978). The distribution of consumption model of prevention of alcohol problems: A critical assessment. *Journal of Studies on Alcohol, 39,* 377–399.

Pittman, D. J. (1980). *Primary prevention of alcohol abuse and alcoholism: A critical analysis of the control of consumption policy.* Cardiff: International Institute for the Prevention and Treatment of Alcohol.

Pittman, D. J. & Strickland, D. (1981). A critical evaluation of the control of consumption policy. *Conference: Control Issues on Alcohol Abuse Prevention: Local, State, and National Designs for the 1980s.* Charleston, SC.

Rehm, J., Ashley, M. J., Room, R., Single, E., Bondy, S., Ferrence, R., & Giesbrecht, N. (1996). On the emerging paradigm of drinking patterns and their social and health consequences. *Addiction, 91,* 1615–1621.

Rosovsky, H. & Romero, M. (1996). Prevention issues in a multicultural developing country: The Mexican case. *Substance Use and Misuse, 31,* 1657–1688.

Saunders, J. B. & de Burgh, S. (1997). The distribution of alcohol consumption. In M. Grant & J. Litvak (Eds.), *Drinking Patterns and Their Consequences* (129–152). Washington, DC: Taylor & Francis.

Saxena, S. (1997). Alcohol, Europe, and the Developing Countries. *Addiction, 92* (Supplement 1), S43–S48.

Sharma, H. K. (1996). Sociocultural perspectives of substance use in India. *Substance Use and Misuse, 31,* 1689–1714.

Single, E., Brewster, J., MacNeil, P., Hatcher, J., & Trainor, C. (1994). The 1993 General Social Survey I: Alcohol use in Canada. *Canadian Journal of Public Health, 86,* 397–401.

Single, E. & Leino, V. E. (1997). The levels, patterns, and consequences of drinking. In M. Grant & J. Litvak (Eds.), *Drinking Patterns and Their Consequences* (7–24). Washington, DC: Taylor & Francis.

Skog, O. J. (1982). *The Distribution of Alcohol Consumption. Part I: A Critical Discussion of the Ledermann Model.* [SIFA Monograph 64]. Oslo: National Institute for Alcohol Research.

Smart, R. G. (1996). Behavioral and social consequences related to the consumption of different beverage types. *Journal of Studies on Alcohol, 57,* 77–84.

Walsh, B. & Grant, M. (1985). *Public Health Implications of Alcohol Production and Trade.* Geneva: World Health Organization (Offset Publication).

World Bank. (1997). *World Development Report 1997: The State in a Changing World.* New York: Oxford University Press.

Xiao Jiacheng. (1995). China. In D. B. Heath (Ed.), *International Handbook on Alcohol and Culture* (42–50). Westport, CT: Greenwood.

Part One

Contemporary Trends

Chapter 2

Sub-Saharan Africa

Alan Haworth and S. W. Acuda

Many factors contribute to the patterns and consequences of drinking. This chapter will discuss several of these factors as they have contributed to patterns and consequences in sub-Saharan Africa. The complexity of these factors, even when discussing an apparently closely linked group of countries, is not always recognized. Although often considered as a single entity, sub-Saharan Africa is comprised of many individual nation states and an even greater number of individual peoples, each with its own historical heritage. Very often, events which began as closely related regional developments—for example, the establishment and expansion of the mining industry—have diverged as countries have gained independence and started to establish individual policies, agendas, and priorities. Thus changing use patterns and consequences may have been of limited duration as political events have occurred and new liberties or economic influences have come into play.

Sub-Saharan Africa is made up of all the African nation states excluding the North African countries of Algeria, Egypt, Morocco, Tunisia, and Libya. Therefore, it includes countries with vast geographic and demographic differences. Additionally, the region was home to many different colonial occupations, including those of France, Great Britain, Belgium, Portugal, the Netherlands, and so forth, thus resulting in significantly varied colonial legacies. There are, however, some general demographic and economic similarities among the sub-Saharan countries: population growth trends, migration, and economic structural adjustment to name a few.

Given the differences and similarities noted above, this chapter presents a regional overview with some analysis of individual nation states. Analyzing the individual countries affords us more specific information about smaller communities and individuals; the broader overview allows us to discern the larger trends. Although we have tried to incorporate data from as many countries as possible, we have not made reference to every country within the region. Our survey includes data primarily from anglophone Africa with some reference to lusophone and francophone Africa. This parameter reflects the availability of data rather than a specific methodological agenda.

An account of drinking and its effects requires the analysis of many kinds of data from many sources. In our discussion of sub-Saharan Africa we will use historical, anthropological, sociological, and medical data regarding alcohol consumption and production, as well as basic economic and demographic statistical information.

Problems arise in writing about trends in drinking in Africa; a central problem is the lack or inconsistency of data. Data obtained from different sources may vary considerably. This is understandable with regard, say, to details of beverage production in a country in which there is, or has recently been, civil war (e.g., Mozambique or Angola). But even basic demographic data from different sources may prove to be difficult to reconcile and we have exercised some judgment in interpreting it.

A problem which is common throughout the region, and one which is directly relevant to this chapter, concerns research and the dissemination of research results (German, 1972; Carstairs, 1973). The problems are many, including a lack of financial support, shortage of qualified personnel, and lack of laboratory back-up for routine investigations, which makes accurate clinical diagnosis quite difficult. Record-keeping and documentation of patients is also usually incomplete because of a lack of facilities and materials, and patients frequently change their addresses and sometimes names. Furthermore, a lack of a common forum for publication of research findings, exchange of ideas, and dissemination of information within Africa means that a researcher based in one country may not be aware of another researcher in the next country who is doing research on a similar topic; and a journal published in one country may not be available in other countries in the region.

The fact that one must deal with groups of countries rather than individual countries reflects the unimportance of Africa within the drinking economy. This is not to say that there is necessarily less drinking in Africa, but that other factors are important in determining the relative consumption of what might be termed cosmopolitan-type commercial beverages. Many countries have a relatively low population, especially in relation to their size, and, hence, the total consumption will be low anyway. The influence of religion must be taken into account and in all the countries there is a large informal commercial sector and an abundant manufacture of beverages, especially in the rural areas, for home consumption. This fact alone makes the task of gathering sufficient data difficult, but in addition, since data are being garnered from many different administrations, there is little uniformity and often an absence of routinely collected statistical information—or it is not kept up-to-date.

Recognizing their limitations, it is our task to take all the available data and put them into a meaningful and understandable format. This involves not only keen judgment but, just as important, it involves establishing a theoretical perspective and framework capable of explaining the many pieces of this complex puzzle. We attempt this step in the first section of our chapter. From there, we present a brief discussion of the basic economic and demographic trends within the region, followed by a section on the historical and traditional aspects of alcohol use and production. Once we have established the current situation in terms of production and consumption patterns, we turn our analysis to the question of consequences, considering a spectrum of alcohol-related problems and their treatment. Although a discussion of the economics of alcohol is present throughout all sections of the chapter, we address the question specifically after our assessment of alcohol's physical and social consequences. The final section of our chapter takes a comparative look at the individual alcohol policies of sub-Saharan nation states, considering how countries seek to control alcohol production, consumption, and consequences.

A THEORETICAL PERSPECTIVE

As one reads the literature in this field it becomes apparent that various professional biases must be present. In discussing the role of the anthropologist (the techniques and insights are still relevant in these days), Mary Douglas (1987) stated that, to become as systematic as the epidemiologist, cultural anthropologists will need to develop new tools. The debate was essentially initiated by Robin Room (1984) when he claimed that anthropologists such as Heath had engaged in problem deflation. Heath (1975) pointed out that initially there had been few anthropological studies focusing specifically upon drinking; rather, writing on this topic had been a felicitous by-product of other research. On the whole, anthropologists did not see drinking as necessarily a problem, even when marked drunkenness was reported. Since the research of sociologists, pathologists, or physicians has usually been instituted because of perceived grave problems (seen, for example, only from the perspective of the accident department), there is a tendency to inflate the problematic nature of drinking. In concentrating upon excess and abuse these researchers were seen as imposing or expressing a strong bias of western culture. Heath (1986), for example, challenged the view that some ethnic groups are biologically vulnerable, that alcohol leads to anomie, and that there is a clear relationship between alcohol use and crime and violence—indeed, as Mary Douglas (1987, p. 4) puts it, "that drunken behavior exemplifies a relaxation of cultural restraints before the leveling effects of nature."

As mentioned above the most prevalent bias in the literature on alcohol problems tends to be found among members of the medical profession. There is not only a conflict in approaches and understanding between cultural anthropologists and epidemiologists but also between behavioral and medical scientists.

There is a real problem, in fact, in ascribing causality to drinking (Pernanen, 1989). Pernanen also discussed, in a later paper (1991), what he describes as the distinction between inference rules based*upon human guidelines, or more generally teleological explanation, and those based on inanimate natural science causality, and sees the tension between the two frameworks as being especially acute in the explanation of alcohol-related behavior:

> There seem to exist a general assumption that the two fundamental explanatory categories are exclusive of each other, i.e., that if something can be explained by the use of a guided rule for behavior or through social definitions or social interaction, etc., it cannot at the same time also be explained by the use of natural level causality. And vice versa. This supposition overlooks the essential temporally extended and *dynamic* nature of any behavioral phenomenon, including as a special case human behavior under alcohol (Pernanen, 1991, p. 8).

In presenting this account we have sought a balance between physiology/pathology on the one hand and social process on the other. An admittedly crude example will help. As we consider the historical context of drinking in southern Africa we will see that the effects of alcohol were constantly being seen through prejudiced eyes. Thus the same concentration of alcohol in an illicit spirit was seen as having a more degrading effect than that in a commercially produced spirit such as whisky. But cheap rum from Mozambique, sold to supposedly vulnerable "natives," was seen as the most harmful, both to morals and to public order. We mention morals because, intermixed with views on the effects of alcohol *per se*, are views on the supposed inferiority of the drinker.

While the layperson and even the anthropologist may think only in terms of drunken comportment (the one inflating the consequences, the other deflating it), the physiologist thinks in terms of rate and amount of change in blood alcohol content, as well as in terms of tolerance and its relationship to previous and current drinking style and experience. Thus the steady drinker may well build up tolerance which protects against the sudden exhibition of intoxication, while the binge drinker, with little previous experience of drinking (an adolescent, for instance), may rapidly become drunk and aggressive after consuming comparatively little alcohol. Though much of this kind of information is available to most people who think seriously about drinking, prejudice tends to overcome reason, especially when matters of deep emotional impact, such as sexual behavior, are at stake. It has recently been persuasively argued by Damasio (1994) that emotion must be an essential component of all reasoning and he provides strong evidence for a neurological basis for this process.[1]

---

[1]We have just referred to the historical context. Ambler & Crush, (1992), within the opening pages of their volume, say this about the historical meaning of alcohol in southern African labor history: "Although many blacks also came to regard alcohol as a source of social decay and a barrier to progress, for most Africans moving into southern Africa's towns and labor camps the preparation and consumption of alcoholic drinks represented a continuity in social and ritual life between the countryside and the town" (Ambler & Crush, 1992, pp. 1–2).

The early ethnographic studies in the dominant functionalist tradition tended to portray drinking in the rural societies of southern Africa as a highly integrated, essentially healthful activity that reinforced the structural order of preindustrial communities. Studies carried out in the 1930s implied that without the restraining influence of "tribal custom," blacks—individually and collectively—could not control the frequency or intensity with which they consumed alcohol. Colson and Scudder, who presented a meticulously documented account of a group of villages they had studied for close to 40 years, are, as it were, tarred with the same brush, as they observed that in a rural area in Zambia a "rising tide of beer" had engulfed an area in which, as recently as the 1950s, the people "never had to learn when to stop drinking, because supplies quickly ran out" and where, consequently, "they drank with moderation" (Colson & Scudder, 1988, p. 5). These authors linked increased drinking to an "African crisis" of social and economic disintegration and decay.

Such an argument has merit, and it was repeated with bland assurance by Mwanalushi (a Zambian) in 1981 in the World Health Organization's magazine *World Health*. Ambler and Crush (1992) draw attention to studies undertaken by other urban anthropologists (Epstein, 1958; Mitchell, 1974) who "largely eschewed moral commentary," describing beer hall drinking within relatively stable communities essentially as an integrated activity reinforcing social norms. These historians, nevertheless, remark that the studies share with other anthropological studies the tendency to romanticize rural African communities as static and coherent and to regard problem drinking—however defined—as an unfortunate, spontaneous by-product of social change. In this sense, Mwanalushi could also have been accused of romanticizing. As will already have been appreciated, the matter is likely to be far more complex.

The book edited by Crush and Ambler (1992) is a rich source of information and a guide to other writing on the historical background to drinking in southern Africa. But the question inevitably arises as to the extent to which current drinking practices are influenced by these historical events; their importance lies more in the major political changes that have occurred in the region as the shackles of colonialism and repression of one community by another have been thrown off. It is now about 35 years since the doors were opened to drinking any beverage in many countries in Africa. Taking into account the relatively small proportion of older people (see Table 2.1), it will be apparent that the majority of even the older age groups, including the present leaders in countries and communities, never personally knew a time when they did not have access to whatever beverage they might wish to drink, provided they had the money.

In former times, there were complex forces influencing which beverage a person might drink, and there is still an aftermath in current beverage alcohol legislation and in current expressed preferences which are associated with different drinking styles. We can only give a very brief overview of some of these forces in this account, but some knowledge and understanding will help in attempting to look at current and possible future trends in drinking and alcohol-related problems.

TABLE 2.1 Demographic data for some countries in sub-Saharan Africa.

	South Africa	Botswana	Zimbabwe	Zambia	Malawi	Namibia	Lesotho	Swaziland
Area: ,000 sq. km	1,221	600	390	752	118	824	30	17
Population: ,000	39,506	1,364	10,819	8,355	9,817	1,521	1,805	861
Population density	32	2	26	10	74	2	56	44
Percent urban population	55.9	21.7	24.6	44.6	13.9	51.3	16.7	26.3
Male life expectancy	61	56	59	54	46	57	59	47
Female life expectancy	66	62	63	57	50	62	62	54
Percentage pop. increase per annum	2.3	3.5	4.5	3.4	3.2	2.7	2.7	1.8
Population aged over 20	51.9	41.4	42.5	42.9	42.3	47.3	52.5	40.4
GNP per capita	$2,071	$1,067	$636	$274	$151	$943	$432	$772
Percent GNP for education	3.8	6	7.9	5.4	3.3	1.9	3.5	5.8
Number of physicians	22,525	156	1,257	821	262	281	114	80
Literacy rate per 100	79	71	76	69	41	73	74	67

Various sources

THE DEMOGRAPHIC BACKGROUND

Many of the countries of sub-Saharan Africa are currently undergoing profound political, economic, and social changes, some of which have been associated with the changing patterns of alcohol consumption and the role of alcohol in the regions.

We have outlined some comparative information on various demographic and economic parameters from a variety of sources in Table 2.1. It is important to remember that, at the time of writing, Angola has not fully emerged from the ravages of internal conflict, and communications in Mozambique are far from good after the recent civil war. In fact, data from these two countries are difficult to obtain and they will be mentioned only in passing in the remainder of this account. It ought to be said, however, that in their recent wars, many children were abducted and recruited into the armed forces. As in many other countries such as Liberia, they were rapidly inducted into a culture of intoxication; the long-term effects and consequences still have to be recorded.

The region is home to literally thousands of different languages, although English and French are widely spoken and the two languages remain official languages in anglophone and francophone countries. The rural people in sub-Saharan Africa are mainly engaged in subsistence farming of cash crops such as maize, millet, bananas, sorghum, palm fruit, and honey—commodities that are also used in the production of drinks.

The distance between the homes of many rural dwellers and major conurbations is significant. There is, however, a high mobility of populations and although many people born in town never experience rural life, many of those going to work in towns, and perhaps spending at least several years of their lives there, especially when migrant labor for work in the mining industry was so important, return to their rural homes. Therefore, there is a strong continuity of experience between urban and rural life, but there are also many differences. For example, while urban dwellers have ready access to sources of a supply of drinks, many rural dwellers are likely to have to rely to a great extent upon homemade beverages, or pay much higher prices for bottled beverages made expensive because of transport costs.

Note the wide range of population densities, per capita GNP, and the percentage of GNP spent on education. The comparatively high literacy rate belies a high dropout rate among girls from formal education in many countries; to earn a living many have to resort to street trading, or making beer. Finally, there is a lack of physicians in all countries except South Africa.

HISTORICAL AND TRADITIONAL ASPECTS OF ALCOHOL CONSUMPTION AND PRODUCTION

So far as is known, brewed beverages made from grains or sometimes fruits were the only kinds of alcohol originally drunk in the region. Indeed, it has been claimed that the mountainous area of Ethiopia in East Africa is one of the seven original growing regions of plants used for the production of beverage alcohol (Platt, 1955). These plants (wheat, barley, sorghum, maize, millet, cassava, and bananas, to mention just a few) have been traditionally cultivated in sub-Saharan Africa for food and cash.

Given the abundant raw materials, beverage alcohol has been widely consumed for many centuries and formed an integral and indispensable part of traditional African village life. No wonder a European explorer who traversed southern Sudan, Uganda, Kenya, and Tanzania in the 18th century remarked on the hundreds of sorts of beer he came across (Platt, 1955). Later, in 1831, Monteiro Gamitto visited what was to become the Eastern Province of Zambia and in his report described the preparation of a brew which took eight days to produce (now known in Zambia as "seven days beer") after which the drinking rarely lasted for more than three days except at harvest time, when people of both sexes and any age would live off this drink for days and eat or drink nothing else (Smith, 1973).

Of two "tribes" (although the word is not fashionable, local usage corresponds more to this concept than "people" or "ethnic group") in the same area Gamitto remarked that the Chewa were distinguished by moderation, sobriety, industry, and activity but the Bisa, living further west, were described as being very intemperate, having beer throughout the year. Livingstone described the Maganja people on the borders of what are now Zambia and Malawi as not a sober people; they brewed large quantities of beer and "liked it well."

In his study Mushanga wrote: "Alcohol played a very important social function in African cultures. Alcohol was always present in meetings when elders settled disputes, after a successful hunt or harvest, and when marriages were arranged. The bride price, usually paid in cows, was traditionally accompanied by several pots of beer" (Mushanga, 1976). A similar practice and situation prevailed in many other countries of Africa (Kilonzo & Pitkanen, 1992; Colson & Scudder, 1988; Robins & Pollnac, 1969; Asare, 1995). For instance, collective work, one of the most remarkable features of traditional rural Africa life (e.g., preparation of fields for planting or building a house), was always cemented by beer.

Beverage alcohol was traditionally made by women. Drinking took place mainly at the end of the working day or in connection with celebrations or ceremonies. Although a few African cultures prohibited women (particularly young women) and children from drinking, most permitted drinking by women, and young people (teenagers) could drink alcohol under supervision or guidance by the elders. Drunkenness in women and children, however, was always strongly disapproved of everywhere.

In most traditional sub-Saharan African cultures the use of alcohol varied tremendously depending on the availability of the raw materials for making it. In a study among the Safwa tribes in southern Tanzania, Harwood (1964) found that there was plenty of alcohol and drinking during or after a season of good harvest, but little or no alcohol during famine or near-famine conditions when most of the grain was reserved as food. The decision to convert food into alcohol during famine times was taken very painfully after careful consultation between the man and his wife. Beer was prepared in this way because it had a constant demand in the community despite the famine, Harwood concluded.

In many rural African societies, beer drinking was the only kind of entertainment in the village and all important events in the village were accompanied or followed by drinking. Traditional village chiefs frequently used alcohol to break up the monotony of village life when people were not occupied elsewhere. Beer was frequently carried to the chiefs as a tribute, used to reward labor, sold for cash, and given as offerings to the gods. An abundance of beer was the villagers' glory and a sign of good times. Without it tribal councils could not be held, and marriages and initiation ceremonies could not take place.

In the Congo, where the main type of beverage alcohol was palm wine, alcohol played a very similar traditional and cultural role (Muokolo, 1990). Alcohol use was occasional and associated mainly with ceremonies. During such occasions drinking—mainly by men—took place in public and could involve the whole clan. To the Congolese, palm wine symbolized everlasting life and was often regarded as a source of life. During religious ceremonies and traditional healing sessions, alcohol was often used to facilitate or induce trance states.

Most households produced alcohol for their own use, for socializing with friends and neighbors, and as a source of cash (Kortteinen, 1989). As Platt (1955) observed in Kenya, a typical villager had to get drunk occasionally even if he was short of food because beer was a social necessity, not merely a source of enjoyment. If he could not find time to give a beer party, even a small one, he could lose his social standing, be considered mean, and would not be asked by neighbors to partake of beer. He would be unofficially, but nonetheless effectively, pushed out of his rightful place in social life. A nondrinker in the village was often regarded or treated with suspicion.

Until just before and after the Second World War the type of alcohol consumed traditionally in much of sub-Saharan Africa, whether fermented from cereals or tapped from palm trees, had a low alcohol content. Such drinks could not be stored for more than a few days and were cumbersome to transport or distribute. Their availability was therefore limited, which restricted regular and heavy use. Furthermore, they were considered to have high nourishment content and were regarded as food in many cultures. Indeed, they were often given to babies, replacing or supplementing breast milk (Muokolo, 1990). Other uses of alcohol were medicinal (Asare, 1995; Muokolo, 1990). Thus beer was said to prevent baldness and stimulate strong hair growth of the fetus. Pregnant women were, therefore, often encouraged to drink it for this purpose. Beer was also believed to stimulate breast-milk production in breastfeeding mothers. Heated red wine was said to relieve dysmenorrhoea, while sugar-cane wine was said to reduce arterial tension and thus be good for people with high blood pressure.

The sections that follow offer an assessment of the role of tradition and history in sub-Saharan African alcohol production and consumption. We consider the relationship between past and present alcohol production and consumption patterns through an assessment of beverage types, costs, and quality. We also look at the movement from home to factory production and the history of state control over alcohol in the region. Limitations of time and space mean that we say little about ethnicity, but the question of styles of drinking in various ethnic groups will need some discussion. The white populations (and other minority ethnic groups such as persons of Asian origin) of these countries vary greatly in number and, in effect, it is only in South Africa that special note will have to be taken of differences in drinking style based upon this criterion. We also discuss the extent to which black élites have taken over some of these other groups' styles in all countries in the region. While the historical context is important in understanding the development of drinking and perhaps in giving clues to present trends, because of the high birth rate and the demographic skew towards youth, many drinking members of the population will have no memory of highly significant historical events (in terms of the development of policies on drinking) which occurred as recently as 25 years earlier.

Control of Access to Alcohol

Africa was effectively divided between the colonizing powers at the Berlin Conference held in 1884–85. An issue at this meeting was that of preventing a massive influx of beverage alcohol. The Brussels Conference of 1889–1890 (convened to terminate the slave trade and create a means by which to control the arms and liquor traffic in Africa) established, through a convention, a prohibition zone between latitudes 20°N and 22°S, crossing the continent from ocean to ocean. In this zone the signatory governments undertook to prohibit the importation and distillation of spirituous liquors in those regions where their use did not already exist—which would usually apply to the nonindigenous population. During the peace conference after the First World War a commission was established to review the documents from Berlin and Brussels, and a further treaty was signed at St. Germain-en-Laye in September of 1919, which prohibited the importation, trade, and possession of trade spirits of every kind and beverages mixed with these spirits in the entire African continent with the exception of some countries in North Africa and the Union of South Africa. The manufacture of distilled beverages of every kind was also prohibited, as well as the importation, distribution, sale, and possession of stills and distillation equipment. This did not mean that no alcohol was being produced. Ambler and Crush suggest that such regulations were more of an attempt at keeping indigenous and settler alcohol practices distinct:

> Outside the Cape Province and Mozambique, Africans were forbidden to consume not only spirits but European beer and wine as well. Such measures appear to reflect a determination on the part of whites to preserve the putative noncommercial, "traditional" character of African drinking and to avoid even the suggestion of

racial mixing in the consumption of alcohol. The Portuguese, however, permitted the development of distilleries to produce rum from local sugar and, after international pressure forced their closure, encouraged a far-flung network of private taverns that purveyed cheap Portuguese-made wines to Africans (Ambler & Crush, 1992, pp. 15–16).

A complex set of regulations and laws was set up in South Africa which prohibited both consumption of beverage alcohol by blacks and at the same time allowed access, by allowing companies to issue limited quantities, by having "closed compounds," and by other means such as the setting up of municipal monopolies for the production of opaque beer (the Durban system) often sold in large structures called beer halls. A beer hall could serve several thousand customers a day in conditions which were, to say the least, not attractive; when beer halls in Zambia were closed, most were converted to markets.

These laws, as it were, rolled onwards from country to country as administrations grappled with the "problem" of excessive African drinking. In Botswana:

> For many years the policy on alcohol in the Protectorate was very closely tied to policies that had been introduced in South Africa ... The Bechuanaland Protectorate Liquor laws were based on the Cape Acts (e.g., Act No. 28 of 1883). Already in April 1892 the colonial state had passed a proclamation that prohibited the sale, exchange, giving, or procuring of liquor for Africans and Indians ... In addition, the proclamation dealt with the problem of drunkenness. It made provision that any person convicted of drunkenness more than four times over a period of 12 consecutive months would, if found guilty on the fifth occasion, be liable to punishment of imprisonment with hard labor ... the town councils in urban communities and district councils in rural areas—were charged with regulating the retailing of sorghum beer ... the legislation specified that retailing of home-brewed sorghum beer was to remain, as in the past, unregulated by government authorities ... One of the proposals made for curbing the availability of European liquor to Africans was to regulate or limit the amount of alcohol that could be purchased by Coloureds. In February 1947 ... [it was] recommended that they be permitted to purchase four bottles of spirits per month (Molamu, 1989, pp. 11–12).

In line with the Kaffir Beer Ordinance of 1911, which had been passed by the Southern Rhodesia (Zimbabwe) legislature, a Native Beer Proclamation came into effect in Zambia in 1914; this was later succeeded by the Native Beer Ordinance of 1930. After Zambia gained its independence in 1964, this became the Traditional Beer Act, with its provisions largely unchanged (Haworth et al., 1981a).

However, a major change took place in the region in the early 1960s; it was decided that Africans could have access to all types of beverage alcohol. A commission had been set up in South Africa (the so-called Malan Commission) to examine the general distribution and selling prices of alcohol. In its report the commission drew attention to the fact that blacks were paying exorbitant prices for the white man's alcohol beverages and, hence, made recommendations which resulted in the Liquor Amendment Act (1961). The new act led to a general lifting of restrictions that eventually became region-wide in southern Africa.

But in the meantime an elaborate system had been set up in every country for providing beverage alcohol, in particular from outlets called shebeens, which initially were illegal and still remain mainly unlicensed. In Botswana it was decided that small-scale enterprise should be encouraged. Shebeens were looked upon from this angle and their operations were made legal. Some shebeens have been licensed in South Africa (3,000, or about 10 percent of the total, are licensed) and Namibia. "Shebeen" is an Irish word used in Africa to refer to a private house where drinks (initially made by the occupant but now more often purchased from commercial sources) are sold for profit. As Louw put it, "In an oppressive society shebeens were symbols of resistance and defiance ... where political discussions and debates and theories took shape. Shebeens were also famous for gambling as well as cultural and musical activities" (Louw, 1990, p. 6). Regarding sales from private homes in the village setting, one vendor in Zambia remarked, in complaining about poor sales, "and ... there were no young women to attract men" (Kay, 1960, quoted in Haworth et al., 1981a).

Moralists (particularly church leaders) have often described shebeens as little more than brothels, but this is far from the case. Many shebeens in Zambia are quiet and exclusive places with a regular clientele where noise and violence are never found, contrasting markedly with the nearby public taverns. May (1994) has pointed out that in South Africa there are at least 30,000 shebeens, compared to only 12,000 legal outlets. He argues for a liberal, effective licensing system in the form of a simplified and more focused liquor act which would be easier to enforce. More recent information suggests that this estimate of the number of shebeens is conservative. The attitude of many politicians seems to be highly ambivalent; Panduwa (1978) has described how local political leaders in the Zambian copper mining region, in fact, controlled the shebeen trade and arranged for unsold Chibuku beer to be delivered to them for after-hours sales.

We shall present data below on preferred drinking places, but it should be pointed out that there have been changes relating to enforcement practices. For instance, the data from Zambia show little drinking around bottle stores; at one time the law prohibiting drinking close to these premises was usually enforced. This is no longer done and some bottle stores have even installed games and provide music. The distinction between bars and bottle stores is disappearing.

The character of drinking places varies from country to country, and the nomenclature can be almost as confusing as that regarding beverage types. A brief comparison of sales practices between Zambia and East Africa illustrates this difference. Beerhalls in Zambia were replaced by municipal taverns, which were in effect small-scale versions of beerhalls that were limited to selling opaque beers. Privately owned taverns also soon sprang up, selling opaque beers. "Tea shops" initially sold bottled beer (and were in effect bars) but such pretense is no longer necessary as bottle stores have taken over. In East Africa, on the other hand, opaque beers were never sold in the same premises as clear beers or European spirits. Rather, opaque beers were always sold in people's homes or in market places.

The pattern of access control established during the colonial period (during which government authorities tried to control who was allowed to produce, where one was allowed to sell, and where and when one was allowed to consume), and the response to that control in the decolonization period, have helped set the stage for today's production and consumption trends in Africa.

Types of Beverage

The nomenclature on beverages today tends to become confused with the nomenclature of control, which in turn is linked with descriptions or regulations as to who may manufacture and sell the beverage. Although there will of necessity be some overlap, we will try to discuss the three topics—types of beverage, production, and control of production and availability—separately.

Beverage alcohol may be classified essentially into five groups: factory-produced, home-brewed, factory-brewed, homemade, and illicit. Factory-produced (sometimes called "Euro") beverages are cosmopolitan-type beverages (e.g., lager, ale, table wine, whisky, etc.) that are formally and commercially sold through an established infrastructure; because of the necessary infrastructure of manufacture and distribution, these beverages are necessarily comparatively expensive. They can be subdivided into those that are produced locally (either brewed or, in the case of spirits, "blended") versus the more expensive imported beverages. Surveys of drinking in South Africa also mention "cider," but we currently have no data on its production and sale.

Home-brewed beverages are usually drunk at home, often in "traditional" fashion. Most home-brewed and similar beverages are produced as a kind of gruel. Because the liquid is unfiltered it is often referred to as a type of opaque beer. Since home-brew is often made from sorghum it is also called "sorghum beer," but this term is also applied to factory brew; in addition, other grains are also used, as well as various fruits.

Swaziland provides a good example of the variety of home-brewed beverages that are available. The traditional home-brew (*umqombotsi*) was believed to have many positive attributes—it was thought to be filling and nutritious and not too intoxicating. Sometimes the grain used in making such beer had been found unfit to eat because of the presence of moulds producing aflatoxin, and it was believed that the process of fermentation destroyed the fungus. A list (taken from the Liquor Licensing Act) includes *mankatshange*, which is the equivalent of the *makanjane* now drunk, a distilled liquor, and several names of beverages which appear to have been obsolete and which were apparently adopted from regulations from South Africa. As in Zambia there is a beverage—*mahewa*—which is thought not to be intoxicating although fermentation does occur. It is given to children, for example. The equivalent beverage, made from a root and known as *munkoyo* in Zambia, is also given to children although it may contain alcohol. Baker describes *marewu* as a nonalcohol beverage drunk in South Africa and, remarking on illicit beverages, states that "A concoction like ... motopi resembled the traditional non-alcohol drink marewu and was extremely difficult to detect" (Baker, 1992, p. 143).

It may be noted that traditional home-brew was diluted when offered to younger persons being initiated into drinking (Richards, 1939). Some home-manufactured beverages are called "wines" although they bear no resemblance to cosmopolitan wines, for they are made overnight or in the space of a few hours by the addition of yeast to a sugar solution which is flavored in some way. Making beer can be hard work and profits may be meager (Kay, 1960), although Colson and Scudder (1988) quite correctly point out that, with no other source of income and with the possibility of increasing the value of home-grown grain, the enterprise was almost essential if common household items, clothing for schoolchildren, and so forth were to be bought.

Factory-brewed beverages (in this terminology distinguished from factory-produced) have a composition based upon "traditional" home-brew. Factory brewing of sorghum beer began in South Africa and Southern Rhodesia around 1910 to supply growing concentrations of black male workers in mines and emerging urban centers. While some centers attempted to supply sorghum beer by supervising batteries of licensed women brewers, the frequent limits on female residence in urban areas and the possibility of generating township revenue motivated most municipalities to experiment with large-scale brewing, either on their own or under contract to private brewing firms. The alcohol content of opaque beer is usually said to be about 3–4 percent by volume, but it varies a great deal according to the length of fermentation allowed. The most common brand of factory brew in the region (called Chibuku) is usually distributed in bulk tankers and the process of fermentation continues. During sale from bulk storage, the beverage may also be deliberately diluted to make it go further.

Homemade (as distinct from home-brewed) beverages are sold for profit by permit. Illicit beverages are also homemade, and include distilled spirits; they are sold for profit without permit. This does not complete the list of types of beverage, however. The term "illicit" is sometimes also used for beverages which have been prepared in a special way, e.g., by the addition of sugar, golden syrup, or honey, which hasten the process of fermentation. The same term is used for beverages to which have been added other (sometimes dangerous) additives such as methylated spirit, battery acid, or carbide, for which the expression "adulterated" is also used; such beverages are often sold illicitly as well, often with exotic or slang names such as "kill me quick." Many of the illicit beverages have a somewhat higher alcohol content (say 6–7 percent) though one, *skokiaan*, is described by Baker (1992) as having quite a low alcohol content but containing a root extract with known narcotic properties.

The Question of Quality

More opinions than facts are usually offered on this subject. Baker (1992) has discussed one issue which rarely attracts enough comment—whether opaque beer, in any of its forms (whether as home-brew or commercially produced), is especially nutritious. There are frequent references, often made with great confidence, to the effect that sorghum beer is as good as food, as nutritious as milk, is full of Vitamin B, or protects against scurvy. To quote Baker, "Management believed that sorghum beer possessed antiscorbutic properties that would improve the diet of the workforce and lead to greater worker productivity. The government and industry paid little attention to those who claimed that the beer had few, if any, positive dietary qualities" (Baker, 1992, pp. 141–142). She goes on to cite other studies casting doubt upon the nutritional content. In any case the modern factory-brewed opaque beers are more often made of a mixture of sorghum and maize and are not especially nutritious.

It is almost certainly claimed more often than actually occurs that home-made beverages are adulterated. Nikander et al. (1991) have given an account of contaminants of "traditional" beverages in Tanzania. They found less evidence of deliberately added substances than the presence of substances such as heavy metals and high concentrations of fossil oils, which could constitute a health risk in regular consumers and reflect the absence of "quality control" in the production of these beverages. One distilled beverage drunk in Zambia (*kacasu*—pronounced *kachashu*—of Portuguese origin) and widely condemned as dangerous (as well as being officially "illicit") is recognized in Malawi as "Malawi gin" and is sold legally there, provided it is sold through official channels where the quality can be assessed. Various investigations of kacasu in Zambia have shown that toxic products, such as methanol, if present, are almost always found in very small amounts; it was proposed by one group of biochemists (Reilly et al., 1974) that the beverage should be commercially sold, and it has been remarked that "shebeen queens"— the women who normally sell such illicit beverages—may remain in business for years without ever making a customer ill, let alone killing off their customers.

The alcohol content varies to some extent, depending on the skill (and the taste) of the maker and/or vendor. It seems that the average drinker likes to be able to predict the effect of consuming alcohol, and this is most easily done with standard bottled beverages. The introduction of a stronger beer in Zambia was not welcome because drinkers were "feeling the effects" too early in the drinking session and hence the expected social intercourse was disturbed.

The Cost of Beverages

This is an important factor in determining both the type of beverage chosen and the amount usually consumed. There is considerable cross-price elasticity with regard to various types of beverage (Kabeta & Sakala, 1993). Homemade beverages are sold for very much less than factory beverages because of the lack of any expensive infrastructure. Costs increase greatly with distance from main urban centers, especially in areas of low population density—hence, the need to appreciate the continuing importance of the distribution of populations in the region and the continuing impetus for home-brewing in many villages.

Despite restrictions and heavy penalties for their manufacture, which date back to the colonial era and are still maintained in many countries today, the distillation and sale of illicitly distilled spirits (*kachasu* in Zimbabwe, *kacasu* in Zambia, *changaa* in Kenya, and *wanege* in Uganda) have survived and flourished throughout sub-Saharan Africa, including West Africa. In one study conducted in Mathari Valley, a slum area of Nairobi in Kenya (Wanjiru, 1979), the distillation and sale of *changa*, as it is called in Swahili, were found to be the major occupations for women living in that area, most of whom supported their families and educated their children with income from this business. A similar situation prevails in Dar es Salaam (Kilonzo & Pitkanen, 1992). In many households, in both urban and rural areas, the brewing, distillation, and selling of alcohol have become one of the main sources of income where cash is becoming increasingly necessary to support the family. In Gambia, where 90 percent of the alcohol is palm wine, a study in a densely populated part of that country near the capital showed that 5 percent of all men were employed in tapping palm wine, while 50 percent of the adults were involved in production and marketing of the local alcohol (Kortteinen, 1989).

Much of the cost in the sale of commercial beverages arises from the various aspects of their production and quality control—packaging and distribution, the profits to be made by vendors and so forth, as well as the amount of excise duty payable. A woman in a city distilling spirits can make a profit while selling alcohol at less than one-fifth the cost of the cheapest commercial beverage and many times less than the cost of imported spirits. An example of the effects of changes in excise duty payable may be taken from Zambia. After Zambian Breweries was taken over, a new management team from South African Breweries arrived in late August 1994, and price reductions were made when the government agreed to reduce excise duty from 125 percent to 100 percent and then to 75 percent; sales improved, mainly at the expense of opaque beer. One year later, the excise duty was increased to 100 percent again and there had to be a price increase, made more marked by the current inflation.

The seesawing sales of clear and opaque beer have been a regular feature of sales reports from Zambia and Malawi. In any particular locality in Zambia there was a month-to-month fluctuation in sales of clear vs. opaque beer, depending upon the way wages were paid. Mosi (a lager beer), being the "high-class" beverage, was purchased when the drinker had money but, as the days after the month-end payday passed, there was a reversion to the less expensive Chibuku, clearly reflected in sales statistics from the Zambian copper mining area (the "Copperbelt") (information from unpublished company sales audits).

All the countries in sub-Saharan Africa are having to cope with considerable economic problems and these are reflected at the household and individual level in drinking style. It has been said that the choice of product mix is not simply a question of availability. It also depends on the resources available to the household, especially labor and working capital, and their opportunity cost. Equally important is the composition of consumer demand, which in turn depends on income levels, the prevalence of wage employment, and the proportion of young workers in the market. This is an important point because so much money is earned in informal trading in urban areas, and very little data are available on its extent and the changes now occurring.

The advent of AIDS brought increased poverty because of the greater number of deaths of persons at the most productive period of their lives, with a corresponding rise in the number of orphans—many of them youths—whose only source of income is street trading and whose only source of recreation is drinking. Unemployment figures for the formal sector vary greatly from country to country, depending upon, for example, the extent of commercial farming, the effects of recent wars, the degree of urbanization, and so forth. The proportion of women in employment also varies greatly.

The Move from Home to Factory Production

One of the themes of this chapter is that of availability and choice of beverage. The historical accounts from the region describe the many motives and activities involving both the enticement and control of African labor. The shift from home to factory production of beverages and the types of beverage offered and being made available is an ongoing process. A summary of Molamu's (1989) case study of Botswana illustrates this process.

For many years, home-brewers met Botswana's entire demand for sorghum beer. They produced small batches, 50 to 200 liters at a time, with simple metal drums, woven strainers, and wooden paddles. Catering to a steadily growing demand, the women home-brewers gradually developed a vast cottage industry. In the early 1980s, roughly 30 percent of all households earned regular income from sorghum beer production, making it the largest nonfarm employer in the country. Several forces combined to transform socially allocated home-brewing into a cash-based cottage industry. First was the gradual emergence of a cash economy, promoted initially by traders who opened up shops in Bechuanaland (the former colonial name of Botswana) in the mid-nineteenth century. Later, the Protectorate government accelerated that monetization by demanding cash payment of a hut tax beginning in 1899 and a supplementary native tax in 1919. Second, mine labor migration to South Africa directly propelled cash brewing to prominence by boosting both supply and demand. On the supply side, many observers have highlighted the causal link between the rise of mine labor migration, the emergence of female-headed households in rural areas, and the beginning of cash home-brewing as these households attempted to support themselves with one of the few marketable skills they all possessed, the ability to brew beer (Molamu, 1989).

We have given some details of the range of homemade beverages and the increase in the range of imported brands. The beverage alcohol industry has always been responsive to changing preferences and, it would seem, also recognizes that the introduction of a new beverage does not always mean the *replacement* of an old one, but, in some cases, heavier drinking by the consumer.

South African Breweries (SAB), for example, not only sells its "traditional" and well-known brands in the region (e.g., Lion Lager, Castle Lager), but also many other brands, some brewed under license to the standards required by the originating company. Thus SAB also produces Castle milk stout, Castle draught lager, Carling Black Label, Hansa Pilsener, Amstel lager, Ohlsson's lager, Heineken, and on taking over the Lusaka factory of what was Zambian Breweries, to become Zambian Breweries PLC, Mosi which had at one time, before independence, been called Castle.

THE MANUFACTURE AND CONSUMPTION OF BEVERAGE ALCOHOLS

Because of the rapid sociocultural changes that have taken place all over sub-Saharan Africa in the last two or three decades, traditional drinking patterns and the role of alcohol have changed dramatically, especially in urban areas (Kilonzo & Pitkanen, 1992; Kortteinen, 1989; Acuda, 1979; Odejide et al., 1990). Alcohol is now being produced more and more for monetary purposes, both domestically and commercially. In addition to the fermented drinks, distilled spirits with very high alcohol contents, whose manufacture and consumption was forbidden during colonial rule, are rapidly replacing the fermented types in both urban and rural areas. Apart from their high alcohol content, the distilled alcohol beverages that are generally quite easy to make can be stored for several days or weeks. They are much easier to transport and distribute and can, therefore, be available at any time and in any place. They are being produced mainly for sale and not for family and home consumption or for drinking with friends. With their easy availability, drinking in the rural areas ceased to be a social activity and became an individualized and atomized activity outside customary roles (Muokolo, 1990).

With the introduction of European types of beverage alcohol (clear beer, spirits, and wines), improved communications, and efficient distribution and advertising, a wide variety of commercially manufactured beers and lagers have become widely and easily available in retail shops and bars alongside the traditional homemade ones. Furthermore, recent economic liberalization policies, adopted by most countries in the sub-Saharan region as part of the economic structural adjustment programs, have removed restrictions on importation of most commodities, including beverage alcohol. Imported beers, spirits, and wines

Per Capita Consumption

One topic must be examined before looking at per capita consumption—that of abstinence. To understand what is meant by abstinence, it is first necessary to define drinking. So much data are obtained from surveys which have not carefully defined what is meant by the researcher. In a study in Zambia it was apparent that drinking tended to be equated with feeling the effects of alcohol, but without attempting to define the term "effects" in any quantitative fashion. Indeed, it was felt that some respondents may have claimed not to have been drinking at all, if they had not felt these "effects." The literature is replete with discussions on defining drinking occasions, determining quantity and so forth, and yet other workers have accepted a positive answer on "ever" drinking (usually in an adolescent) as implying "regular" drinking. The more careful surveys deal with actual, well-defined events, within strict time limits that are defined behaviorally. Is "just having tried" (or consuming one experimental drink) to be equated with being a drinker or with being a current abstainer? One can only say that the expression "abstainer" roughly means that drinking is either totally eschewed or is not currently seen as a major factor in a person's life, in terms of either frequency or effects.

Although few general population surveys have been carried out, the findings have been consistent. Partanen (1990), for example, summarizes work from a number of sources and gives the following proportion of abstainers in two cities in Zimbabwe and in Lusaka, for males and females respectively: Harare (36 percent and 80 percent); Bulawayo (47 percent and 82 percent); and Lusaka (29 percent and 40 percent). He rightly underlines that per capita consumption of alcohol does not make sense without a knowledge of the number of abstainers.

Colson (personal communication) is very doubtful about the high abstention rates reported in the various surveys. However, in a series of studies carried out in Zambia in which a question on drinking was included, the proportion of adult (aged 15 and above) respondents claiming not to be drinking remained more or less constant over a period of 25 years, from 1969 to 1994. The first study was carried out in health centers in the capital city of Lusaka, a rural town, and a rural community; the second, again in several suburbs of Lusaka and a rural community; the third, in a general population survey in several parts of Lusaka; and the fourth, again at a number of health centers in Lusaka. Approximately two-thirds of women and one-third of men stated that they were in effect abstainers in all surveys (Haworth et al., 1981). More detailed data on abstention rates in various countries in the region will be given below.

While per capita consumption rates can be taken as only very approximate indicators of actual changes in consumption, they can be used as indicators both of probable important trends and also of the likelihood of the presence of alcohol-related problems. Rocha-Silva (1994) presents a discussion of the concept and usefulness of per capita consumption, referring to the problems of applying the Ledermann hypothesis and presenting estimates of numbers of people with

TABLE 2.3   Annual per capita consumption of beverage alcohol, South Africa, 1961–1990.

Year	Spirits (liters of pure alcohol)	Beer (liters)	Wine (liters)	Total (liters of absolute alcohol)
1961	0.9	5.2	7.0	2.0
1966	1.14	9.2	8.41	2.6
1971	1.12	12.0	11.28	3.1
1976	1.15	19.2	9.89	3.3
1981	1.39	33.1	9.3	4.2
1984	1.20	39.6	9.7	4.3
1986	1.27	41.8	9.3	4.5
1989	1.07	52.0	9.1	4.8
1990	1.07	52.4	9.3	4.9

Note: Population (1994) 43,931,000.
Source: World Drink Trends (1996).

levels of consumption consistent with alcoholism in South Africa, based upon the assumption of a simple mathematical relationship. It must be assumed that the actual per capita consumption of current drinkers in any population is sometimes much higher than the estimates obtained by categorizing the whole population by age alone. This point is well illustrated by a calculation carried out for drinkers in Lusaka, during the WHO Project on Community Response to Alcohol-Related Problems (Haworth et al., 1981a), in which account was taken of the actual distribution system for the main types of commercial beverage and also the abstention rates in the populations served. It was found that the annual per capita consumption rate for drinkers was 8.63 liters of absolute alcohol in Lusaka, 5.67 liters in Mufulira (a mining town), and 10.28 in Kasama, a rural town (provincial headquarters). The figure of 8.63 liters of absolute alcohol for Lusaka drinkers was equivalent to 552 bottles of beer at the current strength per person per year. Haworth (1984) has also presented a critical discussion of the applicability of the Ledermann hypothesis in considering consumption data from a number of countries in Africa.

Moremoholo reported that the annual per capita consumption in Lesotho is equivalent to drinking 572 cans of beer of 340ml capacity. She remarks however that "sorghum-based beer has been assimilated into the socio-cultural rubric of many communities" (Moremoholo, 1989, p. 60). Moses (1989) reported from Zimbabwe a per capita consumption of 140 pints not including wines, spirits, opaque beer, or home-brew.

Table 2.3 provides information on trends in per capita consumption in South Africa. It is apparent that while beer consumption has risen consistently, the use of other beverages has not kept pace. The South African National Council on Alcohol and Alcoholism fact sheet for 1993 gives the following annual per capita consumption rates in liters: wine 9.06 (liters of actual wine), spirits 1.17 (liters

TABLE 2.4 Percentages of black South Africans consuming specified quantities of absolute alcohol per annum, 1990.

Annual quantity (liters)	Metropolitan areas		Towns		Squatters		Self-governing states	
	Male	Female	Male	Female	Male	Female	Male	Female
Less than 36.5	63.4	81.5	66.4	82.7	62.8	75.2	83.8	95.0
36.5–49.9	15.2	3.7	9.6	4.0	12.2	8.0	4.8	1.3
More than 50.0	21.3	14.8	24.0	13.3	25.0	16.8	11.4	3.7

Source: Rocha-Silva (1991).

of absolute alcohol), malt beer 58.04, and malt and sorghum beer 127 (liters of the actual beverages) (SANCA, 1993). In terms of world consumption, SANCA claims that South Africa ranks 27th for wine, 36th for spirits, 28th for malt beer, and 4th for malt and sorghum beer. The document does not specify which year the figures apply to, but it must be assumed that they are from around 1993 and, as will have been noted, are considerably higher for beers than those shown in the table.

Louw (1990) also gives somewhat higher per capita consumption rates for 1990. He shows a reduction between 1985 and 1990 in the consumption of opaque beer as compared with a rise in clear beer (opaque beer down from 79.88 to 70.5 liters and lager up from 41.18 to 61 liters).

In her study of alcohol amongst Africans in 1990 in South Africa, Rocha-Silva (1991) did not include opaque beer (sorghum beer). She based her estimates on survey data, and thus her figures refer to actual drinkers and not to the general population. She found that very substantial proportions drank on average more than one-tenth of a liter of pure alcohol per day—as many as 35 percent of males living in metropolitan and squatter areas (Table 2.4).

PATTERNS OF DRINKING

Relatively few general population surveys of adult drinking have been carried out in sub-Saharan Africa. We begin by quoting from a summary of the results of a survey carried out in Zambia in 1976 and use this as a basis for comparisons with other countries. It should be noted that such surveys require large resources, and these are in short supply in most developing countries such as those in southern Africa. Rocha-Silva et al. (1995) make some remarks about the validity of the results of such surveys, calling attention to the fact that all data-gathering instruments have built-in validity problems. However, although surveys can only identify cross-sectional and (to some extent) longitudinal trends/patterns, convergence of several lines of independent evidence is fairly widely supported as an indication of an adequate level of quality control (Jessor et al., 1968). In fact, logical consistency between various sets of independently gathered information and between various response sets in a particular study/survey, for example, is heavily leaned on as a criterion. Jessor was one of a group of advisors who worked with teams from several countries in the WHO Project on Community Response to Alcohol-Related Problems; one of the participating countries was Zambia (Rootman & Moser, 1984; Ritson, 1985).

In their report on this project, Haworth et al. (1981a) deal in detail with some of the problems of large-scale surveys using nonprofessional interviewers to administer questionnaires that are long, complex, and detailed. For example, in the Community Response Project, questions were asked in detail about the previous seven days' drinking, the maximum in the past year, and drinking on special occasions. It was evident that both the interviewers and the respondents were not able to cope with an interview of such length and complexity. Examining the drinking on the last two drinking days would have been better than attempting a comprehensive picture of a whole week.

As in the South African surveys to be discussed below, this survey was carried out in several locations which we will call suburban, informal urban, and rural; the word "informal" is now more commonly used than "squatter" or "shanty" compound. None of the locations can be taken as necessarily representative of drinking in Zambia as a whole. In the rural area, 72 percent were subsistence farmers, in the suburban area 61 percent of those in employment were skilled or semiprofessional workers, and in the informal location 61 percent were unskilled laborers. Among the population aged 18 and over, more than 70 percent of females in all three areas reported that they had never consumed alcohol; 56 percent of males were "abstainers" in the suburban area, 41 percent in the informal area, and 34 percent in the rural area.

In all areas, males drank more often and in greater quantities than females. Twenty-seven percent of rural and 23 percent of urban men drank once or twice weekly versus 13 percent and 9 percent, respectively, for rural and urban women; 23 percent of rural and 16 percent of urban men drank three or more times a week, compared to 6 percent and 4 percent, respectively, of rural and urban women. The average amount consumed during any one day ranged from 116 to 190 milliliters of absolute alcohol; the highest intake was reported by males aged 18–29 years or above the age of 50. Put another way, 19 percent of all drinking men and 11 percent of all drinking women drank between 1.35 and 1.8 centiliters of absolute alcohol (the equivalent of 9 to 12 standard 375 milliliter bottles of beer in Zambia) and 35 percent of men and 29 percent of women drank 1.95 centiliters of absolute alcohol or more on the last drinking day.

Very few urban dwellers consumed homemade beverages (and overall, very few admitted to drinking any illicit beverage); commercial opaque beer was consumed more by residents of the informal urban area (64 percent) while a greater proportion of the suburban residents (64 percent) drank bottled beer.

In Zambia, at the time of this survey, the law on drinking from bottle stores was fairly strictly enforced and, hence, few respondents reported the stores as their main drinking place. "Taverns" were looked upon as "downmarket," whether the equivalent of the old beer halls or privately owned (in effect upgraded shebeens), and there was a strong relationship between educational attainment and preferred drinking place: 45 percent for those with no education, 38 percent with primary education, and 19 percent of those with secondary education drank in taverns. The reverse pattern was the case with regard to bars, where 11 percent with no education, 23 percent with primary education and 57 percent with secondary education claimed to prefer drinking. But overall, on the last drinking occasion, 40 percent of women and 23 percent of men drank at home.

Molamu and Manyenyeng (1988) (see also Molamu & Mbere, 1988, which summarizes major findings of the study) carried out a survey in Botswana which was based to some extent upon the methodology of the Zambian survey. The survey was a national one and the sample consisted of 1,406 males and 2,359 females. Fifty-eight percent (rounded figures) of the males and 21 percent of the females stated that they had never consumed alcohol, 46 percent and 17 percent that they had consumed alcohol in the previous year, and 38 percent and 13 percent that they had consumed alcohol in the previous week.

Clear beer was the preferred drink being consumed by 48 percent of the sample, 25 percent reported that they usually drank wine, while opaque beer was consumed by 18 percent. Females over 40 and males over 50 tended to prefer sorghum beer. There was a definite association of beverage type with education. Among females, 52 percent with less than grade 10 education stated that they drank wine, versus about 70 percent of those with a full high school education. Drinking companions for both sexes were mainly friends (except that over half the divorced women stated that they drank alone), and less than 6 percent of men stated that they drank with family members; nevertheless, the majority of respondents gave home as their usual drinking place. Thirty-eight percent of males and 40 percent of females drank only once a week, while 20 percent and 18 percent, respectively, stated that they drank every day.

Several studies of drinking have been carried out in Zimbabwe, including those by May (1973) and Reader and May (1971) in Salisbury (now Harare) and by Wolcott (1974) in Bulawayo. Wolcott wrote a detailed and perceptive sociological account of the beer halls of Bulawayo, Zimbabwe's second (and main industrial) city. Since these studies were carried out some time ago, we will not quote the results in detail, but rather draw on a summary by Acuda (1991). In May's survey in Harare, about one-half the residents drank alcohol regularly and 20 percent of males and 5 percent of females reported alcohol-related problems such as "blackouts," nonspecific complaints of ill health, loss of money, quarrels, violence, and disruption of families. The value of the Wolcott study lies in its description of the integrative aspects of drinking, but Acuda stresses that it also confirmed the high prevalence of alcohol consumption among black Rhodesians.

We have already cited a small-scale study from Zambia which seemed to confirm that the percentage of abstainers was consistent in different locations. A somewhat similar study was carried out in Zimbabwe in primary health care settings (Chinyadza et al., 1993) in which a questionnaire was administered to 483 respondents, 63 percent of whom were male and 37 percent female. Forty-one percent were current drinkers (55 percent of males and 17 percent of females), 16 percent former drinkers, and 43 percent had never consumed alcohol. The most popular drinks were clear beer (46 percent) and opaque beer (45 percent); only 5 percent reported drinking wine and 4 percent drank spirits. Sixty-six percent of males drank 10 "units" or more per day, and on days when the heaviest drinking took place, 38.5 percent drank 21 or more units.

O'Meara (1993), in a Namibian government publication, states that 49 percent of adults abstain, while 13 percent are occasional, 28 percent weekend, and 10 percent regular drinkers. Tichelaar et al. (1992), in a study of plasma lipids and fatty acids in a cohort which included 21 bushmen in Namibia, concluded that differences in blood lipid values could be explained primarily by excessive alcohol consumption and that semiurbanized bushmen, having changed their diets, might be at a greater risk of coronary heart disease. The "alcoholic" population is said to comprise 7.5 percent of adults.

No systematic surveys of drinking by adults appear to have been carried out in Swaziland. Calculations of overall consumption are liable to be misleading since much of the population is distributed in homesteads where home brewing is usual and because there is a large influx of tourists in relation to the size of the total population. Taking the local sales of wines, spirits, and the locally made opaque beer, Mvelo, into account, the apparent annual per capita consumption was 3.519 liters of absolute alcohol. However, 69 percent of sales were in one small area—the so-called "urban corridor" (which is also the center of the tourist industry)—so this figure is manifestly inaccurate.

Rocha-Silva (1987a) reported on white, adult alcohol use in South Africa. In a national sample survey of self-reported alcohol consumption with a 60.4 percent response rate, 3.2 percent of white males and 0.7 percent of white females aged between 18 and 65 years of age on average imbibed at least 10 centiliters of absolute alcohol per day; or 2.0 percent of whites of both sexes. A fact sheet issued by the South African Council on Alcoholism and Drug Addiction in 1993 gave the percentage of those consuming alcohol per population group as: white: 89 percent males, 77 percent females; blacks: 80 percent males, 60 percent females; coloureds: 59 percent males, 27 percent females; and Indians: 49 percent males and 8 percent females (SANCA, 1993).

A series of studies of drinking amongst black South African adults has also been carried out (Rocha-Silva, 1991; and Rocha-Silva et al., 1995). The most recent was a national survey, carried out in 1990 with respondents from metropolitan areas, towns, and squatter compounds (informal settlements) and also from rural areas (the former self-governing states), taking people aged 14 and older as adults. Other studies were made of those aged 18 to 64 in 1982, 1985, and 1990 in Gauteng (which includes the major cities of Johannesburg and Pretoria).

The results cannot be presented in detail, since they are voluminous. The percentages of current drinkers among black men ranged between 80 percent (in 1990 in the national survey) and 54 percent in 1982 in Gauteng (rising to 78 percent in 1990). The equivalent figures for women were 66 percent in squatter compounds in 1990 and 22, 29, and 58 percent, respectively, in Gauteng in 1982, 1985, and 1990. There is evidence, therefore, for a marked increase in the proportion of persons admitting to being current drinkers, especially among women.

In studies carried out in 1962 and 1975, the proportion of current drinkers was 82 and 64 percent, respectively, for males and 45 and 26 percent for females. The question on preferred beverages asked respondents to answer for each category, and hence the percentages, if tabulated, would not add up to 100. When mutually exclusive choices were made, the proportion preferring sorghum beer rose from 48 to 55 percent. It was reported in studies from the 1990s that the proportions in different areas in 1990 ranged from 59 percent to 73 percent—the latter in squatter compounds. The proportion from rural areas was 60 percent. From the later figures it would appear that clear beers are generally preferred with proportions ranging from 73 to 92 percent, but considerable proportions (between about 30 and 50 percent) reported a preference for wines or spirits.

There are incomplete data for women's preferences with regard to sorghum beers. Wine features prominently (73 percent) in the former rural areas and over 50 percent expressed a preference for wine in Gauteng between 1982 and 1990, but there was considerable variation in the preference for clear beers. In Gauteng the proportion preferring clear beer dropped from 77 to 39 percent between 1982 and 1990 and in the national survey in 1990, the proportions in different locations ranged between about 40 and 50 percent. Only in towns (47 percent) and squatter areas (26 percent) did a substantial proportion of people express a preference for spirits.

It is not possible to compare these data from South Africa with the surveys carried out in Zambia and Botswana because of differences in methodology. In particular, the frequency of drinking was recorded in the South African surveys for each beverage separately, and it is difficult to disaggregate these data into overall frequency of drinking even if it is assumed that most drinkers will tend to stay with one or at most two preferred types of beverage. The figures given in the surveys mentioned would seem to imply use of several different types of beverage by many individuals. This seems to be confirmed by the reported frequency of drinking. For example, 85 percent males living in squatter areas reported drinking European beer, 70 percent sorghum beer, 32 percent sorghum-based home brew, 35 percent non-sorghum-based home-brew, 72 percent wine, and 66 percent spirits—all at least once a week.

Regarding the context of drinking, some of the differences reported from Zambia were also reported from South Africa in the National Survey. Whereas both men and women stated that they generally drank at home, much smaller percentages of women reported drinking in shebeens as compared to men. This was less marked in squatter areas, where the ratio was only about two to one (35 percent vs. 15 percent), as compared to 56 percent men and 8 percent women in towns. Similar ratios were found with regard to drinking in bottle stores and clubs/discotheques.

From Nigeria, a study comparing drinking patterns in two Nigerian cities and their surrounding rural areas (Ebie, 1990) found a wide variation in prevalence of drinking and in the types of drinks preferred by the people of the areas. The study found that significantly more residents of Benin City than of Ibadan consumed alcohol. Beer was the favorite beverage in both cities. Seven percent of Benin City residents admitted to consuming alcohol daily, compared to only 0.7 percent of Ibadan residents. As expected, more males than females drank regularly; about 30 percent of the female residents of both cities were abstainers.

Regular consumption of alcohol by schoolchildren was also quite common and involved both males and females. The majority of residents said that they first drank alcohol when aged between 11–15 years.

Compared to the Nigerian study, a general population survey in rural and urban areas of Cameroon (Yguel et al., 1990) found much higher rates of alcohol use and abuse. Over 60 percent of the adults interviewed drank alcohol daily and the average daily level of consumption was quite high, ranging from 58 grams per day for females to 90 grams per day for males. On feast days, men could consume as much as 415 grams of alcohol in a day. Contrary to reports elsewhere in sub-Saharan Africa, which indicated that the educated élite tend to abuse alcohol more than the least educated, the study found in Cameroon that the problem was more acute among those with little or no education.

Also contrary to expectations, the Muslims in Cameroon were found to consume alcohol regularly. Alcohol use was also prevalent among schoolchildren. About 50 percent of the schoolchildren surveyed had consumed alcohol and use of alcohol by children was often acceptable to adults. About 20 percent of the parents interviewed said that they gave alcohol to children aged under 15 years. Similar heavy alcohol use by individuals has also been reported recently in other West African countries, namely, Ghana (Asare, 1995), Liberia (Grant, 1995), and Sierra Leone (Nahim, 1995), although the reports from these countries were not based on epidemiological research and the quantities of alcohol consumed were not specified. A study in Kenya carried out in the mid 1980s as part of a WHO collaborative study found even higher average levels of daily alcohol consumption—106 grams per day for men and 60 grams per day for women (Saunders & Aasland, 1978).

Historical Snapshot: Consumption Patterns in Zambia in the 1970s

To return to the data from the Zambian Community Response Project, the summary offered by Haworth and Serpell (1981) perhaps gives a clearer picture of "typical" heavy drinkers and drinking situations than emerges from the detailed information just presented. It is not possible to interpret the data from other countries without the necessary ethnographic background, and we will make no attempt to go beyond the brief summaries of the numerical findings presented. The following excerpt taken from Haworth and Serpell (1981), illustrates the utility of a multidisciplinary approach in establishing drinking patterns:

> The picture which emerges from our survey of drinking practices in the general population is, above all, one of polarization. On the one hand, we find that more than half of our respondents claim to be total abstainers while at the other extreme we find a hard-core group of regular, heavy drinkers who make up nearly half of the total drinking minority. This group of regular, heavy drinkers, which accounts

for about 15 percent of the total population we surveyed, is probably responsible for more than half of the three communities' total consumption of alcohol. They drink enough to make them drunk at least two or three times a week. Who are they? Two out of three of them are men over the age of 30, most of them married. The heaviest drinkers among them seem to be mainly over 50. We found a similar proportion of regular, heavy drinkers in each of the three communities, and we were unable to detect any significant bias among them in educational attainment, type of job, or occupational status relative to the community as a whole. The close correlation between responses about drinking and those about drunkenness suggests to us that the norm amongst most Zambian drinkers is that one goes drinking in order to get drunk. Drinking in all three communities is largely a sexually segregated activity and scarcely ever involves a married couple drinking together. In the urban areas the men drink about 80 percent of the time in bars or taverns. In the rural area both men and women drink much more often in private houses than men in the urban communities, although again it is the men who are more likely to drink in a bar or tavern. Most of the heaviest drinking seems to occur in taverns, where large quantities of opaque beer are consumed gradually over periods of several hours. The small proportion of our sample who belong to the conspicuous minority, educated, urban sector of the population generally preferred to drink bottled beer in bars. This group seems to include a similar proportion of heavy drinkers to the rest of our sample.

Drinking perceived by most respondents as exceptionally heavy was often associated with some kind of party. But amongst the urban male drinkers an equally common occasion for the heaviest drinking of the month was termed a 'drinking spree.' These sprees feature as part of an urban male folklore in Zambia, and they often coincide with the arrival of a worker's monthly pay. Although a man's wife is never part of a drinking spree, other women may be. We found no evidence that the presence of women in a group of male drinkers has a moderating influence on the amount of alcohol consumed. Such social control as there exists over drinking in the communities we studied seems to be built on the all-or-none premise. Thus the preferred strategy for limiting drinking is total abstention. Drinking by [younger] women is also generally frowned upon in Zambia, and once again we find reported drinking practices conforming with the norms in this respect. The ratio of regular women drinkers to regular men drinkers is about 1:4 in all three communities.

Although the evidence is not too clear on this final point, we suspect that the all-or-none approach to social control over drinking may be more pronounced in the urban communities, than in Mwacisompola. Drinking was admitted to by more of the younger respondents in the rural sample, and more of the drinking reported there was described as occurring in people's homes. We suspect that young people not only reach adulthood earlier in rural communities but that they are also more under the eye of their elders during their adolescence. Villages are probably better able to regulate drinking behavior, so as to minimize its socially disruptive consequences, than are urban 'communities' where anonymity reduced the scope for informal social control. This is not to suggest that greater moderation is exercised in the rural community in respect of the amount of alcohol consumed. But perhaps the violence often associated with drunkenness is more readily contained in the rural setting (Haworth & Serpell, 1981, pp. 7–9).

Consumption Among Sub-Saharan Africa's Youth

There are naturally changing patterns in the process of initiation from tasting to experimentation to occasional to regular drinking. Some authors do not clearly differentiate between these stages and, hence, show a tendency toward problem inflation. It is important to be able to distinguish between the drinking style of a middle-aged regular drinker and the essentially opportunistic binge drinking of a youth. For example, for the occasionally drinking youth the effects each time are likely to be very marked and visible, even with rather moderate alcohol intake. Asking a youth how much he drinks does not help in the sense that there may well be a tendency to exaggerate the amount consumed on a particular occasion. However, there are no systematic data on the tendency to lie.

We shall present survey data below, but it should be noted that qualitative descriptions of drinking styles are of great importance in interpreting the mass of information obtainable. For instance, we can only glimpse at the possible influences of the home on an adolescent's introduction to drinking. Opportunity plays a big part, and this certainly includes the availability of the wherewithal to pay for drinks, or having friends who have money in their pockets. Many small boys in Zambia simply try tasting the beer they are sent to bring home, in open containers, by their parents. Since opaque beer does not have a constant strength it is easy enough for the adolescent to dilute the brew and try some, possibly with his friends. And when money becomes available, the youth can simply purchase, pretending that he has been sent by his parents. It is, however, impossible in a chapter of this length to do more than hint at fleshing out the bare bones of survey data; the rest must be left to the reader's imagination.

Haworth and Nyambe (1979) and Haworth, Ng'andu, Nyambe, and Sin-yangwe (1981b) carried out surveys in Zambia among secondary schoolchildren and college students. In a preliminary secondary school study 336 children in grades 8, 9, and 11 were given questionnaires, and 58 percent of boys and 57 percent of girls reported ever taking alcohol. In the main survey, of 1,836 students (66.6 percent males), 80 percent of the males and 60 percent of the females reported ever taking alcohol. Boys in urban secondary schools reported the least ever use (64 percent) among males, and women attending teacher training colleges (44 percent), the least ever use among females. Choice of beverage among students in this study reflected a number of aspects, notably cash, status, and availability. It is believed by many adults that youthful drinking is mainly an urban phenomenon, especially among boys. The limited data available appear to contradict this view.

An early study by Dewey et al. (1983) compared the drinking habits of upper secondary and university students in Zimbabwe with students at a British university. Abstinence was most marked among the female Zimbabwean secondary school students. In a further study by Khan (1986) only 25 percent of black students at three Harare secondary schools admitted to ever having tried alcohol, and less than 2 percent admitted to regular use.

A more recent study gave somewhat different results. Acuda et al. (1991) carried out a survey of 2,783 schoolchildren in Zimbabwe in 1990. Thirty-eight percent reported ever having consumed alcohol; 7.6 percent had tried it before the age of 10 and 36.4 percent while in the age group up to 14 years. Alcohol had been consumed during the previous month by 12.8 percent, of whom only those aged 20 or more had consumed it on 20 or more days. The proportion consuming alcohol on 1 to 5 days per month increased by age from 4.4 percent for students under 14 years to 10.0 percent for those aged 17–19 years. There were no marked differences between the sexes in frequency of use. Since the survey was carried out in different types of schools it was possible to compare drinking in private and public schools. Sixty-two percent of students at private schools had never tried alcohol vs. only 30 percent at public schools.

In 1982 a household survey of "youths" aged between 10 and 29 years, who were either in or out of school from both urban and rural areas, was carried out in Kenya (Yambo & Acuda, 1983). It was found that 11 percent of males and 4 percent of females were abusers or regular consumers of alcohol, i.e., they consumed alcohol on more than three days in a week. The quantity of alcohol they consumed was not specified. The tendency for them to abuse alcohol increased with age, affecting 8 percent of those aged under 19 years, 14 percent of those aged between 20 and 24 years, and 21 percent of those aged over 25 years. Alcohol abuse was most prevalent among youths from low-income homes and least among those from rural areas. Whereas only 5 percent of youths who were still at school abused alcohol, up to 17 percent of those out of school were abusers. The majority of those out of school were unemployed and most of them also used cannabis, chewed khat, and were regular smokers (WHO, 1985). Similar prevalence rates of alcohol use and abuse by "youths" have also been reported from Ghana (Nortey & Senah, 1990) and Nigeria (Adelekan, 1989).

In a recent paper by Eide and Acuda (1996), an attempt was made to show a correlation between alcohol consumption and "cultural orientation." While careful attention was given to the methodology and use of sophisticated statistical techniques, the measure of alcohol use was "ever use"; the argument that young people are more likely to use alcohol if they are more "westernized" is not convincing, and the simpler explanation of greater availability of cash might be more accurate.

Rocha-Silva et al. (1995) carried out a detailed survey of young persons' drinking in South Africa. The material is detailed and rich, and we present here a synopsis of some of the more relevant findings. A substantial proportion (42.5 percent) of the respondents in this study reported that they had had a proper drink of alcohol at some time in their life.[2] This proportion is substantially lower than the 53.2 percent found in a 1990 study (Flisher et al., 1993) among a somewhat similar age group, but within a more restricted geographical area. The

[2]The use of the word "proper" or a similar expression is meant to remove from consideration those respondents who had just experimented with little more than a sip.

42.5 percent was also substantially lower than the proportion found in a 1989 national study among white Standard 8 and 10 pupils, in which 54.9 percent admitted to the use of alcohol at the time of the study (Department of Education and Culture, 1990).

By far the majority (79.9 percent) of the young people in the 1994 study who said that they had consumed alcohol at some time in their life admitted current drinking (i.e., consuming some form of beverage alcohol in the 12 months preceding the survey); thus 34.0 percent of the total sample reported current drinking. The proportion of current drinkers was somewhat higher than in the 1990 Cape Peninsula study (26.9 percent) (Flisher et al., 1993), possibly because in the latter case the emphasis was on having consumed alcohol at least once in the past seven days.

Current drinking in the 1994 study was somewhat more common in relatively urbanized areas and much more marked among males than females, particularly within the rural areas. Drinkers were found notably in the 18–21 year age group, with males being most prevalent. These included especially those males who indicated that in the 12 months preceding the survey they had taken part in festivities or gatherings (such as birthday parties, weddings, and the unveiling of tombstones) and who resided in metropolitan centers or urbanized towns. Likewise, female drinkers in the age group 18–21 years were especially those who reported that they had attended similar festivities. Drinkers in the next younger age group (14–17 years) showed a similar trend, but, in addition, tended not to have attended church in the 12 months preceding the survey. In the youngest age group (10–13 years), drinkers were found particularly among those who said that they had attended some traditional ceremony or other (*umsebenzi waba phantsi/mosebetsi waba dimo*) in the 12 months preceding the survey.

Regarding the type of beverage alcohol consumed by current drinkers, ordinary beer seems to have been the most commonly consumed beverage alcohol among males, while distilled spirits seem to have been the second, and wine the third most popular type among these drinkers.[3] Female drinkers in the urbanized areas seemed to manifest a fairly similar pattern in terms of beverage preferences, except with regard to homemade alcohol beverages and distilled spirits.[4] In the rural areas wine and cider were by far the most popular among female drinkers. The popularity of wine among young female drinkers generally reflected the preferences of their adult counterparts.

As to the frequency with which various drinks were consumed by current drinkers, it seems that no matter what was consumed, the young people concerned generally reported drinking less frequently than once a week, except for the consumption of ordinary beer and cider by males in the rural areas.

---

[3] Ordinary beer was consumed by 73.9 percent of the male drinkers in the urbanized areas and 76.5 percent in the rural areas; the comparable proportions for distilled spirits were 42.5 percent and 43.9 percent, and for wine 35.3 percent and 41.8 percent.

[4] 45.8 percent consumed ordinary beer, 44.5 percent wine, and 42.6 percent cider.

Indeed, in terms of frequency of alcohol intake, young people in the urbanized areas generally presented a fairly conservative picture compared to their adult counterparts. This applied especially to the consumption of ordinary beer. With regard to distilled spirits, the proportions drinking fairly regularly (at least once a week) among the younger group in urbanized areas seemed to approximate the comparable proportions in the adult group. In the rural areas regular drinking generally seems to have been more popular among the young people in the 1994 study than among the adults in the earlier (1990) study.

With respect to volume of alcohol intake, in contrast to their adult counterparts, the majority of the young current drinkers in the 1994 study reported by far a comparatively low total annual volume of consumption, irrespective of the particular beverage concerned. In fact, the young drinkers mostly reported a beverage alcohol intake of less than 26 liters per annum. Rocha-Silva and colleagues report, however, that what is disturbing is that the volume of absolute alcohol intake, of particularly noteworthy proportions of male drinkers, may be described as heavy by overseas standards, since they imbibe on average at least 7 centiliters of absolute alcohol a day, or an average of 49 centiliters a week.

Rocha-Silva et al. (1995) also examined the age at which young people first start drinking (around 14 years for the majority) and noted that the younger respondents more often reported having been introduced to drink by a member of the family. Having a first drink when older was more likely to be initiated by friends or even by oneself. About 50 percent of all respondents found that their first drink was a pleasant experience, but relatively small percentages stated that they thought they would continue consuming alcohol when older—19.2 percent of rural males, 10.6 percent of urban males, and only 2.8 percent of urban females. It appeared that a person who had refrained from drinking when younger and had a pattern of regular church attendance was less likely to initiate drinking. Half the males and three-quarters of the females reported drinking at home, but shebeens and taverns became more popular with older males in particular, and bottle stores found favor in rural areas. Very small-scale studies show the same pattern (Handunka, 1996).

Regarding attitudes towards drinking, one other finding confirms the social separation of male from female drinking. Only 14 percent or less of boys and girls would allow a boy or girl of the same age to drink. However, 51 percent of boys and 68 percent of girls approved of boys drinking later, whereas only 24 percent and 37 percent, respectively, would approve of a girl drinking later. McMaster and Keshav (1994) report a similar finding from Zimbabwe, where they found that secondary school pupils set normal use for males much higher than that for females. Munodawafa et al. (1992), in a study of 285 secondary school students in Zimbabwe, reported that nearly 17 percent had consumed alcohol and nearly 34 percent intended to consume it during the next year, about half reporting that they expected their parents to be favorable. Nkonzo-Mtembu (1994) in South Africa gathered data from 12- to 19-year olds in two secondary schools. Both sexes of black adolescents had positive attitudes towards drinking alcohol and felt that they could outgrow it. They stated that they had easy access to beverage alcohol.

The Influence of Religion

We may largely discount the influence of Islam in the countries in the southern part of the region. There are two countries with substantial Muslim populations, Malawi (about 15 percent) and Mozambique (13 percent), but little is known of the effect of their religion in these countries. In South Africa there is a much smaller Muslim population. The emergence of a very vocal fundamentalist Muslim group in Cape Town recently, in response to alleged inactivity in combating drug abuse, may well be an indirect indicator that there is also a reaction to the drinking activities of some Muslims. Within eastern and western Africa, however, the percentages of Muslims is much higher. For instance, both Kenya and Nigeria have large Muslim populations. Unfortunately, there has been little study of the effects of the Muslim religion on drinking patterns in these countries.

There are aspects of religion that need examination. The high abstinence rate among women throughout the region has already been noted. During 35 years of practicing psychiatry in Zambia, Haworth concluded that one factor that appeared to be of some importance until recent years was the belief in spirit possession. Although both sexes may be possessed, it occurred more commonly in women, and even in these days at least two or three members of an extended family may be reported to have been possessed. Many women, in particular, would report being prohibited by their spirit from taking alcohol, and in the phenomenology of possession it is well known that alcohol is likely to interfere with the process of entering a trance state.

In their report on the Zambian Community Response Project, Haworth and Serpell (1981) stated that the only religious affiliation which was clearly associated with abstention from drinking was the group of Christian denominations classified as "strict" Protestantism. Within the various denominations, actual church attendance bore no relation to drinking habits, and there were a fair number of regular and/or heavy drinkers whose stated religious faith, if taken literally, would completely prohibit them from drinking.

Another trend has now become apparent, but its influence on overall drinking is difficult to assess—the high proportion of young, well-educated "born-again Christians." These would likely attend churches classified above as "strict Protestant" denominations, and indeed in a recent survey of tertiary-level students many claimed this type of church affiliation. In the Zambian survey, over 50 percent of the students described themselves as "born again," and only a very small minority claimed ever to have consumed alcohol. In the surveys carried out in South Africa, questions were asked regarding church attendance, but not in detail regarding church affiliation.

Advertising and the Media

Parry (1994a) states that in excess of 114 million rand was spent on above-line beverage alcohol advertising in South Africa in 1991, but no information is available from other countries in sub-Saharan Africa.

Tibbs and colleagues (1994) have examined the influence of the media and other factors on drinking among pupils from several schools in the greater Cape Town area in South Africa. Television was rated the most influential *media* source, followed by magazines, radio, and newspapers, but family and friends were rated as being more influential. Marketing strategies may not be directly targeted at youth under 18 in South Africa, but this does not prevent adolescents from being exposed. The authors also draw attention to the sale of alcohol to minors in bars and night clubs, and mention the need to better educate parents— who often introduce children to drinking.

In an unpublished study of 279 primary schoolchildren aged between 10 and 12 years carried out in a suburb of Lusaka in 1987, only 22 percent knew the name of any "European-style" beverage, whereas over 70 percent referred to the main local lager and commercial opaque beer, 46 percent knew of *kacasu*, the principal illicit spirit, and between 10 and 25 percent named various other (illicit) home-brews. This was at a time when the advertising of all beverages was banned in Zambia on radio and television. There were relatively few television sets in use in the suburb studied at the time of the survey. The children were able to recognize that a person had been drinking, first because of the smell and second, because of behavior, but they rarely used the word "drunk" in their descriptions (Haworth, unpublished data).

Many developing countries are being required to carry out economic restructuring programs with an emphasis upon private enterprise. Whereas formerly, the electronic media were essentially used for state propaganda, some have now been privatized and more often use advertising for income generation. This has given increased opportunities to the alcohol industry, and in cases where previously state-owned beverage alcohol undertakings have been sold piecemeal to competing companies, vigorous competitive advertising has resulted. This has occurred in Zambia, which has seen a marked increase in the number of beverage alcohol advertisements since the present government came into power in 1991.

ALCOHOL-RELATED PROBLEMS

It is apparent from the descriptions of drinking styles already given that the assessment of harmful levels of intake can be problematic. Some screening tests for potentially harmful drinking such as the WHO alcohol use disorders identification test (AUDIT) (Babor et al., 1989) ask about actual amounts but, as pointed out by Lutalo and Mabonga (1992), "communal" drinking (that is, where people share drinks from the same container and the alcohol content of the beverage is unknown) presents a problem.[5]

AUDIT has been used in studies in Zambia in primary health care settings, the results being compared with the replies to questions on problems in the community response study of 1976. About the same proportions of men and women reported "memory blackouts," family concern, and accidents or injuries related to alcohol use (4–6 percent) and there was an increase in the proportion of men reporting morning drinking (from 14 percent to 27 percent) and a slight increase for women (from 12 percent to 15 percent). A number of users of AUDIT have used a cut-off point of 8 for the likelihood of alcohol-related problems, and in the Zambian studies the mean score was 9.935 for men and 5.927 for women. But the score is made up of answers to three types of questions, in effect those on frequency and quantity, questions suggestive of alcohol dependence, and questions referring to harmful drinking. The greater part of the scores in the Zambian studies were contributed by the frequency-quantity questions. Of the maximum possible score of 12 for the questions, the mean scores were 5.55 for men and 3.31 for women. Regarding the "dependency score" (maximum 12), the mean scores were 1.416 (men) and 0.8889 (women); slightly higher mean scores were recorded for "harmful drinking."

AUDIT was also used by Chinyadza and colleagues (1993) in studies in primary health care settings in Zimbabwe. In the first study (in which 62 percent of the subjects were males), 41 percent stated that they were drinkers and the majority had tried to cut down, either because of health problems (91 percent of drinkers) or social problems (12 percent), 42 percent of drinkers had felt guilt about their drinking, and 16 percent had neglected important responsibilities. Of the 78 percent of subjects who were given physical examinations, physical disorders were found more frequently (70 percent) in current drinkers than in nondrinkers (21 percent). A second study was part of a collaborative investigation involving Kenya, Mali, and Senegal as well as Zimbabwe. In this study 80 percent admitted to ever having consumed alcohol, 20 percent drank daily or almost daily, and 6 percent were morning drinkers. Forty-two percent admitted that they were attending the clinic possibly because of ill health due to their drinking, and 29 percent reported previous problems with the police. Acuda (1991) does not mention the AUDIT scores of his subjects. The studies are of particular interest because of the apparent high degree of insight into the

---

[5]A scale was, therefore, developed, taking into account the frequency of drinking based simply on how many days a week a person normally drank as one criterion. The other criterion was a score from 0 to 10, based upon descriptions of the effect of alcohol, ranging from no alcohol consumed through "a little excited, normal gait" to "semiconscious, unable to walk." Those whose level-of-drunkenness score was 6 or higher and with a frequency of drinking per week of 5 or more were considered above-average drinkers. The authors were able to demonstrate an association between these scores and a number of medical pathologies such as gout, dilated cardiomyopathy, and epilepsy (Lutalo & Mabonga, 1992).

relationship of drinking to ill health, which was not found in studies carried out in Zambia.

In the community response project carried out in Zambia (between 1976 and 1980) a much more comprehensive list of questions was asked. Conclusions from a detailed examination of these data are summarized below:

> Two rather distinct groups of drinkers were identified who show evidence of facing serious problems. One group consists of older respondents who more often state that they experience morning tremors or take a drink first thing in the morning, and who more often complain of chronic ill health. Despite complaining of these personal consequences, however, members of this group do not tend to report more personal consequences than others—possibly, amongst other reasons, because they less frequently express any wish to cut down on their drinking. The other group of problem drinkers is more clearly delineated and consists of younger, better educated persons, more of whom are in employment. They have more often felt the effects of drink while on the job, done something while drunk of which they were ashamed, and, although not significantly reporting fighting or work accidents more frequently, nevertheless, tend to have higher scores on current social problems. Unlike older respondents, they are much more likely to have had a family member or friend express concern over their drinking, and to have themselves felt that they should cut down. The older age group were less willing to admit having experienced life-time interpersonal problems. It seems that for this group problems either did not occur or were not acknowledged if they were seen as clearly relating to drinking, but were admitted to more readily where the connection was less clear—as when they were more physiological (for instance, shaking of the hands) (Haworth & Serpell, 1981, p. 14).

Few differences were found between the sexes in the proportion of drinkers reporting problems, and these were confined to certain personal consequences of excessive drinking, which were reported more frequently by men than women—feeling that one should cut down or stop drinking, and sometimes being drunk when it was important to stay sober.

Similar questions were asked by Molamu and Manyenyeng (1988) in the general population survey carried out in Botswana. Thirty-one percent of males and 25 percent of females reported having to take a morning drink following previous-day drinking, and 57 percent and 42 percent of males and females, respectively, reported ever experiencing "hangover" symptoms. Of those who experienced hangovers, up to one-half (the effect was more marked among females) experienced them every time they drank. "Blackouts" of memory were reported by 19 percent of males and 10 percent of females, while 25 percent of men and 19 percent of women reported having been offered advice about their drinking by a household member. Three-quarters of women who had separated from their husbands had had concern expressed about their drinking. A majority of both sexes stated that such complaints were raised frequently.

Estimating Alcohol-Related Problems:
The Case of South Africa

Various types of studies have been carried out on various ethnic groups in the South African population, and we shall draw on a number of sources. Parry (1994b), for example, lists surveys carried out in South Africa, giving details of the criteria used for determining the presence of problem drinking. In these studies essentially only one criterion is used in each study for determining the presence of a problem, which may, therefore, vary greatly in severity. In another work, Parry (undated) uses a combined "professional" and lay classification of alcohol-related problems with four categories—"misuse" (a lay term), abuse and dependence (professionally defined terms), and alcoholism, again a lay term—in ascending order of severity. He is very definite in his disagreement with the view of the beverage alcohol industry that alcohol misuse is confined to less than 10 percent of drinkers, and he presents a weight of empirical evidence to support the assertion that this is a gross underestimation of the number of persons at risk of alcohol-related problems.

In terms of survey data, various types of criteria have been used, ranging from the very subjective to the very strictly defined. The "coloured" community (that is, persons of mixed racial ancestry), living mainly in the western Cape region, have long been looked upon as especially vulnerable. Van den Burgh (1983) quotes Dickie-Clark (1966) in describing them as "marginalized" and stated that, although their cultural tradition was mainly that of the whites (with their moderate consumption of alcohol), the misuse of alcohol by coloureds had become so great that various commissions of investigation had been set up. One of the principal problems was the institution of the "tot" system of part-payment of wages to workers in the vineyards of the Cape. Laborers were served cheap, usually unfortified, wine (up to six times during a working day), keeping them slightly intoxicated throughout the day and leading eventually to physical and other complications of abuse. Although an act was passed in 1960, which outlawed the use of wine to partially pay a farm laborer, the practice, according to Louw (1990), still existed.

In Parry's (1994b) review of studies, it was apparent that markedly different estimates—ranging from 8.1 percent to over 32.5 percent in males and from 0.9 percent to 8 percent in females—have been made of alcohol-related problems in the coloured community since 1973. Clearly, the rate quoted depends strongly upon the actual measure being used. It is interesting that the measure Rocha-Silva reported using (in her 1989 paper, quoted in Parry's table), which yielded very high rates among black men, did not do so in the case of this group, usually described as especially vulnerable.

The studies listed by Parry (1994b) relating to black drinking also show a range of proportions of drinkers having problems. In the series of studies carried out by Rocha-Silva et al. (1995) they report a marked increase in the proportions with (potential) alcohol-related problems between 1985 and the later studies using the same criterion.

We have already referred briefly to the drinking styles of white South Africans, and have hinted that this style is increasingly being adopted by black élites in the southern African group of countries. Relatively little global information is available on alcohol-related problems. In an account dating from the early 1980s, van der Burgh (1983) wrote of drinking by whites that both abstinence and problem drinking were regarded as atypical, since the prevailing pattern appeared to be that of moderate drinking.[6]

Rocha-Silva (1987b) also discussed the prevalence of alcohol-related problems amongst white South Africans, and began by remarking on the discomfort associated with the Jellinek-oriented disease (and thus unitary) conceptualization of alcoholism. She carried out a study drawing on routine records of the South African Central Statistical Services (CSS) and the Department of Health and Welfare, while noting that these secondary data were not necessarily less accurate than primary data (e.g., from general population surveys). She quotes the rates of alcohol-related deaths from liver cirrhosis as 8 (1978), 10 (1979), and 13 (1980) per million whites in the respective years—figures that are substantially lower than those reported from European countries with reasonably comparable data. The mortality rates recorded due to alcoholism/alcohol dependence syndrome were 10, 8, and 8 per million for the same years. The CSS recorded the number of white drivers involved in fatal traffic accidents found to have imbibed beverage alcohol as 2.2, 2.9, and 2.4 percent in the same three years. These figures were likely to be underestimates according to Pieterse (1985), who found that 60.8 percent of victims of 1,253 road deaths in 1976/77 had a blood alcohol concentration (BAC) of at least 80 milligrams per 100 milliliters. In the first six months of 1983 the figure was 56.9 percent while 62.9 percent of victims showed evidence of having imbibed alcohol.

Alcohol and Injuries

The Copperbelt—the industrial region of Zambia which contains its mining industry, main urban area, and Lusaka, the capital city—on average accounted for two-thirds (67.2 percent) of all reported accidents in a 10-year period and for just over one-half the deaths (51.8 percent). The mainly rural remainder of Zambia and its two other major towns accounted for only 24.4 percent of accidents but 37 percent of deaths. But what proportion of these accidents was alcohol-related?

In Africa, injuries to unprotected road users (pedestrians and cyclists) are particularly important, though they are often the least likely to be recorded in statistics from the police. Ferguson (1974) found that in a series of 10,000 post mortem examinations on persons dying from unnatural causes in Durban, South Africa, 17 percent died from traffic accidents, of whom 21.5 percent were whites

---

[6]However, using the Jellinek formula he estimated that there were approximately 74,000 alcoholic white men in South Africa in 1980—a rate of 5.18 percent of adults over the age of 19.

(mainly motorists) and 55.5 percent were blacks (mainly pedestrians). Likewise, Patel and Bhagwat (1977), in a similar study in Zambia, found that pedestrians formed 50.2 percent of road accident victims using similar statistics from a large hospital in the main industrial and mining area of Zambia. Over a period of 10 years, the proportion of accidents attributed by the police to alcohol when the driver of a vehicle was involved averaged just less than 1.0 percent, and when a pedestrian was involved 0.42 percent. From information provided by the public analyst, it appears that 53 percent of deceased accident victims in Lusaka (mainly cyclists and pedestrians) in the period 1958 to 1965 had blood alcohol levels of over 150 milligrams per 100 milliliters, while 33 percent had levels below 50 milligrams per 100 milliliters (Haworth et al., 1981a). Patel and Bhagwat (1977) found that 36 percent of 588 autopsies carried out in 1974/75 involved road traffic accidents, and that 58 of the road victims (26.7 percent)— nearly a third of all types of road users—had detectable blood alcohol levels. Only one BAC of less than 80 milligrams per 100 milliliters was recorded, and 42 (72.4 percent) were over 200 milligrams per 100 milliliters.

Kobus (1980) reported on breathalyzer tests given to drivers involved in accidents or suspected for some other reason of being under the influence of alcohol or drugs in Zimbabwe. The law in Zimbabwe mentions two blood alcohol levels: above 80 milligrams per 100 milliliters is referred to as "driving above the limit," and above 140 milligrams per 100 milliliters as "drunk while driving." In 1978, out of 595 analyses only 15 were in the range 80 milligrams per 100 milliliters and 77 percent were greater than 150 milligrams per 100. The average was 202 milligrams per 100 milliliters. Kobus concluded "The average drunk driver is not someone who has had one or two drinks on the way home from work." Similar results were reported in 1979.

Information on alcohol and injury can also be obtained from emergency room studies. In one study (Haworth, 1988), conditions leading to attendance at emergency rooms in Zambia included assaults (39 percent), road traffic accidents (8 percent), work accidents (7 percent), and home accidents (6 percent); sporting injuries, foreign bodies in the eye, and so forth made up the remaining 11 percent. Of the 73 cases of assault, 19 percent were by a spouse, 11 percent by other relatives, 19 percent by friends, and 45 percent by strangers. Four patients did not mention the type of assault. Alcohol was involved in only two of the 14 cases of fighting between spouses. Of the 59 other cases of assault, 30 involved alcohol but not all the assault victims had themselves been drinking. Twenty out of 27 men had been drinking and nine admitted that their drinking had been an important factor; three out of eight women had been drinking and this was considered by them to be a factor. Violent behavior between persons then makes up an important part of casualty work where alcohol may have been an important contributory factor, but elucidating its exact relationship to any particular incident may be difficult.

In the Zambian Project on Community Response to Alcohol-Related Problems (Haworth et al., 1981a) questions were asked of both patients and physicians in order to attempt an assessment of the significance of alcohol. The physicians were asked to indicate whether there were signs that the patient had been drinking or whether he or she appeared "drunk" (this term was not defined). One problem was that the pressure of work was often so great that some doctors were unwilling to provide the information needed and 9 percent of the cases had to be recorded as missing data. The questionnaire used was obviously not always fully understood by the staff filling in the section concerning the patient's drinking. Apart from the question on whether the patient appeared drunk, another asked whether there were other signs of drinking. Of the 41 patients for whom such signs were noted, 51 percent were said to be smelling of beer, 12 percent to have slurred speech, 2 percent to be talkative, and 2 percent to have bloodshot eyes.

Naturally, some patients would have had time to recover from their drunken state by the time they were seen in the casualty department. Twenty-six percent of those who stated that they had been drunk at the time of the incident did not appear drunk to the casualty doctor. Thirty-one percent of those who did appear drunk stated that they had not been drunk at the time of the incident (when, presumably, the effects of drinking would have been manifest). Of the 47 patients who said they were drunk at the time of the incident, the casualty medical officer thought that alcohol was a major factor in approximately 65 percent, a minor factor in 15 percent, and not a factor in 21 percent. There appear to be no special studies of "accident-prone personalities" from Africa, but there have been two reviews from South Africa (Cheetham, 1974; Shaw, 1965).

In the report of a study of patients seen at a hospital in Gaborone, the capital of Botswana, it is not clear how many road traffic accidents resulting in injury actually occurred. Data were collected during the month of December 1986:

> The total number of the sample subjects for the period of observation was 223 . . . 7 were brought in by the police in relation to drunken driving charges. An overwhelming proportion (79.8 percent of 186 patients) were cases of physical injury due to a variety of causes. Over half of the male patients were victims of assault. A significant proportion of these had been drinking prior to the physical assault. Of these, over half reported that the assault had occurred at or near to a drinking outlet. Most of the events occurred mainly in the evenings on weekends (Molamu & Mbere, 1988, p. 107).

Molamu and Mbere (ibid.) also obtained information on rates of violent behavior, possibly associated with drinking, in a number of small towns and other locations in Botswana. In Letlhakane, a town of some 5,169 inhabitants, 94 patients were seen at a local clinic; it was concluded that 39 appeared to have alcohol-related conditions, of whom 12 had injuries.

Chawla (1988), in a review of drug abuse in Zimbabwe, mentioned that drinking was associated with aggressive and violent behavior resulting in admissions to a psychiatric unit. The figures he presents (averaging 14.3 percent of all admissions over the period 1980 to 1985) show no increase in the rate.

Violence and Crime

Although there have been many studies around the world on the relationship between alcohol intoxication and criminal behavior, very few studies in Africa have examined this relationship. In the mid-1960s, Tanner (1970) examined the association between drinking and homicide in Uganda and found that, although there was much drinking in the rural agricultural areas of that country, the drinking party was only infrequently a locale for homicide. He reported that alcohol was present in the blood samples of only 25 percent of cases where men killed men and in only 19 percent of cases where men killed women. During a three-year period from 1961 to 1963, alcohol was involved in only 11 percent of cases of homicide or attempted homicide throughout Uganda.

Replicating Tanner's study a decade later, however, Mushanga (1974) found that alcohol was involved in up to 37 percent of criminal homicides in Uganda. One possible explanation is that whereas in the mid-1960s Uganda was a relatively peaceful country, the mid-1970s, when Mushanga replicated the study, was a period of great political and social instability characterized by extreme degrees of military violence and there was an abundance of guns around. Much more recently, excessive use of alcohol in Uganda has been linked with increasing health and other social problems such as domestic violence, corruption, family breakdown, and increasing numbers of street children. The spread of HIV/AIDS in Uganda has also been partially attributed to alcohol abuse (Kasirye-Lugoloobi, 1995).

Studies of court records have been carried out in both Zambia and Zimbabwe. In Zambia (Okada, 1967), data were collected from all 1,866 cases heard in two urban "local" courts (courts of first instance) in 1965/66. A criminal offense such as rioting, assault, or unlawful wounding was involved in 41.3 percent of the cases, and these made up 71 percent of the offenses, the remainder being "drunk and disorderly." At least a proportion of those who had been injured might have been taken to hospitals or health centers but there would have been no record of alcohol involvement. Gelfand (1971) found that alcohol could have been a factor in between one-half and two-thirds of the cases of homicide tried in the higher courts, but was hardly ever mentioned in cases of assault tried at a number of courts similar to the "local" ones studied by Okada.

In the study by Haworth et al. (1981a) at two police stations in Lusaka, alcohol was mentioned by the complainant in 30 percent of the cases and was noted as a factor by the police (being prompted by having to fill in the study questionnaires) in 35 percent. Overall, the police thought that alcohol was a factor in 55 percent of the cases of assault and in at least 48 percent of the cases the complainant had been drinking. There were some differences in rates of reporting of various types of offenses between the two police stations, which suggested that police attitudes and decisions on how to label behaviors affected the rates at which alcohol was being reported as a factor by these police officers.

It seems that, given the right tools and the correct training, the police are capable of confirming that at least the highly intoxicated have been consuming alcohol. But in general, the ordinary constable seems to be disinclined even to note alcohol as a factor, especially if there is no legal requirement for him to do so. In the study by Haworth et al. (1981a), it was noted at one Lusaka police station that the official diary (the "occurrence book") made reference to alcohol in 13.5 percent of the incidents. In a later study of two very similar police stations, however, in which special (separate) note was taken of whether alcohol had been a factor in incidents dealt with at the stations, it was mentioned in about one-third of all the cases. The fact that the police do not regularly report an alcohol component in many offenses does not mean that this may not emerge if the case comes to trial.

Most of the information provided above is based upon cross-sectional data. But trends in data are of more use to policymakers. Theoretically, the police ought to be a useful source of such data. Haworth has been collecting police data on possible alcohol-related problems in Zambia for a number of years (unpublished as yet in the case of recent years) from Zambia police annual reports. Over the last five years the number of cases of assault, unlawful wounding, and causing grievous bodily harm reported has shown an increase of about 20 percent. However, the number of convictions has consistently been very much less, at only about 15 percent of the cases. On the other hand, the conviction rate for "drunk and disorderly" has been much higher, averaging 99 percent. There has been a marked fall in the number of cases reported, from 22,146 in 1990 to 7,687 in 1994. Convictions for being "drunk and incapable" tended to rise steadily between 1970 (13,351) and 1989 (23,534), an increase of 76 percent; during the same period the population of Zambia rose by about 92 percent. Contraventions of the beverage alcohol licensing laws have also shown a dramatic fall, particularly between 1992 and 1993 (from 1,815 to 293), again with a conviction rate 99 percent.

The number of cars on Zambian roads continues to increase but the number involved in accidents has varied—8,994 in 1987 and 11,664 in 1995, but with a peak of 12,085 in 1992. No information is currently available on whether or not the police attribute an accident to drinking, but between 1964 and 1987 the proportions varied between 0.34 percent (1987) and 4.9 percent (1977). So what is one to make of such figures? The fall in convictions for being "drunk and incapable" and under the Liquor Licensing Act may have been a result of a policy decision by the government which came into power in 1991, according to a police spokesperson. Zambia has fortunately been a very peaceful country politically, but other countries in the region experience high rates of interpersonal violence and even civil war. In our view, if adequate policies are to be developed, data on trends of drinking and on problems will be needed, but this will depend on developing a specific means of collecting valid, reliable, and, hence, comparable data. Means will need to be sought of raising the necessary funding.

Another source of information on the possible relationship of alcohol to violence comes from postmortem studies of victims of homicide and of those dying by suicide. Butchart, Lerer, and Blanche (1994) point out that while women may not usually ascribe violence to their own drinking, elevated postmortem blood alcohol levels indicate otherwise. Loftus and Dada (1992) retrospectively studied 948 cases and found that 52.5 percent of the cases had elevated blood alcohol levels. Lerer (1992) examined the records of female homicide victims and suicides in Cape Town and reported that a blood alcohol level of greater than 100 milligrams per 100 milliliters was found in 56 percent of the subjects.

Duflou-Jalc and Knobel (1988) reported that alcohol was detected in the blood of homicide victims in Cape Town in 62.9 percent of the cases and 8.4 percent had a blood alcohol level greater than 300 milligrams per 100 milliliters. In a much earlier study, based upon records of inquests on persons who had committed suicide in Zambia, Chaplin (1961) found only one case where alcohol was implicated. This finding is an example of a particular focus of interest (Chaplin was interested in relating climatic change to suicide) and may also be explained by the fact that facilities for performing routine blood alcohol estimations were not available, except in Lusaka. Davis and Smith (1982) found that 50 percent of the victims of drowning accidents in the Cape Town area had a blood alcohol level of 100 milligrams per 100 milliliters or higher. But Buchan (1988) has recorded a cautionary note on blood alcohol estimations performed on cadavers, pointing out that they may be artificially elevated due to postmortem changes.

It should be noted that besides injuries resulting from accidents and criminal/violent behavior, there are other acute alcohol-related medical emergencies which may be seen in emergency rooms, for example, alcoholic hypoglycemia. This is a condition which is seen with some frequency in casualty departments in southern Africa and it is neither well-known nor always recognized for what it is. Willcox and Gelfand (1976) reviewed 10 cases of spontaneous hypoglycemia admitted to hospital and discussed the problems of definitely confirming the condition as alcohol-related. Neame and Joubert (1961), reporting from South Africa, found evidence of liver disease in 50 percent of their subjects, but behavioral as well as other health problems were likely to be present.

The Alcohol Dependence Syndrome and Psychiatric Complications of Drinking

Information from psychiatric facilities in various countries gives another perspective on alcohol-related problems. Haworth has pointed out, in describing the situation in Zambia, that the patient exhibiting typical features of alcohol dependence (including one or more episodes of delirium tremens) is not so commonly seen. However, SANCA (1993) estimated that there were 1,025,198 alcoholics in South Africa, which represented 5 percent of those aged over 15 years of age.

Molamu and Manyenyeng (1988) reported on the number of admissions for alcohol dependence and alcoholic psychosis in Botswana between 1980 and 1984. The numbers reported showed a marked increase over the four–five year-period (from 77 to 267 for males, and from 35 to 67 for females) for alcohol dependence and a smaller increase for alcohol psychosis (from 60 to 102 for males, and from 31 to 44 for females). Moremoholo (1989), reporting from Lesotho, stated only that the alcohol-related conditions there were principally vitamin deficiency and alcoholic hallucinosis, which were more common than alcohol dependence.

Malepe (1989), reporting from Swaziland, stated that 20–30 percent of admissions to the only psychiatric hospital were for alcohol- or drug-related psychosis. The rates reported for admissions to the mental hospital in Lusaka, Zambia, have tended to be lower; in 1985 alcohol-related admissions accounted for only 14.7 percent of the total. Buchan and Baker (1974), reporting from the main mental hospital in Zimbabwe, found that 110 white males had been admitted 168 times over a five-year period because of conditions arising from excessive alcohol use. This accounted for 45 percent of all admissions to the hospital; 25 percent of admissions of white females were also for alcohol-related conditions.

The proportion of alcohol-related admissions at the psychiatric unit of the Teaching Hospital in Harare was reported by Buchan and Chikara (1980) to be 25 percent. These authors remark upon the difficulty of distinguishing alcohol-related disorders from other organic conditions. Buchan (undated) also carried out a study in the general wards of the Teaching Hospital in Harare and noted the occurrence of complications of alcohol dependence and the alcohol dependence syndrome itself; this hospital was admitting patients from a more affluent stratum of society at the time. In Chawla's study (1988) of the hospital admitting African patients in Harare, he reported no case of delirium tremens.

Just as there is a dearth of epidemiological data on the relationship between alcohol and health, there are also very limited data on the prevalence of alcohol use and abuse in the general population in sub-Saharan Africa. The earliest prevalence study was done in a rural community in Nigeria in the mid-1970s (Odejide & Olatawura, 1977). The study found that out of 109 randomly selected adults from the community who were interviewed, only nine (8 percent) were found to be "alcoholics." The criteria for alcoholism were not specified. At about the same time a survey of adults from 200 randomly selected households in a rural district in Kenya (Bittah et al., 1979) found that up to 27 percent of the males and 24 percent of the females interviewed could be classified as alcoholics using WHO's 1952 definition of alcoholism (WHO, 1952). This study found that alcohol was widely available in the community concerned and most households brewed or distilled alcohol regularly. Up to 7 percent of secondary school students aged 17–20 years in the district were also "alcoholics" according to the same WHO definition.

Another community study, also in Kenya and carried out at about the same time, but in an overpopulated slum area of Nairobi where 85,000 people lived crammed in a 490-acre piece of land, found alcohol problems to be even more acute (Wanjiru, 1979). Forty-six percent of the male and 24 percent of the female heads of households aged between 18 and 55 years who were interviewed were classified as alcoholics according to the 1952 WHO criteria referred to above. Alcohol, especially the distilled form, was widely and easily available in the slum. However, 54 percent of the females and 27 percent of the males in the area were found to be teetotalers. Since these studies were done in Kenya, the 1952 WHO definition has been superseded and, therefore, the results of these studies should be treated with caution.

The earliest publication from sub-Saharan Africa on alcohol and health came from work carried out in Kenya during the Second World War (Carothers, 1948). In a detailed study of Africans "certified insane" and admitted to a psychiatric hospital in Nairobi between 1939 and 1943, Carothers found that only 0.7 percent of patients admitted during the period had alcohol psychosis "despite heavy consumption of drinks with high alcohol contents by the Africans in the reserves." A similarly low figure was found by Asuni (1974) in a retrospective study of all admissions to the Aro Neuropsychiatric Hospital in Nigeria during the period 1964–1973.

However, subsequent studies, particularly from East Africa, began to show that alcohol psychosis was a major cause of admissions to psychiatric hospitals. For instance, Wood (1975) found that in 1974, 13 percent of all admissions to Butabika Mental Hospital in Uganda were due to alcohol psychosis. Some years later, Cox (1978) found that 8.4 percent of all admissions to the same hospital received the diagnosis of alcohol psychosis on discharge. Later on in Kenya Badia (1985) using the brief version of the Michigan Alcoholism Screening Test (MAST) (Pokorny et al., 1972) as the screening instrument, found that 21 percent of the admissions to Mathari Mental Hospital in Nairobi were due to alcohol psychosis.

A more recent study carried out among consecutive outpatients of a rural district hospital in Kenya (Nielsen et al., 1989) showed that 54 percent of the males and 24 percent of the females met the Diagnostic Interview Schedule (DIS) (American Psychiatric Association, 1980) criteria for alcohol abuse and/or dependence. Two studies in Nigeria among secondary school students (Abiodun et al., 1994) and among university students (Adelakan et al., 1993) found that current use of alcohol was significantly associated with self-reported study difficulties and poor mental health. Another recent study in Tanzania on the role of alcohol in injuries found that up to 29 percent of casualties treated in the emergency department of a general hospital in Dar es Salaam were related to alcohol consumption (Nikander et al., 1992).

We have already remarked that data from the African group of countries are hard to obtain and that they are likely to be unreliable. Several factors account for this. One of the most important factors is that the pattern of drinking in indigenous populations does not usually reflect a steady high intake, and hence it is our impression that typical alcohol dependence of the kind found in many developed Western countries is not so common. A number of the sources mentioned above put much emphasis on psychotic states which are not typical withdrawal deliria. But relying on hospital admission statistics is always problematic. In Zambia, for instance, there is an extensive mental health component in the primary health care provided; and at the same time, the mining industry (which for many years had strong connections with South Africa) may still tend to send senior staff with alcohol dependence problems out of the country rather than utilizing the only (poorly staffed) mental hospital.

The Physical Consequences of Alcohol Abuse

On the whole, mortality statistics from most countries in the region are not of great value. The small number of doctors and lack of medical facilities generally mean that reliable data (for example, from postmortem examinations) are unlikely to be obtainable. We have already referred to some of the few studies relating to accidents and violence, and have mentioned the problems of assessing the extent of alcohol's contribution. Similar problems occur, even with chronic medical conditions—for instance, in assessing the importance of the presence of aflatoxin in grains which may be eaten as well as used for making beer in the etiology of liver cancer. There are many other causes of hepatitis apart from alcohol, for example, viral hepatitis B infection. On the other hand, the contribution of alcohol may not be recognized, as in the case of cirrhosis associated with iron overload from drinking home-brewed beverages in which the slightly acid beer has dissolved some of the iron from the metal drum used in the process (Loewenthal et al., 1967).

A review was made of data on deaths from diseases which might have had some relationship to drinking (pellagra, alcoholic peptic ulcer, and liver cirrhosis) provided by the Zambian Ministry of Health, for a six-year period (during which the population would have increased by almost one-fifth). The proportion of deaths from conditions which might have had alcohol as a factor decreased from 0.818 percent to 0.663 percent and at its lowest, in 1992, was 0.524 percent. Malepe (1989), quoting from the report of a WHO consultancy Haworth carried out in Swaziland in 1982, states that the rate of liver disease over a 10-year period from 1973 to 1982 varied between 0.1 and 0.4 percent of all diagnoses. It is obvious that such data must be extremely unreliable.

Molamu (1989) provided data on liver diseases and mortality in Botswana over an 11-year period (1974–1984) in which there was considerable variation in the number of cases: 33 (12 deaths) in 1975 and 186 (27 deaths) in 1984; whereas in 1982, there were 106 cases with 43 deaths. Molamu admitted that such statistics are unreliable and Edwards et al. (1994) have pointed out that, in the case of liver cirrhosis, there is likely to be a long latency period. Nevertheless, Molamu attributed the rise to an increase in alcohol consumption.

Rees and colleagues (1993) have reported on a study of liver enzyme levels in paint workers in South Africa. They concluded that the rise in gamma GT and other enzyme levels was not due to exposure to solvents but that excessive alcohol use was an important factor. Mohamed, Kew, and Groeneveld (1992) have shown an increased risk for hepatocellular carcinoma in urban South African blacks only in men over the age of 40 who habitually drank more than 80 grams of ethanol daily; hepatitis B was confirmed as a risk factor in younger men and women, but alcohol was the greater risk in the older group of men.

Another example of multiple etiology is that of carcinoma of the esophagus. McGlashen (1969) and colleagues showed that there was an increased incidence in the eastern part of Zambia where the drinking of *kacasu* (an illicit spirit) is prevalent. However, there is also a close association between drinking *kacasu* and smoking home-cured tobacco. In a recent study from Zimbabwe, Vizcaino, Parkin, and Skinner (1995) found no association in a cohort of 826 men and 55 women between drinking and carcinoma of the esophagus.

Lutalo (1993) has shown alcohol use to be associated with gout in Zimbabwe noting that "associated alcohol excess was universal." Coetzee, Yach, and Joubert (1988), in a study of a high-density housing area in South Africa, showed an association between alcohol problems reported by one or more members of a household and the presence of tuberculosis (odds ratio adjusted for employment status 2.2).

There have been very few studies on alcohol and health in the northern part of the sub-Saharan region. Most of the earlier studies were comprehensively reviewed in an article in the *British Journal of Addiction* in 1985 (Acuda, 1985) and in a Nordic Council for Alcohol and Drug Research publication in 1990 (Acuda, 1990). Those reviews summarized the available information in East Africa on alcohol gastritis (Bittah & Acuda, 1979), alcohol-induced hypoglycemia and brain damage (MacSearreigh, 1969), alcohol and heart disease (Ojiambo, 1971), alcohol and gouty arthritis (Mngola & Odeny, 1972), alcohol and eye disease (Bisely & Burkitt, 1974), and alcohol and cancer of the esophagus (Collis, 1972).

Other studies from several parts of Africa have shown that some of the most popular homemade drinks in the region contain various impurities and carcinogenic substances which are potentially damaging to health. Studies in Kenya (Nout, 1981), Nigeria (Obasi et al., 1987; Okoye & Ekenyong, 1984) and Tanzania (Nikander et al., 1991) have found high levels of aflatoxin and other substances such as zinc and iron in samples of homemade beverage alcohol. Earlier studies, which caused a major scare, found high concentrations of nitrosamines in many samples of spirits distilled from maize products in East and Central Africa where cancer of the esophagus was also common (Collis et al., 1971; McGlashan, 1969). Aflatoxin has been implicated in the etiology of liver cancer and nitrasamines have been implicated in the etiology of esophageal cancer (Uwaifo & Bababanmi, 1984; Popper, 1979; Magee & Barne, 1967).

Alcohol and HIV Infection

The WHO estimates that at the end of 1995 more than 18.5 million people worldwide were infected with HIV, including more than 11 million people in sub-Saharan Africa. Current surveillance data on HIV infection in Zambia (Fylkesnes et al., 1997), which (in this brief account of 1996) must also represent other countries in the region, show an infection rate in the sexually active population of about 40 percent amongst the better educated, 25 percent of that population in urban areas, and 13 percent in rural areas. Although overall there is little difference in rates between the two sexes, the rate of discordance in married couples has been found to be 34 percent in large-scale surveys. It is expected that there will be about 90,000 to 100,000 deaths from AIDS in 1997 and the number of orphaned children is expected to reach over half a million by the end of the decade (when the total population of the country will be about 10 million). A secondary effect of the HIV epidemic is a marked rise in the number of persons with tuberculosis; approximately 65 percent of those with pulmonary TB are found to be HIV-seropositive.

Excessive alcohol use has both direct and indirect effects upon the immune system because of liver damage or associated nutritional deficiencies or because of the presence in drinks of fungal toxins such as aflatoxins (Lovelace & Nyathi, 1977). In addition, the social context of drinking may contribute to the risk of having unprotected sex with an infected person. This has been studied in Zambia (Haworth, 1991). It has already been mentioned that a large proportion of male drinkers do not drink with their wives. In this survey of 1,000 respondents carried out in 1990, 60 percent of male drinkers reported drinking in a bar and 8 percent reported having sex with someone other than their regular partner after having been drinking. Twenty-three percent of males who never drank had suffered from sexually transmitted diseases, as against 37 percent of those drinking at least once per week.

Alcohol and Employment

Molamu and colleagues (cited in Zizhour, Zhakata, and Eide (1990)) studied the impact of drinking upon a wide sample of workers and noted that of 506 workers who were drinkers (out of 1,058), 11.1 percent had experienced problems in relation to drinking, but no injuries were reported. Buchan (1988) carried out studies on BAC in workers at a Zambian copper mine. He found that one-third of selected employees (those in jobs which could put others at risk), when given random breath tests before starting work, had measurable BACs; the level was at least 80 milligrams per 100 milliliters in 9 percent of the cases. Of all persons involved in accidents (in any way), 30 percent had measurable BACs and in 5.8 percent of the cases the amount was at least 80 milligrams per 100 milliliters. However, compared to those who were tested before work, this group had spent a much longer time before being tested. The mean BAC in 87 employees tested because they were suspected of being under the influence of alcohol was just over 20 milligrams per 100 milliliters but in one-third of them was less than 160 milligrams per 100 milliliters. Buchan makes the point that there is a case for random testing of all those reporting for work, since it is evident from the random tests performed that a proportion of workers will have consumed substantial amounts of alcohol and this may not have been detected from their behavior.

The International Labor Organization has initiated a number of projects in some southern African countries, advocating the establishment of "employee assistance" schemes and rehabilitation programs. Collaborative work is underway at present in Zambia to assess whether such schemes may be necessary in large industrial firms. One company, after applying a rapid assessment method for potential problems using focus group discussions, decided to adopt a stringent code of conduct supported by a detailed supervisors' guide. It had already been noted from the focus group discussions that the standard of self-discipline among employee drivers was much higher than that of drivers of hired "contract" vehicles. It should be said that employee assistant programs are an excellent way of retaining staff and helping them with alcohol-related problems, provided that they are well organized and that proper attention is paid, for example, to legal considerations, especially regarding confidentiality.

TREATMENT OF PERSONS WITH ALCOHOL-RELATED PROBLEMS

The gross disparities in the funding of health services between countries, and the lack of physicians generally and of psychiatrists, in particular, in most countries, compared with South Africa (Flisher et al., 1996), clearly indicate one problem. But first, perhaps, the question must be asked: What is to be treated? All too often the "wound" (e.g., hypoglycemia or some other condition) is attended to, but not the person and his or her underlying problem. Many persons present for treatment of injuries, for instance, do not see their drinking as problematic, or, when they do, as needing specific medical intervention. Nor are those providing grass-roots treatment for these conditions likely to recognize the "alcohol factor"; they will more likely ignore psychosocial elements in the genesis of the injury or illness they are treating.

Administrators of services share these views, on the whole. If funds are short they must go to the care of the most vulnerable and needy—women of childbearing age and under-fives. And so, for the majority of drinkers in the region, the questions of recognition of their hazardous drinking and of some action being taken to prevent its consequences does not arise. For in this context, "treatment" of hazardous drinking must be taken to mean the secondary prevention of its consequences.

A noteworthy project was recently carried out in several countries worldwide, including Zimbabwe. In this major study (Babor et al., 1994), a total of 1,661 nondependent heavy drinkers were recruited from a variety of settings. Of these 73 percent were assigned to three groups—control, simple advice, and brief counseling—and evaluated some nine months later. The results showed a significant effect of the interventions on both average alcohol consumption and intensity of drinking in the male samples. As Edwards and colleagues (1994) remark in reviewing several studies "the overall conclusion . . . can be the robust assertion that brief interventions . . . are likely to offer significant benefit to men . . . The situation as regards women is at present less clear" (Edwards et al., 1994, p. 192).

Bearing in mind that so much drinking in the region does not correspond in pattern or effects to "dependence," and considering the lack of facilities, such a study would appear to be of great relevance, especially since relatively unskilled personnel can be trained in the techniques of basic counseling, as exemplified in the AIDS field (Haworth, 1989b).

Most countries in the region have adopted and implemented the primary health care strategy for dealing with most health problems, including alcohol-related health problems. But because of the lack of skills in the detection and management of these problems by primary health care workers, the majority of patients attending such facilities with alcohol problems pass through undetected or are not adequately managed. Only those with serious physical or psychiatric complications are referred and receive treatment in tertiary facilities. Even at these levels, they generally receive no more than "first-aid" treatment, usually limited to detoxification and management of the physical or psychiatric complications. A few countries in the region (e.g., Nigeria) have established or attempted to establish specialized treatment facilities. However, such facilities are usually highly centralized, thus making them inaccessible to the majority of patients. They also usually lack adequate resources, especially skilled personnel, and many studies have thrown considerable doubt on their cost-effectiveness (WHO, 1991).

With regard to prevention, most of the countries have set up some form of national coordinating body, committee, or council to coordinate treatment and preventive activities (Giorgis, 1995; Kiima, 1995). Some of the functions of such bodies have included the development and implementation of national policies, the creation of awareness, and preventive education. The coordinating bodies, where they exist, are generally themselves poorly coordinated, usually lack authority and financial support, and are generally ineffective.

The question of the treatment of those who are dependent is another matter. Although we have presented many data, no clear picture has emerged of the existence and extent of alcohol dependence, except in South Africa. And even from that country we do not have sufficient detail in terms of the older definitions of "alcoholism" or of the relatively newer concept of alcohol dependence (Edwards, 1977; Edwards et al., 1977). We do not intend to attempt to enter into the debate on the best method of helping such persons, but will merely mention that many treatment regimes are far beyond the financial capacity of the majority of the drinking population.

Reference must be made to the strength of Alcoholics Anonymous (AA) in some countries such as South Africa. In Zambia the services established by AA made up for the lack of alternative help for the high-earning miners of the Zambian copper mines in the 1950s. At that time racial segregation was practiced in many spheres of life and no black persons were recorded as being members. After independence relatively few black members joined any AA group and the organization's influence has remained insignificant.

Peltzer (1989a) has described the therapy of alcohol-related disorders in a Christian sect in Malawi. He remarks that, as among members of AA groups, the "elder" fellow alcoholic provides a role model, but he also mentions other techniques such as spiritual therapy, including purification, prayers and baptism, and "body" therapy, involving stimulation with a wooden stick and a needle (Peltzer does not go into detail). Peltzer describes the traditional African person as more influenced by "the group" than his modern counterpart and he relates this to a greater tendency to somatic illnesses, including alcoholism in the latter group. He concludes that traditional intervention strategies on a social and community level are no longer effective and that strategies aiming at basic lifestyle changes like those in some healing churches are called for.

It would seem surprising that strong AA groups have not developed. Mention has already been made of the strong evangelical influence promoting abstinence, but in such cases there may also be a tendency to reject the "sinner" from church membership. Antze (1987) has drawn attention to the way that certain traditional cults in Zambia (Turner, 1957) are like AA in forging lasting bonds amongst their membership. As he points out, "The adepts have themselves known the suffering the candidates are experiencing." The reason for the virtual nonadoption of AA in Zambia, and perhaps in other countries in the region, deserves further study, at least in examining whether some of its positive influence at least might be found useful; Peltzer's approach may well prove productive in this context.

SOME ECONOMIC ASPECTS OF ALCOHOL IN SOCIETY

One of the implicit themes of this chapter is that of the symbolism of drinking and drinking styles interacting with economic processes. A particularly good example (which also reminds us that other imponderables may have to be included in any equation of analysis of change) is given by Colson and Scudder (1988). They describe how several interconnected events contributed to the creation of a brewing industry in one part of Zambia and induced people to drink more and more heavily, and go on to cite a 1973 account:

> "Gwembe women would probably never have decided to brew in bulk if (100 litre) oil drums had not become available to them, but it was inevitable that oil drums would become available once the decision was made to build roads.... The link between the building of roads and the expansion of brewing is not an obvious one...." (Smith, 1973).

Proving these types of linkages is, however, difficult given the available data.

We have little aggregate information on the economic aspects of alcohol use for the region. The most abundant information comes from South Africa, some of it provided by May (1994). He states that the South Africa beverage alcohol industry creates direct and indirect employment for over 200,000 people; when their dependents are added the total depending upon the beverage alcohol industry is at least one million. The government makes six times the amount made by the shareholders of alcohol production companies from taxation, and the industry generates four times more tax than the gold mining industry and twice as much as the entire mining industry in South Africa. In 1990, more than R2 billion was received by the state from excise duties and sales tax from the sale of wine and beer, of this R1.6 billion came from beer sales. An economic analysis carried out in Zambia in 1980 similarly demonstrated the extent of the reliance of government on taxation of the alcohol industry sector (Serpell, 1981)

Although the estimation of the costs and benefits of alcohol use is a complex subject in which measurement can be difficult, considerable work has been dedicated to the endeavor. Research conducted in South Africa in 1985 indicated that the total cost of alcohol misuse was R1.178 billion yearly (Langley, 1986). SANCA (1993) estimated that by then costs had risen to R5 billion per year. Parry and colleagues (1996) state that the total cost of alcohol misuse can be divided into core costs (e.g., hospital care, training, research) and related costs such as enforcement, and those arising from accidents, fires, damage to property, and so forth.

A major cost is that of medical expenses. Direct core costs are made up of all costs spent in the direct support and treatment of persons who abuse alcohol. Medical costs can be taken to be any type of care for any alcohol-related condition (e.g., fetal alcohol syndrome), and can also include the cost of rehabilitation, and so on. De Miranda (1988) concluded that in South Africa, 30 percent of beds in hospitals for blacks were for patients with alcohol-related disorders. Indirect costs include losses, for example, from premature deaths. Because they are obviously more dificult to calculate, indirect costs are less often taken into account.

One major feature of the system of municipal beer halls, based upon the "Durban system," was that profits could then be utilized for services to the communities in which the beer halls were situated. As the beer halls were replaced by other types of outlets and as the number of unlicensed shebeens increased, revenues from this source fell. The African National Congress health plan for South Africa calls for a complete transformation of the entire health care delivery system. In order to raise additional sources of finance for the public health service there has been a call for increased excise on tobacco and alcohol products, with the objective of both reducing consumption and increasing revenue.

May (1994) states that in South Africa major increases in taxation of beer in 1991, 1992, and 1993 broke a growth trend in consumption that had started in the early 1980s, and he points out that through a "multiplier effect" this resulted in a net economic loss to the country. Similarly, an increase in excise tax on brandy in 1981 resulted in a sharp reduction in sales.

NATIONAL ALCOHOL POLICIES

One of the main factors which have hindered the development and implementation of effective alcohol control policies in sub-Saharan Africa is the reality of the economic benefits of alcohol to the national economies of the countries in the region through taxation and other measures, although most of the governments are now aware of the negative effects of alcohol abuse on national development (Desjarlais, 1995). Thus in Kenya, although the government recognized that it could regulate alcohol consumption through taxation, the limitation of beverage alcohol outlets, and propaganda, it was also aware of the consequences of such measures, particularly on government finances, employment, foreign trade, agricultural interests, tourism, and political popularity (Kiima, 1995). The major control policies in Kenya have, therefore, been concentrated on limitation of availability through presidential campaigns and decrees aimed at reduction of the number of drinking outlets (ibid.).

In some of the countries the ministries of health and education have conducted preventive education campaigns directed at school-age children or at the general population. The mass media occasionally give prominence to public education messages such as "Don't drink and drive," or "Too much alcohol can be dangerous to your health," but these messages are canceled out by the more powerful and attractive advertisements for drinks. Few attempts are made to curb advertisements. In Ghana, for instance, alcohol is currently widely advertised on television and radio (Asare, 1995). Various television and radio competitions have been introduced, which make it possible for a person to win a crate of beer or even a car using a beer cap (Asare, 1995).

We make no attempt to describe the regulatory laws in each country. Because of their origins and the failure to rationalize them, there are often so many inconsistencies that enforcement is at best only partial. For example, laws referring to the drinking of opaque and clear beer in Zambia give two minimum ages for purchase—16 years for opaque beer and 18 years for clear beer. When the laws were established, however, it was hardly possible to enforce restrictions on underage drinking because few people knew their date of birth. Since much of the youthful drinking took place in traditional contexts age mattered less than perceived maturity, and the amount consumed was under the control of the elders. In towns, however, although it was forbidden for Chibuku to be sold for off-premises consumption, many householders would send 13- and 14-year-old boys with open containers to collect the day's supply (Haworth, 1995a).

In Swaziland, youths were able to obtain spirits from bottle stores without difficulty (Haworth, 1982b), and recent studies in South Africa (Nkonzo-Mtembu, 1994) indicate that beverage alcohol is not difficult for adolescents to obtain. Furthermore, a study in Kenya in 1980 (Mwaniki, 1982) found that the number of official beverage alcohol outlets in that country had risen by 144 percent during the previous 10 years. Drinks were so easily available that even children could purchase them easily. Legal drinking laws were also so permissive that alcohol could be obtained at practically any time of day and night. This situation was further boosted by much advertising in newspapers.

When embarking upon the WHO-sponsored Project on Community Response to Alcohol-Related Problems, the principal investigators in Zambia remarked that the country had been chosen because *inter alia* there had been the necessary political will. This is a most important ingredient for successful policy implementation. At the end of the project, a reporting and planning workshop was held, which made recommendations directed at the agency that would be expected to act. These included the Public Service Commission (the employer of civil servants), the Ministries of Health, Home Affairs (Interior), Education and Culture, Provincial and Local Government, Finance, Labor, and Social Services, and Justice, and, in addition, a number of other institutions such as the university. In each case specific recommendations for action were made, but no central coordinating mechanism was put in place. Subsequently, very little happened, although the recommendations were, in fact, highly practical and in many cases could be effected at little cost. For example, the Ministry of Justice was asked to consider incorporating topics on alcohol-related problems into courses and conferences attended by magistrates; it was recommended that the breathalyzer should be brought into use, and so forth.

It was felt that the results of the survey would provide sufficient basic data for action to be planned and carried out. Since the project had been focused upon the activation of communities, helping community members and leaders to identity problems and possible solutions in light of their participation in the project, this formed an important component of follow-up. But, in fact, community leaders had hardly been involved and found it difficult to relate the results of a large-scale survey to their different situations. Thus renewed efforts were made to seek their involvement through the establishment of action committees. A subsequent report carried a description of the processes of failure.

With regard to the monitoring of alcohol-related problems, Haworth (1989a) proposed that emergency room studies might be most useful. However, it was pointed out that strategies and resources must be fitted very exactly to the needs and infrastructures of the countries. WHO, in the collection of data on drug abuse, has been very conscious of a bias towards control of abuse and not towards a response to health problems; preliminary work has been done on producing a guideline document on the collection of information, including data on alcohol-related health problems. Other factors should be taken into account— for example, the need for a simple saliva-based test or the use of breath tests only for blood alcohol concentrations in countries where the collection of samples of venous blood must be limited because of the high prevalence of HIV infection.

Van der Burgh (1994b), in a paper presented at a meeting of the International Council on Alcoholism and Addiction (ICAA), points out the necessity for keeping in mind cultural and historical traditions, the need to maintain a public health perspective, and finally the need to keep a balance between public health and economic interests.

In 1980 a national plan to prevent alcohol abuse and alcoholism in South Africa was formulated, but it lacked a comprehensive strategy for implementation and did not specify responsible bodies and players. The National Advisory Board on Rehabilitation Matters (which was a board appointed by the Minister of Health) decided in 1988 to revive the 1980 plan. In the new version of the plan it was decided to address the problems of drug and alcohol abuse simultaneously and the plan was presented in scheduled format. A working conference followed and a revised plan was approved in 1992. Four working committees on prevention, treatment, research and control, and law enforcement were established. It was later decided that a coordinating mechanism and infrastructure already existed, and the Interdepartmental Consultative Committee on Social Welfare Matters with its Sub-Committee on Alcohol and Drug Dependence was designated to act as coordinator.

The South African National Council on Alcoholism and Drug Dependency (SANCA) was requested to facilitate a meeting which brought together many players. Lessons learned included the need for political will, awareness, involvement and commitment of the community, the value of popular movements and working together, the need for ongoing research, and finally, the need for a single body to set comprehensive and integrated national alcohol and drug policies.

Yach, Parry, and Harrison (1995) have recently commented on the prospects for substance abuse control in South Africa. After the recent dramatic political changes in South Africa, when the black majority gained power, the Government of National Unity embarked upon a reconstruction and development program. The authors point out that an early draft made specific reference to substance abuse. In March 1995 the Ministries of Health and Welfare set up a national alliance, involving government and nongovernmental organizations to address problems of substance abuse; the question of funding remains. Pretorius (Yach, May, & Pretorius, 1994) has discussed the merits of collection of taxes directly from the beverage alcohol trade and the establishment of a consumer fee similar to Value Added Tax (VAT), so that those who drink more would make a bigger and very direct contribution to revenues. All methods, however, carry the hazard that the revenues collected may not be used for the purposes originally specified. Pretorius argues that specific percentages must be allocated to combating substance abuse.

Parry (undated) advocates 10 strategies with a marked emphasis upon community activation and including action on driving while under the influence of alcohol (and obligatory testing for those exceeding the speed limit by 25 km/hour), focused information (e.g., for youth, pregnant women), coherent licensing policies for beverage alcohol outlets, action to control advertising, and promotion of better media advocacy. It is acknowledged that success can only come from a comprehensive approach and the author was aware of constraints, for example, with regard to enforcement of laws and regulations; he cited studies showing that in 1994, 31 percent of high school students were able to buy beverage alcohol directly.

Becker (1994) has drawn attention to the need for the South African legal system to differentiate between persons who have an addiction and need treatment and those who need education. When a person exceeds the speed limit can the court decide between the alcohol-dependent and the irresponsible? Is medical treatment an appropriate punishment for an offense?

Van der Burgh (1994b) points out that stress is being put upon intersectoral approaches and specialized training by such organizations as SANCA and the National Progressive Primary Health Care Network. He stresses, however, that in the design of future policy it will be essential to give attention to the individual social and cultural factors, and he too underlines the need for community involvement in the design and implementation of "indigenous and culturally relevant community-based prevention and education programmes."

Another approach is that of promoting life skills amongst adolescents, which seeks to give young people the skills and training they need to make informed and healthy choices about lifestyles; the process should ideally incorporate family, teachers, and community. Dealing with entry into the world of drinking can be one of the key areas where a life skills approach would be appropriate.

The beverage alcohol industry in South Africa (including Distillers Corporation, Stellenbosch Farmers Winery, and South African Breweries Beer Division) has set up a committee on the social aspects of alcohol called the Industry Association for Responsible Alcohol Use (ARA—formerly known as the Social Aspects of Alcohol Committee (SAAC)). According to its brochures, the association's activities are based upon principles and data obtained through sound scientific research. Most of the activities can be subsumed under the following headings: self-regulation, research, primary prevention through education, and participation in public policy development (see also Chapter 13).

CONCLUDING REMARKS

Singer (1986) has sought to caution writers that no adequate anthropological account of differing drinking practices can be produced without a theoretical framework and he draws, in particular, on the writings of Engels (1969) (first published in 1895). Singer raises many interesting questions which deserve further exploration, such as how the drinking behaviors and drinking conceptions of micropopulations are influenced by the efforts of alcohol producers and promoters; how the alcohol industry, in turn, responds to segmentation in the market; and, in developing nations, the role of the state in facilitating market penetration and expansion of the alcohol industry.

Such an analysis might have been included here. But this is too narrow a theoretical perspective since, as was pointed out in the opening paragraphs, one must take account of economic and social factors. One must also recognize the complexity of individual human behavior, determined as it is partly by genetic and cultural factors, and also by the influence of a simple chemical substance taken into the body in greatly different quantities and at greatly differing rates (often themselves determined by social and economic factors). The process of analysis becomes daunting indeed.

In *Alcohol Policy and the Public Good*, Edwards and colleagues (1994) correctly assert that alcohol consumption is so important in any society that policymakers cannot avoid considering its effects. These authors have pointed out clearly the lack of data on alcohol from developing countries, particularly from Africa. There is, therefore, an urgent need to stimulate and support research on this commodity, which continues to assume a higher and higher role in the social, economic, and political lives of the people in sub-Saharan Africa. The priority research areas include studies of alcohol production, particularly of domestic and traditional production and their economic impact on the people. There is a need for epidemiological studies on the prevalence of alcohol use and abuse as well as on patterns of consumption and their health and socioeconomic consequences, good and bad. Research on risk factors associated with alcohol abuse among the youth is also needed, in order to give guidelines on primary prevention policies. There is also an urgent need for research on mortality and morbidity resulting from drunken driving and on the role of alcohol abuse in violence, assaults, suicide, and homicide. Such research will enhance our understanding of alcohol's potential harm within particular communities in sub-Saharan Africa, allowing for the formulation of policies and prevention programs aimed at reducing the incidence of harm.

Alcohol Policy and the Public Good presents the kind of daunting survey to which we have just alluded, and it can be argued (Haworth, 1995b) that policymakers in most African countries will have neither the time nor the inclination to study its contents. Will this be the fate of the present chapter? It will certainly inform. It may misguide.

A provocative example of the use of wrong measures, before action is taken, is presented by Garner (1997) in discussing whether the measures chosen as objectives in health aid programs impair their effectiveness. Perhaps we still have to refine our measures so that we can understand the impact of alcohol on society in a truly realistic fashion. Our lack of the right data may lead us to see problems as increasing when they are not and to ascribe them to the wrong sources. A prime example is our lack of data on the home production of drinks.

But at the same time governments are sometimes in danger of ignoring alcohol in society as they concentrate their efforts on action against "drug abuse." There is a marked imbalance in the amount of funding being given to combating drug trafficking and to the treatment and rehabilitation of the relatively few drug addicts found in most countries in the region.

Perhaps, therefore, the most important conclusion from this survey is that, however deficient some of our data may be, there are investigators in some countries of the region who should (indeed must) be involved in assisting in the evolution of rational and well-founded policies regarding alcohol, which must at all times be flexible enough to respond to the inevitable changes. This level of expertise needs to be extended to all countries in the regions. And with this there should be increased collaboration between governments, nongovernmental organizations (sometimes with axes to grind), and the alcohol industry. Finally, there is a need for continued research on simpler methods of detection of alcohol abuse and simple methods of intervention. At the same time there is need to promote wider use of existing simple instruments for detection (Babor et al., 1989) and intervention (Babor & Grant, 1992), which have been developed by the WHO in recent years. With regard to policies, emphasis should not be placed entirely on alcohol control measures; other theories or measures which look at hazardous or harmful patterns of drinking as a basis for prevention should also be developed.

The term "patterns" was introduced as a concept that is useful in considering drug abuse, but Haworth (1995a) extended its application to youthful sexual behavior, especially in relation to the prevention of HIV transmission. This is a very obvious application of the concept (see also Grant & Single, 1998) in that it is based upon the idea that some behaviors are extremely likely to continue in one form or another. It is thus better to aim to minimize any harm that might result from actual patterns of behavior than to adopt an idealistic stance requiring the complete elimination of potentially harmful behaviors. Only a select few will be willing to forgo the pleasures of sex; likewise, it is practically inevitable, as Desjarlais (1995) has argued, that nonmedical use of psychoactive drugs will occur in any society. This argument must apply *a fortiori* to the consumption of alcohol. Such an approach implies that an appropriate response to risky patterns of drinking will be required. Thus responses (be they proactive or reactive) need to be shaped to fit the patterns, and this in turn implies that the particular pattern of drinking behavior requiring a response must be well understood. To appreciate how little we do understand, we mention only the need to know much more about the factors influencing people's choices of homemade vs. factory-made beverages in most African countries. While it may be argued that the guarantee of hygienic production of a beverage of a certain composition should be a strong recommendation when compared with the hazards of drinking a beverage which could transmit cholera, the actual underlying reasons for the choice may relate to quite different views of the costs and benefits of drinking.

In our description of drinking in Africa we have been at pains to stress the diversity of cultures in the continent and to stress also the rapidity of social change. These are just two of the many influences on patterns of drinking, which cannot be described in simple terms, say, of quantity and frequency. We must adopt a multidisciplinary approach to our understanding of drinking, even going beyond the debate between anthropologists and sociologists to which we referred at the beginning of the present chapter. Different patterns of consumption need not only be understood, but also monitored, since we must assume that change is inevitable. This chapter is an attempt to present an overview of a complex phenomenon, but it must also be looked upon as an interim report on the status quo. Each country in Africa with a drinking population needs to develop policies on alcohol which ensure that an increased understanding of that population's characteristics and needs will enable the members to obtain the benefits and pleasures they experience in drinking while being protected in appropriate ways against the ill effects of alcohol.

REFERENCES

Abiodun, D. A., et al. (1994). Psychosocial correlates of alcohol, tobacco, and cannabis use amongst secondary school students in Nigeria. *West African Journal of Medicine, 13*, 213–217.

Acuda, S. W. (1979). Drinking patterns in a rapidly changing culture. In G. Edwards & A. Arif (Eds.), *Drug Problems in the Socio-Cultural Context*. Geneva: World Health Organization.

Acuda, S. W. (1985). Alcohol and alcohol problems research—East Africa. *British Journal of Addiction, 80*, 121–126.

Acuda, S. W. (1990). Alcohol research in developing countries—Possibilities and limitations. In J. Maula, M. Lindblad, C. Tigerstedt, & L. Green-Rutanen (Eds.), *Alcohol in Developing Countries: Proceedings from a Meeting in Oslo, Norway, August 7–9, 1988* (15–27). Helsinki: Nordic Council for Alcohol and Drug Research.

Acuda, S. W. (1991). *Alcohol Consumption and Alcohol Problems in Zimbabwe Today*. The 36th International Council on Alcohol and Addictions (ICAA) Institute on the Prevention and Treatment of Alcoholism, Stockholm.

Acuda, S. W., Eide, A. H., Gudyanga, B. H. T., & Khan, N. (1991). *Epidemiological Study on Substance Use Among Secondary School Students in Mashonaland East and Harare Provinces, Zimbabwe*. International Labor Organization/United Nations Fund for Drug Abuse Control/ZIMBABWE.

Adelekan, M. L. (1989). The epidemiology of alcohol and drug use among youths in Ogun State Nigeria. In *Proceedings of the 35th International Congress on Alcoholism and Drug Dependence, 1* (15–25). Oslo: National Directorate for Prevention of Alcoholism and Drug Dependence.

Adelekan, M. E., Abioduna, O. A., Imouokhome-Obayanb, A. O., Oni, G. A., & Ogunremia, O. O. (1993). Psychosocial correlates of alcohol, tobacco, and cannabis use: Findings from a Nigerian university. *Drug and Alcohol Dependence, 33*, 247–256.

Ambler, C. (1992). Alcohol and the control of labour on the Copperbelt. In C. Crush & J. Ambler (Eds.), *Liquor and Labor in Southern Africa* (339–366). Athens, OH: Ohio University Press.

Ambler, C. & Crush, J. (1992). Alcohol in Southern African labor history. In C. Crush & J. Ambler (Eds.), *Liquor and Labor in Southern Africa* (1–55). Athens, OH: Ohio University Press.

American Psychiatric Association (1980). *Diagnostic and Statistical Manual of Mental Disorders 3rd Ed*. Washington, DC: American Psychiatric Press.

Antze, P. (1987). Symbolic Action in Alcoholics Anonymous. In M. Douglas (Ed.), *Constructive Drinking* (149–181). Cambridge: Cambridge University Press.

Asare, J. B. (1995). Substance Abuse in Ghana. The WHO Inter-Country Workshop on Alcohol and Substance in Africa, Kampala, Uganda.

Asuni, T. (1974). Patterns of alcohol problems as seen in the Neuropsychiatric Hospital, Aro. *Proceedings of the 1974 Workshop of the Association of Psychiatrists in Africa, Nairobi.* Lausanne: International Council on Alcohol and Addictions.

Babor, T. F., et al. (1994). A randomized clinical trial of brief interventions in primary health care: Summary of a WHO project. *Addiction, 89,* 657–678.

Babor, T. F., de la Fuente, J. R., Sounders, J., & Grant, M. (1989). *AUDIT: The Alcohol Use Disorders Identification Test: Guidelines for Use in Primary Health Care.* Geneva: World Health Organization.

Babor, T. F. & Grant, M. (1992). *Project on Identification and Management of Alcohol Related Problems: Report of Phase II: A Randomized Clinical Trial of Brief Interventions in Primary Health Care.* Geneva: World Health Organization.

Badia, P. (1985). *Clinical Presentation of Alcoholism at Mathari Hospital Nairobi, Kenya.* Dissertation, Department of Psychiatry, University of Nairobi.

Baker, J. (1992). Prohibition and illicit liquor on the Witwatersrand, 1902–1932. In C. Crush & J. Ambler (Eds.), *Liquor and Labor in Southern Africa* (139–162). Athens, OH: Ohio University Press.

Becker, K. (1994). The consequences of drunken driving in South Africa. *Medicine & Law, 13,* 11–17.

Beckman, V. (1988). *Alcohol: Another Trap for Africa.* Örebro, Sweden: Libris.

Bisley, G. & Burkitt, W. R. (1974). Eye diseases. In I. C. Vogel, et al. (Ed.), *Health and Disease in Kenya.* Nairobi: East African Literature Bureau.

Bittah, O. & Acuda, S. W. (1979). Alcohol Gastritis at Kenyatta National Hospital. *East African Medical Journal, 56,* 577–579.

Bittah, O., Owola, J. A., & Oduor, P. (1979). A study of alcoholism in a rural setting in Kenya. *East African Medical Journal, 56,* 665–670.

Buchan, D. J. (1988). Studies in blood alcohol in the workers of a Zambian copper mine. *Alcohol and Alcoholism, 23,* 239–242.

Buchan, T. (undated). *Medical Aspects of Alcoholism in Zimbabwe—A Transcultural Study* (unpublished).

Buchan, T. & Baker, A. P. (1974). Psychiatric services in Matabeleland. *South African Medical Journal, 48,* 925–930.

Buchan, T. & Chikara, F. B. (1980). Psychiatric out-patient services in Zimbabwe. *South African Medical Journal, 57,* 1095–1098.

Butchart, A., Lerer, L. B., & Blanche, M. T. (1994). Imaginary constructions and forensic reconstructions of fatal violence against women: Implications for community violence prevention. *Forensic Science International, 64,* 21–34.

Carothers, J. C. (1948). A study of mental derangement in Africans and an attempt to explain its peculiarities more specifically in relation to the African attitude to life. *Journal of Mental Science, 93,* 548–596.

Carstairs, G. M. (1973). Psychiatric problems of developing countries. *British Journal of Psychiatry, 123,* 271–277.

Chaplin, J. H. (1961). Suicide in Northern Rhodesia. *African Studies, 20,* 145–175.

Chawla, S. (1988). Drug Abuse in Zimbabwe. In J. C. Ebie & E. Tongue (Eds.), *Handbook of the African Training Courses in Drug Dependence.* Laussane: International Council on Alcohol and Addiction.

Cheetham, R. W. S. (1974). Road safety and mental health in South Africa. *South African Medical Journal, 48,* 225–229.

Chinyadza, E., et al. (1993). Alcohol problems among patients attending five primary health care clinics in Harare city. *Central African Journal of Medicine, 39*, 26–32.

Coetzee, N., Yach, D., & Joubert, G. (1988). Crowding and alcohol abuse as risk factors for tuberculosis in the Mamre population. *South African Medical Journal, 74*, 352–354.

Collis, C. H. (1972). Cancer of the oesophagus and alcoholic drinks in East Africa. *Lancet*, 1441.

Collis, C. H., Cook, P. J., Foreman, J. K., & Palframan, J. F. (1971). A search for nitrosamines in East African spirit samples from areas of varying oesophageal cancer distributions. *Gut, 12*, 1015–1018.

Colson, E. & Scudder, T. (1988). *For Prayer and Profit. The Ritual, Economic and Social Importance of Beer in Gwembe District, Zambia 1950/1982*. Stanford, CA: Stanford University Press.

Cox, J. L. (1978). Psychiatric diagnosis of 94 male patients admitted to Butabika Mental Hospital, Uganda. *African Journal of Psychiatry, 4*, 103–107.

Crush, C. & Ambler, J., eds. (1992). *Liquor and Labor in Southern Africa*. Athens, OH: Ohio University Press.

Damasio, A. R. (1994). *Descartes' Error: Emotion, Reason, and the Human Brain*. New York: G. P. Putnam.

Davis, S. & Smith, C. S. (1982). Alcohol and drowning in Cape Town: Preliminary report. *South African Medical Journal, 62*, 931–933.

De Miranda, S. (1988). Alcoholism: The incidence, treatment of rehabilitation in the South African population. *Rehabilitation in South Africa, 32*, 83–87.

Department of Education and Culture. (1990). *Care for Our Youth 2000*. Pretoria: Government Printer.

Desjarlais, D. C. (1995). Harm reduction—A framework for incorporating science into drug policy. *American Journal of Public Health, 85*, 10–12.

Desjarlais, R., Elsenberg, L., Good, B., & Kleinman, A., (Eds.). (1995). *World Mental Health: Problems and Priorities in Low Income Countries*. New York: Oxford University Press.

Dewey, M. E., Chambwe, A., & Slade, P. D. (1983). Behaviour patterns of alcohol use among young adults in Britain and Zimbabwe. *British Journal of Addiction, 78*, 311–316.

Dickie-Clark, H. F. (1966). *The Marginal Situation: A Sociological Study of a Coloured Group*. London: Routledge & Keegan Paul.

Douglas, M. (1987). A distinctive anthropological perspective. In M. Douglas (Ed.), *Constructive Drinking: Perspectives on Drink from Anthropology* (3–15). Cambridge: Cambridge University Press.

Duflou-Jalc, L. D. L. & Knobel, G. J. (1988). Homicide in Cape Town, South Africa. *American Journal of Forensic and Medical Pathology, 9*, 290–294.

Ebie, J. C. (1990). The use of different alcoholic beverages in two urban areas of Nigeria. In J. Maula, M. Lindblad, C. Tigerstedt, & L. Green-Rutanen (Eds.), *Alcohol in Developing Countries: Proceedings from a Meeting in Oslo, Norway, August 7–9, 1988* (168–184). Helsinki: Nordic Council for Alcohol and Drug Research.

Edwards, G. (1977). The alcohol dependence syndrome: Usefulness of an idea. In G. Edwards & M. Grant (Eds.), *Alcoholism, New Knowledge, and New Responses*. London: Croom Helm.

Edwards, G., et al. (1977). *Alcohol-Related Disabilities* (WHO Offset Publication 32). Geneva: World Health Organization.

Edwards, G., et al. (1994). *Alcohol Policy and the Public Good*. Oxford: Oxford University Press.

Eide, A. H. & Acuda, S. W. (1996). Cultural orientation and adolescents' alcohol use in Zimbabwe. *Addiction, 91*, 807–814.

Engels, F. (1969). *The Condition of the Working Class in England*. London: Granada.

Epstein, A. L. (1958). *Politics in an Urban African Community*. Manchester: Manchester University Press.

Ferguson, A. L. (1974). Epidemiology of traffic accidents. *South African Medical Journal, 48*, 225–229.

Flisher, A. J, Riccitelli, G., Jhetam, N., & Robertson, B. A. (1996). *Professional Activities of Psychiatrists in South Africa: Implications for the year 2000.* Ninth National Psychiatry Conference, Sun City, South Africa.

Flisher, A. J., Ziervogel, C. F., Chalton, D. O., & Robertson, B. A. (1993). Risk-taking behaviour of Cape Peninsula high school students: Part IV, Alcohol use. *South African Medical Journal, 83,* 480–482.

Fylkesnes, K., Musonda, R. N., Kasumba, K., Ndhlovu, Z., Mluanda, F., Kaltano, A., & Chipaila, C. C. (1997). The HIV epidemic in Zambia—Socio-demographic prevalence patterns and indications of trends among child-bearing women. *AIDS, 11,* 339–345.

Garner, P. (1997). Do objectives of health-aid programmes impair their effectiveness. *Lancet, 349,* 722–723.

Gelfand, M. (1971). The extent of alcohol consumption by Africans: The significance of the weapon at beer drinks. *Journal of Forensic Medicine, 18,* 53–64.

German, G. A. (1972). Aspects of clinical psychiatry in sub-Saharan Africa. *British Journal of Psychiatry, 121,* 461–479.

Giorgis, A. (1995). *Overview of the Supply and Demand Reduction Activities in Ethiopia.* The WHO Inter-Country Workshop on Alcohol and Substance Abuse in Africa, Kampala, Uganda.

Grant, E. S. (1995). *Alcohol and Drug Abuse in Liberia.* The WHO Inter-Country Workshop on Alcohol and Substance Abuse in Africa, Kampala, Uganda.

Grant, M. & Single, E. (1998). Shifting the paradigm: Reducing harm and promoting beneficial patterns. In M. Grant & J. Litvak (Eds.), *Drinking Patterns and Their Consequences* (287–298). Washington, DC: Taylor & Francis.

Haggblade, S. (1992). The shebeen queen and the evolution of Botswana's sorghum beer industry. In C. Crush & J. Ambler (Eds.), *Liquor and Labor in Southern Africa* (395–412). Athens, OH: Ohio University Press.

Handunka, F. (1996). *Drinking among 200 Schoolchildren in Zambia.* Lusaka: University of Zambia, Department of Community Medicine.

Harwood, A. (1964). Beer drinking and famine in a Safwa village: A case of adaptation in time of crisis. In *Proceedings of the East African Institute of Social Research Conference, 1964.*

Haworth, A. (1982). *WHO Mission on the Assessment of the Magnitude and Nature of Changes in Alcohol Consumption and Alcohol-Related Problems in Swaziland.* Assignment Report submitted to WHO (AFRO).

Haworth, A. (1984). *Is the Ledermann Hypothesis Applicable in the Study of the Consequences of Drinking in African Countries?* Conference on Medical Geography, Lusaka, Zambia.

Haworth, A. (1988). Alcohol problems among patients at the UTH Casualty Department, Lusaka. *East African Journal of Medicine, 65,* 653–657.

Haworth, A. (1989a). Alcohol-related casualties in Africa. In N. Giesbrecht, et al. (Eds.), *Drinking and Casualties: Accidents, Poisonings, and Violence in an International Perspective.* New York: Routledge.

Haworth, A. (1989b). *Training Health Workers in Zambia for Counselling for HIV Infection.* Fifth International Conference on AIDS.

Haworth, A. (1991). *Medical and Social Consequences of Alcohol Consumption in Zambia.* The 36th International Council on Alcohol and Addictions, Institute on the Prevention and Treatment of Alcoholism, Stockholm.

Haworth, A. (1995a). *Youth, Drugs and Health in Africa—Linkages.* Expert Group Meeting on Youth, Drugs, and Health, United Nations Economic Commission for Africa and the Commonwealth Youth Programme, Africa Centre, Lusaka.

Haworth, A. (1995b). Zambia: The need for a national "Policy Options Working Group": Commentaries. Alcohol Policy and the Public Good: Further debate. *Addiction, 90,* 1447–1448.

Haworth, A., Mwanalushi, M., & Todd, D. (1981a). *Community Response to Alcohol-Related Problems in Zambia* (Community Health Research Reports 1–7). Lusaka: Community Health Research Unit, Institute for African Studies, University of Zambia.

Haworth, A., Ng'andu, S., Nyambe, B., & Sinyangwe, I. (1981b). *Alcohol and Drug Use Amongst Students in Zambia*. Educational Research Bureau Reports. Lusaka: University of Zambia.

Haworth, A. & Nyambe, B. (1979). *A Preliminary Report on a Study of Alcohol and Drug Use Amongst Students from Five Lusaka Secondary Schools* (unpublished).

Haworth, A. & Serpell, R. (1981). *A Summary of the Final Report on Phase 1. Community Response to Alcohol-Related Problems*. National Conference of Community Response to Alcohol Related Problems. Lusaka: University of Zambia, Institute for African Studies.

Heath, D. B. (1975). A critical review of ethnographic studies of alcohol use. In R. J. Gibbon, & Y. Israel (Eds.), *Research Advances in Alcohol and Drug Problems*. New York: John Wiley & Sons.

Heath, D. B. (1986). Drinking and drunkenness in transcultural perspective. *Psychiatric Research, 23*, 103–126.

Jessor, R., et al. (1968). *Society, Personality and Deviant Behaviour: A Study of a Tri-Ethnic Community*. New York: Holt, Rinehart & Winston.

Kabeta, H. M. & Sakala, S. C. (1993). *Alcohol Consumption Patterns, Preferences, and Attitudes in Zambia* (Consultancy Report 932). Zambia: The Copperbelt University Business Research Centre.

Kasirye-Lugoloobi, R. (1995). *Role of Non-Governmental Organizations in Alcohol and Substance Abuse Demand Reduction Programmes in Uganda*. The WHO Inter-Country Workshop on Alcohol and Substance Abuse in Africa, Kampala, Uganda.

Kaunda, A. T. E. (1995). *Malawi*. Expert Group Meeting on Youth, Drugs, and Health, United Nations Economic Commission for Africa and the Commonwealth Youth Programme, Africa Centre, Lusaka.

Kay, G. (1960). A Social and Economic Study of Fort Rosebery. *Rhodes-Livingstone Communication 21*.

Khan, N. (1986). *Substance Use Among Male Secondary School Pupils: Its Prevalence and Concomitants*. Dissertation. Lusaka: University of Zimbabwe.

Kiima, D. T. M. (1995). *The State of Substance Abuse and the Programme of Activities Against It in Kenya*. The WHO Inter-Country Workshop on Alcohol and Substance Abuse in Africa, Kampala, Uganda.

Kilonzo, G. P. & Pitkanen, Y. T. (1992). *Pombe: Report of Alcohol Research Projects in Tanzania 1988–90*. Helsinki: University of Helsinki Institute of Development Studies.

Kobus, H. J. (1980). Breath analysis for control of drunk driving in Zimbabwe. *Central African Journal of Medicine, 26*, 21–27.

Kortteinen, T. (1989). *Agricultural Alcohol and Social Change in the Third World: Volume 38*. Helsinki: Finnish Foundation for Alcohol Studies.

Langley, M. (1986). *Estimating the Prevalence and Cost of Alcoholism in South Africa*. Johannesburg: South African National Council on Alcoholism and Drug Dependence.

Lerer, L. B. (1992). Homicide and alcohol in Cape Town. *Forensic Science International, 55*, 93–99.

Loewenthal, M. N., Siddorn, J. A., Patel, R. P., & Fine, J. (1967). Haemosiderosis, osteoporosis and scurvy. *Medical Journal of Zambia*, 43–49.

Loftus, I. A. J. & Dada, M. A. (1992). A retrospective analysis of alcohol in medicolegal postmortems over a period of five years. *American Journal of Forensic and Medical Pathology, 13*, 248–252.

Louw, W. (1990). *Social Consequences of Alcohol Abuse in South Africa: Challenges for a Post-Apartheid South Africa*. Belleville, South Africa: Institute for Social Development, University of the Western Cape.

Lovelace, C. E. A. & Nyathi, C. B. (1977). Estimation of the fungal toxins, zearalenone, and aflatoxin, contaminating opaque maize beer in Zambia. *Journal of Food and Agricultural Sciences, 28*, 288–292.

Lutalo, S. K. (1993). Gout: An experience from Zimbabwe. *Central African Journal of Medicine, 39*, 60–62.

Lutalo, S. K. & Mabonga, N. (1992). A clinical assessment of the consequences of alcohol consumption in "communal" drinkers in the Zimbabwean Midlands. *Central African Journal of Medicine, 38,* 380–384.

MacShearreigh, E. T. M. (1969). Chronic neurological syndromes and alcohol induced hypoglycaemia: A hypothesis. *East African Medical Journal, 56,* 577–579.

Magee, P. N. & Barne, J. M. (1967). Carcinogenic nitrosamine compounds. *Advances in Cancer Research, 10,* 163–246.

Malepe, T. B. (1989). Alcohol-related problems in Swaziland. *Contemporary Drug Problems, 16,* 43–58.

May, G. (1994). Licensing as an alcohol control measure within the South African National Control Strategy. National Urbanisation and Health Research Programme, *Urbanisation and Health Newsletters* (67–69). South Africa: Medical Research Council.

May, J. (1973). *Drinking in a Rhodesian African Township* (Occasional Paper 8). Salisbury: University of Rhodesia, Department of Sociology.

McGlashan, N. D. (1969). Oesophageal cancer and alcoholic spirits in Central Africa. *Gut, 10,* 643–650.

McMaster, J. & Keshav, C. (1994). Perceptions of normal alcohol use held by Zimbabwean high school students. *Central African Journal of Medicine, 40,* 88–94.

Mitchell, J. C. (1974). *The Kalela Dance: Aspects of Social Relationships Among Urban Africans in Northern Rhodesia.* Manchester: Manchester University Press.

Mngola, E. N. & Odeny, J. W. (1972). Gouty arthritis in Kenyatta National Hospital. *Nairobi Journal of Medicine, 5,* 6–8.

Mohamed, A. E., Kew, M. C., & Groeneveld, H. T. (1992). Alcohol consumption as a risk factor for hepatocellular carcinoma in urban southern African Blacks. *International Journal of Cancer, 51,* 537–541.

Molamu, L. (1988). Use and abuse of alcohol in southern Africa. In *Proceedings of the Regional Symposium. Gaborone, Botswana.*

Molamu, L. (1989). Alcohol in Botswana: A historical review. *Contemporary Drug Problems, 16*(1), 3–42.

Molamu, L. & Manyenyeng, W. G. (1988). *Alcohol Use and Abuse in Botswana: Report of a Study.* Gaborone: Health Education Unit, Botswana Ministry of Health.

Molamu, L. & Mbere, N. (1988). Alcohol use and abuse in Botswana: A community study. In J. Maula, M. Lindblad, C. Tigerstedt, & L. Green-Rutanen (Eds.), *Alcohol in Developing Countries: Proceedings from a Meeting in Oslo, Norway, August 7–9, 1988* (93–112). Helsinki: Nordic Council for Alcohol and Drug Research.

Moremoholo, R. A. (1989). Use and abuse of alcohol in Lesotho. *Contemporary Drug Problems, 16,* 59–69.

Moses, P. F. (1989). Use and abuse of alcohol in Zimbabwe. *Contemporary Drug Problems, 16,* 71–80.

Munodawafa, D., Marty, P. J., & Gwede, C. (1992). Drug use and anticipated parental reaction among rural school pupils in Zimbabwe. *Journal of School Health, 62,* 471–474.

Muokolo, A. (1990). Alcohol and its main functions in the Congo. In J. Maula, M. Lindblad, C. Tigerstedt, & L. Green-Rutanen (Eds.), *Alcohol in Developing Countries: Proceedings from a Meeting in Oslo, Norway, August 7–9, 1988* (127–133). Helsinki: Nordic Council for Alcohol and Drug Research.

Mushanga, T. M. (1974). *Criminal Homicide in Uganda: A Sociological Study on Violent Deaths in Ankole, Kigezi, and Toro Districts of Western Uganda.* Kampala, Uganda: East African Literature Bureau.

Mushanga, T. M. (1976). *Crime and Deviance: An Introduction to Crimonology.* Kampala, Uganda: East African Literature Bureau.

Mwanalushi, M. (1981). The African experience. *World Health, August,* 13–15.

Mwaniki, B. W. (1982). *Production and Sale of Alcohol and Tobacco Products in Kenya.* Report of the National Environment and Human Settlement Secretariat, Nairobi.

Nahim, E. A. (1995). *Drug Abuse in Sierra Leone.* The WHO Inter-Country Workshop on Alcohol and Substance Abuse, Kampala, Uganda.

Neame, P. B. & Joubert, S. M. (1961). Post-alcohol hypoglycaemia and toxic hepatitis. *Lancet, 2,* 893–897.

Nielsen, M. F., Resnick, C. A., & Acuda, S. W. (1989). Alcoholism among outpatients of a rural district General Hospital in Kenya. *British Journal of Addictions, 84,* 1343–1351.

Nikander, P., et al. (1992). Role of alcohol in injuries treated in the Muhimbili Medical Centre Casualty Department, Dar es Salaam. In G. P. Kilonzo & Y. T. Pitkane (Eds.), *Pombe: Report of Alcohol Research Projects in Tanzania 1988–1990.* Helsinki: University of Helsinki, Institute of Development Studies.

Nikander, P., Seppala, T., Kilonzo, G. P., Hattunen, P., Saarinen, L., Kilima, E., & Pitkanen, T. (1991). Ingredients and contaminants of traditional alcoholic beverages in Tanzania. *Transactions of the Royal Society of Tropical Medicine and Hygiene, 85,* 133–135.

Nkonzo-Mtembu, L. L. (1994). An investigation of the opinions of black adolescents in the Esikhawini area of Kwa-Zulu in regard to the use and abuse of alcohol. *Curationis, 17,* 50–53.

Nortey, D. & Senah, K. A. (1990). *Epidemiological Study of Drug Abuse Among the Youths in Ghana.* Accra: United Nations Educational Scientific and Cultural Organization (UNESCO).

Nout, M. J. R. (1981). *Aspects of Manufacture and Consumption of Kenyan Traditional Beverages.* Dissertation, University of Wageningen, Netherlands.

Obasi, O. E., Ogbadu, G. H., & Ukoha, A. I. (1987). Aflatoxin in burukutu (millet beer). *Transactions of the Royal Society of Tropical Medicine and Hygiene, 81,* 879.

Odejide, A. O. & Olatawura, M. O. (1977). Alcohol use in a Nigerian rural community. *African Journal of Psychiatry, 1,* 69–74.

Odejide, O. A., Ohaeri, J. U., Ikuesan, B. A., & Adelekan, M. L. (1990). Need for cross-cultural collaborative research activities: The promotion of alcohol research in Nigeria. In J. Maula, M. Lindblad, C. Tigerstedt, & L. Green-Rutanen (Eds.), *Alcohol in Developing Countries: Proceedings from a Meeting in Oslo, Norway, August 7–9, 1988.* Helsinki: Nordic Council for Alcohol and Drug Research.

Ojiambo, H. P. (1971). Recent advances in the management of cardiomyopathies. *Nairobi Journal of Medicine, 4,* 99–101.

Okada, F. E. (1967). *Excessive Drinking and Crime: A Survey of Selected Court Cases from Central Province.* Research Unit, Department of Community Development. Lusaka: Government of Republic of Zambia.

Okoye, Z. S. C. & Ekenyong, K. I. (1984). Aflatoxin B in native millet beer brewed in Jos suburbs in Nigeria. *Transactions of the Royal Society of Tropical Medicine and Hygiene, 78,* 417–418.

O'Meara, E. (1993). *A Youth Health Profile.* Windhoek: Republic of Namibia, Ministry of Youth and Sport.

Panduwa, A. (1978). Life in a squatter community. In L. M. van den Berg (Ed.), *Hard times in the City.* Lusaka: Committee on Student Publications, School of Humanities and Social Sciences, University of Zambia..

Parry, C. (undated). *Alcohol Misuse and Responses in South Africa.* Medical Research Council.

Parry, C. (1994a). Alcohol misuse: A significant public health threat facing the new South Africa. National Urbanisation and Health Research Programme, *Urbanisation and Health Newsletters.* South Africa: Medical Research Council.

Parry, C. (1994b). Prevalence of alcohol misuse in South Africa: A review of empirical research. National Urbanisation and Health Research Programme, *Urbanisation and Health Newsletters* (33–38). South Africa: Medical Research Council.

Parry, C., Tibbs, J., van der Spuy, J., & Cummins, G. (1996). Alcohol attributable fractions for trauma in South Africa. *Research, 19,* 2–5.

Partanen, J. (1990). Abstinence in Africa. In J. Maula, M. Lindblad, C. Tigerstedt, L. Green-Rutanen (Eds.). *Alcohol in Developing Countries: Proceedings from a Meeting in Oslo, Norway, August 7–9, 1988* (pp. 70–85). Helsinki: Nordic Council for Alcohol and Drug Research.

Partanen, J. (1991). *Sociability and Intoxication: Alcohol and Drinking in Kenya. Volume 39.* Helsinki: Finnish Foundation for Alcohol Studies.

Patel, N. S. & Bhagwat, G. P. (1977). Road traffic accidents in Lusaka and blood alcohol. *Medical Journal of Zambia, 11,* 46–49.

Peltzer, K. (1989a). Biopsychosocial therapy of alcohol and cannabis-related disorders in the Zion Christian Church (ZCC) in Malawi. In K. Peltzer & P. O. Ebigbo (Eds.), *Clinical Psychology in Africa.* Enugu: Working Group for African Psychology.

Pernanen, K. (1989). Causal attributions in relation to alcohol-related accidents. In N. Giesbrecht (Ed.), *Drinking and Casualties: Accidents, Poisonings, and Violence in an International Perspective.* London: Routledge.

Pernanen, K. (1991). *Causal attributions in relation to alcohol-related accidents.* International Symposium on Alcohol-Related Accidents and Injuries. Lausanne: Swiss Foundation for Alcohol Research.

Pieterse, S. H. (1985). Blood alcohol levels in motor vehicle accident fatalities in the Republic of South Africa. *Acta Medicine Legalis et Socialis, 35,* 250–256.

Platt, B. S. (1955). Some traditional alcoholic beverages and their importance in indigenous African communities. In *Proc. Nutritional Society, 14,* 115–124.

Pokorny, A. D., Miller, B. A., & Kaplan, H. B. (1972). The brief M.A.S.T.: A shortened version of the Michigan Alcoholism Screening Test. *American Journal of Psychiatry, 129,* 342–345.

Popper, H. (1979). Hepatic cancers in man: Quantitative perspectives. *Environmental Research, 19,* 482–494.

Reader, D. H. & May, J. (1971). *Drinking Patterns in Rhodesia* (Occasional Paper 5). Salisbury: University of Rhodesia, Department of Sociology.

Rees, D., et al. (1993). Solvent exposure, alcohol consumption, and liver injury in workers manufacturing paint. *Scandinavian Journal of Work, Environment, & Health, 19,* 236–244.

Reilly, M., Nwegbe, & Ofafor, B. (1974). The methanol, ethanol, and fusel-oil contents of some Zambian-alcohol drinks. *Medical Journal of Zambia, 8,* 13–14.

Richards, A. I. (1939). *Land, Labour, and Diet in Northern Rhodesia: An Economic Study of the Bemba Tribe.* London: Oxford University Press.

Ritson, E. B. (1985). *Community Response to Alcohol-Related Problems. Review of an International Study* (Public Health Paper 81). Geneva: World Health Organization.

Robins, C. M. & Pollnac, R. B. (1969). Drinking patterns and acculturation in rural Buganda. *American Anthropologist, 71,* 276–284.

Rocha-Silva, L. (1987a). Towards a more detailed measurement of quantity and frequency of alcohol intake in Whites in the Republic of South Africa. *South Africa Journal of Sociology, 18,* 133–138.

Rocha-Silva, L. (1987b). The prevalence of alcohol-related problems among White South Africans—Some multisource evidence. *International Journal of the Addictions, 22,* 927–940.

Rocha-Silva, L. (1991). *Alcohol and Other Drug Use by Black Residents of Selected Areas in the RSA.* Pretoria: Human Sciences Research Council.

Rocha-Silva, L. (1994). Alcohol- and other drug-related risks in informal urban settlements in South Africa: A comparative perspective. National Urbanisation and Health Research Programme, *Urbanisation and Health Newsletters* (20–32). South Africa: Medical Research Council.

Rocha-Silva, L., de Miranda, S., & Erasmus, R. (1995). *Alcohol, Drug Use, and Related Matters: Young Black South Africans (10–21 years).* Pretoria: Centre for Alcohol and Drug Research, Human Sciences Research Council.

Room, R. (1984). Alcohol and ethnography: A case of problem deflation? *Current Anthropology, 25,* 169–191.

Rootman, I. & Moser, J. (1984). *Community Response to Alcohol-Related Problems: A World Health Organization Project Monograph.* Washington, DC: National Institute on Alcohol Abuse and Alcoholism.

SANCA (1993). *Alcohol and Other Drug Use, Abuse and Related Problems: Fact Sheet.* Pretoria: South African National Council on Alcohol and Alcoholism.

Saunders, J. B. & Aasland, O. G. (1978). *WHO Collaborative Project on Identification and Treatment of Persons with Harmful Alcohol Consumption. Phase I: Development of a Screening Instrument.* Geneva: World Health Organization.

Serpell, N. (1981). The Alcohol Industry in Zambia. The WHO Conference on Alcohol, Lusaka, Zambia.

Shaw, L. (1965). The practical use of projective personality tests as accident predictors. *Traffic Safety Research Review, 9,* 34–72.

Singer, M. (1986). Toward a political-economy of alcoholism: The missing link in the anthropology of drinking. *Social Science and Medicine, 23,* 113–130.

Smith, V. X. (1973). *Excessive Drinking and Alcoholism in the Republic of Zambia.* Dissertation, Howard University, Washington, DC.

Tanner, R. E. S. (1970). *Homicide in Uganda.* Uppsala: Scandinavian Institute of African Studies.

Tibbs, J., Parry, C., Stretch, C., & Brice, H. (1994). The influence of the media and other factors in drinking among youth. *Southern African Journal of Child and Adolescent Psychiatry, 6,* 39–46.

Tichelaar, H. Y., Benade, A. J., O'Keefe, S. J., Jooste, P. L., Swanevelder, S. A., Van Staden, E. (1992). Plasma lipids and fatty acids in urbanized Bushmen, Hereros, and Kavangos of Southern Africa (Namibia). *Lipids, 27,* 729–732.

Turner, V. W. (1957). *Schism and Continuity in an African Society: A Study of Ndembu Village Life.* Manchester: Manchester University Press.

Uwaifo, A. O. & Bababanmi, E. A. (1984). Liver carcinogenesis in tropical Africa. In A. O. Williams, G. T. O'Conor, G. B. De-Thé, & C. A. Johnson (Eds.), *Virus-Associated Cancers in Africa* (IARC Scientific Publications 63, pp. 59–88). Lyon: International Agency for Research on Cancer.

van der Burgh, C. (1983). Drinking patterns in multi-ethnic South African society. *Journal of Studies on Alcohol, 44,* 446–459.

van der Burgh, C. (1994a). Historical review of the process leading up to the present national strategy against alcohol and other drug abuse in South Africa and the establishment of the Autonomous Substance Abuse Working Group (ASAWOG). National Urbanisation and Health Research Programme, *Urbanisation and Health Newsletters* (79–83). South Africa: Medical Research Council.

van der Burgh, C. (1994b). *Some lessons en route to a national alcohol and drug policy and strategies for the new South Africa.* The International Institute on the Prevention and Treatment of Alcoholism and Drug Dependence, International Council on Alcoholism and Addiction, Stockholm.

Vizcaino, A. P., Parkin, D. M., & Skinner, M. E. (1995). Risk factors associated with oesophageal cancer in Bulawayo, Zimbabwe. *British Journal of Cancer, 72,* 769–773.

Walsh, B. & Grant, M. (1985). *Public Health Implications of Alcohol Production and Trade* (WHO Offset Publication 88). Geneva: World Health Organization.

Wanjiru, F. (1979). *Alcoholism, the Man and His Integration Into Society.* Dissertation, Department of Sociology, University of Nairobi.

WHO. (1980). *Problems Related to Alcohol Consumption: Report of a WHO Expert Commitee* (WHO Technical Report Series 650). Geneva: World Health Organization.

WHO. (1985). Technical Report Series 48. Geneva.

WHO. (1991). *Evaluation of Methods for Treatment of Mental Disorders: Report of a WHO Scientific Group.* Technical Report Series 812. Geneva: World Health Organization.

Willcox, P. & Gelfand, M. (1976). Spontaneous hypoglycaemia in Rhodesian Africans. *Central African Journal of Medicine, 22,* 77–60.

Wolcott, H. F. (1974). *The African Beer Gardens of Bulawayo: Integrated Drinking in a Segregated Society.* [Monograph 10]. New Brunswick, NJ: Publications Division of the Rutgers Center of Alcohol Studies.

Wood, J. F. (1975). Psychiatry: Half a century of growth. In S. A. Hall & B. W. Langlands (Eds.), *Uganda Atlas of Disease Distribution.* Nairobi: East African Publishing House.

Yach, D., May, G., & Pretorius, L. (1994). Tax on alcohol products to supplement funding for primary health care in South Africa. National Urbanisation and Health Research Programme, *Urbanisation and Health Newsletters* (70–78). South Africa: Medical Research Council.

Yach, D., Parry, C., & Harrison, S. (1995). Editorial: Prospects for substance abuse control in South Africa. *Addiction, 90,* 1293–1296.

Yambo, M. & Acuda, S. W. (1983). *Epidemiology of Drug Use and Abuse: Final Report of the Pilot Study in Nairobi City and Kyaune Sub Location, Kenya.* Nairobi: University of Nairobi.

Yguel, J. S., Luciani, S., Duflo, B., M'Bamezoui, C., Froment, A., Bard, D., & Gentilini, M. (1990). Consumption of alcoholic drinks in three different parts of Cameroon. In J. Maula, M. Lindblad, C. Tigerstedt, & L. Green-Rutanen (Eds.), *Alcohol in Developing Countries: Proceedings from a Meeting in Oslo, Norway, August 7–9, 1988.* Helsinki: Nordic Council for Alcohol and Drug Research.

Zizhour, J., Zhakata, E., & Eide, A. (1990). *Drug and alcohol abuse in the workplace.* Pilot survey: Supervisors' Opinion on Abuse Among the Workforce in One Company. Harare, Zimbabwe.

Chapter 3

Asia: An Overview

Shanti Jayasuriya and D. C. Jayasuriya

THE CHANGING SCENARIO

The Asian region—comprised of six of the 10 most populous countries in the world—represents not only one of the largest and most rapidly growing consumer markets, but also an extraordinary diversity of ethnic, social, economic, religious, and political characteristics that make each country's context unique and different from the others. Indeed, within some countries there are significant differences among and between the various different regions, states, or provinces in relation to alcohol use patterns, taxation, and public health problems. Rapidly changing lifestyles, more so in urban areas but also increasingly in rural areas as a result of television and other forms of modern communication, and the opening up of hitherto closed economies are influencing consumer preferences as people demand greater access to choices and options. These trends continue despite the civil unrest that still looms large over certain parts of Asia, making it one of the most volatile regions politically in the world.

The evolution of alcohol policies in the Asian region is best understood in its broader religious, economic, political, and sociohistorical context. Three of the predominant religions in the region (Buddhism, Hinduism, and Islam) expressly exclude the use of intoxicating drinks,[1] although individual commu-

---

[1] A study on alcohol use among ethnic Chinese undergraduate students in Singapore showed that religious values and beliefs were not a significant factor in terms of students' alcohol consumption (Isralowitz & Ong, 1990). These findings, however, need to be viewed with caution because religion is not as strong and domineering a force in Singapore as elsewhere in much of Asia and also because of the multireligious nature of the society (students were asked to indicate the family's religion as: Catholic, Christian, ancestor worshiper, Buddhist, Taoist, Muslim, Hindu, no religion, or other) and the small sample size. In any event, alcohol use is not a major public health problem in Singapore (Hughes et al., 1990). In China, alcohol is consumed as an integral part of religious ceremonies and ancestral worship (Colon & Wuollet, 1994).

nities sometimes choose to interpret this more liberally than others. The case for prohibition, in Pakistan and some states in India, has been based partly on religious injunctions. The need to generate revenue for the state through excise duty and to cater to the ever-growing tourist industry often runs counter to the demand for more restrictive alcohol policies. A public health rationale, founded on mortality, morbidity, accident and crime-related statistics, coupled with social protection rationale, based on the magnitude of the family and community problems occurring in the wake of alcoholism, are thus advanced to reinforce the demand for the introduction of such policies. However, with the liberalization of trade and the influx of foreign investors, and the growth of associated enterprises such as advertising firms, some countries are finding it increasingly difficult to subject the alcohol industry—particularly foreign firms or imported products—to more stringent regulations than are applicable to other consumer products or to those that are domestically manufactured. The new trade regimes that are evolving with the emergence of the World Trade Organization (WTO) have placed the differential—and sometimes arbitrary or discriminatory—excise duties and advertising practices of countries such as Japan and Taiwan under tremendous pressure.

Alcohol policies in the region have thus far evolved in a context where there has been an interplay of a variety of factors. Their future evolution is also likely to take place in such a context, but perhaps with ramifications for trade going beyond alcohol. Because of the revenue generated by taxing beverage alcohol, it has come to assume a special place in fiscal policymaking and every encouragement is given in some countries to the promotion of local products. But in a global scenario characterized by free access to markets, there are calls for a level playing field, which will challenge the entrenched market position enjoyed by domestic manufacturers.

The present chapter considers the role of alcohol and alcohol policies in the broadly defined region of Asia. With few exceptions, alcohol-related issues have received relatively little attention in most Asian countries. Recent information on such countries is more often available in newspaper reports than in scientific literature. Where no other sources are available, reference has been made to such reports.

CURRENT STATUS: EPIDEMIOLOGY, MARKETING, AND USER PROFILES

There are visible signs of alcohol use in all Asian countries, even the few with a policy of prohibition. Even in countries with such a policy, alcohol is generally available to foreigners, and locally produced illicit products can often be obtained with impunity.[2] An emerging problem, and an increasingly dangerous trend,

[2]In Pakistan, for instance, out of a sample of 450 youths admitted to a drug treatment center in Lahore from 1990 to 1992, 366 had reported regular consumption of alcohol (Haq, 1993).

TABLE 3.1 Total consumption of pure alcohol per capita (liters) 1990–1994.

Year	China	Japan	Malaysia	Singapore	Thailand	Viet Nam
1990	2.3	6.5	0.5	0.5	0.3	0.1
1991	2.7	6.6	0.5	1.3	0.3	0.1
1992	2.8	6.6	0.5	1.5	0.4	0.1
1993	3.2	6.6	0.5	1.4	0.4	0.2
1994	3.2	6.6	0.5	1.4	0.6	0.2
1995	3.6	6.6	0.6	1.6	0.6	0.2
1996	3.7	6.6	0.6	1.6	0.7	0.2

Source: *World Drink Trends* (1997).

however, is the smuggling of alcohol. Smuggled products are cheaper because they do not attract import and other excise duties. But at the same time their quality is suspect (*International Wine and Liquor*, 1993), and they are likely to produce more harm (Saroja & Kyaw, 1993) than spirits, wine, or beer even when consumed in lesser quantities. Despite the presence of alcohol products in most parts of Asia, there is still a marked dearth of epidemiological data on alcohol use and abuse. Where information is available, it is often derived from a variety of sources, so that it is difficult to make cross-national comparisons. Though the social and public health problems associated with alcohol abuse are often well articulated, the supporting evidence available is generally anecdotal or based on the results of a study done with a relatively small and unrepresentative sample. While the existence of such problems cannot be gainsaid, the lack of data appears to demonstrate both an unwillingness to study the dynamics of the problem seriously and a reluctance on the part of national governments and research institutions to accord the attention and resources the problem warrants. It is in light of these limitations that the data presented below must be considered.

Many countries have witnessed an increase in the per capita consumption of alcohol (see Table 3.1).

As will be observed from the above table, between 1990 and 1996 there was a substantial increase in consumption in China and a steady rise in Thailand. Both countries have experienced changes in lifestyles created in the wake of industrialization. Other countries undergoing similar changes can expect a regular increase, albeit from a very low base if the figures are compared to European levels.

Alcohol production in the region has steadily increased during the past few decades. In Indonesia, for instance, the production of beer has increased tenfold and the production of wines/spirits fivefold during the past decade (Communicable Diseases Research Center, 1996). There is an expanding market, mainly because of visiting tourists and the expatriate population working in Indonesia. Foreign liquor manufacturers target them, rather than the nationals of this Islamic nation (*Jakarta Post*, 1995). In some countries, consumption figures represent predominantly domestically manufactured beverages.

Recent studies show that drinking is increasingly common among school-going teenagers and that drinks are initially taken at a much lower age than in the past. A study quoted by the *Asahi News Service* (1993) covering 14,000 pupils in some 44 high schools throughout Japan revealed that 17 percent were problem drinkers—a tenfold increase over a decade. Another 43.2 percent acknowledged that they were drinkers. In Hong Kong, a survey (*The Standard*, 1993) covering 110,000 teenagers showed that 75 percent had consumed alcohol before they were 18 years of age, and nearly 15 percent had by the age of 6. Curiosity and the belief that alcohol is beneficial to health were given as reasons for consuming alcohol. In Indonesia, evidence of increasing teenage drinking led in 1993 to the adoption of a series of 77 regulations on the distribution, consumption, and marketing of beverage alcohol (*Indonesian Times*, 1993). A study in Sri Lanka covering some 8,058 schoolchildren between the ages of 12 and 20 in six districts reported that the percentage having ever consumed alcohol ranged from 18.3 to 38.6 percent (Alcohol and Drug Information Centre, 1993). The percentage of those currently consuming alcohol ranged from 3.9 percent in one district to 17.2 percent in another district. Parties and school trips were mentioned as opportunities that easily lent themselves to alcohol use. The study also reported that in families where the father consumed alcohol there was a greater likelihood of the children, particularly males, consuming alcohol.

Chung and colleagues reported that in the Republic of Korea, women with more education tend to consume more beverage alcohol than less educated women (Chung et al., 1992/1993).

The profile of Chinese alcohol dependency in Singapore shows that female drinkers have more depressive symptoms with suicidal tendencies, but no other significant difference in alcohol-related problems pertaining to physical health, work, marriage, finance, and so on (Kua, 1995).

In Nepal, beverage alcohol is culturally accepted and socially tolerated. Among many ethnic groups, alcohol use is common on most occasions. A *Matwali* is one who is allowed to drink beverage alcohol, either regularly or on social occasions, simply by virtue of being born into the group (Shrestha, 1992). Many belong in this category; others are not supposed to drink even on social occasions. There is strong social disapproval of female drunkenness. In rural Nepal, alcohol is used for many ailments.

In Singapore, where drinking is neither a major health nor public health problem, studies among Chinese and Indian student populations have revealed interesting differences between the two ethnic groups. Hong and Isralowitz (1989) found in their study of Indian and Chinese undergraduate students in Singapore that, in general, the Indian students started drinking at an earlier age, had a family history of alcohol problems, and had more behavioral problems associated with drinking. Heok (1987) had similar findings in his study of Indian and Chinese patients in Singapore. He too noted that Indians began drinking earlier and experienced more problems with alcohol and had greater severity of dependence. He was careful, however, to note that although they had a higher level than the Chinese, the Indians had a "moderate degree of dependence" (Heok, 1987, p. 773).

While new distilleries have been set up in many countries, there are some exceptions. In Thailand, for instance, no new distilleries have been approved since 1983. At present there are 19 government-owned and 24 private-sector distilleries. Foreign firms are likely to be licensed as part of the trade liberalization policy, after existing concessions expire in 1999. Thais prefer locally made liquor, in part because of the present excise tax barriers for imports. Annual consumption of locally produced liquor is significantly higher than that of imported liquor (*Bangkok Post*, 1995).

Epidemiological data on alcohol-related diseases in the countries of the region are not readily available. This is not surprising because in most developing countries alcohol-related problems are not yet "officially" perceived as significant or important medical or public health problems. There are also methodological difficulties. As noted by some psychiatrists in Sri Lanka,

"How are figures for mortality of cirrhosis of the liver to be interpreted in a country where viral hepatitis is common and where a significant number of death certificates are issued by indigenous practitioners whose models of disease do not include the pathological entity of cirrhosis? *Per capita* alcohol consumption is no more helpful than liver cirrhosis mortality. Official statistics are rarely up-to-date and not always wholly reliable or easily accessible. The existence of a flourishing industry of illicit brewing makes the value of such statistics as are available even more doubtful" (Samarasinghe et al., 1987, p. 1149).

In some Asian societies, spouses, parents, or children will go to any length to downplay alcohol-related problems of a family member because of the social stigma[3] attached to an "alcoholic." In countries where it is common practice to seek prospective marriage partners through advertisements in newspapers, there is occasional mention of being a "teetotaler" as an added qualification of, or requirement for, the would-be bridegroom.

Globally, alcohol-related health problems affect an estimated 5–10 percent of the world's population annually (Gossop & Grant, 1990). According to the World Health Organization's (WHO) Alcohol and Drug Abuse Global Trends Linkage Alerting System (ATLAS) report, although alcohol consumption in Asia and the Western Pacific is not as marked as in North America and Europe, it nevertheless constitutes a growing health problem. In Sri Lanka, for example, up to 10 percent of all hospital admissions are thought to be alcohol-related (WHO,

---

[3]Mahatma Gandhi, the great Indian social reformer, remarked after a visit to Sri Lanka in 1927 that he was "shocked" to discover that "unlike us in India, the drink habit did not carry with it (in Sri Lanka, then Ceylon) a sense of shame and disrespectability" (Uragoda, 1987). This observation was probably made in response to the situation in a particular locality, because from the beginning of the twentieth century Sri Lanka witnessed a temperance movement which became a major political and social event in the country's colonial history (see also Jayasuriya (1986)).

TABLE 3.2   Global burden of disease, 1990: Alcohol dependence by region (hundreds of thousands of DALYs).

	Sub-Saharan Africa	India	China	Other, Asia and Islands	Latin America/ Caribbean	Established market economies
Males	14.9	16.6	16.6	9.4	14.1	24.5
Females	2.2	2.4	2.4	1.4	2.0	3.7

Source: World Bank (1993).

1992). One study in Sri Lanka (Wijesundere, 1992) assessed the incidence and type of medical complications (of alcohol dependence) among patients admitted to the medical unit of Colombo North Hospital, which is located in an area with a major illicit brewing cottage industry. Out of 707 cases studied, 40 percent were in the age group 30–40 years and had a history of alcohol use for 10 or more years. The survey included 10 females. There was a mortality rate of 8.7 percent. The hepatic complications observed included hepatomegaly (in 87 percent of patients), cirrhosis (49 percent), acute alcoholic hepatitis (12 percent), portal hypertension (16 percent), and haemetemesis and malaena (10 percent). Acute gastritis was found in 69 percent of the patients, and hypertension in 6 percent. Neurological complications noted were hepatic encephalopathy (11.4 percent), hypoglycemic coma (5.25 percent), peripheral neuropathy (3 percent), and epilepsy (2.3 percent). Evidence of incidental infections (e.g., bronchopneumonia, pulmonary tuberculosis, leptospirosis, and amebic hepatitis) were found in 14 percent of the alcoholics. The nutritional disturbances observed were anemia (14 percent), avitaminosis (10 percent), emaciation (10 percent), and obesity (8 percent). The incidence of diabetes mellitus was 2 percent.

The World Bank's *World Development Report* (1993) presented data on the global burden of disease (GBD) for some 100 diseases and injuries, including alcohol dependence. For the purposes of the analysis, the GBD was measured in units of disability-adjusted life years (DALYs) in respect to the loss of life from premature death in 1990 and the loss of healthy life from disability. Table 3.2 shows data on the burden of alcohol dependence related diseases for 1990 for males and females.

While the GBD concept is still subject to further refinement and the figures above must be interpreted with caution, they, nevertheless, show that there is reason to be concerned about the health implications of alcohol dependence.

ECONOMIC ASPECTS

The beverage alcohol industry and licit alcohol products represent a major revenue source for governments in Asia. The illicit industry—the magnitude of which is not known for certain in any country—exacts a heavy price in depriving savings available to families, since governments receive no monetary benefit from its operations.

It is difficult to obtain statistics on the financial significance of the alcohol industry and related industries. Nevertheless, the Indian state of Andhra Pradesh claimed in 1994 that a policy of prohibition would cost the state 12 billion Indian rupees a year (*Asian Age*, 1994e) and a loss of 20,000 jobs (*Financial Express*, 1993). A policy on prohibition meant the closure of some 13,000 country liquor shops and 6,500 Indian-made foreign liquor shops and bars all over the state. Because of these financial consequences the prohibition policies have now been revoked.

In some countries, taxation of alcohol products has been a major issue that has dominated bilateral relationships and trade negotiations. In Japan, the revenue from alcohol production and sales represents 3.3 percent of total tax revenues (*Far Eastern Economic Review*, 1993). For many years the Japanese government has been under pressure to eliminate tax discrimination between locally produced *shochu* and imported spirits such as Scotch whisky and brandy. Attempts have been made to persuade the Japanese to implement a 1987 General Agreement on Tariffs and Trade (GATT) ruling, which requires all spirit drinks to be taxed at similar rates; the Japanese taxed imported spirits at up to seven times the rate applied to *shochu* (*Harper Wine and Spirit Gazette*, 1995). The market share of *shochu* had increased from 61 percent in 1974 to 74 percent by the end of 1994 (McLaughlin, 1995). In 1995 the European Commission initiated legal action against Japan under the tougher rules of the WTO. Import tariffs have since been reduced in Japan (McLaughlin, 1995), and WTO pressure to decrease them more is mounting.

Tariff reductions have been introduced in some countries to ease trade tensions as well as to strengthen chances of entry into the WTO. In 1996, for instance, China reduced the tariffs on more than 4,000 imported products (*South China Morning Post*, 1995). The same motive lay behind Taiwan's decision to end its beer monopoly. Foreign beer sales have increased slightly from 3 percent in 1987, when the market was first opened to foreign beer companies, to 5 percent in 1993, but local beer still accounts for nearly 95 percent of sales (*Asian Age*, 1994a).

As part of their trade liberalization policy, some countries are likely to offer concessions to foreign enterprises to establish distilleries. Thailand, for instance, is reported to be considering liberalizing its whisky production industry when the existing concessions granted to a limited number of distillers expire in 1999. Foreign distillers are initially expected to keep costs down by building bottling plants in the country or forming joint ventures with Thai investors to build distilleries (*Bangkok Post*, 1995).

The economic dimensions of the alcohol industry can be seen from the few published estimates. In the Philippines, for instance, San Miguel, the country's largest brewery and consumer product group, contributes 6.8 percent of the Filipino Treasury's total annual tax income (Luce, 1996). In Papua New Guinea, about one-third of the income of East Sepik comes from taxation on alcohol sales (*Post Courier*, 1993).

In some countries, even with reductions in tariff rates, the prevailing duty is high. In India, for instance, the duty on imported Scotch whisky is 290 percent.

Tariff structures have, in part, encouraged new patterns of beverage alcohol production in Japan, where malt alcohol is taxed according to the percentage of malt. This structure has encouraged increased production in lower malt drinks (Ikeya, 1995a; 1995b).

Tax increases leading to a fall in revenue have resulted in job losses in some countries. In the Philippines, for instance, between 1990 and 1991 the ad valorem tax on beer was raised from 37 to 50 percent. During this period sales dropped by 15 percent, resulting in some 2,700 job losses (*Manila Bulletin*, 1993).

There are few studies that shed light on other economic dimensions of the problem. One study (Suryani, 1990) on palm wine drinking in a Balinese village suggests that there is a relationship between long seasonal unemployment and excessive drinking. With the advent of water for irrigation and the extension of the farming seasons, there was a decrease in palm wine drinking. This was attributed to the fact that less time was available for group drinking.

PUBLIC HEALTH AND RELATED ISSUES

Drink Driving

Road accidents are increasingly being recognized in some countries as a public health problem of concern. In Thailand, for instance, a total of 84,892 road accidents were recorded in 1993. Nearly 75 percent of these had occurred in the capital of Bangkok. Owing to a lack of adequate legal provisions it was not possible to conduct tests for alcohol in the individuals involved. A study of 431 road accidents in rural Thailand in 1991 revealed that about half the bicyclists (45.5 percent) and motorcyclists (56.1 percent) were under the influence of alcohol at the time of the accident, compared to a much smaller percentage of motorists (24.3 percent) (Swaddiwudhipong et al., 1994). Truck and bus drivers found to have taken liquor or amphetamines while driving have had their licences revoked (*Bangkok Post*, 1994).

In Sri Lanka, the number of people detected of driving under the influence of alcohol increased from 118 in 1977 to 1,494 in 1984, but the problem has not been given much attention (Hettige, 1989).

Hong Kong has recently introduced a new law with stiff penalties. The maximum blood alcohol level (BAL) has been set at 80 milligrams of alcohol per 100 milliliters of blood. Violators are subject to a two-year ban on driving, three years in prison, or a substantial fine. The implementation of the law was preceded by a short transitional period and a public awareness campaign (*Hong Kong Standard*, 1995). The police began using breathalyzer tests from mid-

December 1995, but announced that road blocks would be set up only to test people for drunk driving (*South China Morning Post, International ed.*, 1995).

In Seoul, the capital of the Republic of Korea, new regulations were introduced in March 1995 setting a new BAL of 80 milligrams per 100 milliliters as the legal limit. The new policy is to suspend the licence of drivers caught with a BAL above 80 milligrams per 100 milliliters. In the first two months of 1995, police arrested 6,600 persons in Seoul, a 50 percent increase to the corresponding period in 1994. The new regulations also resulted in an increase in arrests of women drivers; during the same period, 167 women were arrested, three times the figure for the corresponding period in 1994 (*Korea Herald*, 1995).

In Malaysia, consumer groups have been calling for tougher laws and a tougher implementation of the existing law throughout the country (*New Straits Times*, 1995b). On the eve of a major antidrinking campaign, the Road Transport Department called for the doubling of penalties, including the permanent revocation of the licence of persistent offenders (*Asian Age*, 1995a). In certain parts of Malaysia, the new law against drink driving was implemented over the Christmas and New Year period at the end of 1995 (*New Straits Times*, 1995a), when more people were likely to consume liquor.

In neighboring Singapore, where legal provision was made in 1985 for maximum BAL and breathalyzer tests, and with a generally low level of accidents involving persons under the influence of alcohol, there have been calls for stiffer penalties and more random checks (Chao, 1992).

Legislative changes have taken place elsewhere in the region as well. In India, for instance, the Motor Vehicle Act was amended in 1995 to make it an offense for anyone to drive after consuming more than 30 milliliters of alcohol (*Financial Times*, 1995). India is reputed to have the world's largest number of casualties from road accidents. In 1994, approximately 60,000 people died in road accidents, while some 300,000 sustained serious injuries (*Globe and Mail*, 1995). Recent years have witnessed a significant rise in the number of vehicles on the roads, and traffic continues to increase with the liberalization of car imports and the emergence of joint ventures for manufacturing. In the Republic of Korea, despite antidrunk driving and road safety campaigns, road accidents have been increasing. In 1995, some 10,530 people died in road accidents, a 2.6 percent increase over the 1994 figure. The cost of road accidents in 1993—in terms of hospital charges, wreckage tow-away charges, and insurance—has been estimated at US $7.7 billion (*Asian Age*, 1996).

Smuggled, Substandard, and Counterfeit Products

The smuggling of beverage alcohol has been reported by several countries. It has been stated that it is difficult to determine the level of alcohol consumption in Indonesia since much of it is smuggled into the country (*Jakarta Post*, 1995). In Viet Nam, it is estimated that 80–90 percent of premium spirits sold in the country are smuggled from other countries through Cambodia or China

(Schwarz, 1995). Viet Nam's high tariff rates are believed to have led to this lucrative business in smuggled drinks. Smuggling also occurs in countries or areas with a policy of prohibition. In Pakistan, the majority of middle-income drinkers are believed to be dependent on smuggled supplies from neighboring India or handouts from the diplomatic corps (*Asian Age*, 1994d).

While smuggled products escape taxation and result in a loss of revenue to the state, it also presents a more serious pubic health problem resulting from a lack of any quality assurance. In India, empty Johnnie Walker whisky bottles, with the label intact, sell for up to a pound sterling, and are then refilled with locally produced spirits. According to 1993 estimates, 60 percent of international spirit brands in India are local counterfeits, 20 percent are foreign counterfeits that have been smuggled in, and only 20 percent are genuine (*International Wine and Liquor*, 1993).

Attempts to discourage smuggling have included the introduction of laws with tougher penalties for smugglers. For example, in 1995 there was draft legislation in Taiwan proposing an increase in the maximum fine from 5,000 to 300,000 Taiwan dollars and jail sentences from one year to between three and seven years (*China Times*, 1995).

Problems with imitation labels have led to litigation in countries such as India. In one such case, the court had to decide whether the picture of a deer on a label was a Scottish stag or an Indian sambar (Tully, 1996).

In India, unscrupulous traders have substituted rectified spirits with methylated spirits, resulting in the deaths or blindness of hundreds of people annually (*Asian Age*, 1994c). In Orissa, more than 200 people died in an incident in 1992 after consuming methanol-contaminated alcohol (*The European*, 1992).

The HIV/AIDS Epidemic

Apart from the effects of a high intake of alcohol on the immune system and the development of progressive dementia (Molgaard et al., 1988), the use of alcohol can also compromise "safe sex" practices, particularly if people then ignore the use of condoms or similar preventive measures. After years of complacency, Asian countries are now coming to terms with the devastating effects of the HIV/AIDS epidemic.

Recent economic studies in Asian countries lend support to the belief that the HIV/AIDS epidemic will have a disproportionately strong effect on those parts of society least able to cope with it (Bloom & Godwin, 1997). These are the very communities where chronic alcoholism can bring in its wake financial and social problems such as loss of employment and inability to undertake long-term treatment and rehabilitation.

In countries such as Thailand, with a well-established sex industry, concerns have been expressed that customers seeking commercial sex workers are generally under the influence of alcohol, so that their vulnerability to HIV is exacerbated (Fordham, 1995).

POLICY DEVELOPMENT AND SELECTED INTERVENTIONS

In the Asian region, the evolution of national policies has been piecemeal, rather than in accordance with clearly articulated objectives, goals, and targets. Even in a country such as Pakistan, with a policy of prohibition, it has been observed that "decisions pertaining to liquor can be sudden and capricious" (*Asian Age*, 1994b). The advertising industry in Malaysia complained in 1995 of the lack of consultation before the government introduced various restrictions (*Business Times*, 1995).

In Japan, the Alcohol and Health Incorporated Association was formed in 1980 with the support of the Ministry of Health and Welfare and the alcohol industry. Alcohol poisoning cases among students have subsequently come down in Japan by almost 20 percent. This is attributed to the educational campaigns promoted by several organizations, including the Tokyo Regional Chapter of the National Federation of University Cooperative Association (*Asahi News Service*, 1994).

Policies have oscillated between the extremes of the pendulum. Attempts to introduce Islamic criminal law in the Malaysian state of Kelantan included a proposal to apply flogging for drunkenness (*International Herald Tribune*, 1993), whereas it has been remarked of alcohol in Pakistan—another Islamic state with prohibition—that "few talk about it, many drink it, and many more would like to, provided they can lay their hands on it" (*Asian Age*, 1994d). Even where drinking in moderation is not tolerated, revenue collection through liquor continues to find favor with politicians and administrators.

Political pressures exerted from outside to abolish total or partial monopolies in favor of domestic firms, as in the case of Thailand and Taiwan (Tyson, 1994), or to eliminate differential taxation that discriminates against imported beverages, as in India, Japan, and several other countries, have dominated the policy development process, eclipsing other policy elements that need to be addressed if a comprehensive policy is to emerge. Alcohol advertising restrictions have also loomed large in trade negotiations, not only in countries with well-established markets and a developed advertising industry, but also in emerging markets in countries such as Viet Nam (*Wine and Spirits International*, 1995). North Korea announced in 1995 that it would allow foreign advertisements on the occasion of the three-day Pyongyang International Sports and Cultural Festival for Peace after a 50-year ban (*Advertisement Age*, 1995).

Alcohol-related issues have been placed on the political agenda in a few countries such as India, where prohibition has become a major issue in some states in the country. The introduction of a policy of prohibition entails far-reaching financial and employment consequences. When one state government in India banned the production and sale of barrack—a locally distilled coconut or rice-based spirit—it was claimed that the ban would cost some 20,000 jobs (*Financial Express*, 1993).

Women have been particularly active in some countries in calling for restrictive policies. Malaysia reported that in 1993 the first antialcohol group in the country had been formed by women. The group, Women Against Alcohol, had called for an alcohol ban (*Financial Express*, 1993).

Public Education Campaigns

Education campaigns for the general public or for selected target groups have been conducted in many countries to discourage excessive drinking and to protect vulnerable groups such as children and youth.

In Singapore in 1993, the traffic police organized a two-month campaign targeting hosts and guests at parties at private houses as well as those held at hotels and clubs. Hosts were sensitized to the need to discourage intoxicated persons from driving (*New Straits Times*, 1995). Health promotion is a major element in the country's national health policy (Chern, 1996).

Warnings on Labels

With a vision of promoting drinking in moderation, some countries require educational messages and warnings to appear on labels. In South Korea, for instance, under the Public Health Law, one of three messages must appear on all packaged alcohol. The warnings are intended to underline the association between excessive drinking and medical problems such as cirrhosis and the increased probability of accidents while driving or working (*Korea Herald*, 1996).

In India, beverage alcohol containers sold in the capital city of New Delhi, and a number of other Indian states require the warning "Consumption of liquor is injurious to health."

Regulation of Advertising

Advertising has assumed an important place in the marketing of beverage alcohol. In China, a five-second daily prime advertising spot on television for an estimated audience of 400 million was reported to have cost a firm that sells beverage alcohol an annual sum of US $128 million (*Reuters Economic News*, 1996).

Advertising restrictions, such as prohibitions on featuring minors consuming alcohol, are in place in many countries around the world (Jayasuriya, 1995), including some developing countries. The rules applicable vary from country to country because restrictions may be classified according to the nature of the product (e.g., beer advertisements may be subject to fewer restrictions than whisky advertisements), the advertising medium (e.g., television, print), or the content.

Surrogate advertising has emerged as a controversial issue in India (*Asian Age*, 1995b). Both multinational and domestic companies have been criticized for using surrogate advertising to gain publicity for their products by visibly displaying them in advertisements for totally unrelated and inoffensive products. Some newspapers have adopted a policy of not allowing advertising via surrogate products.

Treatment Facilities

Hospital-based care for alcohol-related problems seems to be the most commonly available facility, though some countries have other support services and approaches. In China, for instance, community-based family-oriented approaches are being tried out, while Malaysia promotes therapeutic community approaches. Thailand uses low-voltage stimulation as a special service intervention (WHO, 1992). In Sri Lanka, the assistance of Buddhist monks has been enlisted to help persons avoid returning to the use of alcohol (Samarasinghe, 1989).

A notable trend in the region is the increasing involvement of nongovernmental organizations in the provision of counseling, treatment, and rehabilitation services. In Sri Lanka, for instance, Mel Medura, the Alcohol and Drug Information Centre, and Women In Need are among some of the more prominent nongovernmental organizations working with individuals having alcohol-related problems. In countries with overcrowded public hospitals and severe manpower constraints, some of these organizations are able to provide services that are tailor-made to individual and family needs. Well-structured funding mechanisms exist in only a few countries; in some countries such organizations receive a modest state subsidy.

Other Measures

A number of countries have introduced measures to promote drinking in moderation, while a few have introduced restrictive measures to discourage the habit of drinking. In the Indian capital of New Delhi, for instance, a number of such measures were introduced in 1994. The number of annual "dry" days was increased from 27 to 45. With the exception of beer, there is a ceiling on the quantity of beverage alcohol that can be kept in anyone's possession. Restaurant owners are now required to provide separate areas for drinkers. It has been reported that in the wake of these restrictions liquor stalls have been set up outside the city boundaries and are doing a "roaring trade" (Rettie, 1994). When policy differences exist across states in federal systems of administration, problems of this nature are likely to arise.

With a view to discouraging under-20s from drinking, Japan decided in 1994 to phase out some 2 million vending machines throughout the country over a five-year period. One brewer was estimated at selling beer to the value of a billion pounds sterling a year through such machines (*The Guardian*, 1994). Magnetic cards were introduced to allow such machines to be operated; such cards were sold in alcohol beverage shops on proof of identity (*La Revue de Presse*, 1994).

CONCLUSIONS

With changing lifestyles and exposure to more sophisticated advertising in a context where people have the right to choose from different options, many Asian countries are experiencing an increase in the demand for alcohol. This means that a more judicious and balanced approach is needed in the formulation of alcohol policies. Alcohol policies need to be formulated in a context that takes into account the social, religious, cultural, economic, political, and public health dimensions of alcohol use and abuse (Grant, 1985). Piecemeal and *ad hoc* policymaking must give way to a more holistic approach that is based on objective and long-term perspectives. For far too long, Asian countries have been approaching alcohol use and abuse from a narrow and short-term perspective, without adequate consultation from stakeholders and civil society.

REFERENCES

Advertisement Age. (1995, February 20). North Korea to allow first foreign advertisements for 50 years, p. 33.

Alcohol and Drug Information Centre. (1993). *Substance Use Among School Children in Six Districts of Sri Lanka*. Colombo.

Asahi News Service. (1993, September 30). Problem drinking surges at high schools.

Asahi News Service. (1994, April 6). Group urges student to stop guzzling alcohol.

Asian Age. (1994a, September 6). A decade of Taiwan's beer monopoly reaches a dead end, p. B11.

Asian Age. (1994b, July 13). Beer firm in Pakistan languishes despite demand, p. B11.

Asian Age. (1994c, August 17). Health policies fall short of requisite standards, p. 9.

Asian Age. (1994d, June 30). Mansions, malls, alcohol: Islamabad goes Western, p. 7.

Asian Age. (1994e, November 3). Total prohibition likely in (the Indian state) Andhra Pradesh, p. 5.

Asian Age. (1995a, July 1). Malaysia drink-driving curbs, p. 7.

Asian Age. (1995b, January 28). Stiff Bombay measures put liquor ads on the rocks, p. 2.

Asian Age. (1996, January 15). Road accident fatalities increased in 1995 despite anti-drinking driving and road safety campaign, p. 7.

Bangkok Post. (1994, August 21). Road accidents take their toll on society in numerous ways.

Bangkok Post. (1995, April 7). Foreign distillers await in the wings.

Bloom, D. & Godwin, P., (Eds.) (1997). *The Economics of HIV and AIDS: The Case of South and South East Asia*. New Delhi: Oxford University Press.

Business Times. (1995, June 7). Advertisers unhappy over liquor ad ban, p. 17LO.

Chao, T. C. (1992). Drinking and driving in Singapore, 1987 to 1989. *American Journal of Forensic Medicine and Pathology, 13*, 255–260.

Chern, A. S. C. (1996). Health promotion policies in Singapore: Meeting the challenges of the 1990s. *Health Promotion International, 11*, 127–136.

China Times. (1995, February 8). Tobacco, wine anti-smuggling law drafted, p. 30.

Chung, M. H., Chung, K. K., Chung, C. S., & Raymond, J. S. (1992/1993). Health-related behaviors in Korea: Smoking, drinking, and perinatal care. *Asia-Pacific Journal of Public Health, 6*, 10–15.

Colon, I. & Wuollet, C. A. (1994). Homeland, gender and Chinese drinking. *Journal of Addictive Diseases, 13*, 59–67.

Communicable Diseases Research Center. (1996, March 27). Jakarta. Communication.

The European. (1992, May 14–17). Two hundred die after drinking illicit alcohol, p. 4.

Far Eastern Economic Review. (1993, May 13). Problem drinking in Japan, pp. 44–45.

Financial Express. (1993, May 15). No more arrack in Andhra Pradesh.

Financial Times. (1995, February 14). Amendments to Motor Vehicle Act, p. 10.

Fordham, G. (1995). Whisky, women and song: Men, alcohol and AIDS in northern Thailand. *Australian Journal of Anthropology, 6*, 154–177.

Globe and Mail. (1995, March 20). India drives traffic fatalities to new heights, p. A.

Gossop, M. & Grant, M. (Eds.) (1990). *Preventing and Controlling Drug Abuse*. Geneva: World Health Organization.

Grant, M. (1985). Establishing priorities for action. In M. Grant (Ed.), *Alcohol Policies* (Regional Publications, European Series, 18). Copenhagen: WHO Regional Office for Europe.

The Guardian. (1994, November 4). Japanese town bans offending vending machines, p. 16.

Haq, I. (1993). Multiple-drug abuse in a youth clinic sample in Pakistan. *Contemporary Drug Problems, 20*, 87–92.

Harper Wine and Spirit Gazette. (1995, January 13). Japanese budget fails to tackle dispute on tax discrimination against imported spirits, p. 7.

Heok, K. E. (1987). A cross-cultural study of alcohol dependence in Singapore. *British Journal of Addiction, 82*, 771–773.

Hettige, S. T. (1989). Sri Lanka. In T. Kortteinen (Ed.), *State Monopolies and Alcohol Prevention: Report and Working Papers of a Collaborative International Study* (559–589). Helsinki: Social Research Institute of Alcohol Studies.

Hong, O. T. & Isralowitz, R. E. (1989). Cross-cultural study of alcohol behavior among Singapore college students. *British Journal of Addiction, 84*, 319–322.

Hong Kong Standard. (1995, December 1). Government to launch new drink driving law, p. 3.

Hughes, K., Yeo, P. P., Lun, K. C., Thai, A. C., Wang, K. W., & Cheah, J. S. (1990). Alcohol Consumption in Chinese, Malays, and Indians in Singapore. *Annals of the Academy of Medicine of Singapore, 19*, 330–332.

Ikeya, A. (1995a, May 29). Is it beer? For tax purposes, it isn't. *The Nikkei Weekly*, p. 3.

Ikeya, A. (1995b, December 18). Ministry seeks beer-like tax on low malt drinks. *Nikkei Weekly*, p. 3.

Indonesian Times. (1993, December 15). Children start to drink as young as six.

International Herald Tribune. (1993, November 26). Kelantan State Legislature votes for imposition of Islamic law, p. 2.

International Wine and Liquor. (1993, November 12). Counterfeit Liquor. No. 301, p. 3.

Isralowitz, R. E. & Ong, T. E. (1990). Religious values and beliefs and place of residence as predictors of alcohol use among Chinese college students in Singapore. *International Journal of the Addictions, 25*, 515–529.

Jakarta Post. (1995, November 12). Cognac, the finest of all spirits distilled from grapes.

Jayasuriya, D. C. (1986). *Narcotics and Drugs in Sri Lanka: Socio-Legal Dimensions*. Nawala: Asian Pathfinder Publishers and Booksellers.

Jayasuriya, D. C. (1995). *The Regulation of the Advertising of Alcoholic Beverages—Issues, Approaches and Guidelines*. Programme on Substance Abuse Geneva, WHO (unpublished).

Korea Herald. (1995, April 2). Stricter rules for drunken drivers, p. 3.

Korea Herald. (1996, February 25). Health warning on liquor a must, p. 3.

Kua, E. H. (1995). A profile of Chinese alcoholics in Singapore. *Addiction, 90*, 51–56.

La Revue de Presse. (1994). Changes in the law regarding the purchase of alcohol by minors from dispensers. 10, p. 13.

Luce, E. (1996, February 8). San Miguel growth held back at 9%. *Financial Times*, p. 22.

Manilla Bulletin. (1993, March 13). Opposition to beer tax increases, p. 12.

McLaughlin, C. (1995, April 4). European commission moves to fight Japan's whisky barriers. *The Scotsman*.

Molgaard, C. A., et al. (1988). Assessing alcoholism as a risk factor for acquired immunodeficiency syndrome (AIDS). *Social Science and Medicine, 27*, 1147–1152.

New Straits Times. (1995a, December 13). Drink driving law to be imposed, p. 1.

New Straits Times. (1995b, May 8). Public backing for drink driving law, p. 4.

Post Courier. (1993, March 29). Plans to control liquor drinking, p. 13.

Rettie, J. (1994, May 7). Dry disaster for Delhi's drinkers. *The Guardian,* p. 15.

Reuters Economic News. (1996). Chinese beverage alcohol producer gambles on five-second television advertisement.

Samarasinghe, D. S., Dissanayake, S. A. W., & Wijesinghe, C. P. (1987). Alcoholism in Sri Lanka: An epidemiological survey. *British Journal of Addiction, 82,* 1149–1153.

Saroja, K. I. & Kyaw, O. (1993). Pattern of alcoholism in the General Hospital, Kuala Lumpur. *Medical Journal of Malaysia, 48,* 133.

Schwarz, A. (1995, June 8). Hooch trade; firms advertise smuggled goods in Vietnam. *Far Eastern Economic Review,* p. 52.

Shrestha, N. M. (1992). Alcohol and drug abuse in Nepal. *British Journal of Addiction, 87,* 1241–1248.

South China Morning Post. (1995, December 30). Beijing compiles tariff cut list. 2.

South China Morning Post, International Ed. (1995, December 9). Police pledge on road (breath) tests, p. 4.

Suryani, L. K. (1990). Palm wine drinking in a Balinese village: Environmental influences. *International Journal of the Addictions, 25,* 911–920.

The Standard. (1993, September 24). Hong Kong: Children start to drink as young as six.

Swaddiwudhipong, W., et al. (1994). Epidemiological characteristics of drivers, vehicles, pedestrians, and road environments involved in road traffic injuries in rural Thailand. *Southeast Asian Journal of Tropical Medicine and Public Health, 25,* 37–44.

Tully, M. (1996, January 9). India's taste for trickery scotching distiller drive. *The Scotsman,* p. 9.

Tyson, L. (1994, August 24). Taiwan pressed on beer monopoly. *Financial Times,* p. 4.

Uragoda, C. G. (1987). *A History of Medicine in Sri Lanka.* Colombo: Sri Lanka Medical Association.

WHO (1992) *ATLAS.* Geneva: WHO Programme on Substance Abuse, WHO/PSA/92.5 (unpublished).

Wijesundere, A. (1992). Medical complications of alcohol dependence syndrome in Ragama (1988/1989). In *Alcohol, Tobacco & Other Drug Use: Research Abstracts & Bibliography.* Proc. Abstracts of the 103rd Annual Session of the Sri Lanka Medical Association (pp. 3–4). Colombo: Alcohol and Drug Information Centre.

Wine and Spirits International. (1995, April). Vietnam calms anti-advertising stance, p. 6.

World Bank. (1993). *World Development Report.* Oxford and New York: Oxford University Press.

World Drink Trends. (1997). Henley-on-Thames. UK: NTC Publications, Ltd.

Chapter 4

Southeast Asia

Jeffrey Day

The peoples of Southeast Asia's Pacific rim have brought about unparalleled economic change in the region since 1945. The growth, beginning with the U.S. rehabilitation of Japan from 1946 and spreading through that country's interactions with the Republic of (South) Korea, Taiwan, Hong Kong (until 1997 a British colony), and Singapore, has revolutionized production methods, information technology, and the economic base, not only of those countries but worldwide. It has resulted in the four smaller countries and territories being termed Asia's four "little dragons," since none had a population of more than 50 million when the development began. Their expansion, following that of Japan, also awoke a spirit of entrepreneurship in other countries of the rim including Thailand (McGovern, 1982), Malaysia, and most recently, Viet Nam and the Philippines. Backed by the massive population of China, a country that is still relatively economically undeveloped and agrarian, and led by a strong historical association with the West, the Southeast Asian-Pacific rim has grown explosively as an economic force.

As far as the focus of this book is concerned, Japan has a tradition of national production of beverage alcohol stretching back to the 17th century (Day, Jones, & Wilkinson, 1995), which is an embodiment of Asian cultural values. The four "dragons" have developed substantially as alcohol producers and large-scale consumers only since the Second World War. A comparison with Japan has significance in the context of Asian values, the development of commercial production, and present usage of alcohol.

Local conflicts in Indochina have significantly slowed development there, while ideological considerations have been important matters of concern holding back China's development. It is thus appropriate, especially if alcohol use and abuse are judged to be related to national development and if use increases exponentially with national prosperity (as has been seen in Western nations), for Japan and the four "dragons" to be examined as models for alcohol use patterns which may develop elsewhere on the Asian-Pacific rim.

Through the period considered in this chapter (1945–1996), Thailand has been politically consistent in its response to external conflicts. It has succeeded in limiting its involvement with its war-torn Indo-Chinese neighbors. It is, therefore, an appropriate national example of developments in an independent Asian economy interacting with alcohol as prosperity grows. Furthermore, unlike Malaysia, Brunei, and Indonesia, where the nationally accepted Moslem religion forbids alcohol use, Thailand is predominantly Buddhist, giving it a religious attitude towards alcohol which might be described as moderate, whereas in local Moslem countries—Indonesia, Brunei, and Malaysia—official attitudes are totalitarian and prohibit the open sale and use of beverage alcohol. The Philippines and Viet Nam, largely Christian and Buddhist, respectively, have been developing economically for a rather short time after being held back by, in one case, massive political and economic corruption, and in the other by a long period of conflict. It is not yet realistic to examine the situations there in depth. Singapore has a relatively small population, and disclosure of national trends, which may be considered sensitive, is rather restricted. It is, nevertheless, possible to extrapolate some of the tendencies seen in Hong Kong to Singapore in the absence of readily available local data.

China is evidently a study in itself, since although it is in part Asian-Pacific, its hinterland is its chief emphasis, and its northern associations with Russia and Mongolia argue against treating it as part of the Asian-Pacific rim. In addition, attempts to collect relevant data have proved very difficult. It is, therefore, left to researchers in the country (see Shen and Wang Chapter 5) to review the present situation there.

SOCIOCULTURAL AND DEMOGRAPHIC PROFILE

The national populations in the five countries or areas considered in this chapter vary from 125 million in Japan and some 40–60 million in South Korea, Taiwan, and Thailand, to 6 million in Hong Kong. Apart from that territory's special circumstances—of China but not in China between 1841 and 1997—it could be considered as a large city comparable with Bangkok, Seoul, or Taipei. However, these are all national capitals and have an overriding influence on most of the research on alcohol-related sociopathology in the nation. It is, therefore, more appropriate to consider Hong Kong for the purposes of this review, as a nation state similar to Singapore. Hong Kong has within its boundaries as many as five distinct conurbations, each housing more than 500,000 people. Several of these "new towns" are developing a social culture independent of the others. Hence, Hong Kong is more akin to a small state than to a large city.

The total population of the Southeast Asian-Pacific rim is about 681 million (excluding mainland China), so that the five nations studied here represent 31.4 percent of the total. Some 30 percent of the remainder are Moslems and, therefore, can be considered sociologically as nonusers of alcohol. The rest are in two emerging countries, Viet Nam and the Philippines, and in as yet undeveloped nations such as Myanmar (Burma), Laos, and Cambodia. This chapter may, therefore, help to guide national bodies and social scientists in such emerging economies when they review their own situation. It also indicates in macrocosm some of the problems faced by border regions of Moslem countries that share frontiers with adjacent non-Moslem nations. Thailand's southern Had Yai province reports disturbances from Malaysian tourists who habitually become part of the area's weekend population in order to avoid the legal and religious prohibitions on alcohol use in their own country (Day et al., 1995b).

NATIONAL PROFILES

Hong Kong

Hong Kong ceased to be a British dependent territory in 1997. Since 1956, its population has risen from some 600,000 to 6.2 million, and its high per capita income, earned mainly through service industries since the mid-1980s, and its position as the main entrepôt for China (40 percent of trade) have placed it firmly as one of the four "dragons" of Asia. Unlike Singapore, Hong Kong has grown with a minimum of political intervention and, while housing and urban infrastructure have been carefully planned, they have been developed within a free market. It is expected that 70 percent of the population will own their own homes (80 percent in high-rise apartments) by 2000.

Most of the Hong Kong population consists of first- or second-generation Chinese immigrants, many of whom have a great love of the motherland (China) but not, according to local news commentary, its present political regime. A significant section of the population strongly supports the Taiwan regime. Since June of 1997 the stresses related to issues of immigration to obtain a safe passport have diminished. However, some tension is caused by family situations that span the border of what is now the Special Administrative Region (SAR). There is some continued adherence to traditional practices involving wives and concubines, the latter remaining in China when the working husband returns to Hong Kong on weekends. Furthermore, husbands working in Hong Kong whose wives and families are living overseas also cause unusual situations.

Anecdotally, residents of Hong Kong speak of the few bars in the 1970s where only "expatriates" were seen, which have now been replaced by a plethora of similar establishments frequented by young (under 40) local people with little evidence of the predominantly male bias of other Asian countries. These bars are not only a feature of the metropolitan (Central and Kowloon) area of Hong Kong, but extend to former villages, now new towns close to the SAR border at Sheung Shui (Government Information Service, 1990). No detailed breakdown of consumption by type of alcohol is available for Hong Kong. Beers are very popular, but all except one brand are imported, according to the annual Hong Kong Government Statistical Reports. Chinese wine imported from the mainland of China is freely available to people aged over 18 years in shops and supermarkets, and imported distilled beverages—notably brandies—are a prestigious luxury. Impressively expensive and unusual "cocktails" are a feature of bar and club life.

Japan

The economic history of Japan needs no elaboration here. However, its social climate, formerly so resistant to change, is undergoing a revolution as Western values begin to infiltrate more deeply among women and the young. This perhaps inevitable concomitant of prosperity has led to unimaginable stresses as young people question national traditions and as the work-ethic involving total employee loyalty to a single company for life comes under threat because the companies themselves are now dependent on the global economy. Nevertheless, the solid social and material infrastructure built up as prosperity developed has assured national cohesiveness. As Japan has no significant economic drain created by international political and military commitments, social service investment has been high. Challenges to the health and welfare of the population of 125 million from noninfective sources, resulting from changes in diet or social habits have, therefore, largely been met through medical interventions. Alcohol has been a growing social concern owing to very weak control measures and tacit acceptance that its use has become a rite of passage and an outlet for social tensions (Sato, 1975). The preferred drinks have changed in postwar years from sake to beers. Annual per capita consumption of beer was estimated in 1995 at 72.3 liters, compared to less than 8.3 liters for stronger spirits. Imported spirits represented about 25 percent of this quantity (Day et al., 1995a).

Republic of Korea

The end of the Korean conflict in 1953 saw South Korea beginning to emerge as one of Asia's new economic dragons. The country has only six major population centers of more than a million people and a relatively small number of other urban centers; 75 percent of the population lives in these urban areas. It has experienced a fourfold increase in per capita income since 1983. As in Taiwan, there is a significant male:female population imbalance (Gardner, 1986). Unlike Thailand and Taiwan, prosperity had been built upon a solid agrarian base. In 1971, a national movement to ensure continued measurable self-sufficiency was set up in response to the decline in the farming population. This has cushioned the effects of the continuing decline from 24 percent in 1983 to 12 percent in 1993 (Ministry of Health and Welfare, 1994). The country is a politically troubled democracy and the capital lies only about 50km from the demilitarized zone separating South Korea from North Korea, with which a state of war still formally exists, though is prevented from continuing to operate by United States military intervention. Tensions arising from this situation, and those common in other male-dominated modern economies contribute to the concerns related to alcohol use in South Korea.

The beverage alcohol favored in South Korea encompasses a wide range of traditional and local variants. Beer claims about 90 percent of the alcohol market, the remainder going to *soju*, a distilled spirit, and *makkoli*, a fermented but not distilled rice wine. Only about 2 percent of the market goes to imported foreign spirits (Day et al., 1996b).

Republic of China (Taiwan)

This island state, which the mainland of China still considers as part of itself, was created in 1949 when the non-Communist Chinese army migrated there after the defeat of Chiang Kai-Shek. Relations with China have been normalizing as Taiwan has shown its ability to become one of Asia's most successful "little dragons." Since essentially it has only two major urban centers and three minor ones lying along a North-South arterial route, its population of about 21 million is mostly located there. There is a significant ethnic population of aboriginal islanders who are being absorbed into the economic development of the island, but who still remain socially apart in some respects. They play a role in government perceptions of the island's alcohol-related problems. Taiwan families exhibit a significant preference for male offspring, which results in a population imbalance of 109 boys to every 100 girls, compared with a global average of 105:100 (Department of Health, 1994, 1995). This factor has some influence in a situation where alcohol is consumed predominantly by males.

In Taiwan, according to 1996 estimates, beer represented 14 million liters of pure alcohol consumed in 1991 (Day, Jones, & Wilkinson, 1996). This amount was rising by about 1 million liters each year. Rice wine accounted for 28 million liters, but the annual change had been negligible since 1976 (ibid.). Chinese-style wines accounted for about 7 million liters of pure alcohol annually (ibid.). No figures for imported spirits were available.

Thailand

Thailand is a stable monarchy with 61 million people, where a succession of unstable governments has allowed free-market forces to bring about rapid economic development. Socially there has been an inevitable urbanization. However, regional politicians with economic interests viewed the development of special economic zones in China as a model for Thailand and stemmed the unregu-

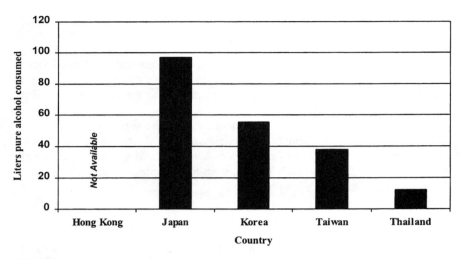

FIGURE 4.1 Aggregate per capita pure alcohol consumption. (*Sources:* Day, Jones, & Wilkinson, 1995a, 1995b, 1996; Day, Wilkinson, & Greene, 1996.)

lated flow of people to the main towns which had rendered parts of Bangkok as sprawling collections of temporary slum dwellings.

Each of the main centers has now, through the distribution of wealth, begun to develop industrial areas. The types of industries are such that massive developments are not necessary, and local prosperity is contributing to the evolution of infrastructure alongside considerable funding for social welfare. Even in Bangkok, where conditions of life had become squalid for many and the infrastructure had begun to break down, the economic improvements are noticeable and social deprivation is less marked than in the 1980s. While the capital is still a social magnet, areas such as Had Yai in the south, Chiang Mai in the north, and Udon Ratchathani in the east are developing as centers of labor with a growing social and material infrastructure. There is an inevitable reduction in agrarian activity, and some social disorder still exists in areas bordering on Burma, Laos, and Cambodia. However, the growing prosperity of Viet Nam has brought significant benefits for Thailand, and will continue to do so until Viet Nam's own infrastructure allows it to take over all entrepôt activities. It is significant that until economic restrictions in Viet Nam were recently lifted, most nonlocal distilled alcohol in Viet Nam was imported from Thailand. Since 1970, when commercial beers as opposed to local began to be brewed on an industrial scale, beer has become the preferred national alcohol beverage, though locally manufactured rice wines and whiskies remain popular spirits (personal communication from sources in Royal Thai government, 1995). No breakdown of consumption by type of beverage is available. Figure 4.1 shows the per capita pure alcohol consumption in 1990 for four of the five countries or areas considered here.

STATISTICAL INCONSISTENCY

Each of the five countries (or areas) approaches the evolving effects of alcohol use by its population from a different perspective. All of them have lexicologically different languages and the people are imbued with national or regional philosophies that are not necessarily congruent with those of the West. Publication of research in a common tongue, English, is of recent date, usually within the last 20 years, and policies on alcohol as a potential social or medical problem have also recently been developed. For example, it is frequently difficult to convey to possible sources of data the differences between someone who is alcohol dependent and someone who is a moderate drinker. Data on the former are relatively simple to access, but for the latter, secondary data often have to suffice to obtain a somewhat clearer picture of developing alcohol use.

There is little consistency in statistical collection methods among different government departments and none among the differing nations. Moreover, the countries have very different views of alcohol and its potential in effecting social and economic change. Thailand has seen the growth of a national alcohol industry from small local manufacturing centers of rice beer and distilled spirits only in the last 40 years, with the emergence of the Boon Rawd Company as its major commercial beer producer. Large-scale national production in Japan can be traced back to the 17th century. The Japanese approach to the situation, which has seen a steady rise in alcohol use by men, and a much more rapid rise in use by women, has been to focus on the medical consequences of alcohol use and their amelioration. Taiwan and South Korea may be said to favor an approach based on social needs and consequences, each country having its own sociological focus. Thailand and Hong Kong have begun to emphasize social harms and their reduction as key issues. In Hong Kong, data concerning illegal drug use among teenage youth have been collected by the government since 1987, while tobacco and alcohol, seen latterly as potential precursors to substance abuse, have been included in such surveys since 1992 (Day et al., 1994, 1996).

National collection of evidence of alcohol's influence reflects these emphases and the use made of such evidence is similarly variously directed. It is, therefore, difficult to compare published rates of use, consumption data, or production figures, since the reasons for collection of each set of figures vary tremendously. Only consumption data can be considered somewhat reliable (see Chapter 3, Table 3.1), but they too may disregard noncommercial local production, which is often of significance in less developed countries such as Thailand.

Hence it may be that only data on changes in the rates of chronic liver disease (CLD) can give a reliable trend for alcohol use in the region, where

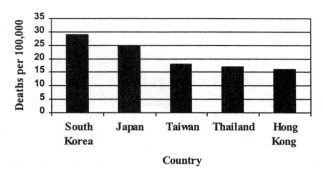

FIGURE 4.2 Deaths per 100,000 from chronic liver diseases in Southeast Asia, 1992. (*Sources:* Government Information Service, 1990; Day, Jones, & Wilkinson, 1995a, 1995b, 1996; Day, Wilkinson, & Greene, 1996.)

the only significant causes of a change in those rates are likely to be diet in general, and alcohol use in particular. Even that approach may not be reliable if the nation's health services are not widely developed, or have only developed in recent times, as in non-metropolitan Thailand or Taiwan. However, it can be shown that, at least in major urban centers, all of these nations have had a well developed service under Western medical regimes for over thirty years, so that their statistics and the conclusions drawn from them may be quite reliable. Figure 4.2 illustrates these rates.

Not unexpectedly, South Korea and Japan, which are known anecdotally for heavy drinking in the male population from early adulthood, have a chronic liver disease (CLD) mortality rate signficantly greater than that of Hong Kong, Taiwan, or Thailand. As drinking is predominantly among males, the mortality rate for males only may be almost twice the rate per 100,000 for the population as a whole. In Hong Kong, where females now drink more frequently, a higher overall rate might be expected because of the nongender-specific pattern of alcohol consumption. However, no gender-related data on CLD rates in Hong Kong are available (Government Information Service, 1990).

A further complicating factor is the high rate of viral hepatitis infection among Southeast Asians. Hepatitis B predisposes carriers towards chronic liver disease. It has in the past, according to the Hong Kong Department of Health, been found among up to 20 percent of the Hong Kong population. With immunization, its spread (by body-fluid transfer) has been curtailed, but it must be a confusing factor in the Thai and Taiwanese data. Correlative data concerning risk from CLD exacerbated by hepatitis infection varies significantly in published sources (Day & Greene, 1997; Day, Jones, & Wilkinson, 1995a, 1995b, 1996; Day, Wilkinson, & Greene, 1996). The validity of a comparative statistical approach towards alcohol-related matters in the Asian-Pacific regions is, therefore, open to question. It seems preferable to emphasize the issues and concerns in each of the countries studied, and to avoid drawing comparative conclusions which may prove to be fallacious.

Governments are inconsistent even in their reporting of consumption figures (Figure 4.1). In Taiwan, for example, which has an alcohol and tobacco monopoly board, it is in the national interest, as a reflection of prosperity, to show consumption rising when there is no perceived detriment to the population. Hence, the recorded increase in per capita consumption of 35 percent from 1984 to 1994 is likely to be accurate. In Japan, where the effects of alcohol consumption are considered to be affecting social order, an increase of only 27 percent was seen over the same period (Day et al., 1995a). In Thailand the reported 50 percent increase from 1987 to 1992 may well be verifiable (Day et al., 1995b). However, consumption also rose by 50 percent in South Korea, and yet this is the only country studied where alcohol consumption was found to be leveling off, while in all others it continues to rise (Day, Wilkinson, & Greene, 1996). In all countries there is recognition that drinking among youth is a serious matter. In Japan this has led to calls for restrictions on sales through publicly sited drink-vending machines (Day et al., 1995a). In Hong Kong, despite its background as a British dependency, there were no specific alcohol control laws, apart from those governing licensed bars and restaurants, until sale to minors (under 18 years) through other retail outlets was prohibited in 1995.

SOCIAL WELFARE AND MEDICINE WITHOUT SYSTEMS

Social Order

In all of the countries there is an increased awareness that alcohol has a significant potential for social problems. However, in Thailand the level of awareness is low except in the capital of Bangkok. The chief concern there was that drunken driving was resulting in a significant loss of life because, until 1995, there was only a rudimentary emergency ambulance service.

In Chiang Mai, the second city of Thailand, the University's medical faculty reported relatively little concern among older people that alcohol consumption among the newly affluent young was growing significantly, because the mostly rural older population had long used locally brewed alcohol as an analgesic to reduce pain and tiredness caused by hard agricultural labor (Day et al., 1995b). Thailand is the only country in the study where rural drinkers still significantly outnumber urban drinkers. In the south of the country, bordering on Moslem Malaysia, the town of Had Yai is concerned with the weekend influx of Malaysians who come to drink there, encouraging the growth of bars and a hospitality industry that negatively influences the town's youth. Increases in car racing in the streets, with consequential alcohol-related road accidents, also cause concern (Day et al., 1995b).

Alcohol consumption has traditionally been a male pastime in Thailand. In Bangkok, however, rates are similar in both genders in the 15–19-year age group. Alcohol was found to have been used by only 32 percent of those aged 15–19 who were apprehended for some crime, while other drugs (excluding tobacco) had been used by up to 49 percent of them (Day et al., 1995b). By comparison, in Hong Kong among noncriminal school students, 70 percent of the same age group had used alcohol but only 14 percent had used other psychoactive substances (Day et al., 1994, 1996).

In parts of rural Thailand, concern is being felt about the consumption of impure forms of locally brewed alcohol, where up to 40 milligrams per 100 milliliters of methanol has been found—a level high enough to cause illness. Academics in this part of the country feel that a regulated alcohol industry would be preferable to harmful local traditional production (Poshyachinda, 1991).

In 1994 in Thailand, nondrinkers outnumbered drinkers in the adult population as a whole by two-to-one. There was a very large regional variation, from almost equal proportions in the northeast to 1:5 in Bangkok (Day et al., 1995b). This contrasts markedly with South Korea and Japan, where over 80 percent of the population reported drinking (Day, Wilkinson, & Greene, 1996; Day et al. 1995a, respectively). The gender bias is also very different. In 1988, the ratio of drinkers in Japan was 1.8 men to each woman, while in Thailand it was reported as five to one in 1994. In Japan 8 percent of women reported daily drinking (Suzuki et al., 1993). No comparable studies are available for Thailand. It might be suggested that Thailand is coming to terms with a phenomenon of developing alcohol consumption in a rather benign way, while in South Korea and Japan it has become a significant social harm.

Thailand has recently joined in supporting a regional body to provide liaison between governments and the alcohol industry, the Asia-Pacific Alcohol Policy Forum (APAPF), which seeks to ensure bilateral responsibility when legislating on alcohol-related issues. The forum has recently released a video and booklet in Thai that illustrate developing social concern, and offer a sensible approach towards alcohol issues in Thailand.

In Japan, a strictly enforced law on alcohol-related driving offenses was passed in 1960 and revised in 1970; breathalyzer testing and enforcement is normal (Hattori et al., 1992). In Thailand an attempt to introduce a law in 1979 was stalled at Cabinet level when ministries failed to agree on responsibility for enforcement (Royal Thai Government, 1991). Moreover, the police could not agree, in 1987, on which type of breathalyzer device should be used (Poshyachinda, 1991). No significant progress had been reported since 1994. However, a "no drink if driving" campaign, financially supported by the alcohol beverage industry, was carried out in 75 provinces in 1995 (Day et al., 1995b).

In Hong Kong, with only some 15,000 road accidents involving injuries annually and no more than 260 fatalities, no drunk-driving laws were in place until 1995. However, with rising affluence and youth road racing becoming a problem, legislation similar to that in Western jurisdictions was introduced.

Over 50 percent of suspects stopped by police under its provisions were reported by journalists to have more than the legal limit of alcohol (50 milligrams per 100 milliliters) in their blood. This strongly supported the public perception of a growing general consumption of alcohol first discerned in a 1983 study of construction site workers in hospital emergency rooms. Of these, 5 percent admitted alcohol consumption within the 24 hours before admission, but 43 percent, in fact, had alcohol levels of 10 to 150 milligrams per 100 milliliters in a blood sample (McQuarrie, 1983).

Taiwan has seen two waves of increase in alcohol consumption, first between 1961 and 1976, and again between 1976 and the present. (Day, Jones, & Wilkinson, 1996). The proportion of drinkers in Taiwan is much more similar to Thailand than to South Korea, with about 30 percent of males and 10 percent of females reporting regular consumption. An emergency room study in 1991 showed that 30 percent of patients had blood alcohol levels between 10 and 100 milligrams per 100 milliliters. Another study of those involved in road accidents showed 47 percent with elevated blood alcohol levels (ibid.). The Taiwanese law, although financially severe, has proved difficult to enforce owing to loose drafting (ibid.). It is significant that alcohol misuse has been recognized as a contributing factor to social problems in all the studied countries in terms of traffic and accident-related matters. Other social issues are seen as relatively insignificant in all but Japan.

Medical Responses

Care of people with alcohol dependence and other alcohol-related problems varies from treatment as a cluster of DSM-IV-defined medical conditions in Japan and South Korea, with full provision of psychiatric services, to some recognition of the long-term nature of the condition in urban areas in Thailand, where psychiatric medicine is considerably under-resourced. In Taiwan there is an acknowledged shortfall in the provision of psychiatric services, so that needs exceed provisions of treatment by up to 80 percent in some categories and up to 50 percent in rehabilitation facilities (Day, Jones, & Wilkinson, 1996). Thus alcohol-related disorders have a low priority.

In Hong Kong, similarly, perception of the problem as a low-priority psychiatric concern can be seen from the fact that there is provision for specific medium-term treatment in only one government-funded nonpsychiatric hospital. Beds in psychiatric hospitals are in short supply, and again alcohol abuse is treated as a low-priority problem. While illegal drugs and tobacco are both mentioned significantly in the Government Year Book for 1997, no mention of alcohol occurs (Government Information Service, 1997). Recent attempts to introduce employee assistance programs, which take account of substance abuse, have met with little response from employers, for whom a substantial labor surplus ensures rapid replacement, even of skilled staff, if alcohol use affects workplace performance. In Japan and South Korea, alcohol-related treatment and rehabilitation may be provided for financially by social welfare assistance. In Taiwan, Thailand, and Hong Kong, on the other hand, only treatment for associated conditions such as depression or liver disorders can be funded through health insurance or public health clinics (Day & Greene, 1997; Day, Jones, & Wilkinson, 1995a, 1995b, 1996; Day, Wilkinson, & Greene, 1996). In South Korea, where data were available on priorities for health research, health education was funded as a second-rank priority together with such fields as occupational health, but drug addiction and alcoholism control were placed in the lowest (fourth) rank (Ministry of Health and Welfare, 1995). Only in Japan has there been specific well-documented and wide study of the medical and social consequences of alcohol use. Studies here have usually been medically initiated and began early, the first being documented in 1975 (Sato, 1975). In South Korea specific studies have been documented from 1987 (Lee et al., 1987; Yamamoto et al., 1987). In the other countries, sporadic work is traceable—in Hong Kong in 1974 and 1983 (Singer, 1974; McQuarrie, 1983), and in Taiwan by Wu Jau-shin (1977) and by Yeh and colleagues (1986). In Thailand no systematic research was published until 1991 (Poshyachinda, 1991)

It may be concluded that alcohol abuse as a serious problem has developed as a function of prosperity in Asia, except where local brewing associated with festivals has caused acute situations (Mougne et al., 1982), but that medical intervention on a systematic basis is rare.

Alcohol and Youth

All the countries or territories reviewed here have become increasingly aware of the problem of illegal substance abuse. However, serious consideration has been given only to opiate abuse which, despite the serious involvement of considerable numbers of individuals, is insignificant when related to morbidity resulting particularly from tobacco use. In Hong Kong there are 38,000 registered heroin addicts, but recent findings indicate that three out of five older male school students have consumed alcohol in a given week (Day et al.,1994, 1996) and about 10 percent of these will eventually become alcohol dependent if minimum norms for other well-studied populations such as those of Europe or America are applied. If Hong Kong has a total male population aged 15 years and over of 2.6 million (Government Information Service, 1990), 260,000 of these will probably become alcohol dependent. Thus the present opiate problem, which is now being addressed with vigor by the government, pales into insignificance when the social and medical needs and costs of its potentially alcohol-dependent population, at present poorly cared for, are considered.

Furthermore, as in Japan and South Korea, young Hong Kong women are beginning to consume alcohol, apparently as a sign of emancipation. Rates of female consumption are similar to those for males, but the median quantities consumed are smaller. The matter is not taken seriously, and only the most cursory alcohol abuse prevention education is provided in high schools. In Japan, however, such education was made obligatory in schools in 1992. (Day et al.,

1995a). Research in South Korea indicates that 84 percent of males and 53 percent of females aged 15–18 years drink alcohol, while only 5 percent of males have used marijuana and 2 percent have used opiates (Lee, 1987). In Taiwan only 11 percent of the same male age group were found to drink in 1995. Females still did not exhibit male patterns (Ko et al., 1992), only 3 percent of 15 to 19-year-old females reported drinking. No similar data are available for Thailand.

In the past, alcohol has not been very popular among some people from Asian populations because of a phenomenon known as "flushing syndrome" that occurs in about 30 percent of individuals who lack aldehyde dehydrogenase iso-enzyme (ALDH-I). Because of low levels of the enzyme, aldehydes in the circulation cause vasodilation and facial reddening. When the enzyme is synthesized by the individual at very low levels, very small quantities of alcohol may cause vomiting without other symptoms of intoxication. Alcohol use has been found to be low amongst those who flush easily. Only ten percent of those who "flush" were alcohol users in one study, whereas 65 percent of those who had mild or no symptoms used alcohol to some extent (Day, Wilkinson, & Greene, 1996).

As the stigma attached to flushing gradually lessens among the young, and as young women in Asia seek emancipation through formerly male rites of passage, it is likely that the proportion of problem drinkers of both genders in these populations will rise steadily.

Haulage of goods from Singapore to Thailand, or from Hong Kong into China, or through the length of Japan or South Korea, leads to the phenomenon of alcohol use by long-distance truckers. This is known to be augmented by amphetamine use, leading to polysubstance abuse problems, which spill over into the youth population when the truckers communicate the effects to young local van drivers who work long hours. Any relationship between alcohol and illegal substance abuse will be addressed not because of the reality that alcohol misuse is more socially and economically significant, but because of the erroneous perception that illegal drug misuse must be controlled at any cost. Thus research linking illegal drug abuse and alcohol misuse will certainly be brought to bear on attitudes of the social use of alcohol, especially by the young.

CONCLUSION

In all of these countries, a rapid rise in prosperity is at the core of the changes in alcohol use. A pure research-based approach to dealing with the situation, as has been preferred in Japan for over 30 years, is not satisfactory where situations develop and change within a few years. Hence, while surveys of youth consumption of alcohol or the gathering of medical statistics can set the background, small-scale ethnographic approaches to observed situations may be more effective in addressing the issues.

The HIV situation in Thailand, perhaps the worst in Asia, is said by those who are involved in preventive education in the sex industry there to be exacerbated by alcohol misuse, which may lead to less careful sexual practices (Poshy-achinda, 1991). This translates into effects upon any situation where prostitution is associated with the entertainment industry, as in Taiwan's capital city of Taipei, Seoul in Korea, or the major cities of Japan. The influence of the entertainment industry itself on national prosperity affects the government's approaches to alcohol use, as does the government's involvement in revenue collection from alcohol sales. The setting of these revenues against related welfare costs as has been seen recently in Australia and Canada (Day & Green, 1997; Collins, 1996), may also influence Southeast Asian attitudes towards alcohol.

Ethnicity is a factor where the Chinese "flushing syndrome" reduces the potential for any or excessive consumption of alcohol amongst that population. If a substantial group of the population is not affected, as in Thailand or Taiwan, demographic make-up must be considered when applying national perceptions locally.

The tendency for the alcoholically intoxicated Southeast Asian not to resort to violence when intoxicated is significant, as is the attitude of women to a drunken partner, albeit they are reported as becoming less tolerant. When a drunken partner commits violent abuse of a spouse, it is likely to be in the home, and, therefore, less likely to be the subject of police intervention. However, the need for help on the part of women, and for facilities for those who are abused by alcoholic partners, is no less than in the West. Thus research derived from a social welfare base must be carefully examined in Asia if the effects of alcohol use habits are to be fully understood.

All of this anecdotal material indicates that the Asian-Pacific rim, with the exception of Japan, is only slowly recognizing the role of alcohol in its developing prosperity. The region may have to use unconventional routes to examine each situation and to react proactively in order to avoid the types of involvements of its youth and its workforce in alcohol misuse that have become burdensome to Western economies.

ACKNOWLEDGMENT

The author is especially grateful to United Distillers (Asia) for funding to carry out the research for this review. However, readers should note that the views expressed above are those of the author and do not represent the views of United Distillers (Asia) or any other industry-related concern.

REFERENCES

Collins, D. J. (1996). *The Social Costs of Drug Abuse in Australia in 1988 and 1992*. Canberra: Commonwealth Department of Human Services and Health, Australian Government Publishing Service.

Day, J. R., Bacon Shone, J., Law, S. W., & Jones, E. C. (1994, 1996). *The health related behavior of Hong Kong adolescents; An overview report and age/gender related data from district based studies*. Hong Kong: Social Sciences Research Centre, University of Hong Kong.

Day, J. R. & Greene, M. (1997). *Sociopathology of alcohol in China* (United Distillers (Asia) Report). Hong Kong: Social Sciences Research Centre, University of Hong Kong.

Day, J. R., Jones, E. C., & Wilkinson, S. (1995a). *Socio-pathology of alcohol in Japan* (United Distillers (Asia) Report). Hong Kong: Social Sciences Research Centre, University of Hong Kong.

Day, J. R., Jones, E. C., & Wilkinson, S. (1995b). *Sociopathology of alcohol in Thailand* (United Distillers (Asia) Report). Hong Kong: Social Sciences Research Centre, University of Hong Kong.

Day, J. R., Jones, E. C., & Wilkinson, S. (1996). *Sociopathology of alcohol in Taiwan* (United Distillers (Asia) Report). Hong Kong: Social Sciences Research Centre, University of Hong Kong.

Day, J. R., Wilkinson, S., & Greene, M. (1996). *Socio-pathology of alcohol in South Korea* (United Distillers (Asia) Report). Hong Kong: Social Sciences Research Centre, University of Hong Kong.

Department of Health. (1994). *The Republic of China Yearbook.* Taipei: Government Information Office.

Department of Health. (1995). *The Republic of China Yearbook.* Taipei: Government Information Office.

Gardner, J. L. (Ed). (1986). *Reader's Digest Atlas of the World.* London: Reader's Digest Association.

Government Information Service. (1990). *Hong Kong—A Review.* Hong Kong: Government Printer.

Government Information Service. (1997). *Hong Kong—A Review.* Hong Kong: Government Printer.

Hattori, H., Komura, S., & Funmo, J. (1992). Legislation on alcohol detection in alcohol-related traffic accidents involving casualties in Japan and Canada. *Japan Journal of Alcohol Studies and Drug Dependence, 27,* 233–240.

Ko, Y-c, et al. (1992). Risk factors related to the use of amphetamines in adolescent students. *Journal of Chinese Psychiatry, 8,* 24–34.

Lee, C. K., Kwak, Y. S., Rhee, H., Kim, Y. S., Han, J. H., Choi, J. O., & Lee, Y. H. (1987). The nationwide epidemiological study of mental disorders in Korea. *Journal of Korean Medical Science, 2,* 19–34.

McGovern, M. P. (1982). Alcoholism in Southeast Asia: Prevalence and treatment. *International Journal of Social Psychiatry, 28,* 14–22

McQuarrie, L. (1983). *Alcohol Use Amongst Patients Admitted to Hospital Emergency Rooms.* Hong Kong: Hong Kong Council of Social Services.

Ministry of Health and Welfare. (1994). *White Paper.* Seoul, Korea: Government Printer.

Ministry of Health and Welfare. (1995). *Cancer Registry Programme in the Republic of Korea, Jan. 1988–Dec. 1992.* Seoul: Government Printer.

Mougne, C., Macleman, R., & Aisana, S. (1982). Smoking, chewing and drinking in Ban Pong, Northern Thailand. *Journal of Social Science and Medicine, 16,* 99–106.

Poshyachinda, V. (1991). *Alcohol and Thai Society.* Bangkok: Chulalongkorn University.

Royal Thai Government. (1991). *Statistics on Alcoholic Beverage Consumption in Thailand and Some Related Problems.* Bangkok: Government Printer, Royal Thai Government.

Sato, A. (1975). *The way Japanese choose liquor: Modern approaches to alcohol consumption in Japan.* Japan.

Singer, K. (1974). The choice of intoxicants among the Chinese. *British Journal of Addiction, 69,* 257–268.

Suzuki, K., Higuchi, S., Yamada, K., Mizutani, Y., & Kono, H. (1993). Young female alcoholics with and without eating disorders: A comparative study in Japan. *American Journal of Psychiatry, 150,* 1053–1058.

Wu Jau-shin (1977). New concepts of alcoholic liver disease and clinical and pathological treatments. *Contemporary Medical Journal, 4,* 156–183.

Yamamoto, J., Lee, C. K., Lin, M., & Hyoung, C. K. (1987). Alcohol abuse in Koreans. *American Journal of Social Psychiatry, 1*(4), 6–27.

Yeh Eng-kung, Hwu Gwai-ho, Chen Chiao-chicy, & Yeh Yuan-Li (1986). Alcoholism: A low risk disorder for Chinese-community surveys in Taiwan. In G. Y. Sun, P. K. Rudean, W. G. Wood, Y. H. Wei, & A. Y. Sun (Eds.), *Molecular Mechanisms of Alcohol*. Taipei: Taiwan National University Press.

Chapter 5

China

Shen Yucun and Wang Zuxin

China is an ancient country with a long history of civilization. Chinese food is renowned both at home and abroad, and alcohol is a significant part of the Chinese diet. Before 1980, in general, alcohol consumption was lower and alcohol-related social and health problems were less serious in China than in Western industrialized countries. From the start of the "open policy" in the 1980s to the end of 1996, China experienced tremendous socioeconomic change and achieved sustained economic growth, with an average annual increase in its gross domestic product (GDP) of 11.8 percent (*Beijing Review*, 1995). In 1996 the GDP was 6,780 billion yuan, with a 9.7 percent increase from 1995 (State Statistical Bureau, 1997). This growth rate was much higher than the world average of 6 percent and an average of 8 percent for Asia as a whole. China's industrialization in recent decades has been accompanied by an improved standard of living and the influence of Western culture, which has included a significant increase in alcohol consumption and related problems. This chapter draws on a variety of sources of information to describe the patterns and problems of alcohol use in China. The material reviewed includes scientific books and papers published in China as well as reports in the official news media. The statistics and research findings set out in this chapter are often difficult to evaluate because of the lack of clear criteria and systematic recording of the necessary information. Nevertheless, they are considered a reflection of the current status of alcohol use in China.

DEMOGRAPHIC PROFILE

The population of China's mainland, excluding the provinces of Taiwan, Hong Kong, and Macao, is now over 1.2 billion—22 percent of the world's total population. Compared with the total of 1133.68 million found in the fourth nationwide census completed on 1 July 1990, the 1995 figure of 1207.78 million represented a 6.54 percent increase, or 74.10 million people. In the 63-month period up to February 1995, the annual growth rate for China—the country with the world's largest population—averaged 1.21 percent (*Beijing Review*, 1996a). By 1996 the total population was 1223.89 million.

In 1949 when the People's Republic of China was founded, its population was characterized by high birth (36 per 1,000) and death (20 per 1,000) rates and a low growth rate (16 per 1,000). In the first 20 years after the founding of the new China, with the success of the public health service and effective control of infectious diseases, there was a trend towards high birth rates and low death rates. This resulted in a high growth rate and a remarkable increase in the Chinese population. Since the 1980s, however, with the introduction of family planning, the birth, death, and growth rates have been significantly lower (*China Today*, 1996), falling to 17.12, 6.57, and 10.55 per 1,000, respectively, in 1995.

In line with its increased rate of national economic development, China has made much progress in its public health services. From 1949 to 1993, the average life expectancy at birth rose from 35 to 69.5 years. The 1993 figure is above the world average of 66 years. With the process of industrialization, changes in lifestyles, and the implementation of family planning policies, the Chinese traditional extended family has decreased remarkably, while the number of nuclear families has increased. In 1995, China had a total of 322.11 million households (1,207.78 million people), with an average of 3.7 persons per family. By that year, the number of males in China had reached 616.29 million, or 51.03 percent of the total population, while the female population stood at 591.49 million, or 48.97 percent. Thus the male/female ratio was 104.19:100. Yet the old tradition of favoring boys over girls is still widespread, especially in rural areas.

China recognizes 56 nationalities. The Han people form the largest group, with a total population of 1,099.32 million. The remaining 108.46 million people come from various other groups. The fourth census (1990) indicated that the proportion of Hans in the total population had decreased from 91.96 percent to 91.02 percent, while the other ethnic groups had risen from 8.04 percent to 8.98 percent. China's urban population has reached 347.52 million, accounting for 28.85 percent of the total population, as against 26.3 percent in 1990 (a rise of 2.62 percent).

The distribution of China's population is unequal. The population density is high in the southeast and low in the northwestern parts of the country, with an average of 236 people per square kilometer in the southeast but only 11 in the northwest. Shanghai has the highest population density (2,118 people per square kilometer), while the least densely populated part of China is Tibet (1.8 people per square kilometer). Such population imbalances are the result of natural, historical, economic, and ethnic factors. The regions of China that are inhabited by minorities cover a vast area; they consist of five autonomous regions, 30 autonomous prefectures, and 124 autonomous counties, with a total area of 6.17 million square kilometers accounting for 64 percent of China's total territory (*China Today*, 1996).

More than 30 sets of characters and 80 languages are used in China. The people of China follow different religions, such as various schools of Buddhism (e.g., Lamaism, Zen), Christianity (Protestantism, Roman Catholicism, the Eastern Orthodox Church), and Islam.

Because of China's enormous population its per capita indices are lower than the world average. Since the founding of the People's Republic the national economy has developed rapidly, and China's total output of manufactured products has become the largest in the world. On the other hand, its enormous population has drained its natural resources and material products, and as a result has held back the rise in China's living standard.

Recently, the national economy showed sustained growth. Statistics indicate that China's GDP in 1996 reached 6,780 billion yuan (US $826 billion), up 9.7 percent over the previous year. The living standards of urban and rural inhabitants have continued to improve. The average per capita net income of the rural population reached 1,578 yuan in 1995, an increase of 5.3 percent over the previous year. For city dwellers, the per capita income available for living expenses averaged 3,893 yuan, an increase of 4.9 percent (*Beijing Review*, 1996b). The average annual wage was 5,500 yuan, up 1.2 percent, with a real growth of 3.8 percent. However, the difference in income growth between provinces and between urban and rural households was still marked, and the real income of some groups declined (e.g., retired, disabled people) (*Beijing Review*, 1996c).

HISTORICAL ASPECTS AND MAIN DRINKING PATTERNS

China is one of the oldest brewing countries in the world. There are many legends and tales that center on this theme. The most famous and widely told ones are of Yi Di and Du Kang. In one story, Yi Di, a woman servant of the emperor's daughter, found that a gruel of grain that had been left for a while tasted sweet and gave her a good feeling. She presented it to the Emperor Yu (Xia Dynasty—2140–1711 B.C.), who drank it all. The emperor supposed that his descendants would disavow his political authority because of his excessive drinking, and so he exiled Yi Di (Du Jinghua, 1992; Liu Jun, 1995).

In another story, Du Kang (Shao Kang), a young shepherd who was the posthumous son of the fifth prime minister of the Xia Dynasty (2140–1711 B.C.), was caught in a shower on a mountain one day. In the rush to drive the sheep home, he forgot his lunch of cooked and husked sorghum that was hanging in a bamboo bucket on a tree. When he returned a few days later it smelled and tasted good. He tried it many times with his family and, finally, a large quantity was produced. Owing to his great contribution, he was called the "God of alcohol," and his name is now synonymous with alcohol (Du Jinghua, 1992; Liu Jun, 1995; Xiao Jiacbeng, 1995).

However, some scholars suggest that the origin of alcohol in China was much earlier than the Xia Dynasty, dating instead from the Shen Nong period of the New Stone Age (approximately 7,000 years ago), when our ancestors settled down and began to farm the land in the middle reaches of the Yellow river. The grain they planted provided an essential prerequisite for brewing. A large quantity of pottery drinking vessels, such as cups with a long foot and two ears, especially made for brewing and drinking, were excavated from a ruin at Da Wen Kou (Shandong province). This ruin has been archaeologically identified as a product of the culture of the New Stone Age of China. It provides strong material evidence that alcohol in China originated 6,000–7,000 years ago from simple natural fermentation (Wan Guoguang, 1986).

Inscriptions on bones or tortoise shells from the Shang Dynasty (16th–11th century B.C.) are where the Chinese word for alcohol first appeared. During the Han Dynasty (206 B.C.–220 A.D.) Zhang Qian was sent on a diplomatic mission to the West. On his return he brought back a fine breed of vine as well as grape wine-making skills. At the end of the 18th and the early 19th centuries, beer, brandy, whisky, and vodka were introduced to China. In 1915, the first domestic brewery in China was founded in Beijing—the Five Star Brewery, formally called the Shuan He Sheng Brewery.

China is known as a country in which alcohol is an important aspect of the culture. Drinking is socially accepted and plays a significant part in major events of daily life. From ancient times, sacrificial offerings were accompanied by alcohol. These customs are also a part of the New Year festival, wedding ceremonies, birthdays, receptions, farewell parties, and so on. Ritual drinking, for example, when offering sacrifices to God, ancestors, heaven and earth, was an important part of these major events in ancient times. After praying, people poured alcohol on the ground for happiness, health, and prosperity. Then they would share and enjoy drinks and food.

Festive Drinking

China has various traditional festivals, and festival activities are closely linked with drinking. For example, during China's most important festival, the Spring festival (Chinese New Year), an auspicious medicinal liquor—*tusu*—made from peppers and cypress leaves, which symbolize luck, health and long life, has been enjoyed by people ever since the Han Dynasty. The Qingming festival (April 5, solar calendar) is a mourning festival, when people pay respect to the dead at their tombs with dishes of food and beverages of alcohol. This festival is still very popular in China. Since grief for the dead is great, alcohol is used to relieve sorrow. Realgar liquor is used for the Duanwu festival (the Dragon Boat festival, held on the fifth day of the fifth lunar month), because it is believed to drive out evil spirits and insects. The Mid-Autumn festival (15th day of the eighth lunar month) is a family reunion day when people join in drinking, talking, singing, and dancing while watching the full moon. The Mid-Autumn festival is still a favorite custom that has been practiced all over China ever since it was a warring state (475–221 B.C.) (Du Jinghua, 1992; Liu Jiuyin, 1995).

Celebrations

Beverage alcohol is typically consumed in China at times of happiness. Weddings are one of the great events in people's lives, and they have long been associated with alcohol. Among both the Han and the Dai, Jingpo and Lahu ethnic minorities, it is traditional for the suitor's family to offer alcohol to the prospective bride's family. Among the Ewenki, it is understood that the parents have approved the marriage once the gift is drunk. At the wedding, the bridegroom and bride must drink a cup of alcohol together, symbolizing their pledge to each other. The bridegroom also must toast each member of the bride's family as well as her relatives and friends (Liu Jun, 1995).

Recreational Drinking

Drinking is also a recreational activity. From the perspective of Chinese culture, beverage alcohol can stimulate the mind and stir the sentiments. As a result, alcohol often goes hand-in-hand with music, dance, poetry, and other literary and art activities. There are a number of drinking games in China. In poetry, for example, players are called on in turn quickly to compose a poem with a specified rhyme pattern. Failure to comply results in a penalty of having to drink a large quantity of alcohol. The great poet Li Bai is famous as the "saint of alcohol" and "alcohol immortal." There seems to be a close association between drinking and poetic inspiration (Du Jinghua, 1992).

Drinking slowly with food is becoming a typical pattern of drinking in China. On the other hand, the drinker's wager game is also very popular. This game entails first proposing a toast, and then submitting to somebody's persuasion after first turning down his request.

VARIETIES OF BEVERAGE ALCOHOL

There are three main types of beverage alcohol in China, which are differentiated by the processing method. The first consists of distilled spirits or liquor (high-strength liquor), in which over 40 percent of the total content is pure alcohol. White spirit, Chinese arrack, and imported or homemade brandy and whisky fall into this category. The second consists of fermented wine (low-strength wine), with an alcohol content below 20 percent, such as beer, yellow rice wine, and fruit wine. The third is *compound wine* (medium-strength wine), with an alcohol content of 20–40 percent. Various kinds of medicinal wines and drinks mixed with fruit juice are examples of compound wine.

Since the materials and technology used in alcohol processing vary from producer to producer, there are hundreds of different country alcohols (mostly distilled spirits), among which eight have been evaluated as famous beverages on the national level, such as Mao-tai (52–53 proof), a top-strength spirit known as state liquor, diplomatic liquor, and *wuliangye*. Mao-tai has been popular among Chinese consumers since the beginning of the century and still commands a huge share of the domestic high-strength liquor market. Another 47 varieties have been rated as superior beverage alcohol. Most of them have won golden or silver medals in international fairs.

Since the foundation of the People's Republic the importation of beverage alcohol has been controlled by heavy duties. Consequently, most Chinese are not yet accustomed to the taste of foreign products. However, the situation is changing. According to trade statistics the sales volume of imported foreign liquors has doubled since 1991. The total sales volume from 1991–95 was about 3 billion yuan, accounting for 5 percent of total alcohol consumption. Since March 1995, customs duties on imported foreign liquors have been cut from 150 percent to 80 percent. Because of the huge profits that selling foreign liquor can yield, many supermarkets, restaurants, and hotels purchase large quantities. Some public officials, eager to impress their guests at ceremonies and banquets, contribute to increased sales. In the last few years, a government-imposed ban on banqueting at state expense has much reduced such status-driven consumption. Sales fell by 40 percent in 1995 compared with the peak year of 1993.

There are two kinds of beverage alcohol that are unique to China. The first is yellow rice or millet wine. This is a fermented wine (about 15–20 proof), which is 10 times richer in amino acids than beer ("liquid bread"), and is referred to as "liquid egg cake." The second is medicinal liquor (e.g., Ehu Ye Qing, Gou Qi Zi), liquors made with traditional herbs for treating or preventing certain diseases.

Since China is now in transition from a centrally planned economy to a market economy and the legal system is not yet complete, some unscrupulous merchants produce illicit beverage alcohol and market it as famous brands, but selling it at a lower price. It is estimated that no less than 1,200 tons of illicitly produced Mao-tai was marketed in 1992, at a value of some 400 million yuan (Xu Penghang, 1995). The total annual output from Mao-Tai Winery is 1,800 tons. Such counterfeiting severely endangers people's health. Six illicit liquor law cases were investigated in Jiamusi (Heinongjiang Province), Shanghai (Henan Province), Jinmen (Hubei Province), Deyang, Yibing (Sichuan Province), and Liuzhou (Guangxi Province), in which 36 people were killed and 89 injured by poisoning from illicit alcohol (Xu Penghang, 1995). The Chinese government is now paying more attention to such cases, and as a result strict measures have been taken. The China Consumers Association, which protects the interests of consumers, is now launching a nationwide program to fight illicitly produced products. In addition, it has initiated a campaign that started in 1995, uniting 10,000 shops in 100 cities to combat counterfeit commodities. It is hoped that as a result of such an action the danger of illicitly produced alcohol will be reduced.

ACCESSIBILITY

The production and sale of beverage alcohol is regulated by licenses issued by the State Council of the Ministry of Light Industry, State Bureau of Industry and Commerce, and its local administrations. Some organizations such as China Sugar, the Wine Group Cooperative, and the China Liquor Business Association are involved in the management and supervision of the production and sale of alcohol. However, in keeping with the development of a consumer economy, a variety of different kinds of domestic and foreign-made drinks with attractive packaging are displayed on the counters of state-owned shops, supermarkets, restaurants, and hotels. Thus, everyone can easily buy alcohol regardless of age and with no limitation on the quantity purchased. Bars and pubs have been opening up in many cities in China. Brewing of beverages such as highland barley wine and sweet wine by peasants themselves is still very popular since they can drink their products when they want without going shopping.

ALCOHOL PRODUCTION AND CONSUMPTION

In 1982, there were 8,600 brewing enterprises in China. Total tax revenue from beverage alcohol was 2 billion yuan, which accounted for 12.4 percent of total food taxation. During the period 1984–94, the gross output of alcohol climbed from less than 6 million tons annually to 23.31 million tons. In 1995, according to figures from the State Statistical Bureau, the output of various kinds of drinks, particularly wines and beer, rose to 24 million tons, roughly four times that of a decade earlier. Total sales hit 65 billion yuan ($7.8 billion).

The year 1988 marked an important turning point in China's beverage alcohol industry. It was not only the first time that alcohol supply fell short of demand, but also the first time that beer output exceeded that of other drinks. From 1979 to 1988, the output of beer increased by an average of 25 percent per year, from 520 tons in 1979, to more than 14 million tons in 1988. The sale of beer accounted for 63 percent of the total beverage alcohol sales volume, and the continuing reduction of spirits to 29 percent in 1994. China is now the second largest beer-producing country in the world after the United States (*World Drink Trends*, 1996).

The growth of the beverage alcohol industry in China reached its peak in 1992 with 45,000 production facilities, only 200 of which were large scale and had advanced technology. Since then, 5,000 small production facilities have gone bankrupt and it is expected that more will follow in the future, owing to the intense competition in the beverage alcohol market over the past three years.

Nineteen ninety-five was another turning point, because for the first time the output of medium- and low-strength alcohol (below 40 percent) exceeded that of high-strength alcohol, accounting for more than 55 percent of output of all beverage alcohol. Concurrently, the proportion of the best quality products was steadily increasing, reaching 1.2 million tons at the end of 1994 and accounting for 21 percent of the output (Zhou Xuanyun & He Guanghua, 1995).

TABLE 5.1   Per capita consumption of absolute alcohol in Chungking.

	1950	1960	1970	1990–1996
Volume of consumption (pure alcohol, liters)	1.27	0.82	1.46	3.47
Change in percentage (1950 = 100 percent)	100	−35*	+14	+173

Source: Zhu Hua et al. (1990).
*National economy as a whole was developing slowly.

Alcohol consumption in China in 1952 was 646,000 tons and per capita consumption was about 1 kg. At the end of the Cultural Revolution in 1978, total consumption had risen to 2.46 million tons and per capita consumption to about 2 kg. Although data on the proportion of different kinds of beverage alcohol were not available, distilled spirits were predominant according to data from the State Statistical Bureau. By 1990, alcohol consumption had reached 14.36 million tons, or about 22 times more than that in 1951 and six times more than in 1978. Consumption increased by 5.3 percent annually from 1952 to 1976 and by 13.3 percent from 1982 to 1990.

Table 5.1 shows per capita consumption of pure alcohol for people aged over 15 years old in Chungking, a suburb county of Kunming City, Yunnan Province.

Beer consumption has also increased substantially. Millions of peasants who never drank beer before have now joined the ranks of beer consumers. In Beijing, for example, the volume of beer consumed was about 30,000 tons during the 1980s; by 1994 the figure had doubled. Until 1995, beer consumption accounted for 65 percent of the country's total alcohol consumption while the demand for spirits had dropped to 30 percent. Yet beer consumption per capita in China is only about 10 liters, as compared to the world average of 21 liters. The per annum consumption of grape wine in China is only 0.05 liters, while it is 100 liters in the developed countries (Wang Jing, 1995). People's purchasing power may to a certain degree reflect alcohol consumption. Table 5.2 is a summary of annual purchases of beverage alcohol by urban households in kilograms per capita:

TABLE 5.2   Per capita annual purchases of beverage alcohol by urban households.

1985	1986	1987	1988	1989	1990	1991
7.8	9.36	9.92	9.45	9.0	9.25	9.45

Source: Statistical Yearbook of China, 1992.

TABLE 5.3 Urban per capita annual purchases of beverage alcohol by income level.

Income level	Yuan per annum	Beverage purchases (kg)
Lowest	1006.54	6.62
Lower	1239.65	7.77
Medium	1671.43	9.40
Higher	2283.08	11.64
Highest	2956.81	14.29
Average total per capita annual purchases		9.45

Source: Statistical Yearbook of China (1992).

The most consistent finding in general population surveys of alcohol consumption in China is that the proportion of female drinkers is very low. If women were excluded from the surveys (as most of them do not drink), per capita consumption of alcohol would double.

An interesting point to note is that annual per capita purchases of beverage alcohol increase with higher incomes (Table 5.3).

POLICY AND PUBLIC OPINION ON ALCOHOL

The general policy for the development of national consumer goods in China is that their production should be given an important place in the national economy, so that special attention should be paid to their quality and function. Concentrating efforts on improving quality, variety, and efficiency improves the ability of enterprises to develop new products, to adapt to market changes, and to intensify technical upgrading.

The development of the beverage alcohol industry enriches people's lives. At the same time, as a popular consumer product, beverage alcohol is also one of the highest taxed commodities. Recently, the Chinese beverage alcohol industry has undergone rapid development, resulting in increased output and quality of drinks.

Along with the development of national production and improved living standards, consumption patterns in the alcohol market are now changing considerably. In the 1950s, the sales volume of high-strength (greater than 40 percent) drinks accounted for more than 80 percent of the alcohol market, while low-strength beverages such as beer (2.5–6 percent), yellow wine (11–18 percent), and grape wine (10–18 percent) accounted for only 20 percent of total alcohol consumption. Recently, the absolute sales volume of both high- and low-strength beverage alcohol has increased markedly. However, high-strength drinks fell back to less than 40 percent of total alcohol sales, while low-strength beverages grew to more than 60 percent. In view of the market environment, the current shortage of grain, and the adverse health consequences of poorly produced beers, the Chinese brewing industry should persist in following the principle of "top quality, low strength, and wide variety." In so doing, "they should gradually achieve four strategic shifts: from high to low strength, from distilled to fermented, from grain-consuming to fruit-based, and from ordinary to superior" (*Beijing Review*, 1996).

From ancient times, many Chinese scholars and classical books on medicine have mentioned the benefits and risks of alcohol. Recent evidence suggests that moderate drinking may reduce the risk of coronary heart disease. This finding has given rise to debate in China. What is the public's opinion and attitude with regard to alcohol? In a public survey conducted in Shanghai in 1993, 481 workers, teachers, businessmen, and soldiers, and 569 college students, nurses, and high school students were given a nine-point questionnaire on drinking-related topics. The results showed that the majority of the people surveyed (912 or 86.86 percent) agreed that the existence of alcohol in society is reasonable, since they considered it necessary for festivals, ceremonies, and social activities, provided benefits to health, and induced joy. They realized, however, that the key is the volume and frequency of drinking. On the other hand, 138 people (13.14 percent) were against drinking because they believed that it was harmful to health, could cause alcohol dependence, and increased family difficulties and crime. They further suggested that alcohol-related health knowledge should be propagated among the masses, and that administrative interventions and legal limitations should be enacted with respect to alcohol. In addition, they supported family intervention and placing warning labels on beverage alcohol containers.

ADVERTISING OF BEVERAGE ALCOHOL

Advertising is an important marketing tool in the beverage alcohol industry. Many advertisements can be seen, not only in the popular press, but in journals, posters, and television programs. China has 280 million TV sets and 400 million viewers watch the news every day. Aware that it might have to cope with competition, Qinchi Winery recently made an astounding 66.66 million yuan ($8 million) bid for five-second advertising spots. It has been estimated that prime-time advertisements have helped to quintuple sales of coconut drinks and increase the sales of Confucian festival liquor fourfold. Advertising has spread the fame of many brands throughout the country. A few years ago nobody had heard of Confucian festival liquor, and now it is one of the best selling liquors in northern China. Advertisements for drinks account for almost 20 percent of all TV advertising. Recently, meetings on commodity ordering, sale and exhibition, commodity fairs, and beer festivals have been frequent. Many large firms have spent huge amounts of money on advertising in order to boost sales of their brands. Larger firms are also sponsoring major sporting and cultural activities.

There is a biennial all-China sugar and beverage alcohol fall commodity fair. Most of the larger producers from across the country attend such occasions, which reveals not only the current strength of the Chinese beverage alcohol industry but also the strong competition, which has never been seen before. Many well-known firms do not mind spending money on advertising and publicity. The head of the Industry and Commerce Bureau of Hunan Province disclosed that total expenditure on advertising reached more than 40 million yuan, and that the volume of business reached over 6.6 billion yuan for the October 1995 fair held in Changsha (the capital of Hunan Province) (*Chinese Broadcasting Weekly*, 1996).

The first advertising law of the People's Republic of China was issued in October 1994 and came into force on February 1995. Article 10 of the law states: "Tobacco advertising through broadcasting, television programs, and news media is prohibited." The prohibition in advertising is not, however, absolute. The law continues, "In China, there are three levels of prizes, the national, ministerial, and provincial. Famous superior liquors, which have won prizes at any of these levels, can be advertised after approval by the State Administration for Industry and Commerce (SAIC)." In 1995 SAIC promulgated several regulations concerning advertisements for medicines, alcoholic drinks, and tobacco. The regulatory measures governing alcohol advertisements ban the following: actions which encourage, entice, or lure people to drink alcohol; images of underage persons; the use of symbols of potency, such as cars, yachts, planes, and unscientific expressions or suggestions of "getting rid of tension and anxiety" and "increasing physical strength"; expressions or suggestions which attribute personal, business, social, sporting, or sexual success to the consumption of alcohol; and comparisons of different kinds of beverage alcohol (*BBC Monitoring Service*, 1996).

THE PREVALENCE OF ALCOHOL USE AND ABUSE

Alcohol use and its related problems are among the most important public health issues, as they can constitute a major risk to human health, well being, and life. This belief has been repeatedly emphasized by the World Health Organization (WHO). Accurate prevalence data are of use in planning mental health services, and provide important baseline information to help plan intervention trials for treating and preventing alcohol-related problems.

Recently, much research has been done to enhance the recognition of the harmfulness of alcohol dependence and alcoholism both to people and to society as a whole. Epidemiological surveys are one facet of this research.

Surveys of Alcohol Use and Abuse in the General Population

It is estimated that approximately 160 million males over the age of 16 years drink frequently in China. If women and children are included, then some 300 million people in total drink. This figure is very close to the total number of tobacco smokers (*Chinese Broadcasting Weekly*, 1996).

In 1982, the first nationwide, large-scale collaborative epidemiological investigation of mental disorders was conducted. It covered 12 regions and was headed by Shen Yucun. A total of 38,136 people of Han origin aged 15 years and older, from 12,000 households in 12 regions (6,000 households in rural and urban areas, respectively) were surveyed. The results showed that the overall prevalence of various forms of psychosis was 12.69 percent, drug dependence 0.39 percent, and alcohol dependence 0.16 percent (0.21 percent in urban areas and 0.11 percent in rural areas) (Collaborative Group, 1986).

The second nationwide collaborative epidemiological survey was conducted 10 years later, in 1993, covering seven regions and using the same procedures. The survey revealed that the overall prevalence of mental disorders was 13.47 percent. The time-point prevalence of drug dependence was 0.47 percent, while alcohol dependence had increased to 0.68 percent ranking third after schizophrenia (5.31 percent) and mental retardation (2.71 percent). The time-point prevalence of alcohol dependence in urban and rural areas was 0.23 percent and 1.06 percent, respectively (Collaborative Group, 1993).

In 1989, a survey of 35,385 subjects in 16 districts and counties of Beijing was conducted using cluster sampling. The study showed that 2,398 people, or 6.78 percent of the sample, consumed alcohol (Wang Anhui, 1994).

TABLE 5.4   Rates of alcohol dependence and alcoholism in some Chinese communities.

Region	Year	Sample		Age (years)	Rate per 1,000	
		Urban	Rural		Urban	Rural
12 regions	1982	19,116	19,021	≥15	0.21	0.16
Shandong	1984	19,160	69,662	≥15	0.31	0.37
Beijing	1983–84	8,740		≥60	2.29	
Chongqing	1985	3,700		≥15	4.55	
Xiangyang	1986	2,571	2,397	≥15	6.61	0.83
Beijing	1991	35,385		≥15	14.30	
7 regions	1993	8,799	10,424	≥15	0.23	1.06

Source: Shen Yucun, 1987.
   Method: House-to-house surveys. Screening forms were developed by the National Collaborative Study Group. Diagnostic criteria International Statistical Classification of Diseases, Injuries and Causes of Death, Ninth Revision (ICD-9).

As the standard of living has improved, and alcohol consumption has increased, the prevalence of alcohol dependence among the Han has increased markedly over time. Some results of recent epidemiological investigations on alcohol dependence and alcoholism in the community are shown in Table 5.4.

Surveys of Alcohol Use in Specific Population Groups

Occupation   In one study, 1,674 individuals with alcohol dependence, who were screened and diagnosed out of 44,920 people from four kinds of occupations (average prevalence 37.27 percent), were analyzed through multivariate analysis. The results of factor analysis and multivariate stepwise regression indicated that the patients' risk manner and volume of drinking were influenced by sex, age, occupation, nationality, education, marriage, and economic status. Among them, gender was the most important factor. The data showed that male physical workers were most at risk among the population studied.

Minorities   Many minority groups in China enjoy drinking. The customs of minorities often favor large quantities of drink. For example, alcohol is consumed as a way to keep warm and overcome fatigue, as part of marriage and funeral ceremonies, and in recreational activities, all of which help form the drinking behavior. The development of the economy as well as the improvement of living standards may also encourage drinking. Table 5.5 summarizes a number of epidemiological surveys on alcohol dependence and alcoholism in minority communities.

TABLE 5.5   Prevalence of alcohol dependence and alcoholism among minorities in regions.

				Prevalence		
Author or unit	**Minority**	**Year**	**Sample size**	**No. cases**	**Rate per 1,000**	**Male/ female**
Lu Qiuyan et al.	Dai	1985	739	26	35.00	26/0
Wan Wenpeng et al.	Bai	1986	370	11	30.00	10/1
Heilongjiang mental hospital	E Lun Chun	1986	1,137	49	43.09	46/3
Sun Mao Sui et al.	He Zhe	1986	638	8	12.54	8/0
Li Tie et al.	Li	1984	662	2	3.02	2/0
He Mutao et al.	Qiang	1984	2,852	14	4.91	12/2
Xiang Mengze	Li Su	1980–83	3,223	1	0.13	1/0
Zhu Hanfu	Korean	1989	44,920		79.61	
Li Qianshi	Korean	1989			68.75	

Source: Shen Yucun, 1987; Li Donggen, 1992.

The highest prevalence rates were found in the Korean E Lun Chun, Dai, Bai, and He Zhe people; the figures were some 3–7 times higher than the highest prevalence rate for the Han. All of the cases had a drinking history of more than 10 years. The age groups with the highest prevalence were the 40–44 year, 50–54 year, and 60 year and over groups. Male prevalence rates were far higher than the rates for females.

In 1986, Li Donggen investigated 1,431 Korean people over 15 years of age, using the Diagnostic and Statistical Manual, third edition (DSM-III) criteria, and found that their lifetime prevalence of alcoholism was 10.7 percent. This figure was very close to those of both the United States (11.5–15.7 percent) and the Republic of Korea (17.67 percent), particularly among men. Li Donggen found that the rate of aldehyde dehydrogenase (ALDH) deficiency (the author did not mention the ALDH-2 subtype) among the Korean minority was 24.8 percent, which is much lower than that of the Han ethnic group (44.0 percent). This suggests that the Korean ethnic group has a higher tolerance to alcohol than the Han (Li Donggen, 1992).

Fang Yiru and colleagues investigated three groups of Han males who were either alcohol-dependent, social drinkers, or nondrinkers. He did so by applying the flushing response test, a drinking behavior questionnaire, and an ethanol patch test. The results showed: (1) the positive rate of flushing response was 21.4 percent for the alcohol dependence group, 62.5 percent for social drinkers, and 69.6 percent for nondrinkers; (2) the positive rates of 30 percent and 70 percent from the ethanol patch test for the alcohol dependence group were 4.8 percent and 11.9 percent, for social drinkers 4.2 percent and 12.5 percent, nondrinkers 34.9 percent and 39.1 percent, respectively. The differences in the positive rates among the three groups were highly significant, suggesting there is a high correlation between an individual's sensitivity to alcohol and the development of alcohol dependence (Fang Yiru et al., 1994; Pan Zhixing et al., 1993).

ALCOHOL-RELATED HEALTH PROBLEMS

Along with the increase of alcohol production and consumption, alcohol-related health problems have also drawn attention. However, research work is just beginning and relevant information is limited.

General Psychiatric Morbidity Surveys

The number of people with alcohol dependence being sent to mental hospital outpatient wards and hospitals for treatment is increasing. A report from Yan Bian (Ji Lin Province, northeast China), a region where the Korean minority is prevalent, indicated that patients with alcoholism accounted for 0–4 percent of total admissions during the period 1964–1979 (mean admissions three cases per year). Subsequently, the number increased significantly to between 30 and 88 cases per year, over 90 percent of whom are of Korean ethnic origin and who constitute between 8 and 23.46 percent of total admissions.

Similar trends are found in other parts of China. For example, a psychiatric hospital affiliated with Hunan Medical University (in South China, where the majority are Han people) admitted an average of only 0.8 patients with alcoholism a year, from 1958 to 1976. Since 1980, however, the number of such patients admitted has increased to an average of 5 cases a year (Shen Yucun, 1987).

The results mentioned above suggest that admission rates for patients with alcohol disorders has increased over time for both Han and minority groups. This may be one of the most striking indications of growing alcohol-related problems in China.

Cognitive Impairment and Cerebrovascular Diseases

Pan Zhixing and colleagues conducted a comparative study of 33 patients with alcoholism and 33 normal subjects by using the Wechsler Adult Intelligence Scale–Revised by China (WAIS–RC) and the Chinese-developed Clinical Memory Rating Scale. The results show that cognition and memory function in patients with alcoholism are significantly ($P < 0.01$) lower than in the control groups (Pan Zhixing et al., 1993).

Some data show that drinking can be a risk factor for apoplexy. A study in Dushan county, Guizhou Province, with a population of 20,000, using cluster samples and house-to-house surveys, indicated that morbidity and mortality from apoplexy increased with years. Second, people who drank over 100 ml of spirits (45–55 percent alcohol) on a daily basis, and who have been drinking for more than 10 years, have a lifetime morbidity of 4.4–5.7 percent, 10–15 times higher than a control group who never consumed alcohol (Chang Zhi et al., 1994).

It is estimated that in China 9,830 people died from alcohol dependence in 1986, 10 times more than 1976. Another paper reported that in the nation as a whole, 570,000 people died from cardiovascular disease caused by excessive drinking in 1987 (Jiang Zuoning, 1995).

Cirrhosis and Cancer of the Liver

Alcohol can harm the liver and induce alcoholic cirrhosis. It is reported that alcoholic cirrhosis accounts for 80–90 percent of liver cirrhosis cases in Western countries. The prevalence of alcoholic cirrhosis is much lower in China, with an average of 7.6 percent of liver cirrhosis cases (Zhou Shisi, 1984). Viral hepatitis endemic in China is the most common cause of liver cirrhosis.

An article on the Zang (Tibetan) ethnic minority reported 41 pathologically confirmed cases of various types of cirrhosis in a hospital in Lhasa, the capital city of Tibet, in 1987; 25 (60.98 percent) of the patients were identified as alcoholic cirrhosis, of whom 20 cases were male and 5 were female. More than half (13) of the 25 patients were peasants or herdsmen. All the patients with liver cirrhosis had a long history of drinking (10–45 years, with a mean 23.5 years) large quantities of highland barley wine amounting to about 2.5–7.5 kg a day, or a mean of 4.2 kg. Thus, these patients ingested about 180–550 g of pure alcohol per day, since highland barley wine fermented from highland barley is a low-strength drink which contains about 7.4 percent alcohol. Tibetans are very fond of highland barley wine, which may be a key reason why cirrhosis among Tibetans is predominantly caused by alcohol, and why the prevalence of cirrhosis in Tibet is 7.6 percent higher than in China as a whole (Zhao Guangbin & Li Lin, 1989).

A further investigation was conducted in an area with a low hepatitis and high liver cancer rate among 202 primary liver cancer cases admitted to the Institute of Prevention and Treatment of Liver Cancer in Qidong County (Jiangsu Province). All patients were male, aged 19 to 76 years, and met the diagnostic criteria developed by a national liver cancer collaborative group; 173 of the cases (85.6 percent) were histologically confirmed. Patients were divided into two groups: an alcohol user group, who had consumed 60 g of spirits per day for more than a year, and a nonalcohol user group. The mean age of onset of illness for the alcohol users was statistically lower than for those who did not drink, suggesting that alcohol use is not a negligible risk factor for liver cancer (Ni Zhiquan et al., 1989).

Cancer of Upper Gastrointestinal Tract

Among Xian inhabitants (northwest China), a case-control study of 138 cases pathologically confirmed as having esophageal cancer (EC), 138 noncancer matched controls, and 5,607 (male 3,739, female 1,868) normal controls was conducted. It was found that smoking was a risk factor for EC. The odds ratio for smokers was found to be 4.12 (95 percent confidence interval 1.57–6.54)—a significant dose-response relationship between the odds ratio and both the level of cigarette use and the duration of smoking. There was no significant association between drinking and EC ($P > 0.05$). This result is quite similar to those of many studies from China. It was assumed that the lower consumption of alcohol in Xian (below 50 g alcohol a week) might be responsible for the absence of drinking as a significant risk factor for EC (Han Chenglong et al., 1988).

A case-control study of 241 persons with stomach cancer in an area with high morbidity and mortality in Hei Long Jiang Province found that the volume consumed and drinking patterns could be important risk factors for stomach cancer. When alcohol consumption was over 5 kg a year and food was not taken while drinking, the risk of stomach cancer was found to increase (relative risks being 1.72 and 1.61, respectively). Drinking alcohol (relative risk = 3.66) increased the risk of stomach cancer more than smoking did (relative risk = 1.82). When both factors (drinking and smoking) were present together, the relative risk was even higher (5.47) (Hu Jinfu et al., 1988).

ALCOHOL-RELATED SOCIAL PROBLEMS

With the development of modern transportation, road traffic accidents have had a negative impact on people's health and public health in general. Mortality figures compiled in 29 provinces across China from 1973 to 1975 showed that death from transportation accidents was the fourth largest cause of death.

Figures from an epidemiological survey on road traffic accidents in Hefei city, Anhui Province, from 1989 to 1991 showed that the accident rate was 324.5 to 218.3/10,000 vehicles, while the fatality rate was 38.8/10,000 vehicles (Wang Yong Zheng et al., 1993). Alcohol-related road traffic accidents and their consequences have not been systematically researched in China.

An article based on data for the whole of China reported that in 1986 there were 26,700 traffic accidents, in which more than 30,000 people were injured or died, due to drivers who were under the influence of alcohol. This was despite the existence of strict laws stating that "driving after drinking is not allowed." It was also reported that in 1995 over one-half the road traffic accidents across the country were associated with drivers under the influence of alcohol (*China Daily*, 1996).

Because beverage alcohol is legal, alcohol's danger and possible harmfulness are not yet fully recognized by either officials or the common people. Information on alcohol-related crime and violence is not readily available in China. It was estimated in 1996 that over 38 percent of mild and serious crimes committed by adolescents were carried out under the influence of alcohol (*Chinese Broadcasting Weekly*, 1996).

An informal survey showed that the incidence of impairment of families and social function was 30.8 percent among a group with alcoholism. An epidemiological study was conducted on alcohol-related social problems among people suffering from alcohol dependence in Yanji city, where the majority of people are Korean and the alcohol dependence rate is the highest in China. It indicated that alcohol dependence in this group had many negative effects: family disruption, 75.7 percent of cases; tense relations with people, 56.4 percent; absence from work, 51.4 percent; irresponsibility in their family role, 50.0 percent; violent behavior, 37.6 percent; traffic accidents, 26.7 percent; being arrested, 9.9 percent; loss of ability to work, 3.9 percent (Li Donggen, 1992).

Another epidemiological study of alcohol dependence among minorities was conducted in the Shimao and Xishuang Banna districts, Yunnan Province, in which 739 people over 14 years of age (males 466, females 273) were investigated. In this group, 26 subjects (all male) were diagnosed with alcohol dependence. Half of those with alcohol dependence had some kind of social problem:

family disruption (36.7 percent of subjects), neglecting their duties (26.79 percent), and fighting and disturbing public order (20 percent) (Lu Qiuyun et al., 1987).

FACILITIES FOR TREATMENT AND PREVENTION OF ALCOHOL DEPENDENCE

Owing to the recent significant increase in the number of people with drug abuse problems in China, many prevention and treatment facilities or centers for substance abuse (primarily heroin) have been set up by the sectors responsible for health and public safety. Some of these centers are attached to mental hospitals. However, there are no specialized institutions for alcohol dependence. People who suffer from alcohol dependence are treated mainly by psychiatrists, since the recognition and knowledge of alcohol-related problems in general hospitals is low. Alcohol abusers use the same public health services as those with other clinical diseases.

According to a report in *Health News*, which is published by the Chinese Ministry of Health, the first Chinese alcoholism club was set up in July 1993 in a municipal psychiatric hospital in Harbin, Heilongjiang Province, northeast China. The club is similar to Alcoholics Anonymous. Activities are held every two weeks. The main therapeutic approaches include individual and group psychotherapy, recreational therapy, the exchange of experiences about how people stopped drinking, and so on. More than 300 members have enrolled, with successful results (Ministry of Health, 1996).

SAVE GRAIN: CURB INTAKE OF SPIRITS

In January 1996, the *Guangming Daily* published a series of reports on "Save grain, curb intake of spirits," thereby launching a publicity drive against drinking spirits and calling on people to lead thrifty lives.

Apart from the fact that drinking alcohol to excess harms health, the use of large quantities of grain for spirits production creates another problem, thus prompting the campaign against spirits. The startling fact that has long been ignored by most Chinese is that every kilogram of spirit on average consumes 2.2 kilograms of grain. In 1994, Chinese distilleries produced 6.51 million tons of spirits. In other words, within one year the Chinese had "drunk down" 14.32 million tons of grain. The problem has become frightening, particularly in China, a developing country that has to feed over 1.2 billion mouths.

Thirty-one government departments and provinces in China have echoed this appeal. To promote the growth of clean and thrifty governance, government officials are determined to wean themselves from drinking spirits during business dinners.

Experts are thus suggesting that people change their drinking habits by filling their cups with red drinks instead of grain spirits. Beers, spirits made from apple and grape, and other fruit drinks will become increasingly popular in China. Undoubtedly, this is a good beginning towards controlling the drinking of spirits, both changing traditional drinking behavior and reducing alcohol-related problems.

ACHIEVEMENTS AND REMAINING NEEDS

Achievements So Far

• During the last two decades, the food hygiene law, which provides both a technical indicator of food hygiene quality and a control system for food hygiene (including beverage alcohol), has been developed and implemented.

• A nationwide campaign against illicit alcohol, which never has a brand, name of producer, or date of production, has been started recently. The number of people dying from alcohol poisoning is reported to have decreased from two or three years ago.

• It is reported that the beverage alcohol consumed last year by inhabitants of urban and rural areas in China required 14,320,000 tons of grain for their production. Thus, the development of low-strength drinks and grape wine became necessary. Some new products have now been developed with a similar color, fragrance, and taste to those of spirits but with a lower alcohol content.

• Efforts are being made to disseminate information and educate the public on the dangers of alcohol and the harm it can cause, focusing especially on high-strength drinks and high-risk population groups.

Remaining Needs

• Training is needed so that community doctors and physicians in general hospitals can learn how to prevent alcohol-related problems or to recognize and manage them at an early stage.

• Further epidemiological investigations on various alcohol-related problems are needed.

CONCLUSIONS

As a developing country, China has experienced tremendous social and economic change from the 1980s onward. During the period up to 1996 the GDP increased by 9.7 percent. Alcohol production and consumption increased simultaneously with the GDP. Meanwhile, as discussed above, the prevalence of alcohol-related problems has increased significantly, especially in areas inhabited by ethnic minorities. Thus, a danger to China from alcohol exists, and has been drawing the attention of medical workers, particularly in the mental health field. Much work has been done recently to reduce alcohol's harmfulness. Generally, however, the recognition that alcohol can harm people as well as society as a whole is still very low.

REFERENCES

BBC Monitoring Service. (1996, February 12).

Beijing Review. (1995). Events/trends: 1994 economy vigorous despite inflation. *38*(3), 5–6.

Beijing Review. (1996a). 1995 sample population survey. *39*(2), 21.

Beijing Review. (1996b). *39*(16), 17.

Beijing Review. (1996c). Statistical communique of the State Statistical Bureau of the PRC on 1995. *39*(14), 22–29.

Chang Zhi, et al. (1994). Alcoholic culture and apoplexy (in Chinese). *Acta Chinese Medicine and Pharmacology, 1*, 2–4.

China Daily. (1996, February 14).

China Today. (1996). *45*, 51.

Chinese Broadcasting Weekly. (1996, June 17).

Collaborative Group. (1986). Collaborative Group of Epidemiological Study on Mental Disorders in 12 Regions. *Chinese Journal of Neurology and Psychiatry, 19*, 70–72.

Collaborative Group. (1993). Collaborative Group Investigation on Alcohol Dependence and Related Problems: Multiple variable analysis on related factors of alcohol dependence. *Chinese Journal of Neurology and Psychiatry, 26*, 3–5.

Du Jinghua. (1992). *Chinese Alcohol Culture*. Beijing: Xin Hua Publishing House.

Fang Yiru, et al. (1994). Investigation on drinking associated problems in different populations in Shanghai (in Chinese). *Chinese Bulletin of Drug Dependence, 3*, 88–92.

Han Chenglong, Li Liangshou, & Fang Zhiheng. (1988). An etiologic research on esophageal cancer of urban inhabitants in Xian city (in Chinese). *Chinese Journal of Epidemiology, 9*, 1216.

Hu Jinfu, Wang Guoqing, & Zhang Shufen. (1988). Alcohol and tobacco: Risk factor for stomach cancer (in Chinese). *Journal of Tumor, 8*, 200–201.

Jiang Zuoning. (1995). Prevention and case of substance abuse in China and its advances in research. In Cheng Xueshi & Cheng Xiuhua (Eds.), *A general situation of Chinese modern neurology and psychiatry development* (in Chinese) (301–311). Beijing: Chinese Science and Technology Publishing House.

Ministry of Health. (1996, April 24). *Health News*.

Li Donggen. (1992). An investigation on alcoholism among Chinese-Korean nationality (in Chinese). *Chinese Journal of Nervous and Mental Disease, 1*, 40–42.

Liu Jiuyin. (1995). *The Science of Drinking* (in Chinese). Shanghai: Shanghai Science and Technology Publishing House.

Liu Jun. (1995). *Chinese Ancient Wine and Drinking* (in Chinese). Beijing: Commercial Publishing House.

Lu Qiuyun, Wang Yufeng, & Shen Yucun. (1987). Epidemiological investigation of alcoholism in the minority areas of Yunnan province (in Chinese). *Chinese Mental Health Journal, 1*, 253–256.

Ni Zhiquan, Zhu Shixiao, & Yuan Aijun. (1989). Analysis of 202 primary liver cancer cases with drinking (in Chinese). *Practical Tumor Journal, 4*, 155–156.

Pan Zhixing, et al. (1993). Intelligence and memory among patients with alcoholism (in Chinese). *Bethune Medical University Acta, 2*, 168.

Shen Yucun. (1987). Epidemiological study on alcohol dependence and alcoholism (in Chinese). *Chinese Mental Health Journal, 1*, 251–256.

State Statistical Bureau. (1997). Macro-regulation with significant achievement. *Xin Hua Agency Digest*, March, 44.

State Statistical Bureau, PRC. (1992). *Statistical Yearbook of China*. Hong Kong: Economic Information Agency.

Wan Guoguang. (1986). *Chinese Alcohol* (in Chinese). Beijing: People's Publishing House.

Wang Anhui. (1994). *China Substance Dependence Bulletin* (in Chinese), *3*, 22.

Wang Jing. (1995, September 13). The road to dynasty. *People's Daily*.

Wang Yong Zheng, Wang Jiyoui, & Xu Rongnan. (1993). An epidemiological survey on road traffic accidents in Hefei during 1989–1990 (in Chinese). *Chinese Journal of Traumatology, 9*(2), 89–90.

World Drink Trends. (1996). *International Beverage Alcohol Consumption and Production Trends*. Henley-on-Thames: NTC Publications.

Xiao Jiacbeng. (1995). China. In D. B Heath (Ed.), *International Handbook on Alcohol and Culture* (42–50). Westport, CT: Greenwood.

Xu Penghang. (1995). Crack down on forged products is not easy and still has a long way to go (in Chinese). *People's Daily*. 13 September.

Zhao Guangbin & Li Lin. (1989). Etiologic and clinical characteristics analysis of liver cirrhosis patients of Zang nationality in Tibetan region (in Chinese). *Chinese Journal of Internal Medicine, 28*, 529–531.

Zhou Shisi. (1984). Clinical analysis of 278 liver cirrhosis cases (in Chinese). *Guangdong Medicine, 5*, 21.

Zhou Xuanyun & He Guanghua. (1995). Brewing industry in China (in Chinese). *People's Daily*. 22 November.

Zhu Hua, Li Jianghua, & Wan Wenpeng. (1990). Trends of alcohol drinking in China, from alcohol consumption point of view in Kunming city (in Chinese). *Yunnan Medicine and Pharmacy of Yunnan, 11*, 217–218.

Chapter 6

India

Mohan Isaac

Alcohol use and the problems associated with it are on the increase in India. Although India is known to be a "dry" culture, alcohol use in some form has always existed in the country. But during the past two to three decades the pattern of alcohol use has been changing. Unlike in Western industrialized countries, reliable data on alcohol production, marketing, and various alcohol-related problems are not readily available in India. There is no systematic recording of most of the necessary information. Research on various aspects of alcoholism, particularly with a public health perspective, has been minimal. However, a variety of indicators point to the changing scenario of alcohol use in the country. The quality of the statistics and research data which exist now is uneven, and it is difficult to make generalizations for the whole country. However, they remain the best sources for the time being and do convey various trends and patterns as well as indicate the current magnitude of the problem. This chapter reviews a variety of sources of information and describes the patterns and problems of alcohol use in India. The materials reviewed include scientific papers published in international and national journals, relevant unpublished reports and dissertations, reports from nonacademic lay literature, and news media.

SOCIOCULTURAL AND DEMOGRAPHIC PROFILE

India is an ethnically diverse country with a population of 896 million (1993), which constitutes about one-sixth of the world's total population (India is the second most populous country in the world after China). About 75 percent of the population lives in rural areas, spread over some 550,000 villages. Thirty-six percent of the population is below the age of 15 years, and 7 percent over the age of 60 years. The life expectancy at birth is 60 years. The adult illiteracy rate is 52 percent in males and is 66 percent in females.

Religion and caste form an important aspect of identity for most Indians. More than 80 percent of India's population is composed of Hindus. The nearly 12 percent of the population of India that is Muslim is outnumbered only by the Muslims in Indonesia and slightly by those in Pakistan and Bangladesh. Christians, Sikhs, Buddhists, and Jains make up about 5.6 percent of the total population. The Hindus follow a hierarchical caste system, which is thousands of years old and consists of hundreds of castes and subcastes. The four large caste clusters called "varnas" (*Varna* is Sanskrit for color), each of which has a traditional social function, are (in order of descending hierarchy based on "purity" and prestige) as follows:

1 Brahmins—priests
2 Kshatriyas—warriors
3 Vaishyas—peasants and traders
4 Shudras—servants.

Outside this caste system is a fifth group formerly referred to as the "untouchables" and now known as "Harijans"; they belong to what are officially designated by the government as "scheduled castes." The scheduled castes account for nearly one-sixth of India's total population. In addition, there are numerous tribal peoples, especially in the northeastern parts of the country.

The people of India have 18 major languages that are officially recognized and hundreds of dialects, which indicate the country's enormous cultural diversity. These languages belong to the Indo-European, Dravidian, and Sino-Tibetan groups. Most Indian languages are derived from Sanskrit, the language of ancient India.

India is a multiparty, federal, secular, democratic republic and has 25 states. State governments have the sole power to legislate in a variety of domains, which include beverage alcohol taxation. Each state is organized into a number of large administrative units called districts.

The country's monetary unit is the Indian rupee. The current (February 1998) exchange rate is around 1 United States dollar = 39 Indian rupees. The gross national product (GNP) per capita was US $340 in 1995. Although India now has the twelfth largest gross domestic product in the world, it is still among the poorest countries and a large fraction of its population continues to live below the poverty line. Until a few years ago, the government promoted a highly regulated economic system in pursuance of its socialist goals and economic policy, popularly referred to as a "mixed economy" policy, but during the past few years a process of liberalization of the economy (involving removal of bureaucratic checks, controls, and industrial licensing procedures) has been initiated, resulting in a faster pace of overall growth and a growing middle class. The enormous socioeconomic and cultural variations that exist in the population make generalization of observations and experiences from one part of the country to another difficult.

HISTORICAL ASPECTS OF ALCOHOL USE

India has traditionally been considered a "dry" or "abstinent" culture. It is important to examine the religious and cultural traditions and drinking practices in Indian society over the years in order to understand its current drinking patterns. Singh and Lal (1979), who reviewed a variety of sources including religious texts, historical accounts, and other manuscripts, describe the attitudes and behavior related to drinking over the centuries in India. They note that there is "no cultural tradition in India which could be described as being clearly and unequivocally against the use of alcohol in any form and under all circumstances." There is evidence to suggest that the Dravidians who lived in South India were familiar with tapping the palm tree and consumed toddy as a beverage. The Vedas (Rig-veda) mention the use of intoxicating beverages such as *soma* and *sura*, indicating that the Aryans who lived in northwest India during the Vedic period (2000–800 B.C.) knew and used fermentation and distillation to make their drinks. Even the great Indian epics of the Ramayana and Mahabharatha make numerous references to drinking. The other castes of Kshatriyas and Vaisyas were permitted to take intoxicating drinks on special occasions. Apparently, drinking was socially accepted among the ruling classes. The ancient Indian medical treatises by great physicians such as Charak and Susruta (dating from around 300 A.D.) make distinctions between normal drinking and excessive drinking. They even mention the good effects of moderate drinking (Hunt, 1987).

The harmful effects of beverage alcohol were also well known from the Vedic period onwards. The Rig-veda includes drinking as one of the seven forbidden sins. Other Indian religions—Buddhism and Jainism—do not allow their followers to drink. During the Muslim rule of major parts of India after 1200 A.D., although drinking was forbidden by the Koran, alcohol was widely consumed. Later, during the eighteenth and nineteenth centuries, after the British and other European colonial powers came to India, alcohol became associated with the "Western way of life" (Wig, 1994). It is likely that social controls and religious teachings contributed to the restricted use of alcohol at different periods in time. Ranganathan (1994a) notes that the Hindu scriptures' reference to drinking as a heinous crime and sin has contributed to "abstinence from alcohol" taking deep roots as a value in Indian culture. Singh and Lal (1979) point out that through various historical periods "although alcohol was frequently referred to as an evil, it was at the same time accepted and glamorized by its use among ruling classes." They note that the Indian culture is an ambivalent one in which "sternly negative and prohibitive attitudes coexist with attitudes actually idealizing intoxication" and, as a result, the consumption of alcohol has never become integrated into normal everyday life.

A recently concluded nine-country survey jointly carried out by the World Health Organization (WHO), the U.S. National Institute on Alcohol Abuse and Alcoholism (NIAAA), and the U.S. National Institute on Drug Abuse (NIDA), which investigated how people from different cultures differentiate between normal and pathological drinking, found that respondents at the Indian participating center in Bangalore had trouble conceptualizing normal drinking. Various indicators for normal drinking stipulated by respondents in Bangalore included "drinking in small quantities," "once or twice a week," on "special occasions," and "not interfering with one's responsibilities, especially with respect to family" (Bennett et al., 1993).

During this century, Mahatma Gandhi, the leader of India's freedom struggle and father of the nation, campaigned against liquor production and sales. The Indian National Congress Party recognized prohibition as one of the main tasks before the country. So, after the country attained independence in 1947, the Indian Constitution incorporated prohibition among the "directive principles of State policy." Article 47 of the Constitution of India states that "the State shall endeavor to bring about prohibition of the use except for medicinal purposes of intoxicating drinks and of drugs which are injurious to health." However, during the five decades since independence, the political commitment to implement prohibition either partially or fully has fluctuated widely in different states, and today it is almost nonexistent anywhere in the country.

POLICY DEVELOPMENTS RELATED TO ALCOHOL USE

As mentioned above, the Constitution of India incorporates prohibition among the directive principles of state policy. Article 47 of the Constitution reads as follows: "The state shall regard the raising of the level of nutrition and the standard of living of its people as among its primary duties and, in particular, the state shall endeavor to bring about prohibition of the use except for medicinal purposes of intoxicating drinks and of drugs which are injurious to health." Production, distribution, and charging of excise duty or tax on alcohol as well as implementation of various measures to reduce or ban the availability of beverage alcohol are amongst the responsibilities of the state governments.

From the early days after independence in 1947, the government of India sought to persuade the state governments to adopt a uniform prohibition policy. Many states, including Madras and Bombay (the present states of Tamil Nadu, Maharashtra, and Gujarat), introduced prohibition during the period 1948 to 1950. The Planning Commission of the government of India set up a Prohibition Enquiry Committee in 1954 to prepare a program on prohibition on a national basis. This committee made several recommendations to implement nationwide prohibition during India's second five-year plan and set April 1958 as the target date for achieving this goal. However, only a few states adopted prohibition either completely or partially. In many states, loss of revenue and the extra cost of prohibition enforcement were major reasons for nonimplementation of prohibition. During the following years, the prohibition policy of the government of India suffered a number of setbacks. In order to promote prohibition, the national government offered to compensate the state governments to the tune of 50 percent of their loss in excise revenue resulting from the introduction of prohibition. However, there were no takers for this offer. A number of states that had introduced prohibition, either partially or completely, again became wet as they could not tolerate the loss of revenue. A comprehensive and critical review of policy and programs related to alcohol use and abuse in India carried out by the Addiction Research Centre in Madras (T. T. Ranganathan Clinical Research Foundation, 1991c) notes that the government's policy of prohibition had failed as early as the 1960s.

The government of India did not give up its efforts to implement prohibition all over the country. It appointed another committee, popularly referred to as the Tekchand Committee (named after its chairman), in 1964 to submit fresh proposals for prohibition. Although the committee prepared a comprehensive report and made excellent recommendations, most of the states did not follow them up. During the 1970s, Tamil Nadu and Gujarat were the only states in the country that continued with prohibition. In 1977, when there was a change of political party at the head of the central government, with a new pro-prohibition prime minister, Morarji Desai, there were again talks of nationwide total prohibition (Sethi, 1978), but this effect too fizzled out soon after.

During the past few years, the liquor policy of the governments of various states has been one of the most controversial issues in the country. Revenue from sale of beverage alcohol now contributes substantially to the state exchequers. The alcohol industry contributes 170 billion (17,000 crore) rupees to different states in the form of various taxes and levies. It was estimated in 1994 that alcohol consumption in the country was growing at a steady 15 percent a year (Chakravarti and Rathanami, 1995). The advent of delicensing and economic liberalization has brought several multinational liquor giants into India and introduced a competitive atmosphere in the liquor trade (Ahluwalia, 1996). There is growing concern in various quarters at the increase in alcohol consumption and the consequent alcohol-related problems in different parts of the country. Now, more than ever before, there is a need for a comprehensive national alcohol policy, which will not only be sensitive to the sociocultural realities and history of drinking practices in the country, but will also take into account various legitimate interests. Such a policy will have to be painstakingly developed and promoted. But there are also major difficulties in the formulation of a comprehensive alcohol policy in a country such as India with its enormous size and diversity. India has an unequal society and the already wide gap between the rich and the poor is growing steadily. Like most other developing countries, India has a large proportion of less well-informed people with little influence on policymakers and little power over what happens to them (Samarasinghe,

1994). In recent years, many alcohol-related policies have been adopted by governments without any public debate or adequate consultation with concerned professionals and behavioral scientists (Janakiramaiah, 1995).

Mass movements have also contributed to policy developments related to alcohol in some of the states in the country. In Andhra Pradesh, what sprang up as a spontaneous agitation by poor rural neo-literate women against the sale of arrack in their village, Dobagunta (Nellore district), spread to the whole state as a mass antiarrack movement spearheaded by rural women. Realizing the appeal of a slogan such as prohibition to the electorate and its vote-catching potential, many political parties and political leaders supported the antiarrack movement. They promised that total prohibition would be introduced in the state if they were voted to power and the winning party did exactly that after gaining a landslide electoral victory. However, total prohibition had to be diluted less than two and half years after its introduction for a variety of reasons, which included loss of revenue, the cost of policing, corruption in the enforcement machinery, illicit distilling, and hooch-related deaths (Ghose, 1996).

The northern Indian state of Haryana is the only state in the country where state prohibition is currently strictly enforced. Total prohibition was introduced in Haryana on July 1, 1996 as the fulfillment of a poll promise by the state's present chief minister, but within months after the introduction it was realized that enforcing the liquor ban was easier said than done (Parihar, 1996). In many places in the state, liquor is freely available but at more than three times the preprohibition price. There is large-scale smuggling of liquor across the borders into the state from the surrounding five states, which are wet. Many illicit distilleries too have appeared in the state. Although prohibition is proving to be a mixed blessing, there is already a growing demand for the prohibition policy to be rethought. Unlike in Andhra Pradesh and Haryana, the arrack ban prior to the general elections imposed by the ruling party in Kerala did not result in victory.

The past few years have witnessed wide fluctuations in the alcohol-related policies of several state governments. Dry laws have been liberalized wherever they existed in the country, thus shifting the focus of policy from prohibition and total abstinence to promotion of temperance (*Times of India*, 1993). Most governments are ambivalent about prohibition. The title of a recent article in a popular news magazine, "To bottle up, or to uncork," exemplifies the dilemma of many governments (Ghose, 1996). A well-known Indian sociologist, M. N. Srinivas, says: "Prohibition means the poor will use illicit liquor, there will be frequent deaths, there will be a rise in lawlessness and organized crime. I believe in a strong temperance movement by the people, not the imposition of prohibition." But Madhu Dandavate, a leading social activist and the chairman of India's Planning Commission, argues that "The issue of prohibition should not be considered in the context of revenue loss alone. The law is unpopular because there are so many proliquor lobbies. The administrative machinery must ensure that the long-term benefits of prohibition are achieved" (quoted by Ghose, 1996).

Many states have set up "temperance boards" to educate people about harmful effects of alcohol, but Chengappa (1986) points out that "most of these boards do little more than release advertisements in newspapers showing a bottle marked with the familiar skull and crossbones."

Alcohol policies in the country have swung from total prohibition to unrestricted sale with no controls. Various restrictive methods whose usefulness has been established elsewhere in the world, such as licensing of places for sale, restricting the consumption of alcohol to a limited number of hours each day, monitoring of advertisements, and differential taxation strategies weighted against spirits, have not been adequately and appropriately implemented in the country. No meaningful and effective health education strategies have been launched. Janakiramaiah (1995, p. 1) notes that "a state policy of restrictions in the context of a concerted middle path strategy involving popular support and professional cooperation is preferable over prohibition and policing."

TYPES OF BEVERAGE ALCOHOL

There are three main types of beverage alcohol available in the country:

- Country liquor
- Indian-made foreign liquor
- Illicitly distilled liquor.

More than 200 varieties of country liquors, which are mostly distilled spirits, are available under different vernacular names in different parts of the country. In English, country liquors are referred to as "arrack." These are distilled from different grains, rice, and sugar cane. Toddy, which is used as a drink in many parts of the country, is produced by fermenting the sap obtained from the incised spathes of various species of palm, especially the palmyra and coconut. Beer and distilled spirits such as whisky, brandy, rum, and gin (brought to India by the European colonialists) produced within the country are referred to as "Indian-made foreign liquor" (IMFL). In 1992 there were more than 200 brands of whisky, 50 of rum, 30 of brandy, 10 of gin, and 50 of beer marketed in the country (Kumar and Dubey, 1992). Until quite recently, wine was not produced in India, but now small amounts are made.

Singh (1978) reported that in Punjab, which is among the states with the highest alcohol consumption, country liquor accounted for 86.5 percent of alcohol sales. Country liquor is significantly cheaper than IMFL and is widely available all over the country, including rural areas. About 15 percent of alcohol consumers surveyed in Punjab admitted purchase of illicit liquor from bootleggers and 45 percent admitted preparing liquor at home for personal consumption. The illicit liquor available in Punjab falls into three categories:

- Homemade for personal consumption
- Homemade for sale in the same rural locality
- Liquor made by professionals for sale in cities and other towns through liquor shops or bars.

TRENDS IN ALCOHOL PRODUCTION AND SALES

Evidence that trends in alcohol-related problems in any country are related to trends in alcohol consumption has been summarized by Edwards et al. (1994). Trends in alcohol production and sales are closely linked to alcohol use (WHO, 1980; Walsh & Grant, 1985). But accurate and reliable data on alcohol production and marketing are often not available, particularly from developing countries. Even when some figures are available, they relate only to the known legal production and sale of alcohol. Information on illegal production (both domestic and commercial) and sale in the black market sector is not available. Such illegal production is known to occur quite extensively in many developing countries, including India. Smart (1991) reported that since the early 1970s many developing countries have shown a large increase in alcohol consumption. Because of the lack of availability of any data, the earliest compilations and comparisons of alcohol use and production in countries across the world have excluded India (Edwards et al., 1994).

A variety of sources, including unpublished reports and reports in nonacademic literature during the past few years, indicate that alcohol production and sale in India have been markedly increasing. These reports refer to various indicators such as government revenue receipts from excise duties or tax on alcohol, an increase in the number of sale points and availability of alcohol, the consequences of illicit alcohol sales, and advertisements for beverage alcohol, as well as actual production figures. Chengappa, a well-known writer and journalist on health-related issues in India, says that "liquor is as easily available as tea leaves in most parts of the country" (Chengappa, 1986). Many news magazines widely respected for their objectivity and accuracy have published extensive cover stories on the "growing malaise" of "alcoholism on the rise" (Kumar & Dubey, 1992; *India Today*, 1986).

Production and Sales

In 1976, liquor manufacturers in India utilized 169.4 million liters of absolute alcohol, enough to manufacture 350 million bottles of rum. The absolute alcohol used by manufacturers rose to 207.9 million liters in 1981, 331 million liters in 1985, and 459 million liters in 1991 (Kumar & Dubey, 1992). The annual per capita consumption in 1991 was estimated at 1.25 liters of absolute alcohol. But that figure also covered women, most of whom in India do not drink. Taking only the men, the figure rises to over two liters of absolute alcohol. Unlike many Western developed countries, where alcohol consumption is socially accepted and integrated in normal daily life, the percentage of the male population who drink is estimated to be lower in India. Thus, if only the drinking male population is taken into account, the figure would be still higher. These figures do not include the millions of liters of illicit liquor produced and sold in most parts of the country. Many knowledgeable persons from the excise and police departments and manufacturers of licit alcohol estimate that the sales of illicit liquor is equal to or even exceed, the official sales of country liquor. The illicit consumption may be anywhere between 20 and 90 percent of the official sales, depending on the district and area of the country concerned. Singh (1978) estimated that if to the total official sales another 50 percent is added as the estimated illicit use, the mean annual per capita consumption in the state of Punjab would be over 10 liters of absolute alcohol.

Illicit Liquor

The most striking evidence of the large-scale production and sale of illicitly distilled liquor is the frequently reported mortality and morbidity, especially blindness, due to poisoning by various types of "hooch." Illicit liquor deaths are reported from almost every state in the country. Chengappa (1986) reported that on average more than 200 people are killed in the country every year from liquor poisoning. A large number of people who become dependent on alcohol shift to illicit liquor because it is cheaper than country liquor. The sociodemographic profile of people who have succumbed to liquor poisoning in different parts of the country indicates that most people who consume illicit liquor belong to the lower socioeconomic strata of society, live in urban slums or rural areas, and are laborers or daily wage earners, many in their twenties and thirties.

At the upper end of the social scale, there is a craze for whisky made abroad, particularly Scotch whisky. Scotch is considered by many to be much safer for the health than Indian whisky. A recent survey in some of the big cities of India estimated that the black market in counterfeit Scotch (Indian whisky in a Scotch bottle) is about 12 million bottles a year. At about 800 rupees a bottle, this amounts to a business of 9,600 million rupees conducted outside the official sales records and taxation system (Fernandez, 1993).

Alcohol Industry

The alcohol industry has been showing steady growth. Against 5 percent in the early 1980s, the annual growth rate of the industry was estimated to be 12 to 15 percent by the early 1990s. The consumption of Indian-made foreign liquor has also gone up considerably. In 1992, 480 million bottles of IFML (whisky, brandy, rum, and gin) were sold, of which 69 percent consisted of whisky (Fernandez, 1993). Beer is gaining widespread acceptance in many states and big cities of the country, resulting in a boom in beer sales. About 500 million bottles of beer are drunk annually. The current process of economic liberalization and relaxation of government regulations has attracted many international alcohol manufacturers to India, "not only to export whisky to India on much easier terms, but also produce their famous brands in India for local consumption" (Saxena, 1994).

Accessibility

Most state governments are liberal in issuing licenses to start distilleries and breweries as well as to open liquor shops. In 1993, the government of Andhra Pradesh granted licenses to open 24 private distilleries and breweries in the state (*Times of India*, 1993). Arrack shops and liquor shops have proliferated in many parts of the country. In Hyderabad, there were about 700 liquor shops, compared to about 1,000 "fair-price" shops, i.e., shops selling essential commodities, in 1992 (Prasad, 1992). For the upper and middle classes, bars and pubs have been emerging in many places. In Bangalore, more than 200 pubs have been opened during the past five years. More than 2,000 beer bars were started in Maharashtra over a period of five years. The regulations on the opening of bars have also been relaxed in other states such as Tamil Nadu (Shetty, 1993). Katiyar (1993) reports that estimates of the turnover of just 10 of Bombay's most popular pubs vary between 100 and 140 million rupees a year. A potential growth rate of 100 percent has been predicted for the city's pubs.

Excise on Liquor

In most states, excise duty on liquor contributes about 10–12 percent of the annual state revenue from all sources. For example, Andhra Pradesh's annual budget for 1991–1992 was 78,000 million rupees. Liquor revenue contributed more than 10 percent of this amount, or 8,400 million rupees. Of this, 6,400 million rupees came from arrack alone (Prasad, 1992). In Maharashtra, annual sales of liquor in its most backward district, Gadchiroli, amounted to 70 million rupees, which was equivalent to the government's support for the district's annual development plan (Bang & Bang, 1991). Many states have registered a considerable increase in revenue from excise on liquor. For example, in 1985 Karnataka state earned about 500 million rupees from excise on liquor. This amount rose to 3520 million in 1992–1993, 4060 million in 1993–1994, and 7134 million in 1994–1995. The increase registered in just one year was over 15 percent (Government of Karnataka, 1993; *The Hindu*, 1996).

Advertisements

Advertising of beverage alcohol is an important aspect of marketing (Walsh & Grant, 1985). In India advertisements of beverage alcohol are not permitted by the rules. However, Saxena (1994) notes that it is difficult to find a magazine without an advertisement for drinks, as the liquor companies in India have perfected "the fine art of bending the rules without breaking them." The brand name of the beverage is advertised using the proxy of soda, snacks, mineral water, or designer glasses, leaving no one in doubt as to what the advertisement actually conveys. Most companies spend huge amounts of money on these ads to boost sales of their brand of drink. Brands are also promoted by many companies by sponsoring major sporting and cultural events.

Liquor Lobby

In most states, arrack is marketed in polythene sachets of 50 ml, 90 ml, and 100 ml. The price of a 100 ml sachet of arrack ranges from 5 to 12 rupees, which compares with a bottle of a local brand (IMFL) of whisky costing 300 rupees. The manufacturing cost of one liter of arrack is about a rupee (Prasad, 1992). The huge profits obtainable from the country liquor trade and beverage alcohol industry make arrack contractors and sellers of other drinks very influential and politically powerful people (Saxena, 1994). In many places, they form cartels and syndicates to monopolize the trade in specific geographical areas. It is widely believed that liquor traders have close links with major political parties and that they are able to influence the liquor policies of the government.

PREVALENCE STUDIES OF ALCOHOL USE AND ABUSE

During the past two decades, several field surveys of general psychiatric morbidity and alcohol use have been carried out in different parts of the country. It is difficult to compare or generalize the results of many of these surveys, since they used varying definitions, criteria, data collection and assessment instruments, and methodologies. The samples studied in many surveys were small and not truly representative of the total population. However, these studies provide certain indications on trends in alcohol use in the community. They can be grouped into three categories:

1 Psychiatric morbidity surveys
2 Surveys of alcohol use in the general population
3 Surveys of alcohol use in specific populations.

Most of the general psychiatric morbidity surveys were carried out during the early 1970s, while the specific surveys of alcohol use and abuse were conducted during the late 1970s. Some surveys have also been completed during the past few years. None of the studies have used standardized interview instruments based on detailed operational criteria of contemporary diagnostic systems such as the Tenth Revision of the International Classification of Diseases (ICD-10)

(WHO, 1992, 1993a) or the revised third edition or fourth edition of the Diagnostic and Statistical Manual (DSM-IIIR or DSM-IV) of the American Psychiatric Association.

General Psychiatric Morbidity Surveys

In the earliest reported field survey of mental morbidity in India, Surya et al. (1964) surveyed a population of 2,731 from 510 households in Pondicherry in southern India and found a rate of 3.6 per thousand for alcoholism. Gopinath (1968) surveyed the total population of a village near Bangalore and found 2.36 per thousand of the population to be suffering from alcoholism. In another major epidemiological study of mental disorders supported by the Indian Council of Medical Research (ICMR), Verghese et al. (1973) surveyed a stratified random sample of 539 families with 2,904 persons in a semiurban area—Vellore town in Tamil Nadu state. All suspected cases were assessed by a psychiatrist and diagnosis was made as per the definitions in ICD-8 (1965). The prevalence of alcoholism in Vellore was 4.8 per thousand. Dube and Handa (1971), who surveyed a large population of around 29,000 in and around Agra in North India, reported that 1.38 percent of the population habitually abused alcohol. Elnager et al. (1971) reported a prevalence rate of 13 per thousand for alcohol addiction in a survey of a small rural community of 1,383 persons from 184 families in the state of West Bengal.

More recently, Premarajan et al. (1993) conducted a cross-sectional study of psychiatric morbidity in an urban area of Pondicherry in South India and found a prevalence of 34.1 per thousand for "alcohol dependence syndrome." When only adult males were considered, the prevalence rose to 66.2 per thousand; no case was identified among women. There were more cases among those who had no schooling, those occupied in unskilled jobs, and those who were married.

These were surveys which primarily focused on the prevalence of disorders such as psychosis, neurosis, mental retardation, and epilepsy in the community. Since most of them used a two-stage design involving an initial screening for probable cases using instruments designed primarily to pick up the disorders mentioned above, it is likely that many persons with alcoholism were not identified during the screening procedure.

Surveys of Alcohol Use in the General Population

Singh (1989), in a review of epidemiological studies of alcohol abuse in India, noted that in spite of the large number of studies, it was difficult to generalize at a national level because of various methodological problems. Different methods of data collection, definition of terms, and categorizations of alcohol consumers are employed by different studies. For example, while some studies categorized the population as "current users" (used alcohol in the past 12 months), "ever used" (used alcohol in the past, but not in the previous 12 months), and "never used" (never used alcohol) (Varma et al., 1980), others grouped the consumers as "normal drinkers" (Lal & Singh, 1978) or as daily users, weekly users, monthly users, yearly users, and lifetime ever users (Sethi & Trivedi, 1979).

Varma et al. (1980) surveyed a representative random sample of the entire adult population of Chandigarh, both rural and urban, and found that 60 percent of the population had never consumed alcohol, while 23.7 percent reported current use of alcohol—the majority of them above 21 years of age. More people of lower socioeconomic status and from rural areas drank country liquor.

A field survey in a rural population in Uttar Pradesh found that 21.4 percent of the population aged above 10 years were substance abusers and alcohol was the most common substance abused. None of the females consumed alcohol (Sethi & Trivedi, 1979). Lal and Singh (1978), in a study of a village in Sangrur district, Punjab, with a population of about 7,000, reported that 49.6 percent of males above the age of 15 years were alcohol consumers. The consumers were classified as mild, moderate, and heavy drinkers on the basis of their average daily intake and frequency of use, calculated as a quantity-frequency index. The mean annual per capita consumption of alcohol for the state of Punjab was also calculated. Applying the Ledermann distribution function and plotting the lognormal curve, it was found that the number of heavy drinkers obtained from the survey was considerably higher than the estimates derived from Ledermann's function. While the lognormal distribution underestimated the number of heavy drinkers, it also overestimated the number of moderate drinkers in the community. Singh (1979) argues that the Ledermann hypothesis, which is based on samples of drinkers from Western societies where drinking is socially approved and indulged in by the majority, may not hold true for a society or culture in which drinking is not widespread. The data from field surveys in Punjab show that while many persons are abstainers, some are drinkers, and quite a few of the drinkers are heavy drinkers. There is also a large sex difference with respect to drinking behavior. Similar results have been found in surveys in another district of Punjab (Mohan et al., 1978). Singh (1979) pointed out that there is a tendency among those who drink in India to indulge in very heavy drinking, in order to get drunk rather than as a mutual social activity.

Surveys from other parts of the country also show similar findings. Ponnudrai et al. (1991) estimated the prevalence of alcohol use in Madras city in the South Indian state of Tamil Nadu, using the Michigan Alcoholism Screening Test (MAST) to be 16.67 percent of the male population. Chakravarthy (1990) reported that 26–50 percent of adult males in rural areas of Tamil Nadu were alcohol consumers and most of them were illiterate. There were only a very few women who were alcohol consumers. Similarly, Mathrubootham (1989) found that 33 percent of the male population in this rural Tamil Nadu sample were current consumers of alcohol, most of them belonging to lower socioeconomic levels and backward or scheduled castes.

In Gadchiroli district, Maharashtra state, Bang and Bang (1991) conducted a survey in 104 villages with the active participation of the local community and the assistance of village health workers, schoolteachers, and local community leaders. The main ill effects associated with liquor as reported by the people were "chronic abdominal pain, loss of appetite, vomiting including vomiting of blood, swelling of feet and abdomen, jaundice, progressive weakness, impotence, family disruption, mental derangement, and death." The survey found that in a population of over 400,000 about 100,000 males consumed alcohol, of whom between 15,000 and 20,000 were addicted to alcohol. The number of people who died the previous year from drinking was about 1,000.

A reliable method for rapidly estimating the number of substance abusers in a community by interviewing the head of the household has been recently described (Mohan et al., 1992). Using this method, it was found that 26 percent of the respondents in an urban slum in New Delhi were substance abusers; most of them abused either alcohol alone or alcohol and tobacco.

Most of the general population surveys carried out in different parts of the country have reported only the prevalence of alcohol use and, in some cases, the pattern of this use. Data on diagnostic assessment of the consumers or the health effects of alcohol on them are not available. A recent house-to-house survey of a population of 32,400 people in eight villages near Bangalore carried out by the Centre for Advanced Research in Community Mental Health (CAR-CMH) of the Indian Council of Medical Research (attached to the National Institute of Mental Health and Neuro Sciences (NIMHANS)) estimated that 1.15 percent of the population suffered from alcohol dependence syndrome according to the ICD-9 definition. In this survey, all the persons indicated as possible cases by the initial stage of screening were assessed in detail by a trained psychiatrist later (ICMR/CAR-CMH, 1990).

The most consistent finding in general population surveys of alcohol use in India is that the proportion of female consumers is very low (below 5 percent). Ray and Sharma (1994) point out that when alcohol use is reported amongst females, they are generally likely to be tribal women or female tea plantation workers. Many studies reported an early age of onset of drinking among regular consumers. As early as 1981, B. B. Sethi, the then editor of the *Indian Journal of Psychiatry*, commenting on the growing frequency of alcohol use among teenagers, observed that "more and more teenagers are now seen consuming alcohol in the parks, on the footpaths, in parked automobiles or in the railway trains. It has frequently resulted in arousal of rage, aggression, fist fights, indiscretion and even transient antisocial acts" (Sethi, 1981).

Surveys of Alcohol Use in Specific Populations

Specific target populations such as university and high school students, industrial workers, and medical personnel have also been surveyed for their alcohol consumption. A multicentered collaborative study carried out in different universities in India found that 10–15 percent of the students were current consumers of alcohol (Mohan, 1981). Other studies have found higher figures ranging from 20 to 32 percent for "ever users" of alcohol (Dube et al., 1978; Varma & Dang, 1979). Singh (1979) and Sethi and Manchanda (1977) reported much higher alcohol use among medical students. Even among high school students in Delhi, 12.7 percent were found to be current users of alcohol (Mohan et al., 1975). Prevalence of alcohol use ranged from 44 to 66 percent among doctors and paramedical staff such as pharmacists (Singh & Jindal, 1980, 1981).

A study of 4,000 industrial workers randomly selected from different factories in Delhi by Gangrade and Gupta (1978) showed that 9.6 percent of the workers were alcohol consumers. A more recent study of industrial workers in Punjab reported that while about 60 percent of the workers were alcohol consumers, many of them were only recreational consumers (Gargi & Goyal, 1992). About half of the workers in Madras Port Trust were found to be regular consumers of alcohol (Chengappa, 1986).

A major drawback of all studies on use and abuse of alcohol is the absence of a consensus on what constitutes an "alcohol problem." Most researchers report only the frequency of alcohol use—"ever used," "occasional use," "use in past year," "recreational use," "current use," "daily use"—and/or the quantity of use—"moderate drinking," "heavy drinking," and so on. There is a lack of consistency in the definitions of these terms across studies. It has been pointed out recently that some of the concepts, criteria, and thresholds for the application of criteria used in the diagnosis of alcohol dependence syndrome internationally are difficult to define, translate, and apply with ease across cultures (Chandrashekhar et al., 1996; Room et al., 1996). There is a need to focus attention on the uniform application of definitions of what constitutes an alcohol problem in the Indian context in future research.

Research in the past two decades on the epidemiology of alcohol use in India shows that although abstainers from alcohol still constitute a majority of the total population, there is widespread consumption amongst the male population. There is a need to carry out multicentered collaborative research on truly representative samples of the population, using currently available sophisticated survey methodology and involving valid and reliable structured assessment instruments based on detailed diagnostic criteria. The research should aim at estimating the prevalence not only of discrete diagnostic categories of alcoholism such as alcohol dependence syndrome, but also of various alcohol use related problems.

HOSPITAL ADMISSIONS FOR ALCOHOLISM

One of the most striking indications of the growing alcohol-related problems in the country is the proportion of patients being admitted to various psychiatric treatment centers in different parts of the country. For example, at the Institute of Mental Health in Madras (formerly the Mental Hospital, Madras), during the period 1953 to 1965 no patients with alcoholism were admitted, and during

1966 to 1981, the percentage of admissions for alcohol problems ranged from 0.1 to 3 percent of the total admissions (Somasundaram, 1985). But today more than 25 percent of the total admissions are constituted by persons with alcohol problems (Palaniappun & Soundararajan, 1994). At the hospital attached to the National Institute of Mental Health and Neuro Sciences in Bangalore, less than 2 percent of all admissions and outpatient consultations in 1980 were for alcohol use related disorders, but by 1990 this figure had risen to more than 20 percent (Isaac, 1990). The number of beds has remained constant at both these hospitals in Madras and Bangalore.

Around half of the patients admitted to psychiatric hospitals in Goa have alcohol-related psychiatric problems (Hegde, 1994). At the psychiatry department of the general hospital in Pondicherry, outpatient consultations for alcohol-related problems doubled from 120 in 1990 to 254 in 1993 (Murthy, 1994).

Similarly, the private sector, particularly private psychiatric consultation practice, has also recorded a substantial increase in the proportion of patients seeking help for alcohol-related problems. While in 1977 alcohol dependence constituted only 1 percent of private practice, it rose to 32 percent by 1988 (Isaac, 1990).

Varma and Malhotra (1988) surveyed 27 general practitioners and found that more than 75 percent of them regularly treated alcohol abusers, who possessed a variety of health, family, and social problems. Gastritis, neuropathy, liver dysfunction, withdrawal, and intoxication were the common problems reported.

In a general hospital survey of problem drinkers, Babu and Sengupta (1997) screened 349 new admissions in the medicine, general surgery, and orthopedics wards with the MAST and the WHO Alcohol Use Disorders Identification Test (AUDIT) (Babor et al., 1992). Problem drinking was present in 14.6 percent of the inpatients. The severity and need for additional treatment was measured with the Addiction Severity Index (ASI). While only 10.3 percent of the problem drinkers met the DSM-IIIR criteria for alcohol dependence syndrome, the majority of them had problems in more than one area. Nevertheless, only about one-fourth the patients were referred to a mental health professional. The findings indicated that alcohol-related problems may exist irrespective of the diagnosis of a dependence syndrome.

Moily et al. (1992) screened 400 new patients attending a rural primary health care clinic using AUDIT, the screening instrument developed by the WHO. The probable cases were interviewed by a psychiatrist using a semistructured interview schedule. Twenty percent of the clinic attendees were alcohol consumers and more than one-half of them were moderate to heavy drinkers. While the majority of them had an associated physical co-morbidity, psychiatric disturbances were evident in 20 percent of the patients.

Some of the trends in the sociodemographic characteristics of drinkers shown by the general population surveys are reflected in data from rural health care clinics. Udayakumar (1992) found that 70 percent of the patients identified by AUDIT and assessed in detail at a rural mental health clinic near Bangalore were illiterate and 45 percent were unskilled laborers. The beverages commonly consumed were arrack and illicit country liquor. The symptoms frequently reported by these patients were tremors, numbness, pains and aches in different parts of the body, decreased appetite, abdominal discomfort, and fits. In a similar patient population from the same clinic, Philips and Sumana (1991) found that only about 3 percent of the patients consumed Indian-made foreign liquor (whisky, rum, brandy, and gin). About 20 percent of the patients started drinking at about the age of 15 years. Most of the patients (60 percent) spent around 500 rupees monthly on alcohol.

During the past decade a large number of deaddiction clinics have been opened in several parts of the country (Jiloha, 1991). The total number of counseling centers, deaddiction clinics, and aftercare homes for substance use disorders run by the voluntary sector was eight in 1986–1987. By 1992–1993, however, this number had grown to 254. Care for alcohol-related problems is predominate in most of these centers (Murthy, 1994; Isaac, 1992).

ALCOHOL-RELATED HEALTH PROBLEMS

Cirrhosis of the Liver and Premature Deaths

Although large numbers of persons with various types of alcohol-related physical problems are seen in general hospitals and internal medicine departments in India, there are no reliable data available on the nature and extent of these problems. Statistics of mortality due to liver cirrhosis are not systematically recorded in the country. Data on the proportion of liver cirrhosis cases that are due to alcoholism are also not readily available. However, other factors such as premature mortality among alcohol dependents give an indication of alcohol-related health problems. In a prospective study of treatment outcome, Desai (1989) followed up 46 patients with a mean age of 39.3 years and an average of 10 years of heavy alcohol use, for 18 months. Only 78 percent of the patients could be traced for follow-up, and of these 5.5 percent had died during the follow-up period, possibly from alcoholic liver disease. Sharma and Murthy (1988) attempted to follow up 71 patients with alcohol dependence diagnosed according to ICD-9 and treated at NIMHANS in Bangalore, four to five years after they were discharged from the hospital. Follow-up information could be obtained for only 53 (74.7 percent), and of these 6 (11.3 percent) had died during the preceding five years. Shankar et al. (1986) studied liver biopsies of 41 alcoholics admitted to NIMHANS and reported that the liver was normal in only 12 percent of the cases. The others showed evidence of alcoholic hepatitis (56.1 percent), fatty liver (14.6 percent), and cirrhosis (9.7 percent). In addition, several studies from different centers in India have shown the relationship between alcohol dependence and a high frequency of alcoholic liver damage or dysfunction (Rajwanshi et al., 1985; Ray et al., 1988; Sarin et al., 1988; Desai et al., 1996).

Cancer of the Upper Gastrointestinal Tract

Information about the risks of cancer of the upper gastrointestinal tract associated with alcohol use is nonexistent in India, except for a study by Jussawalla (1971), which showed a positive relationship between esophageal cancer and alcohol consumption. Zariwala and Bhide (1994) reported that samples of some of the commercial country liquors from Maharashtra and Bihar and toddy from Bihar which they studied were mutagenic.

Cognitive Impairment

Suneetha and Rao (1992) assessed a random sample of 30 alcoholic men admitted to TTK hospital in Madras using a battery of neuropsychological tests. The study was undertaken since it was found that a large number of patients admitted to the hospital showed clinical evidence of neuropsychological deficits. They found that 70 percent of the sample had neuropsychological deficits on day 2, reducing to 60 percent on day 30. There was a positive correlation between the number of years of excessive drinking and the test scores. Narang et al. (1991) assessed the cognitive functions of 30 alcoholics receiving outpatient treatment in Ludhiana and found a significant relationship between their cognitive impairment and the duration of alcohol use.

More than 70 percent of a sample of 50 patients with a diagnosis of alcohol dependence syndrome (ICD-10) assessed on the neuropsychological battery by Shenoy et al. (1996) were found to have significant right temporal lobe deficits and a lesser proportion had frontal lobe deficits.

Road Traffic Accidents and Head Injuries

Alcohol's contribution to road traffic accidents and their consequences has not been systematically researched in India. However, the country's road research institutes estimated that 25 percent of road accidents were alcohol-related and that one-third of the drivers on the highway were under the influence of alcohol (Chengappa, 1986).

Although reliable data on the blood alcohol levels of road accident victims with head injuries is not available, it is estimated that more than 20 percent of accident-related head injury victims seen in emergency rooms have consumed alcohol at some time prior to the accident, although the length of time between drinking and the accident is not generally known. Sabhesan and Natarajan (1987) found behavioral problems and length of hospital stay to be greater in a group of head-injured patients who were alcohol abusers compared to a control group. Sabhesan, Arumugham, and Natarajan (1990), in a further follow-up study of head injury patients, found that irritability and social maladjustment were increased among the alcohol abusers.

Beneficial Effects of Moderate Alcohol Use

Recent evidence, which suggests that moderate drinking may reduce the risk of coronary heart disease, has initiated an international debate on sensible limits of drinking (O'Connor, 1994; Saul, 1994). Although some of the ancient Indian texts such as Rig-veda and Charaka Samhita have also mentioned the positive effects of moderate consumption of alcohol (Hunt, 1987), the public health significance of these recent findings to the current Indian context needs to be assessed. A recent press release from WHO (1994) states that "moderate alcohol consumption for preventive purposes makes little sense in countries where the prevalence of cardiovascular disease is low, including most of the developing world, which represents the overwhelming majority of the world's population." At least one leading figure in the field of alcoholism in India has responded to the debate on sensible drinking by commenting that "the most sensible thing is not to drink" (Ranganathan, 1994a) in the Indian situation.

Two studies on the lipid profile of persons with alcohol dependence in India report higher levels of atherogenic lipids—a finding at variance with several studies in the West which have found a lowering of atherogenic lipids in drinkers along with a rise in protective lipids (Vasisht, Pant, and Sriverstava, 1992; Vaswani et al., 1997). The difference may be attributable to several local factors such as type and amount of alcohol consumed, high fat content of diet and other dietary factors, lifestyle variables, and so forth. The authors point to the need for further study to examine the cardioprotective or atherogenic role of regular low-dose alcohol use in the Indian setting.

ALCOHOL-RELATED SOCIAL PROBLEMS

Family Disruption and Effects on Wives

As elsewhere in the world, there is growing evidence to suggest that alcohol abuse is a major cause of family disruption and marital discord in India. Alcohol contributes to frequent family violence (including "wife-beating") as well as psychopathology in family members. The family disruption initiated by alcohol ends in separation or divorce in many cases. Studies of families and wives of alcohol dependents show that there is substantial dysfunction in all areas of family interaction (Paravathi, 1989; Varalakshmi, 1988; Ganihar et al., 1983). Most of the alcoholic husbands neglected their family responsibilities. A majority of the wives of alcohol abusers reported financial problems, daily quarrels, and physical assaults. Many of the wives suffered from various physical and mental health problems and manifested high levels of stress and stress-related symptoms (Rajendran and Cherian, 1992). Devar, Cherian, and Kalpana (1983), using Beck's depression rating, found wives of alcoholics to be suffering from a depressive state of mind. Ponnudrai and Jayakar (1980), who studied 87 cases of suicide from the city of Madras, found that 6 (12.5 percent) of the 50 females had committed suicide as a result of maladjustment with husbands who were alcoholics. They also found that among the 37 males, 3 (8.1 percent) had killed themselves while they were under the influence of alcohol. Chengappa (1986) observes that "if more families have not broken up, it is because most Indian wives fear the stigma attached to divorce."

Effects on Children

Studies of children of alcohol abusers reveal that they have below-average educational performance and a higher degree of deviant behavior compared to children of nonalcohol abusing parents (Udayakumar et al., 1984). Jayashree (1988) found faulty and inconsistent child-rearing practices in families of alcoholics. Children from these families had poor social adjustment. Somasundaram and Polnaya (1979) reported more than 70 percent alcoholism among the parents of inmates of a government-run institution for delinquent children in Tamil Nadu.

Narang et al. (1996) compared a group of 100 children (between the ages of 4 and 12 years) of alcoholic parents with children of nonalcoholic parents. The children of alcoholics were found to have various disturbances which included somatization, anxiety, conduct disorders, and emotional problems.

Effects on Family Budget

In families belonging to the lower socioeconomic strata with fixed and limited income, frequent alcohol use by any member leads to serious financial difficulties and deprivation of basic needs for the rest of the family. In a study of health behavior of rural populations in 19 villages (in the states of Gujarat, Haryana, Karnataka, Rajasthan, Tamil Nadu, Kerala, Uttar Pradesh, and West Bengal), Banerji (1982) reported that the highest percentages of daily alcohol consumers were among the Harijans (scheduled castes), the landless, and the poor laborers. Philips and Sumana (1991), who studied regular alcohol consumers at the Sakalawara rural health center near Bangalore, report that 60 percent of them spent more that 500 rupees a month on alcohol, 30 percent spent between 250 and 500 rupees, and 10 percent spent less than 250 rupees. Based on the usual monthly incomes of families belonging to the lower socioeconomic class, these amounts represent approximately 15–40 percent of the family income. More than 21,000 working-class families in 50 different industrial centers all over the country were surveyed regarding alcohol use and family budgets by a study team on prohibition. Alcohol use was reported among 10.24 percent of all working-class families (factory workers (9.6 percent), plantation workers (14 percent), and workers in mines (23 percent)). On an average, these families spent 9 percent of their earnings on alcohol (Singh, 1989). A comparison of regular drinkers and nondrinkers among workers at Madras Port Trust showed that nondrinkers "spent 8 percent more on food, 30 percent more on clothing, 168 percent more on health care and 300 percent more on children's education" (Sankaran, 1986).

The amount of alcohol consumed and the proportion of income spent on drinking during the period of three months prior to admission for treatment was calculated in 50 patients admitted to the deaddiction center of the NIMHANS in Bangalore (Leela et al., 1996). It was found that patients consumed on average 240 g of alcohol per day. This amounted to monthly spending of 1,290 rupees (calculation based on the cost of the cheapest drinks). The average monthly income of the group was about 1,300 rupees. At the Bangalore center in WHO's nine-country study on the cross-cultural applicability of terms and concepts used in the diagnosis of substance use related problems, key informants and focus group participants pointed out that economic constraints imposed on the family because of alcohol use by any member should be considered an important component of "alcohol problems" (Chandrashekhar et al., 1996).

Effects on Work

Absenteeism, lowered productivity, and maladjustment at the workplace occur frequently because of alcohol abuse among industrial workers. A study by a sociologist of workers at Madras Port Trust found that heavy drinkers were absent from work on average every sixth day, and as a result nondrinkers took home 50 percent more money than drinkers (Chengappa, 1986). Senthilnathan et al. (1984) studied industrial alcoholics and reported maladjustment among alcohol-dependent individuals as compared to nondrinkers.

Crime and Violence

Information on alcohol-related crime and violence is not readily available in India, but it is likely that alcohol is associated with different types of violence (political, communal, domestic) and crime in the country. Routine scanning of the news media (newspapers in local languages and English) reveals that a variety of petty and serious crimes are committed by people who were under the influence of alcohol while committing them.

Currently available data in India on alcohol's contribution to a wide range of problems, which includes road traffic accidents, nontraffic accidents such as those occurring at home, work or during leisure pursuits, family disruption, crime, violence, and effects on children and work, are grossly inadequate. In future research on alcoholism, there is a need to shift the emphasis from the mere study of the prevalence of alcohol use or misuse to the study of a broad range of "alcohol-related problems" from a public health perspective. Even internationally, it is only during the past decade that alcohol's contribution to traffic accidents and violence has been systematically researched (Heather, 1994). There is an urgent need in the country to generate robust data on the nature and extent of various alcohol-related social problems. Sound social policy decisions on alcohol can only be made on the basis of such data.

OTHER INDICATORS OF GROWING ALCOHOL-RELATED PROBLEMS

Various events and activities taking place in India during the past decade point to growing alcohol-related health and social problems. Some of these are discussed in the paragraphs that follow.

A Growing Number of Treatment Centers

During the past decade specialized treatment facilities for substance abuse have been set up in different parts of the country. These were established primarily because of the problems created by an upsurge in the use of heroin during the mid 1980s in some parts of the country. Drug abuse has been politically more visible in the country than alcoholism and alcohol-related problems (WHO, 1993b). The treatment facilities are organized under the governmental, private, and voluntary (nongovernmental organization) sectors. The Health Ministry of the government of India set up a series of drug detoxification centers, most of them attached to psychiatric hospitals or general hospital psychiatric units. The Ministry of Welfare provided financial support to establish a variety of facilities such as counseling centers, detoxification centers with short-term inpatient facilities for 15 to 60 persons, and aftercare homes for longer term care and rehabilitation. Over the years, most of these centers have provided care for predominantly alcohol-related problems (Jiloha, 1991; Murthy, 1994; Isaac, 1992).

During the past few years many psychiatric hospitals have created additional facilities for substance abuse related problems; examples are NIMHANS in Bangalore and the Institute of Mental Health in Madras. Many of the centers supported by the government of India, such as the facilities at the All India Institute of Medical Sciences in New Delhi and the Post Graduate Institute of Medical Education and Research in Chandigarh, are given the additional tasks of training personnel and researching the area of substance abuse. A specialized institution for management of alcoholism, the T. T. Ranganathan Clinical Research Foundation and its hospital in Madras, was also set up during the 1980s (Cherian, 1986). Most of the centers for substance use related problems in the country are organized in a well-coordinated manner to provide services for abuse of alcohol as well as other substances.

Innovative Treatment Strategies

The total number of beds available throughout the country for management of alcohol-related problems in the various types of treatment facilities mentioned above is only about 5,000. It is estimated that the demand for services currently

far exceeds the available facilities (Isaac, 1992). There is a need to develop innovative, cost-effective, and culturally applicable programs. One such program
developed in recent years is the community treatment for groups of alcohol dependents in rural areas, referred to as the "camp approach" for management of
alcohol dependence. In this approach, persons with problems of alcohol abuse
from rural areas are treated together as a group of between 20 and 30 people, in
temporary treatment settings organized by the local community—the camp—for
an initial period of two weeks. Subsequently, they are followed up periodically
in groups. Ranganathan (1994b) has described the various components of this
treatment package and reports a high percentage (70 percent) of recovery using the approach. Datta, Prasantham, and Kuruvilla (1991) have also reported
high abstinence rates after the community treatment of alcoholics. Provision of
treatment in groups and various sociocultural and religious factors may have
contributed to the better results. The camp approach to alcoholism management
signifies a paradigm shift in the treatment of alcoholism, showing how an empowered community can help itself. A manual describing the methodology of
treatment of alcoholism through rural camps is now available (Ranganathan,
1996).

Involvement of Primary Health Care Sector

There is a growing realization in the country that alcohol-related problems can
be adequately tackled only by providing services through the primary health
care network of primary health centers, taluk (subdistrict), and district hospitals.
Most of the doctors in primary health centers and internists in district hospitals
do not at present possess skills in managing alcohol-related problems. Attempts
are, therefore, being made to train them in assessment and management of these
problems. A model three-week training program has been developed by the drug
dependence treatment center at the All India Institute of Medical Sciences, New
Delhi, and training programs are conducted four times a year. A number of
regional training centers have also been established so that more primary care
doctors can be trained (Saxena, 1994).

Educational and Training Materials

A variety of health educational materials such as pamphlets, information booklets, and self-help guides on various aspects of alcoholism and alcohol-related
problems have been developed in the country during the past few years. These
are meant for persons with alcohol-related problems, their family members,
and the general public. Many of these materials have been produced with financial support from the Ministry of Welfare, the government of India, and
by nongovernmental organizations such as the T. T. Ranganathan Clinical Research Foundation in Madras. Examples of such health educational materials,
which are increasingly being used in the country, are the booklets entitled

New Hopes ... New Possibilities—Comfortable Recovery For Alcoholics and Children of Alcoholics—A Guide to Parents and Teachers (T. T. Ranganathan Clinical Research Foundation, 1991a; 1993a).

Training materials such as manuals for different categories of health and social welfare personnel have also been produced by the T. T. Ranganathan Clinical Research Foundation. These manuals are best suited for the training of community health workers and are used by various centers in different parts of the country (T. T. Ranganathan Clinical Research Foundation, 1991b; 1993b). The need to develop separate manuals for doctors (primary care physicians) has been identified, and this is now in progress at the Department of Psychiatry, All India Institute of Medical Sciences in New Delhi (Ray, 1994).

Community Action Against Alcohol

One of the most visible indicators of the extent of alcohol-related problems is the spontaneous community action against alcohol use and the sale of alcohol in many parts of the country. Many of these "anti-arrack people's movements" and "mass movements" have been spearheaded by women. In many places, the local community has been successful in preventing liquor sales and closing down liquor shops. Thousands of men have reportedly given up their regular drinking habits as a result of the community pressure. Such community action programs have taken place in many states, including Andhra Pradesh, Haryana, Maharashtra, and Bihar (Bang & Bang, 1991; Saxena, 1994; Chengappa, 1986; Prasad, 1992).

Involvement of Nongovernmental Organizations (NGOs)

During the past decade, a number of voluntary organizations carrying out a variety of activities in the area of substance abuse have developed in almost all the states in the country. While many of them are involved only in prevention, awareness building, and education, some provide long-term rehabilitation for persons with substance abuse related problems (Isaac, 1992).

Alcoholics Anonymous Groups

Until a few years ago, there were only a small number of Alcoholics Anonymous groups in India. These groups functioned only in some of the big cities and the participants were English-speaking persons belonging to the middle and upper classes. Today, Alcoholics Anonymous groups conduct their meetings in various local languages. Their numbers have increased and they have spread to more places, including smaller cities such as Nagpur, Cochin, Pune, Mangalore, and Mysore (Chengappa, 1986).

Employee Alcoholism Assistance Programs (EAP)

Many big industries in the country have developed employee alcoholism assistance programs to help their employees with alcohol-related problems. Bharath Earth Movers in Kolar and Bharath Electronics and Motor Industries Company in Bangalore are examples. The T. T. Ranganathan Clinical Research Foundation has developed a training program for factory supervisors to help them to identify alcohol-dependent employees (Cherian, 1986).

National Master Plan (1994–2000)

The government of India formed an expert committee in 1986 to develop a comprehensive strategy for reduction of both supply and demand of all substances of abuse, including alcohol. In recognition of the growing problems posed by increasing consumption of alcohol all over the country, together with abuse of other substances in some parts of the country, needs in this area are currently being reviewed and a national master plan is being developed (Ray and Sharma, 1994). The main goals of this effort are to assess the efficacy of the present strategies for drug abuse prevention and management and develop specific plans for the next five years. The broad areas the plan would cover include:

- The role of state governments in the field of drug abuse prevention
- Procedures for determining financial assistance to nongovernmental organizations
- Measures for coordination amongst various agencies concerned with control and supply/demand reduction of various harmful substances
- Training needs of various categories of governmental and nongovernmental functionaries engaged in substance abuse related activities
- Creation of public awareness regarding harmful effects of substance use
- Measures for prevention of relapse after treatment
- Development of a national-level monitoring system (Murthy, 1994).

The details of the master plan and its position on alcohol-related issues are not yet available.

CONCLUSIONS

There is now a growing body of evidence to suggest that use of alcohol, with the consequent health and social problems associated with its abuse, has been steadily on the rise all over the country during the past two decades. India itself has been going through a period of rapid social change. The demographic profile of the country is in gradual transition, with increasing urbanization and fast-growing cities. While the size of the middle classes has grown in both urban and rural areas, certain subgroups of the population such as illiterate and unskilled workers, landless people in villages, and some of the slum dwellers in urban areas have remained poor or even become poorer. The disposable income of the middle and upper classes has been growing. The country at present is witnessing major changes in its economic policies, with liberalization of the market and the steady introduction of a market economy. Commenting on the growing consumerism in the country, Anthony Spaeth of the *Wall Street Journal* (1988) noted that "the traditional conservative Indian who believes in modesty and savings is gradually giving way to a new generation that thinks as freely as it spends." The availability of satellite television and cable networks as well as videocassette recorders has contributed to the increasing integration of India within the "global village."

All these factors are bringing about various kinds of changes such as the breakup of the traditional joint family system and changes in values and attitudes, including attitudes towards the consumption of alcohol. The cultural and religious controls that prevented people from drinking are weakening. Among the upper and middle classes, alcohol is gaining respectability as a status symbol and symbol of one's westernization. At the other end of the socioeconomic spectrum, alcohol consumption may be the only leisure activity for many. For a large number of poor people, alcohol may be initially a means of coping with deprivation, poverty, and the harsh realities of life. Coupled with these factors is the easy availability of alcohol any time and anywhere in the country. A noticeable trend in the country is the increasing alcohol consumption by groups who traditionally were abstainers, such as women, teenagers, and the rural rich. It is likely that alcohol-related health and social problems are on the rise in India, though their magnitude is unknown. Efforts at prohibition have failed miserably in the past. There is an urgent need for the country to review its alcohol policies.

ACKNOWLEDGMENTS

The author is grateful to Mrs. Shanthi Ranganathan of the T. T. Ranganathan Clinical Research Foundation, Madras, and to Dr. R. Parthasarathy, Dr. C. R. Chandrashekhar, Dr. S. Chatterji, Dr. Prathima Murthy, and Dr. R. S. Murthy of NIMHANS, Bangalore, for providing valuable documents, and to Ms. Jasmine Brügger and Mr. Madan for assistance in typing the manuscript.

REFERENCES

Ahluwalia, B. (1996, October 30). Low spirits—Are Indian liquor makers getting stepmotherly treatments? *Outlook*, p. 54.

Babor, T. F., de la Fuente, J. R., Saunders, J., & Grant, M. (1992). *AUDIT: The Alcohol Use Disorders Identification Test. Guidelines for Use in Primary Health Care*. Geneva: World Health Organization.

Babu, R. S. & Sengupta, S. N. (1997). A study of problem drinkers in a general hospital. *Indian Journal of Psychiatry, 39*, 13–17.

Banerji, D. (1982). *Poverty, Class and Health Culture in India, Vol. 1.* New Delhi: Prachi Prakashan.

Bang, A. T. & Bang, R. A. (1991). Community participation in research and action against alcoholism. *World Health Forum, 12,* 104–109.

Bennett, L. A., Janča, A., Grant, B. F., & Sartorius, N. (1993). Boundaries between normal and pathological drinking: A cross-cultural comparison. *Alcohol Health and Research World, 17,* 190–195.

Chakravarthy, C. (1990). Community workers' estimate of drinking and alcohol related problems in rural areas. *Indian Journal of Psychological Medicine, 13,* 49–56.

Chakravarti, S. & Rathanami, L. (1995, May 15). Invasion of the foreign spirit. *India Today,* pp. 175–177.

Chandrashekhar, C. R., et al. (1996). Bangalore Centre Report. In L. A. Bennett, A. Janča, & N. Sartorius (Eds.), *Use and Abuse of Alcohol and Drugs in Different Cultures—A Nine-Country Study.* Forthcoming.

Chengappa, R. (1986, April 30). Alcoholism, the growing malaise. *India Today,* pp. 72–80.

Cherian, R. R. (1986). Emergence of a day-care centre for alcoholics in India: Its referral system and public response. *British Journal of Addiction, 81,* 119–122.

Datta, S., Prasantham, B. J., & Kuruvilla, K. (1991). Community treatment for alcoholism. *Indian Journal of Psychiatry, 33,* 305–306.

Desai, N. G. (1989). Treatment and outcome of alcohol dependence. In R. Ray & R. W. Pickens (Eds.), *Proc. Indo-U.S. Symposium on Alcohol and Drug Abuse,* (Publication 20). Bangalore: National Institute of Mental Health and Neuro Sciences.

Desai, N. G., et al. (1996). Profile of liver dysfunction in alcohol dependence. *Indian Journal of Psychiatry, 38,* 34–37.

Devar, J. V., Cherian, R. R., & Kalpana, D. (1983). *A Rating of Depression in Alcoholics and Their Wives.* Madras: T. T. Ranganathan Clinical Research Foundation.

Dube, K. C. & Handa, S. K. (1971). Drug use in health and mental illness in an Indian population. *British Journal of Psychiatry, 118,* 345–349.

Dube, K. C., Kumar, A., Kumar, N., & Gupta, S. P. (1978). Prevalence and pattern of drug use amongst college students. *Acta Psychiatrica Scandinavica, 57,* 336–356.

Edwards, G., et al. (1994). *Alcohol Policy and the Public Good.* Oxford: Oxford University Press.

Elnager, M. N., Maitra, P., & Rao, M. N. (1971). Mental health in a rural community. *British Journal of Psychiatry, 118,* 499–503.

Fernandez, V. (1993, July 15). Liquor industry, on a new high. *India Today,* pp. 66–67.

Gangrade, K. D. & Gupta, K. (1978). A study of drug use among industrial workers. A project report of Delhi School of Social Work. New Delhi: University of Delhi.

Ganihar, N. A., et al. (1983). Problems faced by the house-wives of alcoholics. *Rehabilitation in Asia, 7,* 150–154.

Gargi, P. D. & Goyal, B. L. (1992). A study of prevalence of drug use among industrial workers of Punjab, Part 1. In N. G. Desai (Ed.), *Abstracts of 44th Annual National Conference of the Indian Psychiatric Society.* New Delhi: Indian Psychiatric Society.

Ghose, S. (1996, June 5). To bottle up, or to uncork? *Outlook,* pp. 54–57.

Gopinath, P. S. (1968). Epidemiology of mental illness in an Indian village. *Transactions of All India Institute of Mental Health, 8,* 68–73.

Government of Karnataka (1993). Note on excise policy for the year 1993–1994. Bangalore (unpublished).

Heather, N. (1994). Alcohol, accidents, and aggression. *British Medical Journal, 308,* 1254.

Hegde, R. (1994, August 23). Alcohol main cause of mental disorders in Goa. *Deccan Herald.*

The Hindu (1996, February 26). Cabinet panel to study prohibition: Chief Minister.

Hunt, L. (1987). Comment on *Emergence of a day-care centre for alcoholics in India* by R. R. Cherian. *British Journal of Addiction, 82,* 55–57.

ICMR/CAR-CMH (1990). *Longitudinal study of mental health problems in a PHC area.* Bangalore: Indian Council of Medical Research Centre for Advanced Research on Community Mental Health, NIMHANS (unpublished).

India Today (1986). For the fortnight of April 30, 1986. New Delhi: Living Media India Ltd.

Isaac, M. K. (1990). A proposal for starting specialized alcohol and drug abuse services at NIMHANS. Bangalore: National Institute of Mental Health and Neuro Sciences (unpublished).

Isaac, M. K. (1992). *WHO/PSA—Multinational Treatment Mapping Survey—Response from India.* Geneva: Programme on Substance Abuse, World Health Organization (submitted).

Janakiramaiah, N. (1995). State policy on alcoholic drinks: Prohibition or restriction? *Deaddiction Quarterly, 2,* 1.

Jayashree, V. (1988). A comparative study on child-rearing practices in families of alcoholics and adjustmental pattern of their children. M. Phil. (Psychiatric Social Work) dissertation, Department of Psychiatric Social Work, National Institute of Mental Health and Neuro Sciences, Bangalore University, Bangalore.

Jiloha, R. C. (1991). A decade of deaddiction clinics in India. *British Journal of Addiction, 86,* 103–104.

Jussawalla, D. J. (1971). Epidemiological assessment of aetiology of oesophageal cancer in greater Bombay. In D. J. Jussawalla & Sir R. Doll (Eds.), *International Seminar on Epidemiology of Oesophageal Cancer* (Indian Cancer Society Monograph Series). Bombay, India: Indian Cancer Society.

Katiyar, A. (1993, July 15). Bombay pubs—rollicking frolicking fun. *India Today,* pp. 62–64.

Kumar, C. S. C. & Dubey, R. (1992, October 25). One for the road to ruin, alcoholism is increasing alarmingly in the country. *The Week,* pp. 28–31.

Lal, B. & Singh, G. (1978). Alcohol consumption in Punjab. *Indian Journal of Psychiatry, 20,* 217–225.

Leela, S., et al. (1996). The cost of alcoholism. *Indian Journal of Psychiatry Supplement, 38,* 35.

Mathrubootham, N. (1989). *Epidemiological Study of Drinking Behaviour in a Rural Population.* Ph.D. thesis, Department of Psychiatry, Madras Medical College, University of Madras, Madras.

Mohan, D. (1981). Alcohol use among college students. In D. Mohan, H. S. Sethi, & E. Tongue (Eds.), *Current Research in Drug Abuse in India.* New Delhi: Japyce Brothers.

Mohan, D., Desai, N. G., Chopra, A., & Sethi, H. (1992). Rapid survey on substance abuse disorders in the urban slums of New Delhi. *Indian Journal of Medical Research, 96*(B), 122–127.

Mohan, D., Sharma, H. K., Darshan, S., Sundaram, K. R., & Neki, J. S. (1978). Prevalence of drug abuse in young in rural Punjab. *Indian Journal of Medical Research, 68,* 689–694.

Mohan, D., Thoman, M. G., Sethi, H. S., & Prabhu, G. G. (1975). Prevalence and pattern of drug use among high school students: A replicated study. *Bulletin on Narcotics, 31,* 77–86.

Moily, S., et al. (1992). Prevalence of alcohol related problems in a primary health care clinic. In N. G. Desai (Ed.), *Abstracts of the 44th National Conference of the Indian Psychiatric Society.* New Delhi: Indian Psychiatric Society.

Murthy, R. S. (1994). *The laws relating to narcotic drugs and psychotropic substances and alcohol—Indian situation.* Bangalore: National Institute of Mental Health and Neuro Sciences (unpublished).

Narang, R. L., Pershad, D., Gupta, R., & Garg, D. (1991). Cognitive dysfunction in alcoholics. *Indian Journal of Psychiatry, 33,* 297–301.

Narang, R. L., Gupta, R., Mishra, B. P., & Mahajan, R. (1996). Temperamental characteristics and psychopathology among children of alcoholics. *Indian Journal of Psychiatry, Supplement 38*(2), 34.

O'Connor, J. (1994). Sensible drinking. *World Health Forum, 15,* 213–231.

Palaniappun, V. & Soundararajan, M. (1994). A glimpse of deaddiction centre at the Institute of Mental Health, Madras. In V. P. Bashyam (Ed.), *Souvenir of ANCIPS* (117–119). Madras: Indian Psychiatric Society.

Paravathi, K. (1989). *A comparative study on the patterns of violence in families of alcoholics and non-alcoholics and their family dynamics.* M. Phil. (Psychiatric Social Work) dissertation, Department of Psychiatric Social Work, National Institute of Mental Health and Neuro Sciences, Bangalore University, Bangalore.

Parihar, R. (1996, September 15). The other side of prohibition. *India Today*, pp. 72–77.

Philips, T. & Sumana, K. (1991). *An evaluative study on alcoholics in Sakalawara Sub Centre area.* Community Mental Health Unit, National Institute of Mental Health and Neuro Sciences, Bangalore (unpublished).

Ponnudrai, R. & Jayakar, J. (1980). Suicide in Madras. *Indian Journal of Psychiatry, 22,* 203–205.

Ponnudrai, R., Jayakar, J., Raju, B., & Pattamuthu, R. (1991). An epidemiological study of alcoholism. *Indian Journal of Psychiatry, 33,* 176–179.

Prasad, R. J. R. (1992, December 4). A spirited battle, anti-liquor awakening in A.P. *Frontline*, pp. 51–53.

Premarajan, K. C., Danabalan, M., Chandrasekar, R., & Srinivasa, D. K. (1993). Prevalence of psychiatric morbidity in an urban community of Pondicherry. *Indian Journal of Psychiatry, 35,* 99–102.

Rajendran, R. & Cherian, R. R. (1992). *Levels of Stress in Wives of Alcoholics.* Madras: Addiction Research Centre (unpublished).

Rajwanshi, A., Islam, M., Bhagwat, A. G., Kamath, A. S., & Joseph, R. (1985). Alcoholic liver disease in north India—a biopsy study. *Indian Journal of Pathology and Microbiology, 28,* 129–135.

Ranganathan, S. (1994a). The most sensible thing is not to drink. *World Health Forum, 15,* 226–227.

Ranganathan, S. (1994b). The Manjakkudi experience: A camp approach towards treating alcoholics. *Addiction, 89,* 1071–1075.

Ranganathan, S. (1996). *The Empowered Community—A Paradigm Shift in the Treatment of Alcoholism.* Madras: T. T. Ranganathan Clinical Research Foundation.

Ray, R., et al. (1988). Male alcoholism—Biochemical diagnosis and effect of abstinence. *Indian Journal of Psychiatry, 30,* 339–343.

Ray, R. (1994). Training of medical officers for drug dependence care. *Health For The Millions, 20,* 13–15.

Ray, R. & Sharma, H. K. (1994). Drug addiction—An Indian perspective. In V. P. Bashyam (Ed.), *Souvenir of ANCIPS 1994* (106–109). Madras: Indian Psychiatric Society.

Room, R., Janca, A., Bennett, L. A., Schmidt, L., & Sartorius, N. (1996). WHO cross-cultural applicability research on diagnosis and assessment of substance use disorders: An overview of methods and selected results. *Addiction, 91,* 199–200.

Sabhesan, S., Arumugham, R., & Natarajan, M. (1990). Alcohol dependence, head injury, and memory impairment. *Indian Journal of Psychiatry, 32,* 260–264.

Sabhesan, S. & Natarajan, M. (1987). Post-traumatic amnesia longer than four weeks. *Indian Journal of Psychological Medicine, 10,* 79–84.

Samarasinghe, D. (1994). Alcohol policies in poverty and in wealth. *Addiction, 89,* 643–646.

Sankaran, S. (1986, April 30). Quote from "Alcoholism, the growing malaise" by R. Chengappa. *India Today*, pp. 72–80.

Sarin, S. K., et al. (1988). Pattern of alcohol-related liver disease in dependent alcoholics: The Indian dimension. *British Journal of Addiction, 83,* 279–284.

Saul, H. (1994, July 2). The debate over the limits. *New Scientist*, pp. 12–13.

Saxena, S. (1994). News from India. *Addiction, 89,* 883–887.

Senthilnathan, S. M., Sekar, K., Radha, V., & Sheriff, I. A. (1984). Social adjustment of industrial alcoholics. *Indian Psychological Abst, 22,* 913.

Sethi, B. B. (1978). A new era of prohibition. *Indian Journal of Psychiatry, 22,* 1–2.

Sethi, B. B. (1981). Teenage drinking—A plea for intervention. *Indian Journal of Psychiatry, 22,* 1–2.

Sethi, B. B. & Manchanda, R. (1977). Drug abuse among medical students. *Indian Journal of Psychiatry, 19,* 31–39.

Sethi, B. B. & Trivedi, J. K. (1979). Drug abuse in rural population. *Indian Journal of Psychiatry, 21,* 211–216.

Shankar, S. K., et al. (1986). Alcoholic liver disease in a psychiatric hospital. *Indian Journal of Psychiatry, 28,* 35–39.

Sharma, A. & Murthy, R. S. (1988). A 4–5 year follow-up study of male alcoholism. *NIMHANS Journal, 6,* 111–113.

Shenoy, J., et al. (1996). Neuropsychological deficits in patients with alcohol dependence syndrome. *Indian Journal of Psychiatry, Supplement 38,* 84.

Shetty, K. (1993, March 11). Bacchus on the run, state policy on bars confuses serious tipplers. *India Today,* p. 158.

Singh, G. (1978). Issues and approaches in drug abuse prevention with special reference to alcohol use in Punjab. *Indian Journal of Psychiatry, 20,* 217–223.

Singh, G. (1979). Comment on "The single distribution theory of alcohol consumption." *Journal of Studies on Alcohol, 40,* 522–524.

Singh, G. (1989). Epidemiology of alcohol abuse in India. In R. Ray & R. W. Pickens (Eds.), *Proc. Indo-U.S. Symposium on Alcohol and Drug Abuse* (NIMHANS Publication 20, pp. 3–11). Bangalore: National Institute of Mental Health and Neuro Sciences.

Singh, G. & Jindal, K. C. (1980). Drugs on a medical campus, II: Drug use among faculty members. *Drug and Alcohol Dependence, 6,* 123–130.

Singh, G. & Jindal, K. C. (1981). Drugs on a medical campus, III: Drug use among nursing and paramedical personnel. *Drug and Alcohol Dependence, 7,* 31–37.

Singh, G. & Lal, B. (1979). Alcohol in India. *Indian Journal of Psychiatry, 21,* 39–45.

Smart, R. G. (1991). World trends in alcohol consumption. *World Health Forum, 12,* 99–103.

Somasundaram, O. (1985). Alcoholism in Tamil Nadu. In D. Mohan, H. S. Sethi, & E. Tongue (Eds.), *Current Research in Drug Abuse in India.* New Delhi: Jaypee Brothers.

Somasundaram, O. & Polnaya, M. (1979). Juvenile delinquency in girls. *Indian Journal of Criminology, 7,* 11–14.

Spaeth, A. (1988, May 19). A thriving middle class is changing the face of India. *Wall Street Journal.*

Suneetha, V. T. & Rao, A. (1992). *A study of neuropsychological deficits in alcoholic men.* Madras: Addiction Research Centre (unpublished).

Surya, N. C. (1964). Mental morbidity in Pondicherry. *Transactions of All India Institute of Mental Health, 5,* 50–61.

T. T. Ranganathan Clinical Research Foundation. (1991a). *Children of Alcoholics—A Guide to Parents and Teachers.* Madras: T.T.R. Education Foundation.

T. T. Ranganathan Clinical Research Foundation. (1991b). *Alcoholism and Drug Dependency—The Professional's "Masterguide."* Madras: T.T.R. Clinical Research Foundation.

T. T. Ranganathan Clinical Research Foundation. (Addiction Research Centre) (1991c). *A Critical Review of Policy and Programmes Related to Alcohol Use and Abuse in India.* Madras: T. T. Ranganathan Clinical Research Foundation.

T. T. Ranganathan Clinical Research Foundation. (1993a). *New Hopes—New Possibilities: Comfortable Recovery from Alcoholism.* Madras: T.T.R. Education Foundation.

T. T. Ranganathan Clinical Research Foundation. (1993b). *Alcoholism and Drug Dependency—An Advanced Master Guide for Professionals.* Madras: T.T.R. Clinical Research Foundation.

Times of India (1993, February 18). Focus again on arrack. Editorial.

Udayakumar, G. S. (1992). *Patterns and problems of drinking among the patients seeking the services of health care system in rural setting.* Ph.D. thesis. Department of Psychiatric Social Work, National Institute of Mental Health and Neuro Sciences, Bangalore University, Bangalore.

Udayakumar, G. S., et al. (1984). Children of alcoholic parents. *Child Psychiatry Quarterly, 27,* 9–14.

Varalakshmi, G. (1988). *A study of psychosocial problems of wives of alcohol dependents*, M. Phil. (Psychiatric Social Work) dissertation, Department of Psychiatric Social Work, National Institute of Mental Health and Neuro Sciences, Bangalore University, Bangalore.

Varma, V. K. & Dang, R. (1979). Non-medical use of drugs amongst school and college students in India. *Indian Journal of Psychiatry, 21*, 228–234.

Varma, V. K. & Malhotra, A. K. (1988). The management of alcohol-related problems in general practice in North India. *Indian Journal of Psychiatry, 30*, 211–219.

Varma, V. K., Singh, A., Singh, S., & Malhotra, A. (1980). Extent and pattern of alcohol use and alcohol related problems in North India. *Indian Journal of Psychiatry, 22*, 331–337.

Vasisht, S., Pant, M. C., & Sriverstava, L. M. (1992). Effect of alcohol on serum lipids and lipoproteins in male drinkers. *Indian Journal of Medical Research, 96*, 333–337.

Vaswani, M., Hemraj, P., Desai, N. G., & Tripathi, M. (1997). Lipid profile in alcohol dependence. *Indian Journal of Psychiatry, 39*, 24–28.

Verghese, A., Beig, A., Senseman, L. A., Rao, S. S., & Benjamin, V. (1973). A social and psychiatric study of a representative group of families in Vellore town. *Indian Journal of Medical Research, 61*, 618–626.

Walsh, B. & Grant, M. (1985). *Public health implications of alcohol production and trade* (WHO Offset Publication 88) Geneva: World Health Organization.

WHO. (1964). *The ICB-8 Classification of mental and behavioral disorders: Clinical descriptions and diagnostic guidelines*. Geneva: World Health Organization.

WHO. (1980). *Problems related to alcohol consumption: Report of a WHO expert committee* (WHO Technical Report Series 650) Geneva: World Health Organization.

WHO. (1992). *The ICD-10 classification of mental and behavioural disorders: Clinical descriptions and diagnostic guidelines*. Geneva: World Health Organization.

WHO. (1993a). *The ICD-10 classification of mental and behavioural disorders: Diagnostic criteria for research*. Geneva: World Health Organization.

WHO. (1993b). *Annual Report* 1993. New Delhi: WHO Regional Office for Southeast Asia.

WHO. (1994). Press Release WHO/84, Geneva: World Health Organization.

Wig, N. N. (1994). Live sensibly, the rest will follow. *World Health Forum, 15*, 229–231.

Zariwala, M. B. A. & Bhide, S. V. (1994). Mutagenicity of some Indian commercial alcoholic liquor. *Journal of Studies on Alcohol, 55*, 375–379.

Chapter 7

Central and Eastern Europe

Atanas Iontchev

*Here was East and West, North and South. On this street the Tatar prostrated himself,
his face turned toward Mecca, the Jew read the Torah, the German read Luther,
the Pole lit consecrated candles at the foot of the altars in Czestochowa and Ostra
Brama. Here was the center of the earth, the axis of the universe, the accumulation
of brotherhood and hatred, closeness and strangeness, for here were fulfilled the
joint destinies of the peoples most distant one from the other.*

Andrzej Szczypiorski

*Even the relatively straightforward rubric "Eastern Europe" raises hard questions.
. . . Besides the orientalizing undertones which have been exposed as part of an
imperial Occidentalism, the "East" became after Yalta, an official, treaty-sanctioned
Other to the "West". . . . This linguistic curtain may prove as effective as an iron
one in blocking mutual recognition and understanding.*

Randolph Starn

The term "Central and Eastern Europe" has diverse political and social con-
notations beyond the geographical one. Some of the definitions of the region
emphasize an historical evolution: "The area vaguely referred to as Eastern
Europe has no easily defined boundaries, and geographically means the eastern
portion of the continent. But how far? Does it include the western part of Russia
east to the Urals? As a political notion, the term often is applied to the tier of
countries that emerged after the First World War. Personally, with Berend and
Ranki, I feel that Eastern Europe is primarily a historical concept, evolving from

177

the peculiar course of its development" (Rugg, 1985). Other authors are less particular: "Eastern Europe is very diverse. The very question of whether it should be treated as a region—whether there is an Eastern Europe, as distinguished from Central Europe, or East-Central Europe, or Russia—is controversial. So is the question of which peoples, nations, or states should be included if there is a region to be defined. There are no perfect, objective answers to these questions, and I am not offering any in what follows. Whether they are asked, and what answer is offered, depends on whether the questions and answers are useful to specific people at specific times. At most times in history most people have found it itself useful to stress diversity, to focus on the separate experiences of the individual peoples and nations of this part of the world" (Simons, 1993).

In an effort to capture both the diversity and continuity within this region, the present chapter approaches the countries of Central and Eastern Europe as both discrete entities, and as products of larger regional configurations. Consideration is given to the many regional influences (Northern Europe, Eastern Europe, Mediterranean, and so forth) evident in the area. This chapter will examine alcohol's role in the diverse societies known collectively as Central and Eastern Europe. Detailed information will be given about Bosnia and Hercegovina, Bulgaria, Croatia, the Czech Republic, the former Yugoslav Republic of Macedonia, Hungary, Poland, Romania, the Slovak Republic, Slovenia, and Yugoslavia. The countries of ex-Czechoslovakia and ex-Yugoslavia will often be approached as if they were single entities. The figures and table in the chapter relate only to the countries listed above.

The chapter is divided into four sections. The first addresses the historical and cultural factors that have influenced the pattern of alcohol consumption and production in Central and Eastern Europe. The second considers contemporary production and trade of alcohol beverages in the region. This is followed by a section devoted to the problems associated with alcohol consumption and the treatment and facilities available within Central and Eastern Europe to combat them. The last section offers an overview of existing government policies aimed at regulating and controlling alcohol consumption, production, and trade.

INFLUENCES OF HISTORY AND CULTURE ON CONSUMPTION AND PRODUCTION

Influence of Ancient Traditions and Religion

The first historical data about the production and use of beverage alcohol in the lands of Central and Eastern Europe date back to the Hellenic era. The territories of modern Bulgaria, the former Yugoslavia, and Macedonia were once part of the Hellenic cultural domain. The main beverage alcohol produced by the ancient Greeks was grape wine. Divers have recovered beautiful amphoras used as vessels for wine and olives from the wrecks of ancient galleys found close to the shores of Bulgaria and Yugoslavia (in the Black Sea and the Mediterranean).

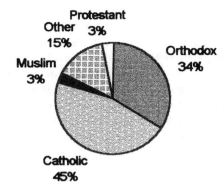

FIGURE 7.1 Religious affiliation, peoples of Central and Eastern Europe. (*Source:* Encyclopaedia Britannica, 1995.)

There are many sources which depict the significance of wine in Hellenic culture and mythology. One of the popular deities in the Greek pantheon was Dionysus—the god of wine and jubilation. The effects of alcohol and drunkenness were used in the stories of the gods and the lives of mortals. Wine was believed to possess spiritual and transcendental power. The poets of ancient times indulged themselves with wine: "I love to sit in the shade with wine to drink, a cake of cheese, goat's milk, and some meat—from a young cow or a kid" (Dawson, 1995, p. 9).

The rise of the Roman Empire and its culture also encompassed the lands and inhabitants of Romania, Hungary, and Czechoslovakia. Like the ancient Greeks, the Romans developed a lavish cuisine and consumed a range of alcohol drinks. They acquired types and products from Egypt, Judea, Thrace, Greece, Iberia, and southern France. The main drinks were wine, beer, and other fermented drinks. For the Romans, meals and drinks were inseparable.

The opulence of the Roman lifestyle contributed to various strategies and procedures for coping with the consequences of excessive alcohol consumption. Ancient recipes are still in use in Bulgaria, Romania, and Yugoslavia. These age-old patterns of consumption have, as we shall see, continued to influence contemporary patterns.

Historical and cultural influences from the distant past were not, however, the only factors that helped form contemporary drinking patterns in Central and Eastern Europe. The role of religion in the evolution of cultural norms and mores should not be underestimated. The territories of Bulgaria and the former Yugoslavia, for example, play host to a mixture of Catholic, Orthodox, and Muslim religions (see Figure 7.1), all of which have exerted their influence on patterns of alcohol consumption.

Religious practices and leaders have strongly influenced contemporary alcohol consumption in many Central and Eastern European countries. When NATO forces arrived in Bosnia in 1994, for example, one of the first steps of the Bosnian Reis-ul-Ulema (Muslim religious leader) was to condemn alcohol consumption and to ask the people to distance themselves from the troops and their attitudes (*The Independent*, 12 October 1994). Another example can be found amongst the migrant construction workers of Bulgaria. These workers, originally from small Muslim villages, work in large cities for about nine months a year. During the active period they live in hotels or lodging houses apart from their families. The stress and unfamiliar environment contribute to enormous daily alcohol consumption. During the remaining three months of the year, they return to their families and Muslim community, and usually refrain from alcohol consumption in accordance with the Koran. In many cases they undergo a slight withdrawal syndrome.

Likewise, the former Yugoslav Republic of Macedonia possesses a religiously diverse population. The ethnic Albanian community in Macedonia is mostly Muslim and officially shares Islam's attitude of strong rejection of alcohol consumption. In the last 40 years, because of the communist suppression of religions, Muslims have become more permissive in practice. "It was a rare event to meet an alcoholic from the Albanian population twenty years ago. By the way, this is not true now. The promise of the strict Muslim prohibition against alcohol brought social-medical problems in that population" (Jovev, 1993, p. 27).

Christian groups throughout Central and Eastern Europe also represent a force in forming today's consumption patterns. Christian clergy and religious organizations are very active in supporting both moderate drinking habits and the treatment of alcohol dependents in Hungary and Poland. Some religious organizations support clubs for people who have recovered from alcohol dependence. The Orthodox Church traditionally does not assist people with alcohol-related problems as a separate group.

Three Historic Regional Patterns of Drinking

Religion and ancient cultural influences represent only a fraction of the many influences that are involved in shaping contemporary drinking patterns. Coupled with geographic and climatic particularities, however, they serve as the foundation of a regional conceptualization of alcohol consumption that further explains contemporary drinking patterns in Central and Eastern Europe. We can distinguish three regional patterns: Mediterranean, Central European, and Northern European. These regional patterns are all represented in Central and Eastern Europe.

Some countries in Central and Eastern Europe, such as Bulgaria and Hungary, have long traditions of wine production and are representative of the Mediterranean pattern. Other countries, such as the Czech Republic, are traditional "beer countries" and exemplify the Central European pattern. Yet others, including Poland, have distilled spirits such as vodka as their favored alcohol beverage, revealing a Northern European pattern. Thus the distinctions between

Mediterranean, Central European, and Northern European traditions that exist in the western parts of Europe are also evident in the countries of Central and Eastern Europe (WHO Regional Office for Europe, 1993).

The Mediterranean Pattern The Mediterranean culture discovered alcohol beverages very early in history and had thousands of years to develop healthy drinking patterns and adequate mores governing alcohol consumption. The legacy of Greco-Roman culture has shaped the drinking patterns of southern Europe. Countries such as Bulgaria, Hungary, Romania, and Yugoslavia illustrate the characteristics of a Mediterranean drinking pattern. The arrival of Christianity did not alter these traditions significantly. Everyday drinking is common. Drinking in the open is acceptable, and taverns play a significant role in society as places for getting together (in many cases the only opportunity for socializing).

In the Balkans, alcohol production and consumption have traditionally been focal points of community life, serving as mechanisms of social integration and reinforcing symbolic ties among local groups. Home meals are served with a glass of wine and some *rakiya* (grape or fruit brandy; *palinka* in Hungary and Romania). Brandy is usually consumed before the meal with salad or appetizers called *meze*. When the drink has a high alcohol content, drinking is accompanied by the consumption of *meze*. Thirty years ago, in a restaurant in Bulgaria or Yugoslavia the construction worker sitting at the next table could be overheard saying that he had had four *rakiyas* for dinner (the *meze* with the drinks were enough for dinner, and were "on the house").

These patterns of drinking have led to a situation in which a relatively large amount of alcohol is consumed without conspicuous intoxication. The "macho" role includes drinking large amounts of alcohol without becoming intoxicated. In rural areas, where wine and brandy are produced, people usually drink wine. The consumption of wine customarily starts at dawn. It is estimated that more than a liter is consumed by dusk. Meals are often taken with wine and sometimes brandy. On special occasions, guests consume different brandies and wines while discussing the virtues of different types of beverage alcohol. In the past, parents fed their babies bread soaked in a mixture of wine and water (the babies used to sleep better after this tonic).

As suggested above, Bulgaria, Hungary, Romania, and Yugoslavia have been wine-producing regions for millennia; and their cultures belong to the Mediterranean tradition where the everyday use of wine is common. Many family and group rituals include the drinking of alcohol, while religious practices and everyday life have adapted to drinking and its consequences. However, attitudes toward drinking can be ambivalent: while society embraces the consumption of alcohol, intoxication in public is considered socially unacceptable. Such attitudes affirm drinking, yet limit the amount of alcohol intake and reduce the frequency of intoxication.

Bulgaria can be used as an almost archetypal example of the Mediterranean pattern. The beginning of alcohol consumption in Bulgaria can be placed somewhere in the millennium before Christ. Ancient inhabitants of the territory produced wine in 2000 B.C. Bulgaria was under Ottoman rule for five centuries, but succeeded in saving its identity as a Christian Orthodox nation, as well as a producer, trader, and consumer of beverage alcohol.

The Central European Pattern   The Central European pattern is also related to an ancient contact with alcohol. The geographical and climatic features of the area determined the production of a different types of beverage alcohol. In terms of consumption, the intake is slow, the beverages are of low alcohol content, and the culture is careful to control intoxication and the circumstances of alcohol consumption.

The Czech Republic is a typical example of the Central European tradition. The main alcohol drink is beer and it is consumed on an everyday basis, although quantities may differ. The beer tradition has its roots in the 13th and 14th centuries. At the turn of the present century, the Czech Republic was highly industrialized and formed part of the Austro-Hungarian Empire. Industrialization continued over a lengthy period, allowing the culture to adapt to the new social reality. Here too, however, alcohol consumption is relatively high. Beer accounts for the bulk of consumption. In the last few years, Czechs have become the biggest per capita consumers of beer in the world, robbing the Germans of that distinction. Figures from 1996 registered annual consumption of beer per capita in the Czech Republic at 160 liters (World Drink Trends, 1997). A 1990 report covering Czechoslovakia as a whole pointed out: "The consumption of beer is especially high in Bohemia (the average for the years 1980–1985 is the highest in the world: 154.0 liters per capita) and in Slovakia it is the consumption of liquors (the average for the years 1980–1985 is the second highest in the world: 13.0 liters per capita)" (Butora, 1990, p. 2).

The Czech culture supports daily drinking of large quantities of beer, and some spirits on special occasions. Pubs are important locations of social life. In the early years of the century, the famous writer Jaroslav Hašek founded a political party that operated from his favorite pub in Prague. The party was preoccupied with the financial burden on the members, which arose from their political discussions accompanied by large quantities of beer. To commemorate Hašek's role in Czech culture, a beer party emerged in Pilsen in 1990 to run for parliamentary elections. The party wanted lower prices, better quality beer, and an annual beer festival. Overall alcohol consumption in the Czech Republic follows the trends in Europe, relative to the increased purchasing power of the population in the last 30 years.

The Northern European Pattern   The Northern European culture accommodated the consumption of alcohol relatively late, after the invention of the alcohol distillation process. This led to the consumption of beverages that contained a high percentage of alcohol. The social environment had difficulty in controlling the intoxication. The pattern of drinking (i.e., drinking spirits fast, to the point of inebriation) was formed in the centuries of hired labor. The workers could ill afford to be drunk during work days. Thus, the habit of "weekend drinking" was instituted. Customarily, the intoxication was severe and had harmful medical consequences in the long term. Research that could explain the relationship of specific medical consequences to this and other types of alcohol abuse would be of considerable interest.

The many influences visible in Poland illustrate the complexity of the history of consumption in Central and Eastern European. Poland was heavily influenced by both Germany and Russia in the formation of its consumption patterns. The following description illustrates the mix of alcohol available and used in Poland. "During the feudal times and as recently as the early part of the eighteenth century, the *dziedzie* (landowner) was largely in charge of the production and distribution of vodka. In addition, he owned the land on which the feudal serfs worked and for which they received wages in the form of coupons redeemable at the *karczma* (local bar). The *karczmas* were forerunners of today's bar, often owned by *dziedzie*, and often rented out. Because Jews were prohibited from owning land, yet literate and sophisticated in handling money, they often managed the *karczma*. The *dziedzie* also owned the *gorzelni* (still) in which the equivalent of today's vodka (*gorzalka*), was distilled from potatoes and rye, as well as the *browarcz* (brewery) where beer was prepared from barley and honey. The *dziedzie* made five times more profit selling alcohol produced from potatoes, rye, barley, and honey than from selling these items on the open market. The tenant, who was the innkeeper, was obliged to sell a quota of alcohol within a specified period of time or pay a heavy fine. Consequently, his patrons' degree of intoxication was irrelevant—what counted was how much money they could spend" (Chase, 1985, p. 420).

A Northern European pattern of drinking can be discerned in Slovakia and Poland (and also in Russia). Polish alcohol consumption can be characterized by "weekend drinking," where people drink large quantities of concentrated alcohol beverages (vodka), and may get drunk once or twice a week. Being drunk is culturally acceptable, but only when the time and place are appropriate. A good description of Polish drinking patterns was published some years ago: "Poles drink in quite a different way from the English and the Welsh. Firstly, they drink mostly spirits—mainly vodka. During each of the last 40 years, more than 60 percent of all alcohol drunk in Poland was spirits. Since foreign spirits, e.g., whisky and cognac, are sold by the government at a much higher price than Polish vodka, most of the spirits consumed is vodka" (Smith, 1982, p. 98). Slovakia also illustrates a Northern European drinking pattern. Although its culture is similar to the Czech culture (Slovakia became a republic in 1992 after the "velvet divorce" of Czechoslovakia), Slovakia has a different tradition of alcohol consumption. In fact, Slovaks' attitudes towards alcohol consumption are closer to those of the Poles: mostly spirits, weekend drinking, and acceptance of drunkenness in public.

The Legacy of State Socialism

While these loose regional characterizations are helpful as a basic tool for characterizing consumption patterns, recent historical occurrences have blurred some of the traditional patterns. Two significant recent influences in Central and Eastern Europe were industrialization and 40 years of state socialism. Because they were interrelated (i.e., they occurred simultaneously, and state socialism encouraged industrialization as a means toward development), the two influences are approached together.

The industrialization and urbanization in the region has transformed the sociocultural context of alcohol consumption. The traditional lifestyle was centered on the extended family, living together, and cultivating family farms. This tradition has given way to the individualism of the industrialized citizen. Following the Second World War, for example, Bulgaria's population was about 30 percent urban; by the 1980s, that figure had reached 60 percent.

These changes disrupted the traditional social networks and changed drinking patterns. The proletarianization of the labor force and the attenuation of community ties have fostered privatism, consumerism, and alcohol abuse. The new individualized life has demanded a deeper understanding of existential needs, potentials, and responsibilities, while isolating people from their childhood social environments. The immense stress of the transition and the lack of a culturally specific means of coping with the new changes resulted in, for example, the world's highest rate of suicide in Hungary and the highest rate of stroke in Bulgaria. These processes may have also contributed to a high per capita consumption of alcohol beverages. Other significant modifications in the patterns of drinking are derived from 40 years of Soviet/Communist rule and the disintegration of that rule in the late 1980s.

In the last 40 years, the regional patterns of drinking were mixed together with different variants, altering the patterns of alcohol consumption. During the period of state socialism one central factor was the growing pervasiveness of the Russian (i.e., Northern European) consumption pattern. In countries formerly characterized by Mediterranean consumption traditions, the use of brandies and vodka became popular. Most of the leaders in these countries underwent many years of training in the Soviet Union and the "Russian way" of drinking became part of the image of a successful person in the communist countries. It has been observed that high-level officials and party leaders often made career moves during parties at which everyone got drunk. Sobriety was unpleasant and threatening to many communist leaders, a perception that stemmed from the belief that drunkenness produces sincerity. This belief affected the structure of career advancement; often, a successful administrative career required an ability and willingness to drink with those who decided who was promoted. Thus, in traditionally Mediterranean cultures, a new type of drinking behavior became acceptable: the everyday consumption of spirits in large quantities, in addition to the usual use of wine as an aperitif or digestive.

As the power of the Soviet Union began to diminish, the validity and sanction of the Russian style of drinking began to be questioned. As early as 1980–81, Solidarność (Solidarity) in Poland accused the government of promoting alcohol as a means of concealing the deeper social problems, while at the same time obtaining more revenue. Under the pressure of this moral challenge, the government tightened alcohol policies. Production decreased and alcohol prices rose remarkably. This policy continued under martial law and was only slightly liberalized during the mid-1980s.

Change was even afoot within the Soviet Union. The alcohol campaign launched in 1985 was symbolically bound up with the policy of perestroika. A moral and public health campaign against alcohol could be viewed as an effort "from above" not only to reduce alcohol-related problems but also to signal the coming of deep political and economic changes.

In other countries of Central and Eastern Europe, Gorbachev's antialcohol campaign was followed with less determination. Nevertheless, in most countries the alcohol question was given higher priority and alcohol policy became more restrictive. In Hungary, the Soviet example legitimized the attempts of some academic circles to increase concern about acute problems, including problems associated with alcohol use (WHO Regional Office for Europe, 1993, p. 5).

The Impact of the 1989–90 Revolutions

The past decade was a time of immense change in political, economic, and moral structures in Central and Eastern Europe. "The 1980s witnessed a deep crisis of the political systems. The beginning of that decade was marked by the Soviet intervention in Afghanistan, the birth of the first independent trade union movement in Poland, and the revival of dissident activities in other countries. Political challenges associated with economic hardship emerged and could not be solved through central planning. Political initiatives were needed for the system to survive" (WHO Regional Office for Europe, 1993, p. 5).

The disintegration of the Soviet empire enabled some countries to develop an independent, democratic political life. For other states, this process was destructive. For example, in Yugoslavia the Soviet breakup triggered military conflict with the war in Bosnia becoming an embarrassing challenge for Western institutions such as NATO and the United Nations. On the other hand, the Czech and the Slovak Republics demonstrated that peaceful separation and good will were possible.

Economic change has produced a crisis in the region that is implicitly related to the previous regimes' national economic structures and Russia's impact on their trade. Traditional trading partners of West European countries (e.g., the Czech Republic and Hungary) were less affected by the Russian market's collapse than were countries such as Bulgaria and Romania, which suffered severely.

The dissolution of societies ruled by the Communist Party left a moral vacuum. In the years of communist regimes, the leadership eroded religion's former role as a moral regulator. The atheistic doctrine of communism replaced religious traditions. While the generation responsible for instituting the current reforms disliked the communist reality, it was not prepared for the free competition of a market economy and democracy. However, the young people adapted better to the crisis period. This difference has also led them to reject the value systems of their parents. In addition, there are signs of a trend towards lower educational levels coupled with higher youth crime rates, increased drug abuse, and other antisocial behaviors. Along with these changes have come changes in the production, distribution, and consumption of alcohol beverages.

After 1989, the restrictions on alcohol production and trade were withdrawn in Russia. As a WHO workshop reported:

> The experiences from the failures have an impact on public attitudes to alcohol control policies. Especially the negative experiences of alcohol policy "from above" during the Gorbachev campaign still create negative attitudes in many countries towards any state regulation of the alcohol market. Alcohol control and concern of alcohol-related problems are associated with the previous regime. Unrestricted marketing and sales of alcohol can (and often are) perceived as symbols of a positive economic development (WHO Regional Office for Europe, 1993, p. 9).

An important issue in understanding the alcohol situation in Central and Eastern European countries is the symbolism involved in drinking Western brands of alcohol beverages, a point also brought out by the WHO workshop. At this workshop it was suggested that Western brands of both alcohol and tobacco had become significant symbols of Western lifestyles. It was argued that this symbolic status was reinforced by Western television programs and advertisements. The elevated position of these products made it all the more difficult for policymakers to control their import, trade, and retail sale. Such products, it was suggested, afforded the people of Central and Eastern Europe a simple means toward getting a feeling of Western lifestyles (WHO Regional Office for Europe, 1993, p. 15).

As the next section indicates, the changes of 1989–90 have also had a significant influence on both production and trade.

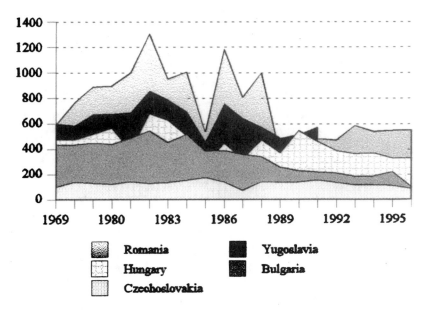

FIGURE 7.2 Wine production in Eastern Europe in 1000 MT per year. (*Source:* FAO Production Yearbook (1969–1996).)

PRODUCTION AND TRADE OF ALCOHOL IN CENTRAL AND EASTERN EUROPE

The production of alcohol beverages in Eastern Europe has long traditions, and it is an important part of the national economy of some countries. Bulgaria, Hungary, Romania, and Yugoslavia are traditional producers of wine and wine products (Figures 7.2 and 7.3). Romania, for example, is the world's 10th largest producer of wine, while Hungary is the 14th and Bulgaria the 18th (*World Drink Trends*, 1997). Central and Eastern European countries are also some of the largest producers of spirits in the world, with the former Soviet Union ranked as the top producer of spirits in the world. The Czech Republic ranks 12th, and Poland 15th (*World Drink Trends*, 1997).

Under communist regimes, the production and trade of alcohol gained the special attention of the ruling parties and was monopolized by the government (i.e., the Communist Party). Moskalewicz (1993) indicated that through the Polish state alcohol monopoly alcohol gained a particular economic significance that had far-reaching consequences for individuals and society alike:

> Its [beverage alcohol] sales provided 10–15% of the state's revenues, often called a "drunken budget." Moreover, beverage alcohol absorbed about one-sixth of the

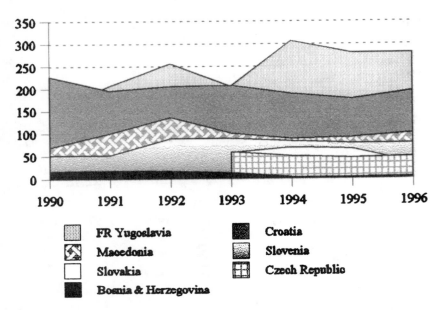

FIGURE 7.3   Wine production in new European republics in 1000 MT per year. (*Source:* FAO Production Yearbooks (1991–1997).

buying power of the population, implying that two months' pay of an average citizen went to buy vodka and, to a lesser extent, wine and beer (Moskalewicz, 1993, p. 265).

Understandably, the governments took good care of the production and sale of alcohol beverages. The export of alcohol yielded even greater profits and "wine" countries expanded their markets in the Soviet Union, Western Europe, Japan, and other overseas markets. In the past eight years, production and trade have undergone a period of crisis. Nevertheless, the trade continued to be substantial.

During the same period, changes in the social structure of the excommunist countries have resulted in the privatization of a large proportion of the alcohol industry. Foreign investments occurred mainly in the beer industry. Only in Macedonia are the production and sale of alcohol beverages still under state monopoly.

Failures in alcohol policy during the 1980s in some of the countries of Central and Eastern Europe also led to the expansion of the black market in alcohol. This formed the basis for the development of a rather "wild market" in alcohol, instead of a Western-style regulated free market, during the transition period (WHO Regional Office for Europe, 1993).

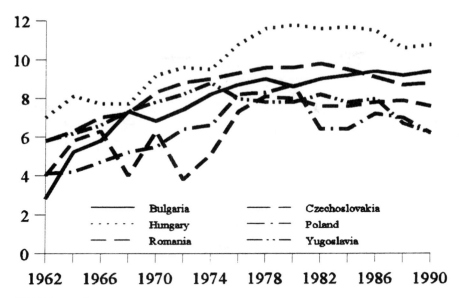

FIGURE 7.4   Per capita consumption of absolute alcohol in some Central and Eastern European countries, 1962–1990. (*Source:* Harkin, Anderson, and Lehto (1995).)

Home production, concealed or underreported in many cases, appeared on an increasing scale in the countries described here as a consequence of the economic crisis. The quality of homemade alcohol was poor, and the incidence of poisoning as a result of the consumption of low-quality alcohol increased. The official statistics, reflected in Figure 7.4, failed to reflect the actual dynamic of alcohol consumption.

ALCOHOL-RELATED PROBLEMS AND THEIR SOLUTIONS

Alcohol-Related Problems

During the stable period of the communist regimes, there was little perception of alcohol-related problems, and the data were limited and not freely available. The WHO database for health indicators contains information on mortality from chronic liver disease and liver cirrhosis for some countries of Central and Eastern Europe (WHO Regional Office for Europe, 1994, p. 3). The mortality from liver diseases is considered an indirect indicator of the trends in alcohol consumption, stemming from the notion that chronic liver failure is contin-

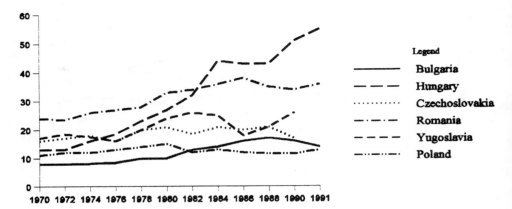

FIGURE 7.5 Standardized death rates on chronic liver disease and liver cirrhosis in some Central and Eastern European countries per 100,000 inhabitants, 1970–1991. (*Source:* WHO Regional Office for Europe (1993).)

gent mostly on alcohol abuse. Reliance upon rates of chronic liver failure as a means for calculating prevalence of alcohol abuse is beginning to wane as other factors, the extended use of fertilizers, for example, are implicated in liver disease.

If we consider consumption and chronic liver failure data from the Central and Eastern European countries we can see some correlation. The data for alcohol consumption (Figure 7.4) shows a significant increase in the 1970s. This seems to be followed by an increase in mortality from chronic liver diseases and cirrhosis (Figure 7.5) at the end of 1980s. That dynamic reflects the natural gap of 15–20 years between the increase of alcohol consumption and the increase of chronic liver mortality.

The data on alcohol morbidity for communist countries were rarely reported to international bodies. The data shown here (Figures 7.6–7.7) were compiled from various sources, mostly reports from professionals in the field of alcohol and drug abuse treatment. The following charts give an overview of the extent of alcohol problems in the countries of Eastern Europe.

Together with the more general problems illustrated in Figures 7.4–7.7, is the significant question of alcohol consumption by young children and adolescents. This is extremely important, since children's metabolisms are highly susceptible to harm from alcohol intoxication, and thus it has long-term health and welfare implications for society's future. Tradition in Southern European countries discourages alcohol consumption in early childhood and limits consumption during adolescence. The achievement of male maturity is usually greeted symbolically by lifting the limitation on alcohol consumption. The majority of

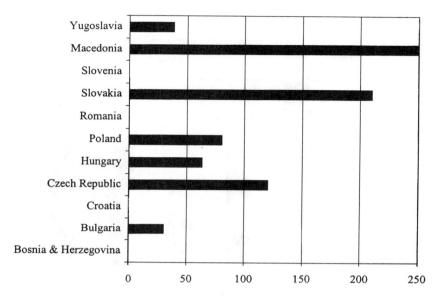

FIGURE 7.6 Alcohol dependence per 100,000 population. (*Source:* Czemy (1993), Harkin et al. (1995), Jovev (1993), Lazarov and Iontchev (1993), Ziolkowski and Ryba-kowski (1993), and Varga (1993).)

schoolchildren drink alcohol, as reported from Bulgaria, Hungary, Poland, and Slovenia. These drinking patterns are usually assumed to represent the patterns of a generic family. On occasion, parents even permit the drinking of spirits. Adolescents copy adult behavior by drinking alcohol at parties. In Slovenia, for example, Kolšek (1994) found the following frequency of alcohol drinking among students 12–15 years of age (Table 7.1).

The picture in the other countries is similar:

- In Poland, between 79 and 85 percent of primary school children have consumed alcohol, and about 16 percent drink regularly (*Warsaw Voice*, 1993).
- In Bulgaria, 55.1 percent of primary school children have drunk alcohol and 1.6 percent consume it regularly (BBC Monitoring Service, 1997).
- In Czechoslovakia, children 9–14 years indicated the following prefer-ences: 69 percent wine, 57 percent beer, and 45 percent liquors. One-third of 9–10 year olds consider eggnog their favorite beverage (Nerad & Neradova, 1991).
- In Hungary, 78.7 percent of boys and 80.4 percent of girls in primary school have tried alcohol, while by the end of high school 100 percent of boys and 94.9 percent of girls have tried it (Nemeth et al., 1994, p. 1455).

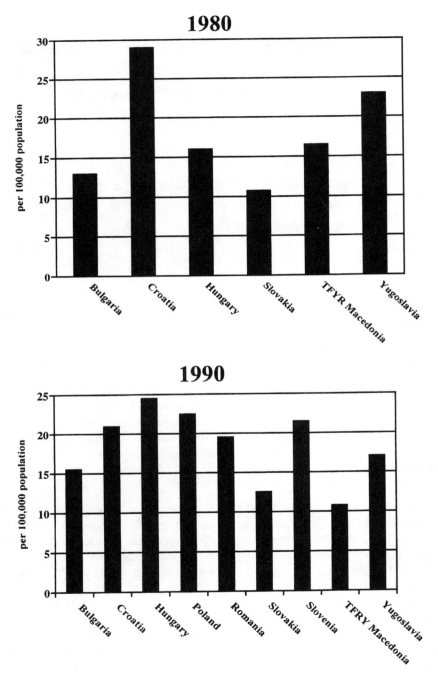

FIGURE 7.7 Traffic accidents involving alcohol. (*Source:* Anderson and Lehto (1995).)

TABLE 7.1 Frequency of alcohol use among junior high students in Slovenia.[1]

Frequency	Percentage of students
More than once a year	51
More than once a month	24.5
More than once a week	14.5
Every day	3.5
Do not drink alcohol	6.0

Understanding Alcohol-Related Problems in Societies: The Influence of Four Models

Excessive alcohol consumption can contribute to medical, psychological, and social problems which may lead to the disease called "alcoholism." Attitudes to and models of alcoholism in Europe have developed over time. Four models have influenced treatment in Central and Eastern Europe: the moral, medical, biopsychosocial, and communist models. Until the turn of the century, the moral model of alcoholism was predominant. In this model, alcoholism and the consequences of drinking were seen as a manifestation of wickedness and were placed in the domain of law enforcement institutions. The development of biological sciences and medicine brought a new understanding of the nature of alcoholism. At the end of the 19th century psychiatry took a huge step forward. Biological explanations for some mental disorders were found and validated. The French psychiatrist, Bail, described anatomical findings among patients suffering from progressive paralysis and showed the relationship between chronic meningitis and mental malfunctioning associated with dementia.

As a result of this new way of thinking about psychiatric disorders and deviant behaviors, a new medical model of alcoholism was developed. The stigma of moral degradation was replaced by a morally neutral view of such disorders as a biological dysfunction. In the years after the First World War, many European countries founded facilities for people with alcohol dependence and opened specialized wards in some psychiatric hospitals. For example, the first alcohol treatment unit in Poland was established in Tarnowskie Gory in 1907; in Czechoslovakia a facility at Tuchlov near Teplice opened in 1924. After the Second World War, in the communist regimes of Central and Eastern Europe, alcoholism was the domain of clinical psychiatry. "In other countries, such as the Soviet Union and Hungary, the concept of alcoholism as a disease is strongly

[1]Reprinted with permission from *Journal of Studies on Alcohol*, Vol. 55, pp. 55–60, 1994. Copyright by Alcohol Research Documentation, Inc., Rutgers Center of Alcohol Studies, Piscataway, NJ 08854.

influenced by a psychiatric approach, referred to as 'biological psychiatry,' which is derived from the study of neurology" (Klingemann, Takala, & Hunt, 1993, p. 222).

In communist countries during the 1950s and 1960s, the totalitarianism of their ideology found expression in a "communist" model of alcoholism. In the words of Klingemann and colleagues, "In the past official ideology in socialist countries of Middle and Eastern Europe claimed that crime, alcoholism, and other forms of 'deviant behavior' would disappear in societies built upon the principles of Marxism–Leninism—a good socialist would not need alcohol. The crime and alcoholism that did exist was attributed to negative infiltration from the class enemy (i.e., capitalism), a relic of former capitalist thought or mental disorder. In any case, the individual, rather than society, was blamed for alcoholism and was typically forced into treatment under the authority of the justice ministry" (Klingemann, Takala, & Hunt, 1993, p. 222). In the USSR a subspecialty in psychiatry called "narcology" was created with a major field known as "alcohol and drug abuse." Narcology was used in all Eastern European countries.

The development of a systems approach in human sciences and biology in the 1970s and 1980s led to a new model of alcoholism: the psychosocial model or model of alcohol-related problems. Many facilities for family therapy, counseling, outpatient treatment, and treatment research operate in Eastern Europe. The predominant public attitude perceives alcoholism as a disease. Most people with alcohol-related problems are referred to psychiatric facilities. In countries where medical care is easily accessible and paid for by the government, the medical professions can more easily promote the medical model of alcoholism. In Bulgaria, for instance, alcohol dependence is classified as a disease and diagnosed patients receive paid leave for the period of inpatient or outpatient treatment. Alcoholic patients are generally treated in psychiatric facilities. There are two psychiatric hospitals that specialize in treatment of alcohol dependents in the village of Mureno and the town of Carvuna. There are also psychiatric dispensaries that operate outpatient facilities for people suffering from alcohol dependence (Lazarov & Iontchev, 1993, p. 1).

Current approaches to the treatment of alcohol dependents are mixed and in many cases three of the models previously described (moral, medical, and biopsychosocial) work in combination. In the last 10 years the diversity of facilities has expanded in response to new political reality and the natural development of science and practice. Treatment and research are now a product of both public (i.e., government) and private initiative. At present, there are six European countries that maintain no national agency for alcohol-related problems: Azerbaijan, Georgia, Italy, Romania, Slovenia, and Ukraine.[2] As a result

---

[2]It should be noted that while Slovenia has no national agency involved in alcohol prevention, it maintains regional agencies. "According to the guidelines of the University Psychiatric Collegiate Body, each psychiatric unit within a general hospital should have a specialized unit

of the difficult economic situation in the Central and Eastern European region, the funding for alcohol research has declined dramatically in the last 10 years. In the communist era all funding was centralized through governmental structures. Now the monolithic governmental structure has gone, and new means of funding and support must be found. Some recently independent countries (e.g., Croatia, Macedonia, Slovenia, Slovakia) do not yet have easily accessible data on the topic.

Common forms of treatment institutions in Central and Eastern Europe are the outpatient and inpatient clinics, which often specialize in the treatment of alcohol- and drug-dependent patients. For example, "In 1990 there were about 180 outpatient centers in the Czech Republic. These institutions conducted 295,357 examinations. Of these, 44,893 were first listed with an alcohol-related diagnosis" (Czemy, 1993, p. 2). At the Croatian Center for Study and Control of Alcoholism, for example, the following numbers of patients are treated annually: 400–600 couples for family therapy or partial hospitalization; 700–800 patients in the Stationery Department; and 500–600 patients in the day-hospital (Lang & Nikolis, 1993). Romania, on the other hand, provides treatment only at psychiatric facilities; only psychiatrists may admit patients, which means that the psychiatric setting is the alcoholic's first contact with treatment (Vrasti & Bucur, 1993).

There are already some nongovernmental organizations and self-help groups in this field, and some international agencies are involved. The programs of the World Health Organization (WHO), and especially the Regional Office for Europe in Copenhagen, play an important role. Furthermore, the United States and other interested countries sponsor many bilateral and multilateral research projects. Since the revolutions of 1989–90, the role of religious organizations has increased. Hungary, for example, has a growing number of nongovernmental facilities that consider such vast therapies as socio-, biblio-, creative, music, and gesture therapies. Occupational and vocational therapy, however, are the most widespread modes of treatment. In Hungary the self-help movement is developing a greater role (Varga, 1993).

Over the past 20 years, various organizations of exalcoholics have gradually developed—AA groups, self-help groups, clubs of exalcoholics, patient clubs, and so forth. The first patient club in Poland was founded in Warsaw in 1948 (Swiatkiewicz, 1992). In the Czech Republic, "thousands of exalcoholics were involved in dozens of sociotheraputic clubs. After the social changes numerous Non Government Organizations (NGOs) have appeared throughout the country. Some of them are interested in the field of alcohol and drug abuse. Most important is, of course, the AA, but foundations like Fit-in, Filia, or Fokus create an alternative to institutional treatment and prevention of alcohol problems"

---

with about 15 percent of its capacity for alcoholism treatment, and a psychiatric dispensary with between 10 and 20 percent of its capacity allocated for alcoholism treatment" (Čebašek-Tratnik, 1992, p. 160).

(Czemy, 1993, p. 4). Likewise in Poland, "It is estimated that there are about 350 Abstainers Clubs and about 400 AA groups. The number of persons involved in both the movements is estimated at 7,000 for the clubs and 6,800 for AA" (Swiatkiewicz, 1992, p. 681).

As indicated above, methods of financing treatment and prevention differ throughout the region. Some Central and Eastern European countries finance treatment through alcohol tax revenues. Poland is one of a few European countries which allocate money from alcohol tax for alcohol-related problems, and especially for the treatment of alcohol-dependent patients. The facilities provided include some 460 outpatient clinics and about 3,300 beds in 70 alcohol treatment units (most of them forming part of psychiatric hospitals) (Ziolkowski & Ribakowski, 1993, p. 1). The Former Yugoslav Republic of Macedonia also allocates money from alcohol production and trade tax revenue for the prevention of alcohol-related problems.

Research into the treatment of alcohol-related problems in Central and Eastern Europe is most often conducted in university psychiatric departments and other specialized treatment facilities. Many countries in the region (Bulgaria, the Czech Republic, and Croatia to name a few) take part in WHO initiatives on alcohol prevention, the promotion of health, early intervention, and so forth.

LEGISLATION, POLICY, AND PREVENTION OF CONSEQUENCES

Eastern European countries have a long history of preventive action against alcoholism. Wald, Morawski, and Moskalewicz (1986) offer an impressive chronology of Polish alcohol policy and movements. Their chronology starts in the late 17th century when F. Jan Stanislaw Papczynski founded the abstemious Order of Marians. The spread of the temperance movement at this time was largely motivated by moral concerns. After the partition of Poland in 1875, temperance, they argue, was linked with patriotism. In 1818 the first Polish scientific study on alcoholism, *On Drunkenness* by Jakub Szymkiewicz, was published. The beginning of the 20th century saw the first surveys on alcohol use by Polish children and youths, as well as the opening of the first Polish treatment center in Tarnowskie Gory in 1907 (Wald, Morawski, & Moskalewicz, 1986).

In other countries, the temperance movement was also a part of national liberation ideology at the end of the 19th century. In the years after the First World War, the recognition of alcoholism as a medical condition was the main manifestation of the shift from the moral to the medical model of alcoholism. It was then that specialized treatment facilities were founded, and the legislation reflected the medical model, including alcoholism in the list of diseases. In the 1950s, in most of the Eastern European countries, new laws were passed providing for treatment of intoxicated people disturbing the community in special facilities. These facilities carried various names: detoxification centers in Czechoslovakia, and sober-up stations in Poland, Bulgaria, and else-where (Smith, 1982). In this type of center, intoxicated people received med-ical care. In Czechoslovakia these centers were under the supervision of the Ministry of Health. "The first was started in 1951, the Anti-Alcoholism De-partment of the Charles University in Prague. This was the first detoxification health care center anywhere in the world, and its founder, Dr. Jaroslav Skala, is known by the nickname of 'Father of the Detox'" (Nerad & Neradova, 1991, p. 86).

In some countries, the centers were under police supervision, and a fine was imposed at the time of discharge. From the legal viewpoint, the treatment of patients with alcohol-related problems followed one of two main modalities of treatment: voluntary and compulsory. While there are differences among the countries, they are not significant. The basic point is that only medical consider-ations, usually stated in court, could lead to compulsory treatment. In Bulgaria, for example, the process involves the district attorney, the local police precinct, a medical expert, and the local court, all of them subsequent to a civil action by relatives. Treatment, even if compulsory, is covered by paid leave of absence from work.

In the 1970s and 1980s, many governments recognized alcoholism as an important problem for their countries' economy and undertook preventive action. This mostly took the form of preventive programs in the work environment and schools, coupled with mass media campaigns. In the late 1980s the Gorbachev administration in the USSR started a restrictive program limiting the sale of alcohol beverages to fixed hours and locations. Restaurants and bars served alcohol according to a schedule prescribed by the authorities. After 1989, the countries of Central and Eastern Europe joined the European Union (EU) in its Action Plan for Prevention of Alcoholism in Europe and harmonized their legislation with the requirements of the EU. At present, all countries in the region considered here have developed national alcohol policies, and in all of these countries but Romania and Slovenia, there are national agencies working on alcohol prevention. Most of the countries are participants in various WHO programs under its policy of Health for All by the Year 2000, such as the health-promoting schools project.

Drinking and Driving Regulations

Throughout Central and Eastern Europe, drinking and driving legislation is strict. In the Czech Republic, Romania, and Slovakia the authorities tolerate no alcohol in the blood. Croatia, the former Yugoslav Republic of Macedonia, and Slovenia maintain the zero alcohol standard only for professional drivers, with a less stringent upper limit for blood alcohol concentration (BAC) of 50 milligrams per 100 milliliters for other drivers. Romania frequently uses random breath testing. Bulgaria, Hungary, and Poland tolerate a BAC of 50 milligrams per 100 milliliters for all drivers.

Violators of drunk driving laws can, in all Central and East European countries, have their licence suspended after the first offense, while the penalty varies depending on how far the driver exceeded the BAC limit. The Bulgarian authorities use traffic police with breathalyzers and subsequent blood testing in designated hospital laboratories to enforce its drinking and driving laws. For second offenses, Bulgarian authorities may permanently revoke the individual's driving license.

State Regulation of the Beverage Alcohol Industry

All Central and Eastern European countries enforce a minimum age requirement of 18 for the purchase of alcohol in public places. Restrictions on the sale and advertising of alcohol beverages have shifted in the last 10 years. There is a broad range of policies on the advertisement of alcohol beverages. Slovenia has a total ban on alcohol advertisement. Poland, Romania, and Macedonia all have limited restrictions, primarily geared toward the broadcast media. While Hungary has official restrictions, they are only loosely enforced. In Slovakia alcohol advertisements are limited through the use of a voluntary code. Bulgaria has the most liberal regulations, permitting most forms of alcohol beverage advertisement.

Privatization of the production and sale of alcohol and the attempts of the administrations to continue to work with older models is leading to rapid changes in legislation. The major trend is the adaptation of legislation to EU norms, reflecting the countries' aspirations to join the EU. As with advertising, there is a wide array of policies on the regulation and licensing of the production and sale of beverage alcohol. All the Central and Eastern European countries have partially or completely privatized production and sale except for Macedonia, where these functions are still under state monopoly. Among the other countries the spectrum of licensing and regulation policies regarding both production and sale is broad. In Croatia, for example, production and distribution are unlicenced, while Slovakia and Hungary regulate production and sale through various licenses and taxes.

With respect to pricing, the changes have had varying effects in the different countries. Prices of drinks within the past 10 years have, for example, increased in Poland, Romania, Slovenia, and Macedonia, while they have remained stable in the Czech Republic and Croatia (Harkin, Anderson, & Lehto, 1995, p. 50). The illegal production of alcohol beverages has risen significantly in the Central and East European countries. At the moment the governments can only guess at its scale. As indicated above, there have been some attempts to limit this phenomenon. Along with the general regulation of the market, other regulations are being devised that are specifically aimed at decreasing illegal alcohol production and consumption—special labeling, excise bands, police seizure of illegal factories, and so on.

In the absence of effective regulation and control of alcohol retail, whole-sale, and import trade, there are several problems that seem to be particularly important:

- Large-scale smuggling of alcohol beverages;
- The exploitation of loopholes in new foreign trade legislation to import alcohol without paying duties and taxes;
- Trade in low-quality alcohol, sometimes containing dangerous levels of methanol or other impurities;
- Trade in counterfeits of well-known western brands of beverages;
- Trade in beverages with extremely high alcohol content, e.g., German Royal Vodka, with a 70 percent alcohol content, which is one of the favorite spirits at the moment in Poland, the Baltic countries, and Russia.

CONCLUSION

The Central and Eastern European region has a long and rich tradition in the production, trade, and consumption of alcohol beverages. The heritage of an-cient cultures and more recent historical developments have determined three basic drinking patterns observable throughout European civilization: the Mediter-ranean, the Central European, and the Northern. Production and trade of alcohol beverages are an important part of the economy for most Central and East-ern European countries. The current per capita annual consumption of alcohol is relatively high, and the Czech Republic is the reigning world champion in beer consumption. The social response to the consequences of excessive al-cohol consumption is complex and clearly depicted in the culture, attitudes, and the behavior of the different countries. The treatment and prevention of alcoholism have centuries-old traditions, and are among the region's contri-butions to European civilization. Over the years, four models of alcoholism can be discerned according to the prevailing philosophy at a given time: the moral model, the medical (biological) model, the bio-psycho-social model, and the "communist" model. The first three models are applied in conjunction in Central and Eastern Europe at present, and corresponding institutions exist to care for the alcohol-related problems. The courage and wisdom of the peoples of Central and Eastern Europe in today's difficult economic circumstances are the best promise for the constructive coexistence of alcohol and society in the future.

REFERENCES

Anderson, P. & Lehto, J. (1995). *Evaluation and monitoring of action on alcohol: Targets, indicators, and monitoring and reporting systems for action on alcohol* (WHO Regional Publications, European Series 59). Copenhagen: World Health Organization, Regional Office for Europe.

BBC Monitoring Service—Eastern Europe. (1997, March 4). Bulgaria: Drug and alcohol use among Bulgarian minors growing, but not that terrible yet.

Butora, M. (1990). *Alcoholism in Czechoslovakia in the last thirty years: A neglected burden for the reforms.* XII World Congress of Sociology, Madrid, July.

Čebašek-Tratnik, Z. (1992). Organizacija zdavnijehja odvistnosti od alkohola v Sloveniji (The organization of treatment of alcohol dependence in Slovenia). *Zdravstreni Vestnik, 61,* 159–161.

Chase, C. (1985). Alcohol consumption—An indicator of malfunction in contemporary Poland. *East European Quarterly, 18,* 415–429.

Czemy, L. (1993). *Alcoholism treatment and alcoholism related research in the Czech Republic.* Didactic Workshop on Alcoholism Treatment Research and Evaluation, June 16–19. San Antonio, TX: National Institute on Alcohol Abuse and Alcoholism.

Daly, E. (1994, October 12). Bosnia: Iman tries to ban beer and bacon. *Independent,* p. 11.

Dawson, I. (1995). *Food and Feasts in Ancient Greece.* Parsippany, NJ: New Discovery Books.

Encyclopaedia Britannica: Britannica Book of the Year 1994. (1995). Chicago, IL.

FAO Production Yearbook. (1969–1996). FAO Statistics Series 125. Rome: Food and Agriculture Organization of the United Nations.

FAO Production Yearbook. (1991–1997). FAO Statistics Series 125. Rome: Food and Agriculture Organization.

Harkin, A., Anderson, P., & Lehto, J. (1995). *Alcohol in Europe—A Health Perspective.* Copenhagen: WHO Regional Office for Europe.

Jovev, J. (1993). *Addiction Diseases.* Parallel 23 (monograph). Skopje, Macedonia: Publishing House.

Klingemann, H., Takala, J., & Hunt, G. (1993). The development of alcohol treatment systems: An international perspective. *Alcohol Health & Research World, 17,* 221–227.

Kolšek, M. (1994). Alcohol consumption among junior high school students in the community of Litija, Slovenia. *Journal of Studies on Alcohol, 55,* 55–60.

Lang, B. & Nikolis, J. (1993). Didactic Workshop on Alcoholism Treatment Research and Evaluation. Center for Study and Control of Alcoholism and Other Addictions, 16–19 June. San Antonio, TX: National Institute on Alcohol Abuse and Alcoholism.

Lazarov, F. & Iontchev, A. (1993). *Alcohol treatment and treatment research in Bulgaria.* Didactic Workshop on Alcoholism Treatment Research and Evaluation, 16–19 June. San Antonio, TX: National Institute on Alcohol Abuse and Alcoholism.

Moskalewicz, J. (1993). Privatization of the alcohol arena in Poland. *Contemporary Drug Problems, 20,* 263–275.

Nemeth, J., Swaim, R., Katona, E., & Oetting, E. (1994). Substance abuse among Hungarian students. *International Journal of Addictions, 29,* 1443–1467.

Nerad, J. & Neradova, L. (1991). Alcohol and drug problems in Czechoslovakia. *Journal of Substance Abuse Treatment, 8,* 83–88.

Rugg, D. S. (1985). *Eastern Europe.* London: Longman.

Simons, T. W. (1993). *Eastern Europe in the Postwar World.* New York: St. Martin's Press.

Smith, R. (1982). Polish lessons on alcohol policy. *British Medical Journal, 284,* 98–101.

Swiatkiewicz, G. (1992). Self-help abstainer clubs in Poland. *Contemporary Drug Problems, 19,* 677–687.

Varga, G. (1993). *Data on alcohol-related problems, therapy, and research in Hungary.* Didactic Workshop on Alcoholism Treatment Research and Evaluation, 16–19 June. San Antonio, TX: National Institute on Alcohol Abuse and Alcoholism.

Vrasti, R. & Bucur, M. (1993). *On the treatment of alcoholism in Romania and related features.* Didactic Workshop on Alcoholism Treatment Research and Evaluation, 16–19 June. San Antonio, TX: National Institute on Alcohol Abuse and Alcoholism.

Wald, I., Morawski, J., & Moskalewicz, J. (1986). Alcohol and alcohol problems research in Poland. *British Journal of Addictions, 81,* 729–734.

Warsaw Voice. (1993, October 10). Young people and alcohol, p. 7.

WHO Regional Office for Europe. (1993). *Alcohol policy during extensive socioeconomic change.* Report on a workshop on alcohol and market economy, Krakow, Poland, 4–5 June.

World Drink Trends. (1997). *International Beverage Alcohol Consumption and Production Trends.* Henley-on-Thames: NTC Publications.

Ziolkowski, M. & Rybakovski, J. (1993). *Alcohol dependence in Poland: Current situation, treatment, and research.* Didactic Workshop on Alcoholism Treatment Research and Evaluation, 16–19 June. San Antonio, TX: National Institute on Alcohol Abuse and Alcoholism.

Chapter 8

Russia

Andrei Vroublevsky and Judith Harwin

In its Constitution, the World Health Organization (WHO) defines health as "a state of complete physical, mental and social well-being and not merely the absence of disease or infirmity." This aspiration could not be further removed from the situation in Russia today. The nation's health is in a critical state. Most dramatic and disturbing of all are the recent data on mortality and life expectancy. In 1994, the average length of life in Russia was 57.6 years for men and 71.2 years for women (*Sovershenno Secretno*, 1995); only seven years earlier the figures were 64.9 and 74.6 years, respectively. Taking a longer view, the picture 30 years ago was quite different. In the mid 1960s, Russia's mortality rates were broadly similar to those of Japan and the U.S. (Chen, Wittgenstein, & McKeon, 1996). Today life expectancy has plummeted to levels found in developing countries such as India and Bangladesh, although the latest figures suggest a slight leveling off for men (MONEE Project Database, 1995, 1996). The significant decrease in male life expectancy is closely connected with the rise in mortality rates from cardiovascular diseases and accidents. Here the increasing stress associated with economic and political instability, and the attendant increase in alcohol abuse, play a very important role (Leon et al., 1997).

Alcohol is a well-known traditional pharmacological agent for coping with stress, which often contributes to people's greater consumption of alcohol, and accordingly, puts them at higher risk of cardiovascular disorders and accidents that can lead to premature death. Indeed, alcohol is estimated to account for 20 percent of premature deaths (Barr & Field, 1996). This reason alone would merit a discussion of the role of alcohol in Russian society today, but the issues go further and raise basic questions of policy, both present and future.

Russia's alcohol situation today confronts society with a major public policy crisis. Consumption levels are high, alcohol-related health morbidity has increased in the last few years, and so have a wide range of social problems from alcohol-related crime to suicides. The situation calls for a major public policy intervention as many have been arguing for some time. But what has been the government's response to the escalation of harm, and how can lessons learned from the past be applied to tackle the future effectively? These are the main questions that this chapter will seek to address, focusing particularly on the last 15 years—the watershed years for Russia, as they encompass the collapse of the old political order and the shift to democratization and market reforms. The authors argue that it is impossible to understand the trends in alcohol consumption and the public response without an appreciation of the wider political and economic environment and the legacy of the past. Russia's alcohol problems today mirror all the major restructuring issues facing policymakers, since they raise basic questions of the proper role of the state and the market. In the current drastic economic situation, it seems highly unlikely that the chaotic situation, in relation to alcohol consumption and policy, will be brought under control in the near future.

The chapter is divided into four main sections. First, it reviews drinking patterns and public policy in the final years of the socialist regime. It then reviews current consumption trends, and goes on to analyze their relationship to a range of indicators of medical and social dysfunction. In the final sections it considers the implications for future public policy and draws brief conclusions.

LESSONS FROM THE PAST: CONSUMPTION TRENDS IN THE LAST YEARS OF SOCIALISM

High levels of alcohol consumption, particularly the widespread use of spirits, are deeply ingrained in Slavic culture, especially among Russian males. The widespread cultural tolerance for heavy drinking may help to explain why the Communist Party decided to tackle alcohol-related harm only three times during the past 40 years. It adopted antidrunkenness measures in both 1958 and 1972; more than 7 million people were picked up from the streets by the police after the resolution of 1972 in a single year (*Sovershenno Secretno*, 1995). However, it was the Gorbachev antialcohol campaign of 1985–87 which was the most comprehensive attack on alcohol ever to be launched by the Party. Indeed, Gorbachev was strongly and personally committed to the campaign. While it was conceived with the best of intentions, its short-term successes were far outweighed by its long-term negative repercussions. In 1984 consumption levels were at their highest, just before the new antialcohol legislation of 1985 was adopted. According to data from the Russian Federation State Committee on Statistics (1993), per capita consumption in 1984 was 10.45 liters of absolute alcohol (see Table 8.1).

TABLE 8.1 Per capita alcohol consumption, 1984–1991.

Year	Absolute alcohol (liters)
1984	10.45
1985	8.80
1986	5.16
1987	3.90
1988	4.40
1989	5.29
1990	5.56
1991	5.57

Source: Russian Federation State Committee on Statistics (1993).

By 1987 consumption had fallen sharply to a low of 3.9 liters. These data are based on the sale of all types of beverage alcohol. The reduction was achieved by draconian measures possible only in a society where the state holds total power and is the major owner of land and property. Between 1985 and 1987 vineyards totaling 265,000 hectares of land were destroyed in the USSR, with a value of 2 billion roubles (in 1991 prices). At the same time 20 beer production plants with modern imported equipment were shut down and practically all the hop plantations needed to produce high-quality beer were destroyed.

Production of vodka and wines fell by more than one-half in the former Soviet Union and exports also dropped substantially, thereby decreasing the considerable income derived by the state from the alcohol industry. However, alcohol consumption also fell, as did some alcohol-related problems such as suicide rates (Varnik & Wasserman, 1992). There is also evidence to suggest that alcohol mortality declined over this period, especially among males. Over the 1984–87 period deaths from alcohol-related causes in the Russian Federation dropped from 23.0 to 9.1 per million population. This meant a substantial decline in mortality from conditions such as alcoholic cirrhosis of the liver, alcohol poisoning, chronic alcoholism, and alcoholic psychosis (Ryan, 1995).

It was however, a pyrrhic victory. Most commentators are in agreement that Gorbachev's campaign had wide-ranging and long-lasting repercussions, most of them negative. In the first place, the campaign did not even achieve the drop in consumption that the official figures appeared to suggest. A study carried out by researchers at the Institute of Psychiatry, Russian Academy of Medical Sciences (Ministry of Health, 1994), found that even during the period of maximum alcohol regulation (1985–87) real per capita alcohol consumption decreased by less than 25 percent, from 14.2 to 10.7 liters (see Table 8.2).

This study, conducted in 25 regions of Russia with a population of 57.6 million people, showed that while the level of illicit spirit production was relatively stable in the three years preceding the Gorbachev campaign, it shot up

**TABLE 8.2   Per capita absolute alcohol consumption in
25 regions of Russia, 1981–1992.**

Year	Total (liters)	Officially recorded (liters)	Unrecorded (liters)	Unrecorded (as % of total)
1981	13.7	10.7	3.0	21.9
1982	13.4	10.4	3.0	22.4
1983	14.1	10.6	3.5	24.8
1984	14.2	10.8	3.4	23.9
1985	13.3	9.1	4.2	31.6
1986	10.6	5.1	5.4	50.9
1987	10.7	4.2	6.5	60.8
1988	11.0	4.6	6.4	58.2
1989	11.8	5.6	6.2	52.5
1990	11.8	5.8	6.0	50.9
1991	12.6	6.3	6.3	50.0

Source: Ministry of Health (1994, pp. 37–40).

between 1985 and 1987. It reached a maximum in 1987 of 6.5 liters, a stagger-
ing increase of some 90 percent in unrecorded per capita alcohol consumption
from the prevailing level of 3.0–3.5 liters between 1981 and 1984.

The campaign also had an impact on patterns of consumption and the resulting trends have persisted into the 1990s. According to official data, in 1984
beer was the preferred drink, followed by wine, and with spirits in third place.
But by 1987, consumption of spirits had moved into second place while wine
drinking had fallen. This change is explained partly by the reduced availability
of cheap wines, which had been so popular before the start of the Gorbachev
campaign, and by the decline in access to good-quality, cheap beer and the
general restrictions introduced under the antialcohol campaign. These official
figures, based on state trade data, are likely to distort the real picture, because
they do not include home-brewed alcohol, usually spirits, which are equal in
strength to vodka. The acute shortages of sugar reported during this period were
widely attributed to the rise in home-brewed spirits. Data from the USSR State
Committee on Statistics show that in 1987 1.4 million tons of sugar were used to
produce two billion liters of illicit spirits (with the same proof levels as vodka)
(*Rossiyskaya Gazeta*, 1992).

Thus the policies pursued in the Gorbachev campaign, although lessening
the amount of licit alcohol consumed, encouraged illicit production and resulted
in increased consumption of illicit and potentially dangerous alcohol. Apart
from the massive black market that ensued, the quality of alcohol deteriorated
and the government lost massive sums in tax revenue. The campaign also had
profoundly negative political consequences. Many commentators believe that it
damaged relations with the wine-producing countries of the South—Moldova
and Georgia in particular—contributing, some claim, to the rise of national

liberation movements in these two countries (Gerner, 1995). Certainly it created fertile ground for the subsequent deregulation that followed in the transition years by hardening public opinion against state interventionism (Loukomskaia, 1997).

THE TRANSITION YEARS 1989–1995

Between 1990 and 1995, per capita consumption of alcohol more than doubled. According to a recent report from the Russian Presidential Commission on Women, the Family, and Demography, average per capita consumption has now reached 13 liters per year, 5 liters more than the level WHO considers dangerous (*Moscow Times*, 5 May 1997). The Russian Longitudinal Monitoring Survey, which is a periodic survey of households, found that consumption peaked at 60 grams per day in 1993, at the height of the most difficult transition years for Russia. It has fallen back somewhat since then, though levels remain relatively high at approximately 40 grams per day (*Moscow Times*, 5 May 1997). Interestingly, this same survey found that there had been a change in the numbers who reported drinking beverage alcohol over the period 1992–96, the total dropping from 85 percent to 71 percent of all men in 1996 with a corresponding fall among women from 60 percent to 44 percent. It is unclear how reliable these self-reported figures are; they may well underestimate true consumption levels.

Some surveys suggest that most of the alcohol consumed is spirits, which are estimated to have reached a share of around 80 percent of all beverage alcohol drunk today (Loukomskaia, 1997). A wide range of new vodkas has come on to the market. The multinational giant Smirnoff reentered Russia in competition with its own Russian relative, Smirnov, which stayed in Russia after the 1917 Revolution. Quite remarkably, by 1995 Russia was Smirnoff's third largest market after the United States and the United Kingdom according to the Economist Intelligence Unit (1995). The fact that its vodka costs $10 a bottle in comparison with the more typical price of the equivalent of $1.5–2 for national products has not hindered its growth on the Russian market. Vodka generally has become a fashionable drink. Some new brands have even been named after well-known Russian personalities. For example, Zhirinovsky and Kalashnikov both now have vodkas named after them, a somewhat dubious appeal, perhaps, to nationalist sentiment.

Alcohol has become far more available. Until new measures were introduced in the summer of 1997, it was sold in the small kiosks that are found on most Russian streets and could be bought at any time of day or night. It has also become far cheaper, in relation to both average wages and food costs. When compared with food costs, the real price of alcohol fell by two-thirds over the 1990–95 period (*Trud*, 1996), the price of strong drinks remained relatively low. This is partly because liquor stores and other trade establishments receive beverage alcohol in large quantities from wholesale markets within the

Commonwealth of Independent States (CIS), Belarus, Moldova, and Ukraine, and also from illegal and semilegal Russian production. As might be expected, the wholesale prices in these markets were low at about one-half that of the official Russian alcohol-producing factories. These lower prices were partly the outcome of more favorable taxation and duties in other CIS countries compared to Russia. The consequence of these fiscal policies has been to precipitate a shift to cheap alcohol, often of low quality. According to tentative data, the share of the alcohol market controlled by the state in 1995 was less than 50 percent. The president of the distilling lobby Spirtprom has claimed that counterfeit spirits now occupy 80 percent of the spirits market.

MEDICAL AND SOCIAL CONSEQUENCES OF ALCOHOL USE AND ABUSE TODAY

Medical Aspects of Alcohol Abuse

The part played by excessive alcohol intake in medical and social dysfunction today is a crucial issue, but problems with data collection and measurement make the determination and interpretation of underlying trends very difficult. This is particularly the case with some of the medical evidence on trends relating to alcoholism and alcoholic psychosis. For example, the official statistics for alcoholism incidence (all new cases) and prevalence (the total number of registered cases) seem to suggest that both conditions are less frequent than 10 years ago (see Table 8.3).

However, these figures may be misleading in the sense that they partly reflect the decline in the availability of services for alcohol dependents since 1989. As can be seen from Table 8.4, the number of specialized hospitals, beds, outpatient departments, and physicians has diminished substantially because of a range of political, economic, and social factors.

Moreover, the official figures are not supported by epidemiological survey evidence. While the proportion of the population officially recorded for alcoholism in 1990 was 1.8 percent, the Epidemiological Department of Russia's State Research Center on Addictions calculated a real rate at least 1.7–2 percent higher. This higher figure would suggest that between 3 and 3.5 percent of the population should be recorded for alcoholism. But even the official figures paint an extremely worrying picture. When the data are broken down by sex, males recorded and treated for alcoholism in 1990 constituted 5 percent of the able-bodied population. While the incidence of female alcoholism is considerably lower than for males, the women's share in the overall incidence of alcoholism is rising. In 1993 they represented some 30 percent of all new cases (see Table 8.3). Until that year female alcoholism had been falling from its 1985 peak. What is more, as Table 8.3 shows, the share of alcoholic psychosis appears to be increasing among all new cases of alcoholism. The proportion of alcoholic psychosis rose by one-third from 1993 to 1994, when the level was 3.5 times

TABLE 8.3 Prevalence and incidence of alcoholism and alcoholic psychosis in Russia (per 100,000 population).

Year	Incidence					Prevalence					Incidence		Prevence	
	A	AP	AP/A	FA/A	AA/A	A	AP	AP/A	FA/A	AA/A	FA	AA	FA	AA
1976	181.0	25.0	13.8			995.0								
1980	244.0	27.0	11.1			1461.0								
1983	264.1	21.1	8.0			1793.6	37.1	2.1	n.a.	n.a.	n.a.	n.a.	n.a.	n.a.
1984	243.5	20.5	8.4	23.8	4.6<	1802.0	35.4	2.0	21.9	1.0	57.9	11.2	395.0	17.8
1985	266.1>	16.7	6.3	24.1	8.6	1959.2	29.2	1.5	21.8<	1.3>	64.2>	23.0>	427.1	25.3>
1986	242.5	6.9	2.8	24.7	9.3>	1985.7	14.3	0.7	22.4	1.2	60.0	22.6	445.6	24.6
1987	224.0	5.5	2.4<	24.1	9.0	2013.5>	11.7	0.6	24.4>	1.1	54.0	20.2	491.3>	22.3
1988	198.9	5.1<	2.6	23.3	7.8	2005.5	10.9<	0.5<	22.9	0.9	46.4	15.6	458.7	18.8
1989	190.5	7.5	3.9	21.9<	7.6	1886.8	14.7	0.8	22.9	0.9	41.7	14.4	433.0	16.4
1990	152.0	9.7	6.4	24.4	6.1	1790.6	17.5	1.0	22.9	1.0	37.1	9.3	410.7	18.7
1991	115.3	10.5	9.1	25.9	6.7	1727.5	18.7	1.1	23.4	1.1	29.9	7.7	403.9	18.4
1992	103.3<	13.3	12.9	27.6	9.0	1658.5	22.3	1.3	23.8	0.8	28.5<	9.3	394.4<	13.4
1993	145.4	32.1	22.1	29.1>	5.2	1656.8	47.6	2.9	24.2	0.6<	42.3	7.6<	400.5	10.6<
1994	160.?	47.?	29.?	n.a.	n.a.	1648.?	68.?	4.?	n.a.	n.a.	n.a.	n.a.	n.a.	n.a.

Source: Department of Medical Statistics, Ministry of Health.
A = All alcoholism in total, including alcohol psychoses
AP = Alcoholic psychosis only
FA = Female alcoholism
AA = Adolescent alcoholism
< = Minimum level
> = Maximum level

209

TABLE 8.4 Services for alcoholics in Russia.

Indicator	1989	1992	1993
Number of hospitals	18	13	12
Number of outpatient departments	321	247	233
Number of beds	81,160	43,309	38,418
Number of physicians	5,349	4,006	3,944

Source: Department of Medical Statistics, Ministry of Health.

higher than in 1984. This is a worrying trend, which may indicate that cases are becoming more severe.

These national trends mask important regional variations for both alcoholism and alcoholic psychosis. In 1992 the highest prevalence of alcoholism was recorded in some areas of the far east (especially Kamchatka, Magadan, and Sakhalin), western Siberia, central Russia and the northwest region. Areas with low rates in 1992 included some areas of the North Caucasus and the Volga region (see Table 8.5).

Similar regional variations were also found in the incidence of alcoholic psychosis. In 1984, continuing a pattern already in evidence in the 1970s, the highest rates were found in the far east of Russia while the lowest levels were recorded in some North Caucasian territories. These trends were maintained in 1992, the far east region remaining an area with some of the highest rates—it included parts of eastern Siberia, the northwest region, and also central Russia. But even though these data point to underlying continuities in the trends, there are also regions where the correlation does not hold well. For example, Altai Territory had a high prevalence of alcoholism but a low rate of alcoholic psychosis, while the converse was true of Orel. More work needs to be done to explain these interregional variations and trends over time. Earlier studies have highlighted the influence of local tradition and culture, the rural/urban divide, the availability of services, and the numbers of migrants (Urakov & Mirosničenko, 1989). All these factors can increase or decrease the level of risk in a given area. For example, one study of inhabitants of the far north of the former Soviet Union found that rates of uncontrolled drinking were far higher among migrants than in the indigenous population (Urakov & Mirosničenko, 1989).

The role of alcohol in mortality is one of the most closely investigated topics at the present time. Building on earlier inquiries (UNICEF, 1994; Ryan, 1995), Leon and colleagues were the latest to examine the interrelationship between alcohol and mortality trends (Leon et al., 1997). The authors analyzed the 10-year period 1984–94, which coincided with marked fluctuations in alcohol consumption as well as changes in mortality rates. They concluded that alcohol abuse does indeed play a significant part in mortality patterns from a wide range of causes, including alcohol poisonings, accidents, and violence. In all of these causes of death, the highest rates occurred in the young and middle-aged pop-

TABLE 8.5 Comparative estimates of indicators of alcoholism in different areas of Russia, 1984 and 1992 (per 100,000 population).

Area/territory	1984			1992		
	Prevalence	Incidence	Psychosis-incidence	Prevalence	Incidence	Psychosis-incidence
Altai	2589.0	392.0	8.0	2352.0	124.1	7.5
St. Petersburg	1871.0	170.0	33.0	1462.9	95.3	20.1
Orel	1766.0	190.0	41.0	1928.2	184.3	7.1
Perm	2512.0	237.0	20.0	1920.6	93.6	18.8
Lipetsk	2262.0	234.0	28.0	2074.2	130.7	9.5
Astrakhan	1766.0	237.0	29.0	1650.5	116.6	14.6
Tula	1879.0	208.0	33.0	2404.0	74.5	14.4
Murmansk	2058.0	243.0	25.0	1831.9	111.5	27.2

Source: Based on unpublished data collected for the Ministry of Health under regulations requiring each area to present annual information on these indicators. At the end of each year, the data are aggregated to produce overall indicators for Russia.

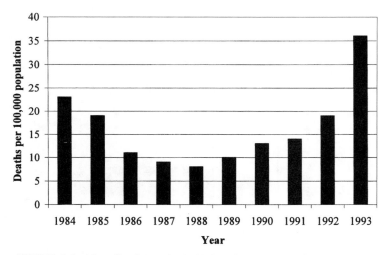

FIGURE 8.1 Mortality from alcohol-related causes in Russia, 1984–93.

ulation (under 45 years of age). This is consistent with the findings elsewhere, that alcohol poisoning resulting in death is less common in older than younger age groups. The authors also implicated excessive drinking in a range of other causes of mortality such as infections and parasitic diseases as well as different forms of coronary heart disease—principally hemorrhagic stroke, cardiomyopathy, and arrhythmias. Of particular interest is their tentative conclusion that it is the pattern of binge drinking, as well as the high consumption levels, that is resulting in the high rates of the specific forms of coronary heart disease noted above.

Further support for this strong and growing interrelationship between alcohol abuse and mortality trends is shown in Figure 8.1. The alcohol mortality rate was lowest in the 1986–89 period (8.8–10.6 per 100,000 population) but rose after 1990 to 35.9 per 100,000 population in 1993, four times as high as in 1988, and significantly higher than 1984 levels. Statistics show that one-half of all lethal accidents other than traffic accidents in the city of Moscow in 1995 involved people in a state of acute alcohol intoxication (*Arguments and Facts*, 1996).

Figure 8.2 shows that mortality from accidental alcohol poisoning in Russia was also at its lowest from 1987 to 1989. It then increased very significantly, particularly from 1992 onwards. In 1994 the mortality level was much higher than in 1984, reaching 36.9 per 100,000 population (compared to 19.6/100,000 in 1984). In 1995, 72.5 percent of all deaths connected with acute poisoning (except suicides) in Moscow city (2,661 of 3,668) were caused by alcohol or alcohol-substitute intake (*Arguments and Facts*, 1996). Some experts believe that alcohol is responsible for more than 500,000 deaths every year in Russia

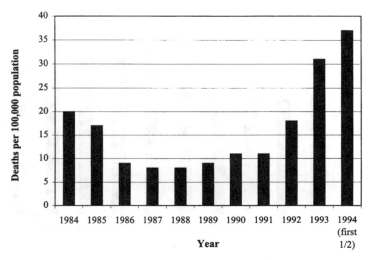

FIGURE 8.2 Mortality from accidental alcohol poisoning in Russia, 1984–94.

(*Komsomolskaya Pravda*, 1996; *Arguments and Facts*, 1995), and others believe it is even more. Some have estimated that every year each liter of pure alcohol per capita consumption kills 132,000 people, in addition to the natural attrition of the population. That is why participants at a recent conference in Moscow entitled, *"The Situation in Russia and Ways to Make It Healthier"* called alcohol "the main killer of Russians." There have been many incidents that reveal the dangers of some kinds of alcohol products. For example, poisonings in the city of Volgograd were caused by a cheap and highly toxic vodka called "Petrov." It came as a bulk purchase from the Baltic and was sold in cans with a high acetone content. People came to call it the "black death" (*Komsomolskaya Pravda*, 1996).

Alcohol is significant not only in mortality, but it also plays its part in causes of morbidity. This was brought out clearly in an important booklet entitled *Towards a Healthy Russia* (Ministry of Health, 1994). It reports on studies which found that morbidity levels among abusers of alcohol were twice as high as among nonabusers. Somatic disorders such as diseases of the liver and pancreas, other gastrointestinal disturbances, and cardiovascular diseases were all prominent among causes of morbidity. Specific disorders of the central nervous system such as encephalopathies and peripheral disorders such as polyneuritis, were also frequently found. Strong direct correlations between liver cirrhosis mortality rates and per capita alcohol consumption have also been established in the population and it has been shown that alcohol cirrhosis comprises a very substantial proportion of all cases of liver cirrhosis. Moreover, one-quarter of the patients with alcoholism suffer from pancreatic disorders usually found in combination with liver disorders. In Moscow, a comprehensive project was

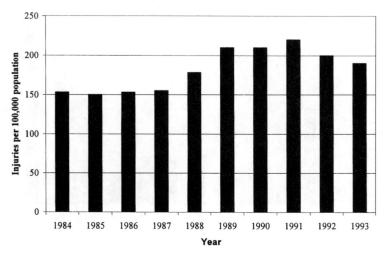

FIGURE 8.3   Number of persons injured in traffic accidents in Russia, 1984–93.

conducted in which cardiovascular diseases were monitored during the period 1984–93 (*Moskovskaya Pravda*, 1996). It was found that alcohol abuse had a strong influence on the premature death of people with cardiovascular disorders.

The Social Repercussions of Alcohol Abuse

The social repercussions of alcohol abuse in the transition period after 1989 are also very worrisome. Figures 8.3 and 8.4 outline the dynamics of traffic accidents in Russia over the period 1984–94 indicating the numbers of people injured and killed. The figures show a direct correlation with movements in per capita alcohol consumption levels. From 1988 to 1993, the annual number of persons nonfatally injured increased by almost 40 percent and the mortality level almost doubled (it rose by 82 percent). The State Research Center on Addiction undertook a special study (Zerenin and Peshkov) on the distribution of road accidents according to type of violation of traffic rules for drivers in 1991. It found that drunk driving caused 23.9 percent of all traffic accidents. The authors also found that in 29 percent of all traffic accidents, intoxicated pedestrians were to blame.

Another important indicator of the negative effects alcohol is exerting on social life in Russia today is the number of crimes committed by persons in a state of acute intoxication. As can be seen in Figure 8.5, the percentage of crimes in Russia committed by intoxicated persons is substantial; it was estimated that, in 1994, they represented more than 40 percent of all crimes. It was found in St. Petersburg in 1995 (*Sevodnia*, 1996) that the number of premeditated murders, thefts, and robberies decreased by 5.6 percent from 1994 levels, but

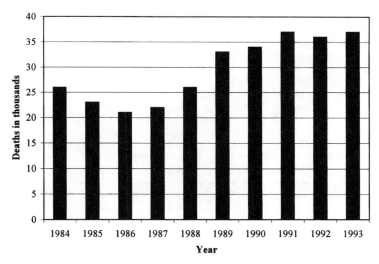

FIGURE 8.4   Number of traffic accident deaths in Russia, 1984–93.

that the number of murders committed and serious injuries inflicted by people who had been drinking increased by 22.6 percent over the same period. This trend is not confined to adults but is also apparent among the young. Rates of monitoring of youths for alcohol-related problems by juvenile authorities increased sharply from 14.8 per 1,000 youths in 1990 to 27.3 in 1994 (UNICEF,

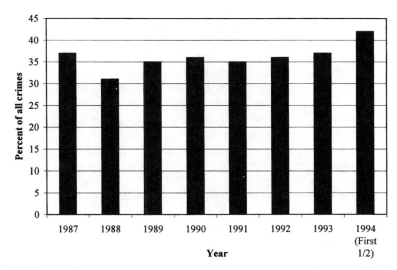

FIGURE 8.5   Crimes committed under alcohol intoxication in Russia, 1987–94.

TABLE 8.6   Number of minors on the records of internal affairs agencies in Russia by cause.

	1990	1991	1992	1993	1994	1995
Misdemeanors	245,342	219,040	278,246	320,906	392,364	446,265
Alcohol abuse	122,630	106,219	118,760	162,174	236,378	269,086
Too young to sentence	54,635	53,477	66,556	73,946	82,543	88,891
Drug abuse	9,127	7,643	3,402	4,133	5,573	10,813
Other	154,018	147,805	93,058	95,144	120,852	125,644
Total	585,752	534,184	560,022	656,303	837,710	940,699

Source: MONEE Project Database, UNICEF ICDC; Russian Children's Fund, 1995; 1996.

1997), while the number of children monitored by internal affairs agencies for alcohol use more than doubled between 1989 and 1995. Table 8.6 illustrates these trends.

These trends are worrisome in their own right and point to a rise in behaviors associated with problematic drinking among young people. The effects of alcohol abuse on family life has been insufficiently studied and received far less attention than its influence on mortality, etc. But there is also more direct evidence of the growing role alcohol is playing in crime committed by juveniles. The number of crimes committed by young people while under the influence of alcohol climbed 121 percent between 1989 and 1995 (UNICEF, 1997).

The effects of alcohol abuse on family life today have not received as much attention as its influence on mortality or crime trends. Yet it seems likely that its role is significant. Indeed, the very substantial increase in the number of Russian children who have lost a parent through death—up by an estimated 500,000 in the period 1990–95—is the result of the marked increase in excess mortality in men and women in their prime childrearing and childbearing years. One-half the excess mortality, which has been calculated at 1.5 million people, has occurred in this age group of people under 45. As indicated earlier, alcohol abuse has played its part in these figures. The consequences of these excessive deaths on family functioning are wide-ranging; not only is family income sharply reduced, but the emotional repercussions on children and any surviving partner are considerable. Where there is no partner, the risk of admission to public care for the surviving children increases.

The rise in alcoholism may plausibly be linked to the increase in the children entering public care in the transition period. Alcoholism traditionally played a substantial role in court-ordered admission to care in the 1970s and 1980s, and compulsory admissions because of unsatisfactory parenting more than trebled in the period 1991–94 (Harwin, 1996). Although there are no published figures available, it seems likely that the rise in alcoholism may have contributed to these child protection trends. Child homelessness too has been linked directly to parental alcohol dependence. The privatization of housing under the legislation introduced in 1991 failed to make any arrangements to protect the rights of minors who under former socialist legislation had been entitled to a share of the family accommodation. Stories began to appear in the press on the plight of children made homeless by their alcoholic parents who had sold their apartment and disappeared with the proceeds, leaving children to survive on their own. The newspaper *Izvestia* reported that in Moscow alone, out of 100,000 homeless children, one-third had lost their homes because of the housing privatization program (Harwin, 1996). Alcohol abuse has also been cited as a factor in domestic violence, although it is by no means an automatic correlation (Meek, 1995).

It will be apparent from this brief review that alcohol-related harm has escalated over the transition years and has had serious negative consequences for both health and social welfare. It is equally clear that the kinds of public policy that were adopted by Mr. Gorbachev are neither politically feasible today nor indeed desirable. But it is also very obvious that Russia urgently needs an effective alcohol strategy. The present situation is very costly to individual well being and to society in general. Not only is the public purse deprived of desperately needed taxation revenue through illicit production and sales, but health and welfare services have to bear the financial repercussions of the rise in alcohol-related harm and the economy suffers further from lost days at work. How these major problems can be tackled at such a difficult time, when Russia is facing so many major restructuring issues, is indeed a complex matter. But before recommendations for future policy can be identified, the first question that needs to be addressed is what policies have been adopted up to the present time.

ALCOHOL POLICIES AND THE PREVENTION OF HARM

The strategies adopted so far have focused on three main elements:

1 Policies on the rights of patients suffering from alcoholism;
2 Measures aimed at regulating the alcohol market;
3 Prevention strategies.

Policies on the Rights of Patients Suffering from Alcoholism

In the past, state policy deliberately isolated alcohol-dependent patients from society. Even as recently as 1985, during the last government antialcohol campaign, alcohol dependents were often compulsorily treated in institutions usually reserved for criminals. Patients were required to attend outpatient alcohol treatment units and were allowed no say in their treatment procedures. Persons defaulting on treatment could be subjected to compulsory treatment. Over the last few years, treatment policies have become more liberal, with movement away from an exclusive focus on obligations and towards a better balance between rights and obligations. A first step forward was taken with the adoption of the Law on Psychiatric Assistance, which came into effect on January 1, 1993. Later that year, in July, a more comprehensive law was adopted entitled "The Fundamentals of Russian Federation Health Legislation," which set out the rights of all patients. According to "The Fundamentals," patients' rights include:

- The principle of confidentiality, whereby information on health status and diagnosis cannot be divulged;
- The right of voluntary consent to any medical intervention;
- The obligation of health staff to provide patients with truthful information about their medical condition request;
- The right to call on an attorney's services;
- The possibility of recourse to a higher authority or court in the event of any violation of rights.

Since the introduction of the new law, all other regulations contradicting these principles have been abolished. As of July 1, 1994, the application of compulsory treatment for alcoholism stopped (apart from convicted criminals suffering from alcoholism). But despite these positive steps, a number of matters concerning the legal rights of patients with alcoholism still remain unresolved, such as the question of the long-term rehabilitation of these patients.

Measures Aimed at Regulating the Alcohol Market

The Russian state monopoly on alcohol was officially repealed in May 1992, thereby ending the state's 70-year period of control over alcohol production, sale, and prices (Loukomskaia, 1997). For the first time, any state, private, or cooperative enterprise could sell alcohol, needing only a license from the local authority. Private enterprises were entitled to import and sell alcohol at free market prices, with the result, as seen earlier, that huge amounts of alcohol products were brought in from abroad with no obligation to pay taxes or duties. While in the days of the state monopoly tax revenues ranged from between 30 and 50 percent, estimates in May 1997 cited a paltry revenue of only 3–5 percent, despite spiraling consumption (Ulyanova, 1997).

The first real attempts to regulate the alcohol market and protect domestic manufacturers more effectively came in the first half of 1996, when some important import, tax, and price controls were introduced. As of January 22, the government introduced fixed taxation on beverages stronger than 28 percent ethanol, equivalent to no less than 10,000 roubles per liter (*Moskovskaya Pravda*,

1996). In March 1996 the Russian Ministry of the Economy introduced regulations fixing minimum prices for hard liquors (more than 28 proof). These prices differentiated between Russian manufacturers (15,720 roubles per liter) and imported products (40,000 roubles per liter). The regulations did not cover other countries of the Commonwealth of Independent States, where other limitations were in force (*Komsomolskaya Pravda*, 1996; *Moskovskii Komsomolets*, 1996). New import quotas were also to be introduced in 1996, set at a maximum of 20 percent of the domestic market. In the light of these developments the Ministry of the Economy claimed that the state monopoly of beverage alcohol was returning (*Arguments and Facts*, 1996).

A new presidential decree was introduced in 1997 to tackle illegal alcohol production and sales. As of July 1997, any drinks with an alcohol content of more than 12 percent could only be sold through food stores. This measure was a direct attack on the kiosks which, together with wholesale food stores, according to First Deputy Prime Minister Nemtsov, were responsible for the sale of approximately 80 percent of beverage alcohol sold without payment of excise duty according to the BBC Monitoring Service (May 7, 1997). By cutting out the kiosks, the government also expected to be able to exercise better control over the quality of alcohol. This fiscal strategy is clearly important, but it is still too early to judge its impact and whether it will be enforced. Indeed, there are major obstacles to regulation, with a powerful mafia and evidence that tax evasion is rampant—not just by foreign manufacturers, but also by domestic producers. To cite one widely reported case, the huge Russian distillery, Cristall, which used to make alcohol for the tsars, was investigated for tax evasion on its exports (*Impact International*, 1997). There are also competing interests which create additional obstacles. The attempt to limit imports, according to Reuters News Service (October 9, 1996), was strongly resisted by the European Union, which claimed that its exports would have dropped by 75 percent from 1995 levels had the quotas been introduced and argued that the controls would have contravened an interim trade agreement. It is worth noting that these measures were postponed in late 1996.

More generally, there are a number of measures that are still needed to bring about better regulation of the alcohol market in Russia. These include:

- Strict quality control of beverage alcohol;
- More effective prosecutions to fight illegality and corruption in the sale of alcohol products;
- Use of mass media to encourage people to drink alcohol in socially acceptable amounts and settings.

Prevention Strategies

Prevention strategies are concerned with the promotion of healthy lifestyles and are a vital component of any effective alcohol policy. They involve clear policies on advertising, the introduction of education and media campaigns to promote safe drinking, and the provision of nonstigmatizing early intervention services. By no means do these all need to be provided by the state; many can also be delivered effectively through the voluntary and private sectors.

It is in this sphere of prevention that policies are most visibly missing. As already made clear, Russia is a high-consumption society with patterns of drinking that also promote risk. Yet the opening of the Russian beverage alcohol market was accompanied by uncontrolled advertising, which additionally promoted alcohol as a highly glamorous product, so that its appeal to youth in particular was increased. Although controls were introduced in 1995 following a presidential decree which banned the advertising of both alcohol and tobacco on TV and in the press, far more needs to be done to help encourage safe drinking and to promote and foster the movement toward responsible advertising. In the first place, there needs to be some agreed upon targets as to what constitutes safe drinking. Without these, it is impossible to mount any effective public education and health campaign. The public also needs to be made aware of the risks of excessive consumption. But Russia, in general, has an indifferent track record for all programs aimed at promoting healthy lifestyles. Excessive drinking, smoking, poor diets, and lack of exercise are rarely seen as targets of public policy. This does not lessen the need for far more proactive planning; policy merely becomes harder to introduce because it is not building on any existing tradition. Moreover, the huge psychosocial shocks of the transition and the widespread poverty have undoubtedly increased the vulnerability of the population in seeking relief from stress and the uncertainties of the future. Introducing measures directed at controlling consumption levels may also seem politically unacceptable and smack too much of the old totalitarian past. Programs will require considerable sophistication and sensitivity in their design. Nor is there any tradition of community-based counseling programs. As already suggested, treatment has been highly stigmatizing and Western commentators have noted the emphasis on medical rather than social measures (Fleming, 1996). The activities of nongovernmental organizations in this field have been limited. Creating a suitable therapeutic and counseling infrastructure is vitally needed to bringing about effective early intervention. There are plans to reintroduce a federal program on substance abuse which will seek to develop comprehensive prevention policies; it is much needed.

Future Research Priorities

According to an unpublished joint paper (Ministry of Health) prepared by researchers from the Russian State Research Center on Addiction and the Russian Ministry of Health, areas for future research will be focused on alcohol-related harm reduction. The following fields of inquiry have been identified as the most urgent:

- Comprehensive comparative epidemiological studies using broad screening methods that take into account gender, age, type of beverage consumed, place of residence, and quality of diet in order to clarify the situation and answer the question: "How much do people really drink?"
- Development of scientifically based, early preventive measures aimed at children, teenagers, and young adults;
- Studies oriented towards the reduction of alcohol-related toxic effects and somatoneurological disturbances;
- Research on effective ways of rehabilitating alcohol dependents and abusers.

The Federal Program on Substance Abuse recognizes that alcohol problems relate to society as a whole and not just the medical community. It hopes to implement measures at the state, regional, and city level that are compatible with the priority areas listed above.

CONCLUSIONS

The extreme political, social, and economic changes in Russia since the fall of socialism have created a difficult context in which to formulate and implement government policy. As the above analysis illustrates, alcohol policy is no exception. While the relative openness of the alcohol market was understandable in the context of broader economic and political climate, and indeed inevitable, its consequences have been almost exclusively negative in the short term. This is not a plea to restore the old order, which indeed did little to tackle alcohol matters in any effective way—in fact there are some early signs that government policies are beginning to be more proactive—but is rather a commentary on the failings of policy since perestroika. The new government will need to find the correct balance between state and market, and between the freedom of the individual and the role of the state in shaping alcohol-related behaviors. Finding such a balance is difficult for any government no matter how longstanding and stable, suggesting that the task that lies ahead in Russia, at least in the short term, is likely to prove particularly difficult.

REFERENCES

Arguments and Facts (Аргументы и Факты). (1995, December). No. 51.
Arguments and Facts (Аргументы и Факты). (1996, February). No. 5.
Arguments and Facts (Аргументы и Факты). (1996, February). No. 7.
Barr, D. & Field, M. (1996). The current state of health care in the former Soviet Union. *American Journal of Public Health, 86,* 307–312.
BBC Monitoring Service. (1997, May 5). *Russia: First Deputy Minister Nemtsov says state alcohol monopoly is to be strictly enforced.* Original source: Interfax, Moscow.

Chen, L. C., Wittgenstein, F., & McKeon, C. (1996). The Upsurge of Mortality in Russia—Causes and Policy Implications. *Population and Development Review, 23*, 517–530.

Economist Intelligence Unit. (1995, December 6).

Fleming, P. (1996). Drug and alcohol user treatment/intervention services in Russia—A Western Perspective. *Substance Use and Abuse, 31*, 103–114.

Gerner, K. (1995). *Nordisk Alkoholtidskrift, 12*, 80–88.

Harwin, J. (1996). *Children of the Russian State.* Aldershot: Avebury.

Impact International. (1997, January 15). pp. 19–20.

Komsomolskaya Pravda (КОМСОМОЛЬСКАЯ ПРАВДА). (1996, January 23).

Komsomolskaya Pravda (КОМСОМОЛЬСКАЯ ПРАВДА). (1996, February 22). N 34.

Leon, D., et al. (1997). Huge variation in Russian mortality rates 1984–94: Artefact, alcohol, or what? *Lancet, 350*, 383–388.

Loukomskaia, M. (1997). Recent alcohol policies in Russia. *Alcogolia, 9*, 37–42.

Meek, J. (1995, June 2). Moscow wakes up to the toll of violence in the home. *The Guardian.* p. 2.

Ministry of Health. (1994). *To a healthy Russia.* Moscow: Research Center for Preventive Medicine.

MONEE Project Database, UNICEF ICDC; Russian Children's Fund. (1995; 1996). As reproduced in UNICEF (1997). *Children at Risk in Central and Eastern Europe: Perils and Promises.* Economies in Transition Studies, Regional Monitoring Report 4. Florence, Italy: International Child Development Center.

Moscow Times. (1997, May 5).

Moskovskaya Pravda (МОСКОВСКАЯ ПРАВДА). (1996, February 22). No. 35.

Moskovskaya Pravda (МОСКОВСКАЯ ПРАВДА). (1996, March 26). Your Health (ВАШЕ ЗДОРОВЬЕ) (supplement). No. 3.

Moskovskii Komsomolets (МОСКОВСКИЙ КОМСОМОЛЕЦ). (1996, February 26). No. 37.

Rossiyskaya Gazeta (РОССИЙСКАЯ ГАЗЕТА). (1992, June 3).

Russian Federation State Committee on Statistics. (1993). *Russian Federation External Trade.* Moscow: The Committee.

Ryan, M. (1995). Alcoholism and rising mortality in the Russian Federation. *British Medical Journal, 310*, 646–648.

Sevodnia (СЕГОДНЯ). (1996, January 25). No. 83.

Sovershenno Secretno (СОВЕРШЕННО СЕКРЕТНО). (1995). No. 12.

Trud (ТРУД). (1996, February 3). No. 21.

Ulyanova, Yu. (1997, May 5). *Izvestia.*

UNICEF. (1994). *Crisis in Mortality, Health, and Nutrition.* Economies in Transition Studies, Regional Monitoring Report 2. Florence, Italy: International Child Development Center.

Urakov, I. & Mirosničenko, L. (1989). Union of Soviet Socialist Republics. In M. Plant (Ed.), *Alcohol Related Problems in High Risk Groups* (100–112). EURO Reports and Studies 109. Copenhagen: WHO Regional Office for Europe.

Varnik, A. & Wasserman, D. (1992). Suicides in the former Soviet republics. *Acta Psychiatrica Scandinavica, 86*, 76–78.

Chapter 9

Latin America

Enrique Madrigal

Most Latin American countries, while they constitute distinct and sovereign states, also share and preserve a common historical and cultural heritage. At the same time, these nations, and some societies within those nations, are part of complex and diverse aggregates which challenge all efforts to draw general conclusions in any field of study.

It might be sensible, then, to recognize from the outset that geopolitical, ethnographic, demographic, educational, economic, and other attributes form the foundation of social and individual values, attitudes, and behaviors. These attributes are constantly and dynamically reinforced or modified as a result of changing circumstances such as migrations, input from modern mass media of communication, changing opportunities and options, and, very importantly, shifts in the political and socioeconomic conditions.

Alcohol-related issues in Latin American countries have undergone change according to differing historical, socioeconomic, and political circumstances. Thus it is appropriate to review alcohol-related matters from the vantage point of some of the disciplines that contribute to this field, namely, sociology, anthropology, psychology, and the biomedical sciences. At the same time, the complex and specific issues relating to regulation and control of the production and commerce of beverage alcohol are the domain of legislators, policymakers, law enforcement, and the socioeconomic sciences.

Some authors argue that there has been a predominant trend to approach alcohol-related matters from the standpoint of alcohol's harmful consequences to individuals and society. By and large, the major thrust has been to place problem drinking in the context of normative drinking and normative drinking in the context of prevailing local cultural patterns (Singer, 1986).

Indeed, issues involved in so-called socially accepted or moderate levels of consumption, as opposed to problem or hazardous drinking, have been vigorously debated.

Latin America was also influenced by the first global attempts to reach a consensus on the definition of the problem. In 1952 a WHO Expert Group defined pathological use of alcohol as "any kind of drinking which in its extent goes beyond the traditional and customary 'dietary' use, or the ordinary compliance with the social drinking customs of the whole community concerned" (WHO Expert Group on Alcoholism, 1952).

Nevertheless, this initial assessment had to be rapidly withdrawn, since its objective of making a distinction between cultural prescriptions and problem drinking did not please French or Finnish policymakers, as they considered that in their own cultures people who engage in some socially acceptable drinking practices that were not perceived as hazardous—such as heavy wine drinkers who developed a withdrawal syndrome when weaned from alcohol or eventually suffered from cirrhosis—could not be given a double message. In Finland, the custom of boisterous and casualty-ridden binges among some workers was also considered normal behavior, and WHO's initial definition may have been interpreted as disregarding necessary social safeguards.

This situation confirmed the dictum about distinguishing drinking practices in a multicultural scenario as "different strokes for different folks," which is the predominant perception in regard to popular ideologies of drinking.

Cultural issues, by and large, are conspicuously omitted from all international public health criteria. That is why a thorough review of "wet" and drinking societies from a historical and sociocultural perspective is essential for decision-making when appropriate policies and plans are being drawn.

Scope of the Chapter

The aim of this chapter is to provide an overview and examination of the role of alcohol in Latin America, with an emphasis on Central and South American cultures. Topics to be examined include: sociodemographic profiles; production, distribution, and regulation of beverage alcohol; levels of consumption; and the harmful consequences of problem drinking and alcoholism.

This chapter is intended to review different facets of alcohol and drinking practices, as well as some of the responses related to policymaking, diagnosis, treatment, and prevention of alcohol-related problems in Latin America. At the same time, it will discuss inputs from other areas of inquiry, such as some aggregates of socially accepted drinking styles, ideologies about alcohol, sets of comportments and attitudes, and any other issues considered salient or relevant in these countries. In this respect, and notwithstanding some medical and social consequences, alcohol consumption in its ordinary form is also valued as a public phenomenon, associated with both sociability and pleasure among different groups in the region. Indeed, drawing the line between moderate and problem drinking is really more complex than just setting a limit to consumption; perhaps the two modes constitute separate territories.

A comprehensive but selective list of country reports and other material from the local literature in this field will be reviewed. In addition, it is appropriate to include sociodemographic data from various international reports, survey and risk behavior studies, and theses, dissertations, or nonpeer reviewed publications which may be rich in anecdotal material that characterizes certain drinking patterns, even though not usually discussed in technical reviews.

The need to draw on less traditional published material stems from the virtual abandonment of some facets of drinking behavior by the scientific community. This neglect may hamper the possibility of approaching alcohol-related issues in a more comprehensive manner. It may not be necessary to go to extremes, as argued by some sociologists regarding strict public health supply reduction points-of-view, which do not consider that sociability and pleasure deserve a legitimate status or are fit subjects of scientific inquiry (Gonzalez, 1984)

On the other hand, some customs rooted in historical events may have to be included in the picture, since the goal of a dry society in Latin America, needless to say, may not be a feasible alternative.

A brief historical overview is important to examine some of the plausible foundations that explain the past and current social integrative functions of drinking. These documentary observations are hard to extrapolate to present conditions, in view of the predominance of current transcultural influences and the appearance of stronger marketing trends in the area of alcohol products. Yet it is argued that some social groups are still deeply rooted in traditional patterns of drinking, as documented by Heath (1991).

At the same time, this chapter contemplates the possibility of introducing a sequential order to the discernible stages of the natural history of alcohol consumption in selected Latin American countries, and of suggesting how some plausible explanations of the current state of the triad "alcohol, health, and society" might be constructed in modern times.

POLITICAL AND DEMOGRAPHIC CHARACTERISTICS

Central America comprises seven countries, including Belize, which is more politically linked with the Caribbean Commonwealth and CARICOM. There are also two Spanish-speaking countries in the Caribbean—Cuba and Dominican Republic—together with the free associate state of Puerto Rico, a nation that fully shares its cultural heritage with the rest of Latin America. Last, the more extensive territory of the region is South America, consisting of 12 countries and other political territories, for a total population of about 250 million. These countries are in different stages of economic development. For example, Central America's economy is based on agriculture, mainly bananas and coffee, and it has a total population of nearly 30 million. The Spanish-speaking Caribbean comprises Cuba, the Dominican Republic, and Puerto Rico, for a total population of approximately 22 million. This is the most politically diverse subregion, with an economy depending on agriculture and tourism.

In the second half of this century South America has made a major leap forward in industrial development, especially Brazil and Argentina. Agriculture is also a predominant factor in the economy of less developed countries, although mineral resources and oil are also strong in countries such as Venezuela, Peru, Chile, Argentina, and Ecuador. During the last two decades most countries have enjoyed political stability, as opposed to the turbulent times typical of the decades of the 1950s and 1960s, a condition epitomized in the pejorative appellation "banana republics." Some data on specific issues related to economic conditions will be discussed in the corresponding section below, in relation to alcohol as a commodity.

With the exception of Brazil, all other countries have a common heritage, as their history was linked to the Spanish colonial empire for several centuries. As such, they share Spanish as a common language, but some native languages are still spoken in countries such as Guatemala, Bolivia, Ecuador, Peru, and Paraguay. Indeed, the indigenous population has been estimated at 40 million in the Americas. It is commendable that at least one of the surveys (Paraguay) was also conducted in Guarani.

The ethnic composition of Latin America is very rich and varied. Some countries are considered quite homogeneous. In countries such as Costa Rica, Chile, Uruguay, and Venezuela the indigenous population is relatively small. In Panama, the Dominican Republic, Colombia, Brazil, and Cuba there are large black or mixed populations, while Guatemala, Peru, Bolivia, and Ecuador have a substantial proportion of indigenous people, reaching 45 percent (perhaps more in Guatemala) of the population in some countries. White populations derive from the original Spanish settlers and more recent migrations, notably from Italy, Germany, and Portugal (Caetano & Carlini-Cotrim, 1993).

HISTORICAL NOTES ON DRINKING PRACTICES

Pre-Columbian Times

This section is intended to examine some early historic issues concerning beverage alcohol. While some of the early behaviors or customs regarding the use of alcohol by the different cultures evoke more curiosity than scientific interest, it is plausible that remnants of these practices may still be present in certain societies and contribute to the present sociocultural context of drinking.

Beverage alcohol was used long before there was any written history. It has been pointed out (Mariategui, 1985) that primitive peoples faced their surrounding environment and the unknown with great fear, and that alcohol provided an appropriate vehicle to relieve anxiety and to participate in special ceremonies and community gatherings. There was also some use of alcohol to alleviate pain and minor ailments (Mariategui, 1985).

As a very early discovered product, alcohol became more easily available when humans first made use of stone and metal instruments, and agriculture became more advanced. At that time, cereals complemented other vegetables (mostly fruit, but also roots and tree barks) that were used for home-brewed products in Mesopotamia and among early American cultures thousands of years ago.

The history of alcohol and humanity has been exhaustively reviewed in many contexts. Richly detailed chronicles from early Mesopotamia, China, Persia, India, and a wealth of other cultures point to the very early bonding of ancient peoples to the production and consumption of alcohol, as well as other psychoactive substances (Escohotado, 1989).

In the New World, the pre-Columbian use of different psychoactive substances has contributed to current attitudes, behaviors, norms and practices, at least in sociocultural enclaves where modern marketing and communication media have not reached out significantly. Among these cultures, alcohol was discovered, probably by chance, through the deposit of airborne yeasts in leftover fruit juice or cereal preparations which yielded the fermented beverage. Hence, it is believed that different civilizations incorporated distinct drinking behaviors, encompassed in their own traditional attitudes and norms. Later on in history, influence over this behavior shifted to the realm of individual motivations, dietary customs, medicinal discoveries or misconceptions, rituals, celebrations, the enhancing of conviviality, and so on.

Any examination of the use of beverage alcohol—or psychoactive substances—during the years previous to the discovery of the American continent must take into account the significance of these behaviors in places where centralized and structured civilizations existed, such as the Gulf of Mexico (Olmec, Toltec, and Maya civilizations) in North and Central America, and the Inca Empire in the Andean region. It has been documented that the Aztecs had an abstemious culture, and that peoples from other areas in North America, Amazonia, and the Parana River were typically nomads and hunters who had no use for such home-brewed products.

As for the availability and variety of alcohol and other substances in these areas, two main characteristics of Latin America are the abundance and exuberance of plants containing psychoactive substances and the existence of links between the consumption of alcohol and psychoactive plants and religious cults, in both great civilizations and small communities (Escohotado, 1989).

For instance, the Olmec, Toltec, and Mayan civilizations took advantage of the richness of honeys produced by bees of different species. Bird droppings probably kindled the fermentation process in these rich mixtures, which contained levulose, a more potent and flavorsome sweetener. The high content of this sugar was actually an advantage for the production of more exotic and tasty home or tribal brews (Escohotado, 1989). The Olmec and Mayan civilizations discovered a very rich mixture of fermented honey and mixed it with the bark of the balque tree to use as an integral part of their ceremonies.

This particular observation prompted Levi-Strauss to write about products "of different aromas, but always of indescribable richness and complexities ... exquisite to the point of being intolerable on occasions" (Escohotado, 1989). More precisely, the bees and wasps in Latin America produce honeys which may not only be intolerable to your taste, but are also inebriating in the strict sense. Such is the case of the *trigona* bee, also called "the witch bee," *feiticeira*, in Brazil. Some of their honeys are toxic, and are used for fishing or hunting. Some groups ferment these concentrated mixtures, and produce some highly intoxicating brews, used also in combination with hallucinogenic substances to produce daturas (mixtures of alcohol and hallucinogens) (Escohotado, 1989).

From early times, according to historical accounts most drinking practices were linked to religious rituals, as part of structured and meaningful ceremonies, and they involved an élite of healers and priests. Some cultures had well-controlled celebrations or ceremonies involving the larger community, usually related to special events such as changes of season and agricultural festivals.

More progressive cultures, on the contrary, established strict means of control. The Aztecs, for example, considered the effects of alcohol quite damaging, because it could cloud the alertness of warriors, putting safety in jeopardy under the ubiquitous threat of their traditional neighboring tribal foes and the "conquistadores." Therefore, they instituted a prohibition code which limited the use of alcohol or any psychoactive substance to mostly ceremonial occasions.

As for the Andean-based civilizations and their conquered territories, fermented maize was also considered a sacred beverage. Celebrations were accompanied by this product in many ceremonial ways, and social control was very strict in regulating the occasions when drinking was allowed. Hence, early codes were established containing punitive measures to discourage uncalled-for transgressions of social norms.

These early traditional practices (i.e., drinking during special occasions only) also arose from the fact that, while the climate favored the production of fermentable goods such as maize and some fruits, these drinks easily spoiled, so they had to be freshly made and then consumed only on special occasions, and almost to total depletion.

Colonial Period

During the colonial period, alcohol played an important role as part of a social meltdown following the cultural devastation and alienation of previously well-established societies. In this sense, indigenous groups had to adjust to new social censoring codes that addressed drinking behaviors that already had well-formed social controls. They had to grapple instead with harsh sentences and beatings.

One gets a sense of the Spanish missionaries' understanding of drunkenness in the following passage: "People prone to wine drinking, turning them into beasts without law or reason, and in this state they fall into the practice of sodomy and they disrespect mothers and children" (Mariátegui, 1985).

During colonial times, alcohol was blamed for all manner of sins and social problems, including idolatry, rebellion, poverty, infirmity, violent crimes, infidelity, and incest. Chronicles from Andean countries are replete with alleged observations about religious raptures that were judged to be heretical and a pagan interference with evangelization.

In contrast to these early chronicles that demonized drinking, other Hispanic hierarchies took advantage of alcohol and drugs to enforce hard labor in the silver mines of Potosi. In fact, this might have been a turning point, using alcohol as a barter commodity to avoid paying wages.

This was probably a significant stage in the region, where drinking became a weapon or a value scale by which the use of these products by subordinates was either forbidden or controlled. The lower classes from that time on were despised as drunkards and untrustworthy individuals (Escohotado, 1989; Menendez, 1983).

It is also interesting to note some relevant documentary studies in other regions, such as Central America, where there still seem to exist some remnants of colonial control practices in current formal and informal responses to alcohol-related situations.

A recent unpublished thesis (Salazar, 1994) prepared for the Faculty of Social Sciences at the University of Costa Rica thoroughly reviews drinking patterns and control measures introduced during the colonization period, which were initially implemented to tackle social problems. Later on, these early responses turned into restrictive and fiscal measures, forming a possible foundation for current control measures in the region.

This thesis describes how, from very early in the 17th century, the Representative Captain for the Crown of Spain, at his designated headquarters in Guatemala, kept tight control over wine procurement on the isthmus, including allocations to the Franciscan Order, which had been commissioned to evangelize the region.

Later on, when trade in wine and spirits from Peru began, via Panama, fiscal complications developed as increasing profits from contraband competed with the established revenue collecting system for the Crown. Thus new taxes became essential to keep control of the areas under domination and to be able to divert some revenues for the officials' own political needs and ambitions.

This situation remained more or less stable during the 17th century, when sugar cane plantations became more profitable. Distilling then turned into a lucrative industry, reinforcing the early policies of Guatemala's royal authorities to raise more revenues from this commodity. Thus, after years of piecemeal operations, including fines and imprisonment for breaking the fiscal code, as well as profiting from licensing and taxes, the local hierarchy decided on further controls and increases in revenues by establishing a central alcohol depository in Costa Rica. When this enterprise became more profitable, some subsidiaries were established, but alcohol continued to be produced mostly from this central depository, which continues as the current state monopoly, the National Industry of Distillates, founded in Costa Rica in 1850.

Central America's history may epitomize the advent of the stage when alcohol became a more profitable commodity. At that point, trade, regulations, industry, and marketing took over infrastructures that were previously culturally controlled.

The initial *cedulas reales*, or royal ordinances, during the colonial period, may not have been quite uncommon. In Venezuela in 1731, for example, a decree limited the production of some beverage alcohol and banned aguardiente (a still popular sugar cane distillate, also known as *guaro, cachasa,* and many other names). By the mid 19th century, there are indications that penalties were again imposed for inebriation. Colombia also went through a similar control process, which at one point prohibited the production and distribution of fermented sugar cane products (*chicha*).

In terms of patterns of alcohol consumption, most societies have experienced enormous change. The initial traditionally stable and "culturally controlled" codes of behavior evolved during the second half of the 19th century as a result of the development of a medley of production, trading, and lifestyles. Thus it is not possible to view alcohol consumption in its totality through any one discipline on its own.

From this brief historical review, it might be plausible to conclude that: (a) early drinking styles were effectively regulated by pervasive norms, which enhanced the socially integrative function of this behavior; (b) during the colonial years, the behavior was seen as primitive and sinful, perhaps contributing to problem drinking styles on the part of certain ethnic groups; and (c) later responses included both the introduction of fiscal controls to increase revenues and restrictive ordinances to suppress undesirable drinking-related comportments.

While these early responses of the type seen in Central America, Venezuela, and Colombia probably set the stage for later alcohol policymaking, Latin American countries have experienced more profound changes with regard to early traditional and socially controlled drinking practices. It is interesting to note that legislation, including bylaws, is similar to that of industrialized countries with regard to fiscal measures, but restrictions are in general more punitive and contrast more sharply with current tolerant attitudes in the general population. At the same time, early forms of socially integrative drinking are found in selected ethnic groups in the region. Heath (1991), Mariategui (1985), and Menendez (1983) have made important contributions to the study of these exceptional ethnic groups.

The question arises, whether some present-day alcohol codes are still based on early attitudes to public drinking and social disorganization, on fiscal measures to collect taxes and fines. It is common knowledge that most legislation may be outdated in Latin America, but it might be worthwhile to review these texts and promote the adoption of regulations more up to date and oriented towards reality.

SOCIOCULTURAL ASPECTS OF DRINKING

Reflecting on drinking patterns and the harmful consequences of alcohol, Jellinek (1960) advocated the attainment of a sort of ecological homeostasis offering a balanced coexistence with alcohol, by which "there would be no harm to the individual, society, or both" (Jellinek, 1960).

If this earlier conceptualization came from a respected thinker who is chiefly identified with the so-called medical model of alcoholism, it would only be fair for sociology to follow up and help to clarify the different facets of drinking practices as a broad domain of acceptable or socially sanctioned alcohol-related behaviors. Thus it is relevant to review some of the issues covered by sociology and anthropology, as a counterpoint to the strict medical model or the disease conception of alcoholism.

This approach recognizes that humanity's long contact with alcohol must be considered as a social act (Heath, 1990), as well as learned behavior, both of which suggest that the influence of the sociocultural context is very significant.

Heath suggests that this fact should be taken into account when trying to discern the dynamics of alcohol drinking patterns in any culture: "Culture is to behavior as grammar is to language. We learn often without knowing that we are learning. Accepting the importance of culture does not mean that all people act the same, as there is a range of acceptable variation with respect to most beliefs and practices" (Heath, 1989).

Within this topic, genetics, as well as sociocultural and environmental factors, should not be considered as opposing, dichotomous issues, but rather as complementary contributions to understanding the etiology and dynamics of the processes involved in alcohol-related behaviors (Heath, 1989).

Heath (1989) also made an important contribution by better defining the range of environmental factors, including surroundings, religion, values and attitudes, sociocultural issues in general and, most of all, the structure of normative behavior.

As supported in practice by the examples offered below in the domain of ideology and norms, it is most important, according to Heath, to make a clear distinction with regard to

- normal norms—those that refer to people's conventional mores; these are frequently encountered in candid surveys, where people simply try to comply with what the social mores are supposed to be;
- normative norms—which pertain to what may be the equivalents of taboo restrictions among primitive peoples;

- modal norms—which are basically the trends of the times, or what most people do anyway. They form the perfect mechanism to avoid the first set of norms, and include early teenage drinking binges at more permissive gathering places, getting drunk on special occasions, and so on.

An understanding of attitudes and norms is more important than most other criteria, including availability and formal constraints, for any prevention approach may otherwise be missing an important element regarding motivation and collective rationalizations for not refraining from collectively accepted drinking behaviors.

Thus alcohol policymaking, following these criteria, must take special measures to ascertain whether or not it is plausible to promote or enhance moderate drinking practices under certain conditions.

There are many studies about drinking practices among ethnic groups, by Heath and other authors, which thoroughly describe sets of distinctive characteristics among the groups' ancestors in pre- and post-Columbian times. Other less well-known, yet very relevant studies, such as the study by Kirberg and Maass (1985) of drinking habits among Aymara communities in Iquique, Chile, depict common integrative functions of drinking behaviors similar to these reported by Heath among the Gamba in Bolivia. In these examples, drinking takes place during community or family festive occasions as well as in religious, agrarian, and health-related rituals ("Salute to the sun," "Shopping for stars," etc.).

Other studies about modern patterns of drinking are scarce, especially regarding attitudes and behaviors, formal and traditional norms, and socioeconomic factors.

Menendez (1983) reviewed the Latin American literature on sociocultural approaches to alcohol-related matters. He added some reflections on this subject, and suggested the need to review the then predominant "disease-oriented" approaches, in view of the richness of drinking practices in terms of cultural variables. This author proposed the term "alcoholization" as opposed to the medical or problem-oriented terminology current at the time, in order to contribute to a better understanding of the multiple facets of drinking, as well as neglected issues of popular ideology.

This last topic is seldom recorded or reflected in the application of regular survey questionnaires. In this respect, the insights of Gonzalez (1984), who studied drinking practices through a participatory observation method, as opposed to formal responses obtained by professionals in Costa Rica, are more indicative of the role (sometimes positive) of alcohol in some societies.

By contrast, the reports from attitudinal studies in the region (in El Salvador, Paraguay and Dominican Republic, *inter alia*) (FUNDASALVA, 1991; Ministry of Public Health and Social Welfare, 1991) are more closely related to Heath's concepts of normal and normative norms in head-on collision with actual drinking practices. In these situations, most respondents (a) despise alcohol dependent people, (b) do not perceive some forms of drinking practices as harmful or obnoxious, and (c) do not experience significant social pressure to check these social behaviors.

The explanations by Menendez (1983) and Gonzalez (1984) are compatible with the socioculturally constituted nature of drinking behavior (Singer, 1986) as they relate to (a) intracultural variation in drinking patterns, and (b) the sociocultural and psychosocial functions of drinking and drunkenness. These views from Singer are crucial to a further understanding of the need to study different risk or protective environments that may otherwise be neglected in general surveys.

At the same time, there is a need to ponder carefully the effect of previous cultural assessments of drinking as a low-class behavior, and to project problem drinking to the lower socioeconomic classes. As reflected by the vignette on Central America (Salazar, 1994), and earlier in Peru (Mariátegui, 1985), it is historically relevant to keep in mind early colonialist stereotyping drinking behaviors as a sign of degeneration among Indian populations and slaves. It is not at all uncommon to find strict regulations on drinking among minorities that are still based on these attitudes.

One rather controversial and bold position is the approach of Cavanaugh and Clairemont (1985), who are more inclined to strictly follow the distribution theory approach to problem drinking. These contributions are parallel to Ledermann's log-normal distribution of alcohol consumption, in the sense that free markets, liberal policies, and inadequate restrictions would account for increased average drinking, with an additional ripple effect on the skewed end of the curve, representing problem drinkers and alcohol dependents.

On another level, the approach advocated in the recent guideline book on this subject by Edwards and colleagues (1994) takes stock of these positions, and strictly recommends no-nonsense policymaking to bring down per capita consumption as the fundamental step to reduce alcohol-related problems in any given society.

On the other hand, Heath (1990) considers that it is quite likely that people would not refrain from purchasing alcohol in spite of strict fiscal or sales control, nor will they stop problem drinking in spite of strict constraints. This point may better reflect consumption trends, which in some Latin American countries with problem drinking may be more related to uncontrolled cultural and individual patterns, in line with Singer's observations, than to simple issues of availability. Indeed, this situation is taking place with much lower purchasing capacity than in industrialized nations, in respect of both price and income elasticity, as well as a low and stable per capita consumption.

Heath (1989) also notes that social scientists often have to rely on natural experiments for evidence. From this viewpoint, the fact that official and popular attitudes towards the use of alcohol and alcohol-related problems differ not only among various cultures, but also shift—often diametrically—to an opposite position within a single culture over only a few decades strongly suggests a few points that appear simple but may be crucial (Heath, 1989).

These various approaches to a common problem may be summarized as follows:

- Problems emerge not from an inert substance, but from the interaction between it, the user, and the context;
- Drug users, including alcohol abusers, are not just "organisms" affected by a chemical; those individuals should be viewed as a complex biopsychological system;
- In practical terms, this means that the user also comprises a personality (influenced by expectations, values, attitudes), a unique life history (influenced by all sorts of teachings and experiences), and a distinctive combination of status, many of which imply very different roles (female, adult, mother, sister, etc.). All these possible attributes have no direct link with the use of any particular drug, but they all come into play in the style of use and its consequences.

Thus, many significant problems associated with drugs (and, in this instance, by extension alcohol) can best be viewed as social constructs. Such problems are then based on clusters of attitudes and associations in the minds of peoples, which makes it important to gather particular observations in systematic aggregates, in order to ascertain social impact.

For instance, taking the axis of religion as a criterion, Latin American societies incorporated a certain degree of permissiveness to drink, partly because the predominant Roman Catholic faith is not proscriptive, by comparison to Judaism and other religions, either prohibiting alcohol, or limiting use to strict religious ceremonies. At the same time, the way people in many countries refer to "normative behaviors" as opposed to actual "modal norms" or drinking practices, reflects a social double standard, which becomes part of this equation.

Did this series of events translate into setting up early precursor policies to control drinking? The answer is partially positive, as suggested by the trends noted in the Central American vignette about state monopolies and the conspicuous punitive measures against alcohol intoxication and related behaviors causing disturbance. On the other hand, never in its history, has Latin America experienced any temperance or prohibitionist influences of the kind seen in Germany, Sweden, or the United States. This fact alone should be sufficient to indicate the need to make a critical appraisal of any approaches rallying the world to a single distribution theory paradigm.

As a counterpoint to previous concepts, and reaching beyond the realm of culture and drinking, Cavanaugh and Clairemont (1985) and Singer (1986) argued that anthropology has failed to systematically consider the world-transforming effects of global market and global labor processes associated with the evolution of the capitalist mode of production.

In that context, social and anthropological approaches, no matter how appealing to some policymakers, could be preempted by the economic reality, stemming from an organized international corporate gluttony. Indeed, this paradigm is very appealing to those involved in the field of alcohol policymaking, and it is certain that some measures will have to be taken regarding the broad field of availability, which definitely cannot go unregulated. On the other hand, it may be wrong not to consider the dynamics of drinking practices in depth in Latin America, since the economics of beverage alcohol may have their main influence in determining markets share, in settings characterized by paradoxical stabilization of consumption but overburdened by problem drinking.

At this point, to complement what has been discussed so far, it may be useful to consider further in the following section how alcohol abuse itself comes to play a major role beyond historical and socioeconomic factors.

In the realm of public health, the many facets of disability, premature mortality, social dysfunction, and decreased productivity have broadened the discussion on whether these problems also have a negative impact on health and socioeconomic development.

THE ISSUE OF "PROBLEM DRINKING" AND HEALTH STATISTICS

The World Bank's 1993 "World Development Report" on investing in health provides selected health indicators and socioeconomic data in order to present a general picture of socioeconomic conditions in the region. In this preview of a trend-setting publication on health statistics, the World Bank proposed some innovative indicators such as the "burden of disease," which offers criteria to estimate both mortality and days lost for disability related to any particular disease.

These criteria have the advantage, in assessing the impact of alcohol abuse and alcoholism, of taking into account other factors than statistics on mortality. The World Bank duly defines the criteria to make explicit the concept of "disability adjusted life years" or DALYs.

In this approach, the burden of disease takes into account years lost for premature mortality, as well as those lost as a consequence of disease-related disability. Table 9.1 depicts a comparative distribution between other mental health profiles and alcohol dependence, including other regions, the established market economies (EME), demographically developed nations, and world figures. Other relevant data include levels of production and consumption, as well as the most recently available figures on mortality from liver cirrhosis.

Based on these indicators, the following comments endeavor to deal with the way that macro-economic issues, the production and marketing of beverage alcohol, and (in a subsequent section) survey and more specific health statistics combine with the sociocultural factors depicted in the previous section. This exercise is aimed at raising questions for discussion, rather than laying down dogmatic solutions to problems already acknowledged as complex.

TABLE 9.1   Burden of disease by cause expressed as disability adjusted life years × 100,000 DALY*, 1990.

Disease	Gender	LAC†	EME‡	World
Communicable, maternal and perinatal	Male	226	66.8	3057.7
	Female	207	48	3182
Non-communicable	Male	228	630.6	2981.6
	Female	212	334	2772
Neuro-psychiatric disorders	Male	46.8	78.2	499
	Female	35.7	62	426
Alcohol dependence	Male	14.1	24.5	116.2
	Female	2	3.7	17
Cirrhosis	Male	8.7	11.7	88.5
	Female	2.7	6.5	40.8
Injuries	Male	117.2	78.8	1092.1
	Female	37.2	32.1	533.9

Source: World Bank Report (1993).
*DALY: 100,000 of disability adjusted lost years
†LAC: Latin America and the Caribbean
‡EME: Established Market Economies

Most economic indicators point to the presence of a market for alcohol production and consumption in Latin America that is already stable. If this argument is valid, as stated in the previous section, it may be sensible to examine other relevant factors that could contribute to the current situation of alcohol-related matters in Latin America.

Some observations have to do purely with economics. In addition to common and generally applied criteria, such as income and salary elasticity, vis-à-vis the relatively low real price (inflation-adjusted) of alcohol, it may be argued that Latin America cannot be taken for granted or, in other words, be lumped together in some broader market analysis to decide the need and means to increase alcohol controls.

Production and consumption are higher in countries with developed or established market economies (EME), which according to the 1993 World Development Report (World Bank, 1993) averaged a GNP per capita of $21,050 in 1991, than in Latin America and the Caribbean, where the figure was just $2,390 (almost the level of countries placed by the Work Bank in the category of "severely indebted nations") (World Bank, 1993). At the same time, while the rate of inflation averaged 4.5 percent in developed nations, Latin America has grappled in recent years with inflation rates as high as 416.9 percent, with an average of 208.2 percent. If these trends continue, with an average annual growth rate of −0.3 percent (the rate for high-income economies is 2.3 percent), there is no possibility that Latin American economies will recover and rise to the level of "consumer nations" in international trade markets.

If these observations are accurate, as the data suggest, policymakers of alcohol-related matters should consider carefully whether most effort should be geared to the control of the availability of beverage alcohol, or whether other factors, such as sociocultural practices and public health deficits, should be targeted to reduce undesirable or harmful patterns of drinking.

By and large, the short route has been taken so far, giving predominance to reviewing the legislation and seriously advocating more efficacious action to curtail alcohol availability. Other specific areas of control and prevention are then relegated to program managers, who are usually not capable of reaching out to a significant portion of the population at risk, and therefore maintaining a position where individual responsibility is the major factor.

Nonetheless, market regulations and allowances mean that trade and consumption of beverage alcohol are governed chiefly by offer and demand (with the exception of countries where the government is more substantially involved in the production and sale of alcohol, such as Costa Rica (Bejarano, 1995), Paraguay and Uruguay (PAHO, 1990).

In Costa Rica, the National Alcohol Industry (Fabrica Nacional de Licores), founded in 1850, produces and distributes most popular distillates, including a 30 percent sugar cane distillate (*guaro*), and other popular and relatively inexpensive rums and gins. All revenues are earmarked for state institutions, and a minimal payment (approximately $150,000) goes to prevention. In Paraguay and Uraguy, the governments are in charge of producing and distributing distillates from different sources, including industrial alcohols. Apart from these examples, the general practice is that the state does not get involved in the business of alcohol production and commerce.

It is worth examining some series of data from unpublished PAHO sources dealing with trends on availability and consumption of beverage alcohol. For instance, per capita consumption of alcohol in South America increased just 2.4 percent from 1970 to 1980, while the average increase for all of Latin America was 0.36 liters of absolute alcohol per capita. This trend has continued in many countries, for which estimates are available to 1994. The average per capita consumption of 10 countries increased by 0.32 liters from 1980 to 1994. In fact, major producing countries Argentina and Chile reduced consumption between 1970 and 1994 by 6 and 0.4 liters, respectively, while Uruguay and Brazil increased their consumption by 0.29 and 2.6 liters.

Argentina has also experienced changes in consumption rates for spirits, wines, and beers. In 1980 the per capita consumption of distillates was 1.3 liters of pure alcohol, but by 1993 had decreased to 0.3 liters, while beer consumption increased to 27.1 liters and wine fell from 76.3 to 43.2 liters. Total per capita consumption dropped from 11.6 to 6.5 liters within the same period.

Interestingly, Argentina has experienced a rapid change from wine to beer production, while keeping spirits consumption low. Chile continues to have, as stated above, a high mortality rate for cirrhosis, while per capita consumption of pure alcohol has tended to taper off from 7.4 liters in 1982 to 6.3 liters in 1991. Beer has remained stable with a total consumption of 2,670,000 hectoliters in 1990 and 3,943,960 in 1994.

Other countries with a high per capita consumption of beer are Brazil (62,555 million hectoliters), Colombia (21,000 million hectoliters), and Canada (62,500 million hectoliters).

In Central America, Costa Rica is considered by many to be a country that has carefully recorded production and consumption trends for decades, and since 1974 no illicit distillates have been detected, after an intensive control program lasting some 10 years. Thus, issues of production, availability, and consumption are possibly free of bias, assuming, as seems to be the case, that the records are reliable. Per capita consumption in 1970 was 2.23 liters of pure alcohol. By 1980 it had increased to 3.03, but had fallen again in 1990 to 2.6 liters.

Chile has come to the attention of several national scientists in the field because of the puzzling and complex situation regarding alcohol as a priority public health matter. The reasons are multiple, but the major problem, as mentioned above, is the high risk for the population of developing cirrhosis of the liver (around 27 per 100,000),which affects the country endemically. Per capita consumption from 1970 to 1994 has hovered around 6 and 7 liters of pure alcohol, while the mortality rate for cirrhosis remains in the upper 20s, down from the mid 30s in the 1980s. In 1989, 3,551 Chileans died from cirrhosis of the liver, the highest figures along with Mexico and Puerto Rico (and the same number of deaths as Argentina, which has more than twice the population of Chile).

Another interesting figure indicates that Argentina lowered alcohol consumption from 1970 to 1994 by almost half (-44 percent). Chile, on the other hand, increased consumption by 15 percent during the same period.

The most outstanding beer production changes are: Brazil $+388$ percent; Colombia $+68.9$ percent; Paraguay $+216$ percent; and Uruguay $+39$ percent. During this period, the United States and Canada lowered their consumption by 1.5 percent and 7.7 percent, respectively. Of course, these data must be weighed against demographic changes, but new industries and marketing are definitely important factors, as stated above.

There are also indications, although not well substantiated, that Brazil and Ecuador may be substantial producers of illicit alcohol. Estimates vary, but some figures suggest as much as 20 percent for Chile and up to 50 percent for Brazil and Ecuador. These observations are subject to confirmation.

In addition, Ferrando (1989) reports that some 4.4 percent of consumption is accounted for by toxic alcohol, popularly known as *salta p'tras*, *racumin*, and *capitan* in Peru.

It may be concluded that there is an apparent homeostasis taking place, in spite of the documented high production of beer and some spirits. Indeed, an open, free-market situation, suggested as being significantly linked to problem drinking by some experts (Singer, 1986), has long been in place, particularly in this past decade, but it has not been translated into higher figures of consumption, according to the reports available.

Interestingly, though, reports from countries with very low consumption, such as Peru, reflect the endemic use of toxic homemade distillates, which are responsible for periodic mass catastrophes. Thus Latin America's lower per capita consumption is not necessarily reflected in fewer alcohol-related problems. This would likely be true regardless of whether some countries experience underrecording of consumption due to homemade or small-industry production of home-brews and distillates, as well as contraband.

At the same time, some of the countries have gone through demographic changes, as a result of which population profiles may tend towards older strata and decreased rural populations. However, demographic characteristics indicate that most countries present a predominance of younger age groups in their population profiles, so that the adjustment of per capita consumption for age may not make a big difference at this point.

It is interesting to note that most global or regional proposals to curtail availability stem from European and other developed country models. But, as discussed above, these countries have at least 10 times the average Latin American per capita income and, consequently, a much higher per capita consumption of alcohol, which can be attributed exclusively to consumer power.

These strong economies, comprising the major wine, beer, whisky, and vodka industries of the world, can only be compared to the United States. This means that the remaining more than half a billion inhabitants of this region will have to be provided with more sensible policies to deal with problem drinking, in view of the fact that these other measures do not seem to match regional trends, when socioeconomic conditions and sociocultural context are taken into account.

The recent book by Edwards and colleagues (1994) has been received as a trendsetter for policymaking in the world. Yet curiously, only one paragraph is dedicated to the Americas, and refers merely to "the lack of reliable information in developing countries" (Edwards et al., 1994). While some of the collaborating scientists listed in the publication are from the region, none of the authors included in the book are from Latin America.

Among the few issues raised in this publication, mortality rates for cirrhosis are adjusted correctly to the European rate, and, therefore, they appear to be much higher than the usual crude rates that policymakers use as a criterion in Latin America. These adjusted rates are obviously based on the 17 percent difference in the populations under 15 years of age (19 percent in Europe and 36 percent in Latin America). It would be sensible, perhaps, to estimate per capita consumption in a similar way and not to base it on the general population figures, thus obtaining higher rates for the age groups more prone to drink.

Once these adjustments are made with regard to levels of drinking in 1970, when younger populations were larger, as opposed to today's demographic profiles (still young but living longer), then the production and marketing trends for beverage alcohol should still be somewhat lower, based on the small average increase in per capita consumption over the last 20 years depicted above.

In other words, alcohol-related problems depicted as creating social disturbances and psychosocial problems such as violence and accidents, let alone alcohol dependence, are allegedly increasing in Latin America. But the question is, what is the risk factor in this equation? Is it related to uncontrolled production and marketing? Or is it the social and/or demographic conditions in line with those theories that suggest an increased consumption of alcohol among stress-ridden social groups? Or, as suggested in this chapter, is it just that sociocultural issues and the history of drinking have to be assessed more thoroughly in order to plan better solutions?

In addition, in Latin America it has been found that countries with higher mortality rates from liver conditions also present other acute and chronic infectious and degenerative liver conditions linked to poor living conditions and hygiene, as well as malnutrition.

Determining the validity of these points is crucial from the standpoint of policymaking. In fact, there is still a strong tendency to recommend that government curtail the availability of alcohol products by means of taxation or, in general, by imposing restrictions on production and sale.

Further, as will be discussed in the section on legislation, many countries make substantial efforts to pass laws and statutes to impose special constraints on times when sales are permitted, the regulation of licenced premises, and many other similar measures, when enforcement is reportedly very lax throughout the region.

As stated above, it has been atypical for Latin America to be successful in passing strict legislation to curtail the availability of beverage alcohol. Heath (1989) is of the opinion that this approach will not stop people from buying or producing their own beverages, and that restrictive measures will not curtail problem drinking. In fact, serious problem drinking is taking place in the region in spite of the low figures for per capita consumption discussed in this section.

So, is it appropriate to control the marketing and promotion of beverage alcohol in order to restrict the general population's contact with these products, or would it be more worthwhile from the point-of-view of public health to target pervasive abnormal patterns of consumption or problem drinking?

Eventually, this situation will have to be examined to ascertain if hazardous patterns of drinking stem from other problems with broader impact, such as drinking patterns linked to poor socioeconomic conditions, mass internal migrations, and many other possible risk factors. If the root problems of those groups are not addressed, and care and prevention do not reach out to them, it would certainly be futile to enforce strong marketing restrictions for the general population, since these problem drinking niches will continue to deteriorate medically, psychologically, and most of all, socially.

At the same time, authors such as Singer (1986), Skog (1995), Edwards and colleagues (1994), and Cavanagh and Clairemont (1985) have taken strong positions in recommending tougher public health measures, based on the argument that an already high per capita consumption would be responsible for further "skewing" to the right in Ledermann's distribution curve (levels of problem drinking) (Edwards et al., 1994), or, similarly, that aggressive free marketing would have a strong influence on consumption (Singer, 1986; Cavanaugh & Clairemont, 1985).

Furthermore, some authors (Edwards et al., 1994) argue that a safe level of per capita consumption should ideally be less than five times the corresponding individual safety limit. In this respect, countries at high risk for coronary and heart disease (CHD) are recommended not to surpass an annual per capita consumption of three liters of pure alcohol, while in low CHD risk countries the level should be substantially lower. Therefore, according to these authors, the health benefits of such a healthy lifestyle approach would be null, or not significant, in terms of the general population.

It may be tempting to take these assertions at face value, since they are the product of very sound public health studies. Nevertheless, it might be appropriate, as suggested above, to review some of the issues pertaining to actual data for per capita consumption in the Americas, as well as the new approaches to health-related statistics recommended by the World Bank. Unfortunately, the setting of reliable standards regarding more recent indicators for assessing the burden of disease is still far from perfect.

Another pertinent issue in the few countries where a state monopoly is in place is whether current trends toward the privatization of state-managed businesses, generally considered to be nonthriving and weakly promoted industries, will turn them into more aggressive private enterprises. This is feared as a possible future factor, within the conventional concept of offer and distribution (Ledermann's log-normal concept), leading to increased alcohol-related problems (Bejarano & Amador, 1995).

ASSESSMENT SURVEYS AND OTHER STUDIES

By the mid 1960s, Horwitz, Marconi, Addis, and Mariategui had set the stage with a first look at drinking and alcohol-related problems in Latin America.

Thereafter, the pace was somewhat slow, a few studies being conducted in the 1970s, mostly in Chile and Costa Rica by Juan Marconi and the National Institute on Alcoholism (Costa Rica). At that point, most of the topics reflected in the questionnaires given pertained to the field of problem or excessive drinking and alcoholism, according to Marconi's and Jellinek's criteria. Interestingly, early data estimates were more or less homogeneous: 10 percent of problem drinkers and 5 percent of alcoholics, across the board. Distributions of frequencies and further analysis for causality or associations with more rigorous probabilistic approaches were not included.

By the middle of the 1980s, the high level of enthusiasm produced a continuous flurry of national, city, and special population surveys, supported by local and international agencies such as Pan American Health Organization/World Health Organization (PAHO/WHO), Commission Interamericana para el Control del Abuso de Drogas/Organization of American States (CICAD/OAS), U.S. Agency for International Development (USAID)/Development Associates, and even Funcación de Ayuda Contra la Drogadicción (UNFDAC) (now United Nations International Drug Control Programme [UNDCP]).

A review of some of these studies shows that lifetime prevalence in most countries hovered around 65 percent to 80 percent of the population aged 12 years and older. Unfortunately, not much emphasis has been put on further analysis to ascertain degrees of associations in the areas of attitudes, behaviors, and other sociocultural or economic factors. A few highlights are summarized in the few examples where this information is available.

Caetano and Carlini-Cotrim (1993) reviewed the topic of research in South America, and concluded that recent trends in this field indicate a broader focus and a more sophisticated methodological approach. Epidemiological surveys have studied not only severe forms of drinking, but also a range of drinking patterns and problems. They point to several factors enhancing this approach, and the expressed need to develop local methodologies to reinforce health and social resources to better diagnose and plan national or community comprehensive programs (Madrigal, 1989). A set of important, culturally adjusted and validated tools are already in place, including WHO's Comprehensive International Diagnostic Interview (CIDI), International Classification of Diseases, 10th edition (ICD-10), Diagnostic Interview Schedule (DIS), Diagnostic and Statistical Manual, 4th edition (DSM-IV), Munich Alcoholism Test (MALT), Michigan Alcoholism Screening Test (MAST), CAGE, Alcohol Use Inventory (AUI), Drug Use Screening Inventory (DUSI), and a set of "quick and dirty" epidemiological surveillance questionnaires for ER, detention and treatment centers by PAHO/CICAD. A promising arena is the area of prevention research, as the Drug Screening Interview (DUSI) is being implemented in Chile, Colombia, Venezuela, and Central America.

Twelve-month, and current (last 30 days) prevalence of alcohol consumption in several countries provide more reliable figures for the population, since most surveys did not specify the exception "more than a few sips" when surveying lifetime prevalence and the culture is permissive, so that most people have tried alcohol on multiple occasions in their lives. Table 9.2 illustrates prevalence rates for some selected countries.

Apart from national averages, Chile presents an interesting situation. In this country, European traditions are quite salient, and it is also regarded as ethnically homogeneous and well educated. Thus regular consumption of wine is culturally accepted. The mortality rate from cirrhosis of the liver is one of the highest in the world, as discussed in the section from consumption statistics (crude rate 27/100,000, vs. a standardized European rate of 46.2).

Nevertheless, it is important to further analyze the last national survey in 1995 (National Council for the Control of Narcotics, 1996), in which 86 percent

TABLE 9.2 Prevalence rates in selected countries of the Americas alcohol consumption: 15 years of age and older.

Country	Ever used %	In last year %	In last month %
Bolivia: 1992[1]	68.7	58.9	42.1
Canada: 1994[2]	88.2	72.3	n.a.
Chile: 1996[3]	–	60.6	39.9
Colombia: 1996[4]	–	59.8	35.2
Costa Rica: 1995[5]	62.3	40.3	24.8
Mexico: 1993[6]	74.6	51.6	42.9
Paraguay: 1991[7]	36.5	31.6	25.8
US: 1994[8]	84.2	66.9	53.9

[1] El Uso Indebido de Drogas en Bolivia (Illegal Drug Use in Bolivia). Población Urbana—1996. Centro Latinoamericano de Investigación Científica, Bolivia (Bolivia: Latin American Center for Scientific Research).

[2] Canadian Profile 1997, Alcohol Tobacco and Other Drugs. Canadian Centre on Substance Abuse. Addiction Research Foundation, 1997.

[3] Estudio Nacional de Consumo de Drogas. Informe final (National Study on Drug Consumption: Final Report), 1996. Consejo Nacional para el Control de Estupefacientes. Ministerio del Interior, Chile (National Council for the Control of Narcotics. Interior Ministry, Chile).

[4] Segundo Estudio de Consumo de Sustancias Psicoactivas en Colombia 1996 (Second Study on the Consumption of Psychoactive Substances in Columbia, 1996), 1997. Coloquio: Revista de la Dirección Nacional de Estupefacientes. No 3, Marzo de 1997 (Conference: Journal of the National Narcotics Administration Number 3, March).

[5] Consumo de Drogas en Costa Rica. Resultados de la Encuesta Nacional de 1995 (Consumption of Drugs in Costa Rica: Results of the 1995 National Survey), 1996. San José, Costa Rica: Instituto sobre Farmacodependencia y Alcoholismo (San José, Costa Rica: Institute of Drug Addiction and Alcoholism (IAFA)).

[6] Encuesta Nacional de Adicciones, Tabaco (National Survey on Addictions, Tobacco), 1993. Secretaría de Salud de los Estados Unidos Mexicanos (Mexican Ministry of Health).

[7] Estudio sobre Salud Mental y Hábitos Tóxicos en el Paraguay (Study on Mental Health and Substance Abuse in Paraguay), 1991. Ministerio de Salud Pública y Bienestar Social (Ministry of Public Health and Social Welfare).

[8] National Household Survey on Drug Abuse: Main Findings, 1994. SAMHSA. U.S. Department of Health and Human Services.

of men and 92 percent of women who reported drinking during the previous 30 days did so "for an average of only five days or less" (the amount drunk is not discussed in the report). Only 4 percent of men and 1.3 percent of women reported drinking on 15 or more days of the month.

Interestingly, 24 percent of drinkers during the previous 30 days were found to be high-risk or problem drinkers through the application of a locally validated questionnaire EBBA (Escala Breve del Beber Anormal (Brief Scale for Abnormal Drinking)). This approach revealed that, while most drinkers during the previous month belonged to the higher socioeconomic strata, 73 percent of problem drinkers belonged to lower income groups.

These important insights should be taken seriously by the local authorities, since Chileans combine episodic drinking, daily wine consumption, and now problem drinking among the lower socioeconomic strata.

The relevance of these findings is related to the high prevalence of problem drinking and a high mortality for cirrhosis of the liver. A possible explanation of this situation might stem from the higher medical and social risks among the populations concerned, making them vulnerable to chronic liver problems (nutritional deficiencies, adverse social conditions, homelessness, severe stress, and poor hygienic conditions).

It is also noted that Chileans consume more distillates (8 times) per capita than Argentineans. On the other hand, both countries consume approximately equal amounts of beer, though in Argentina the switch from wine to beer has been more evident during the last decade.

There are many ways to speculate about these differences between two countries that share similar ethnic and cultural backgrounds and are the main wine producers in Latin America.

It may be that, over time, local patterns of consumption, as well as the greater prevalence of problem drinking among lower socioeconomic strata in Chile, account for the higher alcohol-related morbidity and mortality there.

Argentina has not carried out representative surveys to estimate national levels of consumption. It is reported that 95 percent of the total grape harvest is devoted to wine production. This corresponded to approximately 283,673 hectares of vines, for a total crop of over 25 million metric tons. In terms of benefits for Argentina, this is equivalent to 17,708 jobs (1.3 percent of the manufacturing work force) and 0.02 percent of the GNP.

Duties on wine represent 3.4 percent of total internal taxes, while alcohol beverages as a whole account for 6.33 percent (1988). In 1985 total tax revenue on beverage alcohol was $46.5 million. In terms of control, there is a completely free and open market policy, with no restrictions on promotion or advertising.

In sum, the role of alcohol, at the current level of consumption in these two countries, is very hard to determine in reference to causal factors of two highly prevalent chronic disorders (CHD and cirrhosis), which may be influenced by this substance. In one case, alcohol is a potential protective agent, since Argentina is the highest red meat consumer country in the world, but enjoys relatively low cardiovascular disease rates, and in the other it is a possible risk factor for chronic liver disease.

Accordingly, public health policies in this field should perhaps be more carefully weighed, and other contributing aspects must be examined, such as patterns of consumption, co-morbidity, and basic attitudes and values about drinking.

Bringing together the sets of data and criteria presented and discussed above, the finding with regard to problem drinking may be summarized as follows:

• Latin America is characterized by high prevalence rates of problem drinking, accompanied by relatively low per capita consumption figures (albeit contested on the grounds of lack of reliability and because of illegal channels of production, as well as the need to standardize for the population aged 15 and older).

• The prevalence of excessive drinking is relatively high, ranging from 15 percent to 34 percent. In the few countries that measure them, self-awareness or perceptions by others of these abnormal patterns of consumption are relatively low, indicating that the region enjoys a permissive environment for drinking.

- Public opinion is based on local ideology, normative behavior, and mass communication. In this respect, a polarity has been established, where low perception of problem drinking leads to social pressure to drink (everyone thinks that it is the thing to do). Other attitudes, such as those fostered by social values about alcohol and strong differences of opinion with regard to alcoholism as a vice or a disease, make it difficult to convey health messages in this field.

- Poorly studied profiles and subcultural patterns of drinking among certain low socioeconomic strata accounts for the more dramatic and sustained socially and medically harmful effects of alcohol, reflected in surveys as problem drinking.

- Legislation and overall responses to alcohol-related issues are structured to deal with fiscal and normative issues, leaving out the important aspects of education and support for healthy behavior and lifestyles.

Taking into account the previous two sections dealing with alcohol-related statistics and epidemiological or special studies, it might be useful to consider the following issues:

- While average levels of consumption tend to be low in all countries surveyed, there is a lack of information regarding groups that may be using alcohol harmlessly and the special factors that affect individuals who develop problem drinking and addiction.

- Drinking styles in countries that share similar population profiles, such as the Southern Cone countries, are conducive to different effects among drinkers. In Argentina, where there is a stronger alcohol (wine and beer) industry than in Chile, the burden of disease is much lower, as judged by the mortality rates from liver cirrhosis and disability-adjusted life years lost from alcohol dependence and its complications.

- Studies that apply screening questionnaires to detect problem drinking can have a complementary value to help to solve contradictory findings. Such is the case in Chile, where over 80 percent of reported drinkers said that they consumed alcohol on fewer than five days a month during the last 30 days. Nevertheless, when those drinkers were screened with the brief problem drinking instrument (EBBA), 24.5 percent were diagnosed as problem drinkers.

- When these figures were further analyzed to determine specific socioeconomic differences, it was found that over 60 percent of those screened as problem drinkers belonged to lower socioeconomic levels, whose living conditions, employment status, nutritional deficit, and so on, have deteriorated with the current trends to develop free market economies and reduce social welfare.

• On the other hand, countries where per capita alcohol consumption is very low have not only experienced a partially documented increase in accidents, violence, and other social consequences of inebriation, but symptomatic drinking (to alleviate personal or social distress) may be atypically increased.

These previous considerations need to be taken further for sound policy-making, and it may be sensible to readdress the following issues: (a) whether problem drinking is the cause of all those evils on its own; or (b) if controls were weakened whether there would be a higher supply, and hence these problems would worsen. What seems to require serious attention is that, in spite of a market that has remained stable for some 30 years, problem drinking is dangerously high and, indeed, is showing a strong tendency to increase in intensity and frequency in Latin America.

Accidents

Alcohol-related injuries from a variety of causes other than war are allegedly well documented by law enforcement and forensic agencies, although there are very few adequate reporting systems to record what seems to be common knowledge and a cause of concern among the public.

It has been suggested (Rosovsky & Borges, 1992) that accidents linked to the consumption of alcohol are also related to other circumstances, such as socioeconomic conditions, levels of consumption among different groups, safety measures, personal behavior, and enforcement measures.

In general, it may be stated that accident- and violence-related mortality affects men more than women, and the main causes are traffic accidents, homicide and, less frequently, suicide (Rosovsky & Borges, 1992).

Alcohol-related accidents and violent deaths are difficult to document, mainly because many deaths occur long after the incident, as reported by Rosovsky and Borges (1992). Sometimes relatives of the victims intervene to avoid autopsies as well. The studies in Costa Rica and Medellín are also important, since these are probably two of the most accurately timed case-of-death reports linking alcohol to violence, suicide, and traffic accidents.

Because of the lack of established criteria, the reported range of alcohol-related traffic accidents is from 3.4 percent to 55 percent (Rosovsky & Borges, 1992). In Costa Rica, at the beginning of the 1990s, five out of 10 violent deaths were related to traffic accidents and 46 percent of vehicle operators dying at the time of the accident had positive blood alcohol levels.

These situations persist, in spite of apparent full awareness of the authorities. Legislation is quite explicit with regard to problems related to "driving under the influence" (DUI) and "driving while intoxicated" (DWI). Yet enforcement falls short. In Bolivia, traffic accidents involving a positive blood alcohol concentration (BAC) comprise 19 percent of all accidents. In Brazil, 25 percent of vehicle operators involved in traffic accidents had some degree of alcohol in their blood. In Ecuador, one-third of all accidents are considered to be related to alcohol ingestion.

In Peru, it was reported that alcohol was a factor in 17.35 percent of traffic accidents, 50 percent of aggressive behavior, and 30 percent of incidents of marital violence. Another study indicated that 50 percent of traffic deaths were associated with alcohol consumption. Alcohol dependence is reported to range between 2.68 percent and 18.6 percent in some communities, and it is estimated that the problem affects 2 million Peruvians.

In other studies of different risk populations, alcohol has been found to play a role, sometimes as the primary etiological agent, and in other instances as a promoting factor in problems such as those referred above. For instance, in a survey of inpatients in a substance addiction treatment unit, alcohol was found to be the primary drug in 41.3 percent of the subjects, while the figures for coca paste, marijuana, and cocaine were 30.7 percent, 20 percent, and 3.4 percent, respectively (Torres & Murrelle, personal communication). At the same time, 72 percent were diagnosed as alcohol-dependent or high-risk drinkers, while alcohol was determinant of depressive symptoms in almost 26 percent of all cases of depression.

In another study in Medellín, Colombia, of 496 cases attending or taken to the emergency room of a city hospital, positive blood alcohol levels were found in 42 percent of personal injuries, 40 percent of traffic accidents, 30 percent of suicidal patients, and 10 percent of work-related accidents. In a forensic study, 33.6 percent of the cases linked to possible homicide, 33.3 percent of suicides, and 60 percent of traffic fatalities tested positive for blood alcohol.

A further survey carried out in Medellín in 1992 (Torres, 1992) applying the CAGE questionnaire found that 32.9 percent of people came within the rating of high-risk or alcohol-dependence (42.3 percent for men when desegregated), with a 16 percent alcohol-dependence rate among the urban population of Medellín. The authors indicate that Medellín has been under tremendous social pressure because of violence and drugs (which may explain the high prevalence due to stress in the population).

TEENAGE DRINKING

The onset of drinking needs careful attention when considering issues pertaining to psychosocial development and teenagers' interaction with prevailing drinking practices in any given society. Adolescence is the gateway to lifetime attitude and choices among the different possible options and lifestyles.

The onset of drinking usually takes place around the age of 15 in most Latin American countries, and the last-month prevalence and current drinking ranges from 10 percent to 20 percent among teenagers.

There are few studies at present that permit consistent conclusions on this topic. These include in Chile (National Council for the Control of Narcotics, 1996) an executive report about the metropolitan and national study on school populations carried out in 1994 and 1995, Costa Rica's (Sandí, 1995) *Adolescence and drug consumption*, and a Bolivian study by Alcaraz and colleagues (1994) on *Prevalence of drug abuse among urban students in Bolivia*. While each of these studies has singular characteristics which make them difficult to compare, there are also some interesting common findings.

Both the Chilean and the Costa Rican studies applied the same instrument, a validated Spanish version of Tarter's DUSI. This instrument encompasses the gathering of data, including levels of consumption, and also the analysis of frequency and intensity, as well as an assessment of risk and protective factors. In Bolivia, an instrument was designed to estimate levels of prevalence among 12 to 21-year-old urban populations (use ever, last year, and last month). It was also possible to compare two studies (1993 and 1996), which was valuable for observing trends during the period. Chile and Costa Rica carried out their studies on a representative sample of the national population. The age distribution ranged from 12 to 18+ year-olds in Chile, 12 to 19 years in Costa Rica, and 12 to 21 years in Bolivia.

In Chile (National Council for the Control of Narcotics, 1996), 72.7 percent of adolescents reported that they had consumed alcohol at least once (76.18 percent of males and 69.45 percent of females). Urban adolescents reported a higher prevalence of 79.3 percent (79.2 percent for males and 79.4 percent for females). In Bolivia (1994) ever-use prevalence was 57.8 percent (65.7 percent for men and 49.5 percent for women). The Costa Rican study did not include ever-use prevalence.

Last-year prevalence was as follows: at the national level Chile reported a 62.7 percent prevalence among the adolescents surveyed and 70.8 percent among an urban sample. The figure in Bolivia was 50.9 percent (59.3 percent males and 42.2 percent females) and in Costa Rica 50.8 percent (51.6 percent males and 49.6 percent females).

The figures for last-year prevalence suggest gender differences. Such differences were present in Bolivia, while minimal in both Chile and Costa Rica.

Last-month prevalence figures for 1995, available for Chile and Bolivia together, indicate that 37.5 percent at the national level and 44.9 percent of urban samples consumed alcohol during that period. In Bolivia 29.7 percent of students (38.3 percent of males and 20.7 percent of females) reported drinking in the past month.

Students from urban areas in Chile had a higher prevalence of drinking than at the overall national level, and also higher than their peers in Bolivia. This is a relevant insight, since there has been concern that urban teenagers in most Latin American countries have developed a particular pattern of consumption, namely, binge drinking during weekends, which entails multiple consequences, such as driving while intoxicated, violence, drag racing, and unsafe and premature sex.

As for the average age of onset, these studies report certain areas in common (Costa Rica 11.2 years, Chile 13.3 years nationally and 13.2 in urban areas, and in Bolivia 10–15 years).

Knowledge about the age of onset of drinking is important for planning preventive approaches. These results of studies may also indicate what ages are most at risk, and prompt the setting up of programs dealing with refusal skills, early interventions, and specific approaches both to family and through one-on-one counseling to deal with the abnormal factors usually present in teenage drinking. Fortunately, many countries are now paying greater attention to these early experiences about drinking, their context, and the triggering causes. There are, at present, several special population studies and monitoring programs underway, as well as systematic applications of risk scales, usually based on the DUSI, which in due time will give a better picture of these risky behaviors.

For instance, Chile and Costa Rica carried out a logistic regression analysis on risk and protective factors within the several domains of the DUSI: mental health, aggressiveness, temperament, isolation, assertiveness, impaired peers, family, and school adjustment. The scores derived from the different domain categories were matched with other variables such as age, gender, and drug use reported in the study. The results were clear with reference to age, school problems, and aggressiveness, which were the most significant risk or predisposing factors.

In Costa Rica, with similar results, controlling for age and social class, the most significant levels of risk were linked to behavioral and emotional problems and poor utilization of leisure time. Alcohol was suggestively linked to rebelliousness and depression as well, but with weaker statistical associations.

One question that is particularly difficult to answer through these research approaches is how traditional drinking styles and, according to Cavanaugh and Clairmont (1985), Singer (1986), or Edwards et al. (1994), unsafe levels of availability are incorporated, and to what degree, in these risk scales. It may be argued that permissive societies, for instance, those where early drinking experiences are sanctioned as "desirable macho behavior," play a substantive role in molding decision-making attitudes among adolescents, facing either peer pressure or any other opportunities allowed in their cultural settings. Unfortunately, there are not many studies in Latin America on attitudes among adolescents and/or students, but most experts believe that this question may not only be relevant, but—it is sensible to assume—very valid as well.

Among earlier studies, Alban (as cited in Sandi, 1995) in Costa Rica surveyed a group of 10th and 11th graders; 70 percent of the students showed some "indifference" to alcoholism, although 19 percent admitted to having an alcohol dependent parent. They expressed awareness of the harmful consequences of excessive drinking, but also a clear intention to get drunk. These attitudes and behaviors are very similar to later studies by Sandi (1995), as reported above. Another salient conclusion for the understanding of these earlier drinking styles is that in spite of students' frequent positive answers about their own drinking or smoking behaviors, the perception of harm is very low. Obviously, this may be related to "acceptability and denial of the consequences" (Sandi, 1995), at both the individual and cultural levels.

These authors, Sandi and Miguez, expressed some concern that in the first national survey in Costa Rica in 1970, there were no problem drinkers registered among teenagers, while in 1990 in a study of a representative sample of 10th and 11th graders, it was reported that 13 percent were rated as excessive drinkers.

To conclude, it may be useful to refer to another study carried out in Costa Rica (Bejarano, 1995), which refers to the reported levels of drug consumption and risk perceptions among university students at four different centers. This survey was done sequentially in 1992, 1993, and 1994 and it covers older populations than those depicted above. While this group ranged from 19 to 30 years of age, some of the conclusions may reinforce the data obtained on the issue of perception of harm related to alcohol consumption in prescriptive societies. Interestingly, in all but one university center, the older the individual the lower was his/her perception of harm. This may indicate that the process of socialization is more firmly incorporated in early adult life, and the prevailing attitudes of a "permissive culture" are progressively reinforced. It is proposed that this phenomenon is closely related to issues such as the perception of social and individual harms linked to drinking behaviors. At the same time, according to Heath's conception of social control, this may be a good example of the social cross-purposes that occur when having to confront "normal," "normative," and "modal" norms in permissive societies.

The data gathered in this interesting study lead to the finding that alcohol drinking during the previous week increased at all centers. Also, drinking in the previous 24 hours increased by 5 percent from 1992 to 1994.

These few studies on teenage and young people's drinking point to the need to gain further insight into the extent of the problem in Latin America. A relatively early age of onset, for instance, causes some concern in view of the subsequent developmental risks related to problem drinking. The potential to continue systematically to study risk factors (age of onset, increase in problem drinking with age, school problems, issues of gender, impulsiveness, and aggressive behaviors) as well as protective factors (stable family life) such as those suggested by the Costa Rican and Chilean studies is quite encouraging. As this research makes progress across Latin America, school and community-based prevention programs can be duly enriched by these insights as part of the design review and monitoring process.

LEGISLATION

The Appendix shows some examples of legislation approaches implemented in several countries during a span of approximately 20 years.

Notwithstanding the fact that in most Latin American countries there are regulations and some legislation to control alcohol availability, the corresponding enforcement mechanisms are not always as effective as intended by the legislators and policymakers involved in their promotion and adoption.

For example, in all countries with the exception of Chile, the minimum drinking age is 18 (in Chile it is 21). Nevertheless, this measure is hardly enforced in any country. The same is true of restrictions on drinking at certain venues and occasions.

Bearing these limitations in mind, there are regulations in Chile and Venezuela to restrict drinking according to time of day and the venue. In Colombia, there are restrictions on the opening hours allowed for bars. In El Salvador, which has some regulations on advertising beverage alcohol, there are no regulations with regard to the number of licenses or opening hours for bars or liquor stores. One country, Brazil, has included penalties and fines to discourage drinking in the workplace.

In Paraguay, the production of alcohol and tobacco consumption dates back to colonial times, and today they have become the legal drugs approved by social consensus. Alcohol is an ubiquitous component of all celebrations, as an indispensable facilitator for every festive occasion, whether in the family or community, and for all socioeconomic levels, including young people's parties. There are no laws or ordinances dealing with the licensing of outlets and free sale is common, except during public spectacles taking place at night. Paraguay's health code prohibits sales to minors. There are specific standards to regulate the advertising of beverage alcohol, and taxation on these products is relatively high. A state entity, the Paraguayan Alcohol Administration (APAL) has a monopoly on purchasing, distributing, and ensuring quality control of all alcohol products. Nevertheless, 41.6 percent of alcohol products are imported, and in 1987 there seemed to be an increasing trend.

In both Central and South America, the estimated degree of exposure of the public to alcohol advertising is believed to be high. Some authors consider, as in the Dominican Republic, that targeting younger groups is one of the factors in the early onset of drinking, between the ages of 14 and 17 years (Jutkowitz, 1992).

In Costa Rica, in that same year, 1992, there was a total of 81,586 advertisements, of which 60 percent were beer commercials, for a total investment of $3 million, or 58 percent of all advertising expenditure.

Though few countries regulate advertising, some, such as Venezuela and Costa Rica, have specific legislation in this area. There is a total ban on alcohol advertising in Venezuela (radio and television), while Costa Rica has had a National Institute on Alcoholism and Drug Abuse screening and clearance procedure for all beverage alcohol advertising implemented since 1975.

For more than a decade, investment in advertising in Chile has been reported to exceed $14 million, mostly allocated to television commercials.

ALCOHOL POLICIES

While some countries of the world enjoy a long tradition in the formulation of alcohol-related policies, many of them, especially in Latin America, are without such public health measures. A public health approach is lacking and no standards are applied to the advertising of alcohol.

At the beginning of the 1960s, very few countries had formulated explicit national policies in relation to this problem. Based on such policies, only four countries in the whole continent were able to develop national programs. These policies covered only a few of the issues, in spite of the 10-year regional health plan approved by a special meeting of ministers of health held in 1972, which recognized alcohol-dependence as a threatening health problem for member countries.

Things have not changed much since then, as most of the measures proposed relate to fiscal objectives such as taxation, production, and sales. Some of those active in this field complain about the lack of public health input to these measures, although it is recognized that some of the issues fall in some other areas of responsibility, for example, public drunkenness and violence belong to the area of public order.

It would be desirable for national planners to make an effort to define strategies, not only to bring down levels of consumption, but also to address certain attitudes and behaviors in each cultural setting, and even to intervene effectively to solve the rooted social problems that are fundamental for certain strata. In Costa Rica, and perhaps in all countries of the region, many people drink to get drunk, sometimes fast. Therefore, any intervention to create awareness and measures to counteract this behavior would be beneficial in curtailing problem drinking.

Further reflections on this topic may again point to sociocultural characteristics that some, regrettably, turn into caricatures to explain the origin of problem drinking. This may explain the resistance to reality test the sensible drinking that takes place on a substancial scale in practically all countries of the region. In fact, it is plausible to suspect that this shadowy area where consumers shift from sensible or moderate drinking to harmful patterns may be affected by the following factors:

• Alcohol-related policies, by and large, have been prompted by fiscal motives, and are blind from the public health perspective;
• Early or timely responses to the educational or health care needs of problem drinkers have been inadequate, and punitive measures through law enforcement channels do not provide opportunities to coordinate with treatment or support services;
• Vulnerable groups have not found an adequate level of care and protection from hazards involving crime, malnourishment and, in general, the absence of minimal provisions for human needs and social welfare. This may well be the case of the unemployed, uneducated, homeless, workers in areas that force them into an unprotected nonnurturing environment (hard labor), people deprived of basic social needs and security, those involved in mass migrations to unfriendly and harsh environments, and so on;
• Some law enforcement measures are still geared to restricting drinking in particular venues and at particular times as in earlier stages in societies con-

cerned, with no regard for the sociocultural evolution of thinking, education, and lifestyles. Such is the case of banning alcohol, especially at drink outlets on elections or certain holidays, at times when alcohol is available at other outlets, so that potential troublemakers can procure and even stock alcohol for the "dry" periods;

• As a corollary, a cultural perception of drunkenness is as an alien or "rogue," lifestyle, contributing to some people's lack of awareness about their own limits as part of a more privileged group of society. Examples of this are driving under the influence, failure to acknowledge the possibility of agreeing to a designated driver on appropriate occasions, inability to perceive social clues as to when drinking behavior turns insulting or embarrassing, not knowing "how much is really too much," and so forth;

• It appears that population approaches to early detection and care for drinkers have been found wanting in most countries. For instance, very few care facilities apply adequate questionnaires or procedures to detect, treat, or refer patients admitted for alcohol-related problems (trauma, gastro-intestinal disorders, depression, suicidal acts, marital difficulties, etc.).

In sum, as discussed in the section on the historical aspects of drinking and policymaking, some of the responses of the colonial era (Salazar, 1994) are still part, and at times the whole, of the repertoire of responses to alcohol in changing times. The tempting solution of advocating and legislating to decrease the availability of alcohol is based on generalized formulas that still need to be time- and field-tested. There is an indication that production and distribution trends, at least for licit products, have remained stable for decades. On the other hand, there seem to be high-risk situations related to unwanted patterns of consumption that may merit more determined efforts at early identification and intervention. In terms of prevention, a plausible population approach to be recommended to countries would be to extend and intensify programs aimed at better environments and sensible drinking lifestyles through a health promotion approach.

Assisting schools of medicine, education, psychology, and social science as well as postgraduate or continuing education programs, including the community- and primary-care level is a fundamental step, as needs assessment, planning, implementation, and evaluation go far beyond just the setting of the policies at the national level.

PROMISING APPROACHES

Caetano and Carlini-Cotrim (1993) reviewed alcohol research in South America, and concluded that recent studies in this field have a broader focus and a more sophisticated methodological approach. Epidemiology surveys have examined not only severe forms of drinking, but also a range of drinking patterns and problems. They point to several factors enhancing this approach, and the expressed need to develop local methodologies to reinforce health and social resources to better diagnose and plan comprehensive national or community programs. A set of sound, culturally adjusted, and validated methodologies is already in place.

These authors underscored that researchers in Latin America have stopped relying as heavily as they did on foreign methodologies and have begun to discover suitable ways of designing their studies to fit the context of their societies and history.

There is obviously still a long way to go in this direction, but it might be appropriate to start promoting research to tackle some of the following questions:

- Are there any genuine integrative drinking styles in different groups or defined communities in the region? Is this possible in light of the globalization taking place all over Latin America? And in this connection, how far can these integrative drinking styles protect these groups as role models for moderate or harmless drinking? What could the protective factors be in this situation?
- With regard to risk factors, it is sensible to continue all feasible lines of well-designed research in this field. There is a need to continue the identification of these factors and their sequence of interaction, and define which are directly involved in early problem drinking. The combination of serious, disciplined understanding, and risk determination may jointly contribute to the development of new paradigms of prevention based on more solid evidence.

CONCLUSIONS AND RECOMMENDATIONS

- It is suggested that due consideration be paid to special issues such as attitudes, values, and behaviors at both the individual and social levels, in order to study and reflect adequately on alcohol consumption and dependence.
- The two prevailing approaches to the study of this problem—the medical and sociopolitical models—are somewhat limited. The medical model may tend to hinder alternative and multidisciplinary initiatives to tackle the problem in all of its dimensions. The sociopolitical model has been very insensitive to the natural history of drinking practices, and has not given sufficient emphasis to anthropological approaches.
- It is important to pay sufficient attention to the natural history of alcoholism, in order to answer questions about the sequential steps that lead drinking to affect some individuals, but not others.
- It may be useful to appeal to policymakers to initiate a process of careful review of current approaches, and to ponder the possibility of looking for alternative and more modern policies.
- It is essential to tackle the issue of culture, which when studied comprehensively and integrated with individual psychosocial factors may be crucial in explaining most drinking practices in a given society.

- It is important to seriously address further research on "cultural" traditions and integrative drinking in different societies, to show whether they still exist or, if they have disappeared, what were the factors involved. Could such societies or groups be used as models to set up moderate drinking programs at the community level? What could be the best strategies for this purpose?

- It is also important to trace and rediscover, within the current social context, historically based attitudes on drinking styles. In such cases, what were the dynamics involved in turning earlier, more controlled drinking practices into problem drinking. Are they really problem drinking or integrative drinking styles, judged from a medical viewpoint?

- One major topic is the need to review current assessments of drinking and related problems that have been evaluated through the tinted glass of different cultures. This is particularly relevant in the case of the adoption of goals which may be more appropriate for the so-called established market economies, especially in North America and Western Europe, where factors such as taxes and inflation-adjusted prices have proved to have far greater impact in controlling drinking problems. There is no need to take an extreme position in this respect. However, it is not infrequent for these dominant ideas to be transplanted wholescale to Latin America without taking local values and traditions into consideration. This may be unwise, especially if the roots of problem drinking are mostly associated with particular culturally influenced drinking styles. At the same time, it is appropriate to ponder a prevailing trend in Latin America, characterized by a very slow increase in per capita alcohol consumption, accompanied by insidious abnormal patterns of drinking which seem to be quite independent of average levels of consumption at the national level.

- The most challenging question for policymakers is to respond to the possibility of promoting moderate and integrative drinking practices through health promotion. It can be argued that this may not be feasible with teenagers, not only because they distrust the sometimes contradictory messages from their elders, but also because they would find it very difficult to absorb messages to drink moderately when surrounded by so many opportunities for drinking during that stage in their development.

- It may be sensible at this time not to rush into intensive programs to encourage integrative patterns of drinking, in view of the caveats pertaining to specific issues raised by the globalization and heavy promotion of beverage alcohol, which may displace most traditional products. In this respect, it may be wiser to devote further study to the dynamics of harmless drinking and set up programs to promote moderation in broader social groups. Adolescents could then be integrated into these societies where more moderate drinking practices prevail, as opposed to the contradictory environment characterized by the aggressive promotion of beverage alcohol and by the problem drinking, especially intoxication of their elders, that they witness at the present time.

APPENDIX

Review of legislation in some Latin American countries.

Country	Date	Legislation	Substances	Description
Panama	May 1979 No. 129	Decree	Alcohol & Tobacco	All advertising must be priorly approved by the Ministry of Health. Establishes sanctions.
Dominican Republic	June 1956 No. 4.471	Health Code	Alcohol	Health Education: Refers to the promotion of health education to implement "campaigns" against alcoholism.
Costa Rica	June 1984 No. 15.449-S No. 16.008-S	Decrees	Alcohol	Established compulsory labeling for all beverage alcohol, including imports. Specific sanction. Subsequent amendments regulate content and size of warning labels.
Costa Rica	Aug. 1987 No. 17.659-S	Executive Decree	Alcohol & Other Substances	Establishes statute for the National Institute on Alcoholism and Drug Dependence.
Costa Rica	Oct. 1987 No. 17.757-G	Executive Decrees	Alcohol	Alcohol trading, approval of regulation aspects of the National Bill on Alcoholic Beverages. It covers issues on sale outlets, sales regulations, and specific clauses to deal with penalties for violators such as cancellations of licenses, etc.
Bolivia	Jan. 1978 No. 15.272	Supreme Decrees	Alcohol	Suspension of imports banning beverage alcohol.
Argentina	Sept. 1983 No. 22.914	Bill	Alcohol	Regulations and standard for admission, covering minors, custodial court orders, and voluntary commitments.
Colombia	April 1983 No. 13.920	Resolution	Alcohol & Drugs	Regulates "standards of organization for specialized services on alcohol and drug dependence."

Country	Date/No.	Type	Topic	Description
Colombia	Feb. 1986 No. 30	Bill	Alcohol & Drugs	Adopts a "national stature on drugs and narcotics." Includes standards to implement educational and preventive campaigns on alcohol and tobacco, import controls, and violations and penalties.
Colombia	Dec. 1986 No. 3.788	Decree	Drugs, Alcohol, & Tobacco	Refers to bylaws for Bill No. 30, refers specifically to educational programs at the school level, and preventive campaigns against alcohol and tobacco.
Ecuador	March 1988 No. 9.939	Resolution	Rehabilitation, Mental Health, and Alcoholism	Approval of standards of care in mental health units of alcohol treatment and rehabilitation; regulations are not included.
Ecuador	March 1979	Constitution	Drugs, Tobacco, and Alcohol	Refers to the constitutional right for health and social services, including programs to combat alcoholism and other dependencies.
Nicaragua	Nov. 1979 No. 153	Decree	Alcohol and Drugs	Distance from alcohol sales outlets must be minimum 400 meters from educational centers, hospitals, churches, etc.
Nicaragua	Dec. 1980 No. 596	Decree	Alcohol	Forbids sale of beverage alcohol to minors under age 18.
Nicaragua	May 1991	Regulation	Alcohol	Furthers bylaws on sales in restaurants and bars, including schedules.
Peru	March 1969 No. 17.505	Code	Alcohol & Drugs	Contains regulations pertaining to control of alcoholism and toxic habits.
Venezuela	Dec. 1978 No. 2.999	Decree	Alcohol	Bylaws on alcohol and derivatives: definitions, registers, distilleries, aging. Regulations for alcohol consumption on planes, boats, and sports centers: imports, exports, taxes, and inspection.

(continued)

257

Country	Date	Legislation	Substances	Description
Mexico	Feb. 1985	Regulation	Alcohol	Regulation and organizational chart of the National Anti-Alcohol Council.
Mexico	July 1986 No. 23	General Sanitary Codes	Tobacco, Alcohol & Drugs	General applicable dispositions to the control of tobacco and alcohol (Articles 185–193).
Mexico	Jan. 1988	Regulations	Alcohol & Food Products	Regulates production, imports and exports of food products, including beverage alcohol as well as procedures and requirements for sales of these products.
Chile	Aug. 1980 No. 4.710	Decree	Alcohol	Establishes an "Intersectoral Commission on Primary Prevention on Alcoholism" at the school level.
Honduras	Oct. 1987 No. 308-87	Resolution	Drugs & Alcohol	Pertains to treatment and rehabilitation, recognizing legal basis for the "Foundation of Pioneers of Tegucigalpa."
Honduras	Feb. 1983 No. 131	Constitutional Decree	Substance Abuse & Alcoholism	Establishes the Honduran Institute on Prevention for Alcoholism and Drug Dependence (IHADFA).
El Salvador	May 1988 No. 955	Decree	Tobacco, Alcohol, & Drugs	Actions to treat and rehabilitate substance dependence. Regulates movie and TV ads, warning labels of tobacco products, and imports of controlled drugs.
Guatemala	Sept. 1985 No. 740.85	Resolution	Alcohol & Drugs	Establishes a "National Commission on Alcohol and Drug Abuse," to plan and oversee programs to deal with addictive disorders.
Paraguay	Dec. 1980 No. 836	Sanitary Code	Tobacco, Alcohol, & Drugs	Establishes regulations to control production, consumption, and advertising of tobacco and alcohol products.

Country	Date / No.	Type	Alcohol & Institutions	Description
Honduras	Oct. 1989 No. 136–89	Decree	Alcohol & Institutions	Bylaws dealing with National Institute (IHADFA), its objectives, official coordinating agency, and normalization in the field of addiction and dependence.
Costa Rica	April 1991 No. 20.310	Decree	Alcohol	Approves Regulation NCR 110:1990, further defining rules for alcohol distillation and quality control.
Guatemala	Jan. 1992 No. 85.491	Resolution	Alcohol	Schedules for sales and law enforcement in regards to bars, drinking in public places, regulations for other commercial outlets. Severe penalties for selling alcohol to minors. Controls possession of arms in drinking venues.
Panama	Dec. 1990 No. 30	Bill of Law	Alcohol & Tobacco	Establishes new regulations and penalties for sales or provision of beverage alcohol to minors.
Peru	Nov. 1991 No. 691	Decree	Tobacco & Alcohol	In a package to protect consumers, regulates publicity and establishes the National Council on Publicity.
Ecuador	June 1992 No. 2.369	Resolution	Alcohol & Tobacco	Bans tobacco and alcohol from educational venues. Regulates consumption among staff and forbids commercial promotion of these products in educational centers.
Panama	May 1992 No. 299	Decree	Alcohol & Tobacco	Regulates publicity on alcohol and tobacco. Classification of beverage alcohol. Warning labels on alcohol and tobacco products.

Source: Bolis (1993).

REFERENCES

Addiction Research Foundation. (1997). *Canadian Profile 1997: Alcohol, Tobacco, and Other Drugs.* Toronto: Canadian Centre on Substance Abuse, Addiction Research Foundation.

Alcaraz, F., et al. (1994). La prevalencia del uso de drogas: Poblacion Urbana Estudiantil (*Prevalence of drug abuse among urban students in Bolivia*). La Paz: Centro Latinoamericano de Investigacion Cientifica (CELIN). Bolivia.

Bejarano, A. (1995). Estudio sobre consumo de drogas y percepciones de riesgo en estudiantes universitarios con carné 1992 (Study of drug consumption and risk perceptions among university students enrolled in 1992). San Jose, Costa Rica: Instituto Sobre Alcoholismo y Farmacodependencia.

Bejarano, J. & Amador, G. (1995). El Monopolio de la Producción de Alcohol (The alcohol production monopoly). *Revista del Colegio de Médicos y Cirujanos, Costa Rica (Journal of the College of Physicians and Surgeons, Costa Rica).* September.

Bolis, M. (1993). Legal Data Bank (Working Document). Pan American Health Organization.

Caetano, R. & Carlini-Cotrim, B. (1993). Perspectives on alcohol epidemiology research in South America. *Alcohol Health and Research World, 117,* 244–250.

Cavanaugh, J. & Clairemont, F. F. (1985). *Alcoholic Beverages: Dimensions of Corporate Power.* New York: St. Martin's Press.

Edwards, G., et al. (1994). *Alcohol Policy and the Public Good.* Oxford: Oxford University Press.

Escohotado, A. (1989). *Historia de las Drogas.* (History of Drugs). Madrid: Alianza Editorial.

Ferrando, D. (1989). *Use and Abuse of Drugs in Peru.* Lima: Centro de Información educación para la Prevención del Abuso de Drogas (CEDRO).

FUNDASALVA. (1991). Conocimientos, actitudes y prácticas sobre drogas y drogadicción en población general entre 15 y 54 años del Area Metropolitana de San Salvador, Volume 1.: San Salvador (Knowledge, attitudes and practices regarding drugs and drug addiction among the general population between the ages of 15 and 54 in the San Salvador metropolitan area, Volume 1). San Salvador: FUNDASALVA.

Gonzalez, H. (1984). *Ideologies of drinking: Public and professional ideas on drinking in Costa Rican society.* Dissertation for Doctorate in Public Health. Graduate Division, University of California, Berkeley, CA.

Heath, D. B. (1989). Environmental factors in alcohol use and outcomes. In H. W. Goedde & D. P. Agarwal (Eds.), *Alcoholism: Biomedical and Genetic Aspects* (312–324). New York: Pergamon Press.

Heath, D. B. (1990). Anthropological and sociocultural perspectives on alcohol as a reinforcer. In W. M. Cox (Ed.), *Why People Drink: Parameters of alcohol as a reinforcer* (263–290). New York: Gardner Press.

Heath, D. B. (1991). Drinking patterns of the Bolivian Camba. In D. J. Pittman & H. R. White (Eds.), *Society, Culture, and Drinking Patterns Reexamined* (Alcohol, Culture, and Social Control Monograph Series). New Brunswick, NJ: Rutgers Center for Alcohol Studies.

Institute of Drug Addiction and Alcoholism. (1996). *Consumption of drugs in Costa Rica: Results of the 1995 national survey.* San José, Costa Rica: Instituto Sobre Alcoholismo y Farmacodependencia (IAFA).

Jellinek, E. M. (1960). *The Disease Concept of Alcoholism.* New Haven, CT: Hillhouse Press.

Jutkowitz, J. M. (1992). *Survey on Drug Prevalence and Attitudes in Domincan Republic.* Washington, DC: Development Associates.

Kirberg, A. & Maass, J. (1985). Observaciones sobre habitos de ingesta de alcohol en una comunidad Aymara del altiplano de la Provincia de Iquique (Observations on alcohol consumption in an Aymara community in the highlands of the Iquique Province). *Separata de la Revista De Psiquiatria (Journal of Psychiatry, Supplement),* Hospital Psiquiatrico Doctor Jose Horowitz Barak, Año II, No. 7.

Latin American Center for Scientific Research. (1996). *Illegal Drug Use in Bolivia*. Bolivia: Latin American Center for Scientific Research.

Madrigal, E. (1989). Alcohol research in Latin America: Cup that is bubbling. *British Journal of Addiction, 84*, 243–244.

Mariátegui, J. (1985). Concepción del Hombre y Alcoholismo en el Antiguo Perú. *Anales de Salud Mental, 1*, 33–49.

Menendez, E. (1983). Socioantropología del proceso de alcoholizacion en America Latina 1970–1980 (Systematic analysis of socio-anthropological works on the alcoholization process in Latin America 1970–1980). *Acta Psiquiatrica y Psicologica de America Latina, 29*, 247–256.

Ministry of Health. (1993). *National Survey on Addictions, Tobacco*. Mexico City: Ministry of Health.

Ministry of Public Health and Social Welfare. (1991). Proyecto Marandu. Estudio sobre Salud Mental y hábitos tóxicos en el Paraguay (Marrandu Project: Study on Mental Health and Substance Abuse in Paraguay). Asuncion: Ministry of Public Health and Social Welfare.

National Council for the Control of Narcotics. (1996). *National Study on Drug Consumption: Final Report*. Santiago: Ministry of the Interior.

PAHO. (1990). *Bulletin of the Pan American Health Organization, 24*, 86–96.

Rosovsky, H. & Borges, G. (1993). Accidentes y Alcohol en America Latina (Accidents and alcohol in Latin America). In *Hacia un Enfoque Multidisciplinario* (147–157). Mexico City: Consejo Nacional contra las Adicciones.

Salazar, D. (1994). Las Bebidas Espirituosas en el Siglo XVII. En Vida cotidiana en el Siglo XVII (thesis). Universidad de Costa Rica, Facultad de Ciencias Sociales, Escuela de Historia, 253–346.)

SAMHSA. (1994). *National Household Survey on Drug Abuse: Main Findings*. Washington, DC: U.S. Department of Health and Human Services.

Sandi, L., et al. (1995). *Adolescencia y consumo de drogas en Costa Rica* (Adolescence and drug consumption). Editorial, UNA—Instituto del Niño, IAFA.

Singer, M. (1986). Toward a political-economy of alcoholism: The missing link in the anthropology of drinking. *Social Science and Medicine, 23*, 113–130.

Skog, O. J. (1995). Paper presented at the WHO Working Group on Alcohol and Health Implications for Public Health Policy, Oslo, Norway, 9–13 October 1995.

Torres, Y. (1992). *First National Household Mental Health Survey, Columbia*. Bogotá: Luís Amigó University Press.

World Bank. (1993). *World Development Report*. New York: Oxford University Press.

WHO, Expert Committee on Mental Health. (1952). First Session of the Alcoholism Subcommitteee, WHO Technical Report Series, No. 42. Geneva: World Health Organization.

Chapter 10

Mexico

Maria Elena Medina-Mora

The use of beverage alcohol is part of the Mexican culture, as it is an important means of social integration, but at the same time it is associated with adverse health and social consequences. Alcohol abuse is the biggest single risk factor for health, accounting for 9 percent of the burden of disease in Mexico from both acute and chronic conditions (Frenk et al., 1994), a high proportion of that figure being explained by the way alcohol is consumed. Public health interventions to control this problem yield a high level of return on investments, thus ranking high as a priority from the cost-benefit viewpoint.[1]

The aim of this chapter is to provide an up-to-date assessment of drinking practices in Mexico, a country that is undergoing major socioeconomic change. It includes a discussion of policy developments and cultural barriers to implementing policies oriented toward the promotion of moderation in the consumption of alcohol and thus the reduction of alcohol-related problems.

It is divided into seven sections:

- The introductory section contains a brief description of the country in terms of its demographic profile and health status in order to provide both a framework and to position the alcohol phenomenon in the overall and socioeconomic setting of the country.
- Historical aspects: this section provides a description of alcohol use from colonial times to the present day, with an emphasis on cultural aspects,

---

[1] The estimate was based on an assessment of the burden of disease as measured by healthy days lost due to premature mortality or disability (DALYs) and on an analysis of the cost-benefit of different interventions (Frenk et al., 1994).

again to provide a frame of reference, but also to introduce Mexico's cultural setting derived from the mixture of two cultures with different drinking values and norms in order to understand the role of alcohol in society, the prevailing drinking norms, and problems and the cultural diversity still prevailing in the country.

• Availability of alcohol: this section describes trends since the 1970s in global availability and type of beverage produced.

• Patterns of use: this section emphasizes the demand side of the phenomenon, describing the main results of local and national surveys and variations by groups of the population, and providing a framework to understand the major health and social problems associated with this practice.

• Health and social consequences: this part includes a description of the social costs of the alcohol problem to the Mexican population and its evolution, based on available statistics and on specific studies addressing accidents, violence, and health problems.

• Social response: this section describes recent and current alcohol policies over the past 10 years, with emphasis on the current program.

• Conclusions: a final section summarizing major research and policy issues that deserve reconsideration.

SOCIODEMOGRAPHIC PROFILE OF THE COUNTRY

Sociodemographic Transition

Several demographic trends are likely to influence drinking behavior—the distribution of drinking in the population and the way it affects society. Among the more important are the increase in absolute numbers of the drinking population, the integration of females in the economy and their increased access to alcohol, an important modification of the religious composition towards more Protestantism, bringing with it different norms and values related to drinking, and an accelerated process of urbanization and acculturation resulting from intensive international migration of seasonal workers, with continual changes of residence between Mexico and the United States.

Another important factor is that in Mexico the mortality rate started to decrease in the 1930s but it was not until the 1960s that a similar trend was observed for the fertility rate. As a result the population increased substantially; it doubled between 1930 and 1958, doubled again by 1981, and according to projections will double yet again by 2020. Also there has been a considerable drop in the fertility rate since 1970 which has modified the demographic composition of the population. The proportion of young people is decreasing (from 43 percent in 1950 to an estimated 35 percent in 2000), while that of old people is growing (from 4 to 7 percent in the same period). The adult drinking population will not increase as a proportion of society but is growing in absolute numbers (from 13.7 million in 1950 to an estimated 56.1 million by the year 2000).

Since the 1980s the status of women has altered radically. The fall in fertility from 7 children per woman in 1970 to 3.4 in 1990, to a further estimated 2.75 by the year 2000 has given them more time for themselves, apart from raising children. Nowadays the proportion of males and females in secondary school (7–9 years of school completed) is almost equal, as is a strong presence of women in the final stages of labor training programs. The proportion of females among the economically active population increased from 15.2 percent in 1970 to 29.2 percent in 1990. The predominance of young, single women has changed as more married mothers join the workforce, as a result of the increase in the availability of positions for women, the recession in the economy, and the rise in unemployment among males (INEGI, 1990). Along with these changes, women now have more occasions for drinking.

Another important demographic trend expected to influence drinking be- havior is migration, both domestic and international. Mexico has changed from being a rural country with only 25 percent of its people living in cities in 1970 to being a mainly urban society, wherein 75 percent of the population live in cities. Several studies have documented a higher level of inebriation in rural communi- ties (Maccoby, 1965; Natera, 1977; Berruecos & Velasco, 1977; Medina-Mora et al., 1988) and also some evidence that males modify their drinking habits after migrating by reducing the number of drinking occasions (Cuevas, 1991).

More recently, a new process of acculturation has been observed as a result of the intensive international migration to the United States. A large number of undocumented workers do seasonal work on the other side of the border, continually changing residence between the two countries. For instance, 72 per- cent of the workers who crossed the border through five major cities between March 1991 and February 1992 had previous experience of crossing the border. The majority of international migrants are adult males involved in small-scale agricultural production, though there is an increase in the rate of migration of females and more educated male workers (Bustamante, Santibañez, & Corona, 1994). Patterns and norms of substance use are also influenced by this process of acculturation.

Another recent important demographic change is the change in the religious affiliation of Mexicans in the last two decades. In the 1970 census, 96.2 percent of the population considered themselves Roman Catholics, but this proportion fell to 89.7 percent in 1990. The growing group of Protestants of different denominations have definite and clear temperance values for drinking that differ radically from the original Catholic values that do not prevent people from drinking.

Health Status of the Mexican Population

In the latter part of this century there have been substantial advances in the health status of the population. Life expectancy has increased in the nearly two decades since 1980, with UN estimates for the years between 1995 and 2000 standing at 75.5 years for females and 69.5 years for men. Mortality among children under five years of age fell by 37 percent, and maternal mortality by 44 percent, between 1980 and 1992. In just two years, from 1990 to 1992, coverage of comprehensive immunization programs for children under five years expanded from 46 percent to over 92 percent.

In spite of these advances, Mexico faces two overlapping health challenges. On the one hand, it must overcome the epidemiological backlog represented by diseases related to underdevelopment such as common infections, malnutrition, and maternal and perinatal deaths. On the other, it has to tackle emerging problems associated with population aging, industrialization, and urbanization, such as cardiovascular diseases, cancer, mental illness, addictions, and injuries.

In 1991, Mexico lost 12.8 million healthy life years, measured in disablity-adjusted life years (DALYs), through premature mortality and disability. The population under the age of five years accounted for one-third of the burden of disease, the losses being mostly due to premature death from communicable diseases. One-fifth was associated with accidental or intentional injuries, in males between the ages of 15 and 44 years. Of the DALYs lost for these causes, 56 percent were due to injuries; the breakdown by specific causes shows that injuries from motor vehicle accidents and homicide headed the list. One-half of the total burden resulted from noncommunicable diseases, notably cardiovascular disease, neuropsychiatric conditions, including alcohol dependence, and diseases of the digestive tract. Alcohol was the leading risk factor, accounting for 9 percent of the burden.

A study conducted in 1989 estimated that 71 percent of the population lived below the poverty level, 45 percent being extremely poor (Boltvinik, 1994). With a considerable inequality in the distribution of health problems, the burden of infectious diseases, malnutrition, and reproductive health problems is 2.2 times greater for a rural inhabitant than for a town dweller. Life expectancy in two poor states to the south, Chiapas and Oaxaca, was comparable in 1991 to that of poor developing countries, while that in Nuevo Léon was comparable to that of several European countries (Frenk et al., 1994).

In spite of the fact that the number of medical care units in the National Health System increased by 75 percent between 1980 and 1992, and that social security covers 60 percent of the Mexican population, 21 percent of the population still has no access to medical care (Frenk et al., 1994). Treatment for alcohol problems is quite unavailable (Campillo, 1995). It is within this context that alcohol-related problems and possible solutions must be considered.

HISTORICAL ASPECTS OF ALCOHOL USE

All cultures where beverage alcohol is consumed establish their own rules as to the way substances may be used. This includes establishing the types of substances that are made available, the occasions and circumstances of use, and the groups of individuals that may consume them.

Mexico is a society formed by a process of interbreeding (*mestizaje*) of a multiplicity of ethnic groups and people of Spanish origin. Before the Spaniards conquered this region of the world there were 82 ethnic groups. Each of these cultures shared some norms relating to alcohol consumption, but also differed in some aspects. After three centuries of Spanish domination, a new culture emerged that spoke a different language and had a different religion while still preserving the norms, values, and beliefs of the indigenous cultures. Despite the fact that the vast majority of the population is of mixed origin (*mestiza*), there are still 5 million people who speak an indigenous language (7.5 percent of the total population aged 5 years or older) (INEGI, 1990) and 57 different languages are spoken. Although there are some shared common norms relating to substance use among these ethnic groups, the norms differ in many respects.

The indigenous cultural norms on alcohol use strongly influenced the manner in which alcohol was consumed by the emerging Mexican population. That manner differed both from the original Indian practices and from the Spanish way of drinking alcohol; the prevailing Indian regulations were weakened and the Christian norms on drinking were not adopted.

During pre-Columbian times, the types of beverage alcohol consumed in Mexico were derived from fermentation. The most common was a beverage produced from a Mexican agave, *pulque*. The general pattern of use was communal drinking in rituals associated mainly with agriculture, religion, and life events such as being born, getting married, and dying (Taylor, 1979).

Some descriptions (Corcuera de Mancera, 1991) of drinking practices during precolonial times suggest differences in norms on drinking and inebriation for different subgroups of the population and for different circumstances.

Inebriation was allowed under certain circumstances, for example, during the festival of Izcali. During this festival, drunkenness was not only permitted, but was a community practice for everyone, males and females, young and old. This drunkenness was public and was aided by the *tabemero* who kept a constant stream of alcohol flowing.

The Mendoza Code mentions 60 years as the age when people could start drinking without restrictions, while other sources mention 50 years; this was true for both genders. It was said that "drunkenness provided old people with a sense of plenitude and realization that coincided with the decline of natural life ... by that age, blood cooled and alcohol was a remedy for getting warm and going to sleep." During the festival of Tlaxuchimaco, ... "old men and women drank alcohol, got drunk, and fought each other."

Pulque served various purposes. It was used for religious purposes and produced ritual inebriation accepted by society. At the same time, it was a popular secular beverage for restricted use, though abuse was condemned and punished by society. It was also a fated beverage, and men and women born under the sign of the rabbit would be inevitably inclined to drink (Taylor, 1979).

Violation of norms was severely punished. The transgressor was rejected by society as a whole and the price for momentary loss of individual control and the social repercussions of this behavior was isolation. Although the severity of the punishment could vary, it was always applied immediately without opportunity of appeal, and was thus quite effective. European Christian culture also had a normative discourse that regulated ritual and secular use of alcohol, but without effective means for limiting immoderate drinkers (Corcuera de Mancera, 1991).

The Spanish Conquest radically modified the indigenous patterns of alcohol use, which changed from occasional use limited to certain festivals, to indiscriminate secular use. The Spaniards introduced distilled beverages and considerable amounts of alcohol were consumed, including pulque, wine, and brandy. According to Taylor (1979), three main factors accounted for the increase in consumption: the inclusion of a larger proportion of *macehuales*[2] in the population of drinkers, the adjustment of ritual inebriation to numerous festivals in the Catholic calendar, and the commercialization of pulque.

Other reasons might be related to the absence of laws or dispositions that limited alcohol abuse, together with a decrease in the rigor employed by the Indian authorities, who had lost their prestige and political liberty, and thus also a decrease in the rigor with which abuse was prosecuted (Rojas Gonzalez, 1942). No replacement regulations were immediately introduced by the Spaniards who often considered alcohol to be the reason for all misdeeds among the Indians.

Nowadays patterns of alcohol consumption among indigenous cultures show important variations, an example being the complete integration of alcohol use in all aspects of life among the Chamulas of Chiapas (Bunzel, 1940) and the strict limitation of alcohol use to certain occasions among the Tarahumaras of Chihuahua (Kennedy, 1963).

The Tarahumaras consume a fermented beverage known as *tesgüino*. They usually drink in a group and use is almost always linked to religious ceremonies, civil events, or a collective work activity. No guilt is associated with behavior while intoxicated, because responsibility is attenuated under the influence of alcohol.

On the other hand, de la Fuente (1955) described the Chamulas as an "alcoholic culture" because he believed that beverage alcohol was central to Chamulas social life and culture and, excepting those who adopted Christianity, the Chamulas consumed large quantities of alcohol. Binge drinking and intoxication during festivities could last a week (Bunzel, 1940). Initiation to alcohol use occurs early in life and systematic consumption in early adulthood is the norm when civil or religious positions are occupied. Alcoholism is common among those who have occupied such positions. Among the Chamulas, therefore, alcohol consumption per se is not condemned if drinking and inebriation are linked to a group social function. It is condemned, however, when it becomes a "vice" not associated with social activities.

---

[2]*Macehuales* were the lower social group formed by the poorer and simpler citizens (those who could only travel by foot).

Great ambivalence towards alcohol use and abuse has also been described among cultures of Nahuatl origin. Antisocial behavior while intoxicated was rejected, as was frequent consumption of alcohol, especially if it was associated with intoxication, because it was considered a sign of weakness. At the same time, the alcohol dependent was seen as a victim of destiny and as a person who was not responsible for his problems (Madsen & Madsen, 1969).

In these cultural antecedents we may find the roots of many norms and practices observed today in Mexico, among them the use of alcohol linked to festivities, where binge drinking is a common practice, the permissiveness towards inebriation, regulations that are directed more towards for whom and in what circumstances drinking is allowed than to moderation, and a marked ambivalence with regard to alcohol seen as a part of everyday life and as responsible for all problems.

ALCOHOL-RELATED NORMS AND ATTITUDES

Cultural expectations are reflected in social norms defined as rules concerning a given practice in a given cultural setting. These rules are specific to a given status, defined by gender, age, type of occupation, socioeconomic status, and so on, and to the different situations in which individuals find themselves. In this section, the cultural norms now prevalent in Mexico are described as a basis for further analysis of drinking patterns and problems derived from the different ways in which alcohol is consumed.

Some problems are related to drinking practices. Thus it is expected that excessive drinking will cause problems to the individual, but its manifestation will also depend on other factors that interact with drinking behavior such as social tolerance. A problem will arise when someone's behavior violates what is generally accepted or constitutes a social norm (Roizen et al., 1980).

Local studies conducted using these assumptions (Calderon et al., 1981; Medina-Mora et al., 1988; Medina-Mora, 1993) have shown that in Mexico today norms are still more directed towards defining who may drink than towards moderation. It is believed that young people under 16 years of age and people aged over 65 years must not drink. The norm is also more restrictive for females. Occasional inebriation among males is considered appropriate, but females are not supposed to drink. These double standards are supported by both men and women, young and old (Medina-Mora, 1993).

Alcohol fulfills an important function as a means of social integration, and indeed this is the reason for drinking given most frequently by people interviewed. There is also considerable ambivalence towards drinking. For instance, only one-half of the persons interviewed in a household survey conducted in central Mexico (Medina-Mora, 1993) agreed with the statement "Drinking is one of the pleasures of life," while only one in three considered that "Taking a drink is a way of being friendly." The same proportion (32 percent) considered that getting drunk was only an innocent way of having fun, and one in four

(24 percent) agreed that "it is good for people to get drunk once in a while." There was also general agreement with the statements "Attention should not be paid if a drunken man says something inappropriate" and "One must excuse his outspokenness." These data suggest that there is not a straightforward normative structure governing what is expected in relation to the amount consumed or inebriation.

Furthermore, there seems to be no clear differentiation between drinking and excessive drinking, as is shown by the fact that 83 percent of the sample from this study stated that "Nothing good can be said about drinking" and 93 percent said that "Drinking is one of the main reasons why people do things that they should not have done." Alcoholism is considered simultaneously a disease and a vice: 94 percent of respondents considered that alcoholism was a disease; 95 percent considered that if an alcoholic did not seek help the problem could become worse; and 87 percent considered that alcoholics needed to remain abstinent for the rest of their lives. Nonetheless, more than 80 percent also considered that an alcoholic was a morally weak person, and a substantial proportion (71 percent in rural and 62 percent in urban areas) considered that the majority of alcoholics drink because they want to do so.

Results from this and other studies have shown that the Mexican population has a considerable misunderstanding of the similarities between different beverages, as well as of the effects of alcohol, for example, the amount of alcohol required to impair the ability to drive or operate machinery. These studies open important avenues for preventive education.

The above-mentioned study conducted in central Mexico also explored social controls on drinking and attitudes towards control measures. It was evident that religion—in this case, Catholicism—plays a secondary role as a control of alcohol abuse. Only 47 percent of the males and 56 percent of the females agreed with this reason for not drinking as compared with health concerns, cost, making one do things that one regretted later, or loss of control, which were endorsed by more than 90 percent of the sample. In fact, religious festivals were usually related to intoxication; during these occasions binge drinking is common.

In the months prior to the survey, restrictions on alcohol availability had been imposed, including limits on the hours and days alcohol was sold: 87 percent of the people interviewed were aware of these measures; 73 percent agreed with them and considered that they could have positive effects; 37 percent saw benefits related to a possible decrease in violence or accidents; 15 percent reported benefits for the family; 17 percent considered that restrictions could benefit the health status of the population; 12 percent disagreed with the measures; 10 percent considered that they could have unwanted effects such as an increase in legal violations; and 1.4 percent considered that they violated the right to buy and consume alcohol or affected commercial interests. In general, attitudes toward restrictions were more positive among the rural population, and rural and urban dwellers who were less educated and had lower incomes.

In spite of the apparent acceptance of the measures, results from the study also showed that violations of the norms did occur. Just less than one-half (40 percent) of the people interviewed said that it was easy to buy alcohol at night, despite the regulations. Observations from other sources also suggest a possible increase in the local and illegal production of alcohol, involving adverse health consequences and in some cases linked to increased mortality.

Unfortunately no national data are available on normative beliefs and values which might enable these findings to be generalized. Regional variations can be expected, as well as modifications in cultural perceptions linked to other variables, such as the increase in the number of women participating in the country's labor force, with a consequential liberalization of cultural restrictions on drinking, and an increase of Protestant influence promoting abstention. In fact this change of religion among some Indian communities is the cause of social conflict in some regions, where the local authorities control trade in alcohol and the income generated from this activity.

TRENDS IN ALCOHOL PRODUCTION AND SALES

According to Rosovsky (1985; 1994), the beverage alcohol industry in Mexico has grown rapidly since the 1940s, mainly as a result of the expansion of foreign producers as well as local industrial growth. It has been dominated by a few powerful transnational corporations, is vertically integrated, and has led to the development of other manufacturing industries such as glass, thus representing an important source of income for the country. Firms compete for the consumer market using a variety of promotional strategies, effective distribution, and costly advertising, reaching the most remote parts of the country.

Per capita consumption has been studied using self-report in general population surveys (Medina-Mora et al., 1991) and through figures for the production and sale of beverage alcohol (Rosovsky et al., 1992). Both methodologies have advantages and disadvantages, mainly linked to underreporting and to the failure to include local and illegal production. In any case they can be complementary, especially if the data obtained are consistent.

The population between 15 and 65 years of age interviewed in the 1990 national survey on addictions (Medina-Mora et al., 1991) reported an annual per capita ethanol intake of 4.6 liters. The per capita intake of drinkers was 5.6 liters, and when only males were considered the rate reached 8.1 liters. It was found that the 25 percent of drinkers with the heaviest intake consumed 78 percent of the total alcohol.

This estimation of per capita intake was compared to an estimate obtained through sales figures.[3] The rate estimated from sales was 4.4 liters, while the rate estimated through self-report was 3.71 liters, for the urban population aged

[3]In order to make the estimates comparable, use of pure cane alcohol and of pulque were deleted from the estimated total obtained from the self-report.

15 to 65 years. The shortfall of 16 percent may be due, in part, to the proportion consumed by the population over 65 years of age and by the rural population not covered in the survey, which is estimated to represent 25 percent of the total population of the country. Surveys conducted among rural populations have indicated that rates of both abstainers and heavy drinkers are higher in this sector (Medina-Mora et al., 1988).

Per capita consumption of alcohol in the population aged 15 years and over, estimated from legal production, reached 5 liters in 1994. Per capita intake for the population as a whole has increased considerably in the last 20 years or so, from 2.1 liters in 1970 to 3.5 liters in 1994, an increase (variation rate) of 62 percent. Data published by Rosovsky et al. (1992) showed a steady increase from 1970 until 1980, when they showed a decrease and then rose again after 1986, reaching a peak in 1991. Data from *World Drink Trends* (1997) indicate that per capita consumption is on the rise, chiefly aided by an increasing per capita consumption of beer. This expansion is related partly to the widening of the drinking population and also to other factors such as the increase in supply that occurred when Mexico signed the General Agreements on Tariffs and Trade (GATT) agreement resulting in a reduction of taxes for foreign beverages from 80 percent to 10 percent of their price.

According to production figures, beer is the beverage most widely consumed, accounting for 70 percent of the ethanol produced, followed by spirits (27 percent), and to a lesser degree table wines (1 percent). Nonetheless, this last product has increased more than any other, with a increase of 388 liters from 1970 to 1991. Another new phenomenon in the country is the increasing share of new beverages such as coolers (5 percent ethanol) and cocktails (12 percent ethanol) aimed mainly at the younger end of the consumer spectrum (Rosovsky , forthcoming).

Estimates based on self-report suggest a smaller share of beer in overall consumption[4] at only 58 percent of total intake, coupled with higher proportions of spirits with 37 percent, and wine with 5.3 percent. Self-report data also provide information on unrecorded beverages. By this method it was possible to estimate a per capita intake of pulque for the urban population aged between 15 and 64 years of 0.515 liters, and of per capita intake of 96-proof alcohol of 0.235 liters. Pulque accounts for 9.12 percent of the total per capita intake of drinkers, and 96-proof alcohol for 4.2 percent.

Interesting gender differences were observed. While for both groups beer (51 percent for males and 45 percent for females) and spirits (32 percent and 30 percent, respectively) are the preferred beverages, females more often consume wine (per capita intake of this beverage accounted for 12 percent of female alcohol consumption, as compared to 4 percent of male alcohol consumption), while

---

[4]These percentages were obtained after deleting pulque and 96-proof alcohol from total per capita estimates.

males consume greater amounts of 96-proof alcohol (5 percent of consumption as compared to only 0.4 percent for females). A slightly larger proportion of females (13 percent) consumed pulque, as compared to males (9 percent).

Despite the increase in per capita consumption observed in the last 20 years, it remains 4.9 times lower than consumption in the United States, 4.3 times lower than in Spain, and 2.9 times lower than in Chile. Another interesting feature is that while in these countries there is a tendency for per capita intake to decrease (Edwards et al., 1994), in Mexico the opposite trend is observed. Part of this low level of consumption is due to the high rates of abstention, mainly among females, but also, as mentioned, because the illegal and local production of noncontrolled beverages is not included in the Mexican estimates.

PATTERNS OF ALCOHOL USE

Alcohol Use Among the General Population

The relationship between alcohol availability and problems associated with alcohol use is not clear; while per capita intake is lower in Mexico than the level observed in other countries, problems seem to be more frequent. At least part of the explanation for this puzzle might be found in the way alcohol is consumed. This section, therefore, reviews patterns of consumption.

Daily consumption of alcohol is not a common practice in Mexico. Only 17 percent of the urban adult population of the country interviewed during a household survey conducted in 1989 (Medina-Mora et al., 1991) reported drinking once a week or more often. Use to the point of intoxication is, however, frequent; 31 percent of drinkers reported at least one event of intoxication the year preceding the survey. Overall 7 percent of drinkers reported the same frequency of drinking and of getting drunk. When this was controlled by frequency of use it was found that 72 percent of those persons drinking daily or almost daily also got drunk with the same frequency. In other words, the European pattern of frequent consumption of low quantities of alcohol does not seem to characterize the culture.

There is a big difference in the drinking habits of men and women, 63 percent of the female population are abstainers[5] as compared to only 27 percent of males. When females drink they usually do so infrequently,[6] while the most typical pattern for males is one of moderate frequency[7] associated with high quantities;[8] 14 percent of males were classified as heavy drinkers[9] as compared

[5] Abstainer: person who reported not having consumed beverage alcohol during the year previous to the survey.
[6] Infrequent drinking: less than once a month.
[7] Moderate frequency of drinking: at least once a month, less than once a week.
[8] High quantity: five or more drinks per sitting.
[9] Heavy drinker: person who reports five or more drinks per sitting, once a week or more often.

to only 0.6 percent of females. Among males, drinking categories that include low quantities of alcohol intake per sitting are not very common (6.7 percent[10] and 3.1 percent[11]). In the adult population, the highest rate of frequent high and heavy drinking is observed in the middle age groups (30 to 49 years of age), although recent trends show an increase in use and abuse among male and female adolescents (Rojas et al., forthcoming). Other studies have documented higher levels of alcohol consumption among young females with higher incomes, who had liberal attitudes toward drinking (Medina-Mora, 1993).

Cross-cultural comparisons of patterns of alcohol use among Mexicans in Mexico and the population of Mexican origin living in the United States (Caetano and Medina-Mora, 1988) have suggested that when Mexican men migrate to the United States, they modify their use patterns by adopting the more frequent drinking pattern preferred by Americans, maintaining, however, the high quantities per occasion common in Mexico. When males born in Mexico have lived five years in the United States, their pattern of drinking is more similar to the American way of drinking than to the pattern followed in Mexico. On the other hand, migrant Mexican women do not alter their abstinence or low-frequency drinking. However, the first generation of women born in the United States shows a distinct decrease in the number who are abstainers. Among Mexican American females a high level of acculturation and liberal attitudes were found to increase the probability of drinking.

Patterns of Intake for Different Types of Beverage Alcohol

As already noted, beer is by far the most frequently consumed beverage, followed by spirits. Beer accounts for 50 percent of consumption and spirits for 32 percent. Pulque is the next beverage in terms of intake, though with a smaller proportion of the total, 9.12 percent, followed by wine and pure cane alcohol with almost the same share of the overall intake (4.5 percent and 4.2 percent, respectively). Wine and pulque are consumed significantly more frequently by women, while pure cane alcohol is more often reported by men.

Gender differences are also important when the drinking patterns of persons reporting use of different beverages are analyzed. For instance, more than one-half (68 percent) of male drinkers of pulque are heavy drinkers, while female drinkers are more often frequent low drinkers (59 percent). Wine is more often consumed by more moderate male drinkers (only 30 percent of those reporting having ingested this beverage were heavy consumers of alcohol).

Pure cane alcohol intake is more often reported by male and female heavy drinkers (82 percent). It is interesting to note that although pure cane alcohol

---

[10]Moderate low drinker: person who consumes alcohol at least once a month, less than once a week, and did not drink five or more beverages per sitting in the last year.

[11]Frequent low drinker: person who consumed alcohol once a week or more often, but did not drink five or more beverages per sitting in the previous year.

is more often consumed by heavy drinkers, it is not exclusively their domain. A proportion of moderate and infrequent drinkers also report its use, especially females. This confirms previous indications that pure cane alcohol was becoming part of the alcohol use culture in Mexico.

Data from the latest household survey yielded similar results, 66 percent of the population interviewed reported having had a drink in the past two years, and 8 percent were former drinkers. Beer was the most common type of beverage (71 percent), around one-half of the drinking population (49 percent) reported spirits, and one-fourth (28 percent) consumed table wine. Coolers were taken by 10 percent, 5 percent reported having drunk pulque, and less than 1 percent consumed 96° proof alcohol (Dirección General de Epidemiologiá, 1993).

Previous studies conducted among urban and rural populations in a region in central Mexico have documented a higher rate of abstention and alcohol-related problems among the latter, which also report higher frequencies of pulque and 96° alcohol intake, while wine and distilled beverages are more common among the urban population. Wine consumption was more often reported by females and younger drinkers, who often limited their intake to one or two drinks per sitting and thus had fewer alcohol-related problems. At the other end of the scale were drinkers of 96° alcohol, who showed the highest frequency of intoxication and of related problems. Drinkers of other beverages were situated between these two extremes (Medina-Mora et al., 1988).

Underage Drinking

The national survey on addictions of 1993 reports a rate of alcohol consumption in the two years previous to the survey of 54 percent among the population between 12 and 18 years of age, as compared to 70 percent among the adult population between 19 and 65 years of age. In both groups males report higher rates of consumption than females (about one female for every three males) (Dirección de Epidemiologiá, 1993).

Surveys among high-school students report similar results. About one-half of the country's high-school students had consumed alcohol on one or more occasions in their life, one-third had drunk during the 12 months previous to the survey, and 15 percent had drunk during the past month. Forty men and 10 women in every thousand had drunk one or more drinks per session, once or twice a week, and 25 percent of males and 13 percent of females reported at least one problem related to their drinking behavior. The most frequent problem recorded was the desire to take less (28 and 13 percent for males and females, respectively), followed in considerably smaller proportions by having seen a physician or counselor (7 and 3 percent, respectively), and police problems (5 and 0.76 percent, respectively) (Medina-Mora et al., 1993).

Seventy-five percent of male drinkers from urban regions of the country and 56 percent of females reported having started to drink alcohol before they were 18 years of age (Dirección de Epidemiologiá, 1993). Moreover, data from high-school students show a steady increase in the rate of use and abuse of alcohol among adolescents, both males and females. For example, 45 percent of males under 14 years of age had tried alcohol, rising to 83 percent of those aged 17 years, and 86 percent of those who had reached the legal age for drinking (18 years), with no sharp increase on reaching this age (Medina-Mora et al., 1995).

According to the 1993 National Addiction Survey, beer (18 percent) and spirits (6 percent) are the preferred beverages among the age group between 12 and 18 years. Coolers (2.7 percent) occupy an important place and are consumed with the same frequency as wine (3 percent). For every three adolescents who consume beer, there is one who reports the ingestion of coolers. The proportion in the general population (12–65 years of age) is eight beer drinkers to one person who consumes coolers (Dirección de Epidemiologiá, 1993).

The national school surveys of 1986 and 1991 reported no variation in the rates of use among urban students: 57 percent and 50 percent, respectively, reported having drunk alcohol. In Mexico City, there was an increase in the proportion starting use in the 30 days previous to the study from 15 percent in 1989 to 24 percent in 1993. The increase was observed in both males and females but was more marked in the former. This use trend coincided with an increase in the social tolerance towards the consumption of one or two drinks once or twice a week during the same period (Rojas et al., forthcoming).

ALCOHOL-RELATED PROBLEMS

Two sources of data are available to assess the rate of alcohol-related problems in a society: personal reports of drinkers interviewed through surveys, and routinely maintained statistics.

Six percent of the national urban sample, aged 18 to 65 years, met the International Classification of Diseases—10th edition (ICD-10) criteria for dependence (WHO, 1992). This was true for 12.5 percent of the male population but for only 0.6 percent of the female population. The most frequent symptom reported was a sense of impaired control.

One of 10 males in the population reported having work problems due to alcohol intake, but only in one-half the cases did they mean losing or nearly losing a job. Although the rate of problems seems unusually high, persons who reported ever having problems also reported consumption of significantly higher quantities of alcohol and had patterns of heavier drinking. This was true for all types of problems investigated. It is interesting to note that people who reported problems at work or with the police, or had had accidents other than automobile accidents, drank higher quantities of alcohol. Even more interesting is the fact that except for family and—in a lower proportion—health problems, other types of consequences are more prevalent among nondependent drinkers. For instance, only 18 percent of persons reporting being involved in a car accident due to alcohol intake were dependent on alcohol, confirming the finding already reported by Rosovsky et al. (1988) that alcohol-related injuries seen in casualty departments in Mexico may be more related to acute intoxication than to chronic ingestion.

Although people with a pattern of heavier than average drinking are more likely to suffer from consequences of abuse, the majority of persons with problems (73 percent) are not heavy drinkers, which reinforces the need to address acute intoxication as a goal of problem prevention.

Rates of consumption are lower among adolescents, but some of the consequences related to drinking are more frequent. In the last national survey on addictions, the group between the ages of 12 and 18 years reported a higher proportion of problems with the police, friends, and in bars or other drinking places. In turn, adults over 35 years of age report the highest rates of work problems and those related to their health (Dirección de Epidemiologiá, 1993).

In Mexico, admissions to emergency wards among people who had drunk alcohol in the six previous hours are higher than the figures reported in other countries (Cherpitel, 1993). In a study conducted in the eight most important hospitals for treating emergencies in Mexico City, it was reported that 20.9 percent of people admitted for injuries had positive blood alcohol levels (Rosovsky et al., 1988), while a similar study conducted in California reported positive readings in only 10.9 percent of the admissions for similar causes (Cherpitel et al., 1993). In Mexico the proportion of positive cases increased to 38 percent when only the cases involving violence were considered (Rosovsky et al., 1988).

Alcohol and suicide have also been linked. In a study conducted in Mexico City, it was found from autopsy records that alcohol was present in 38 percent of those who had committed suicide in a period of a year. Psychological autopsies revealed a history of alcohol problems in 24 percent of the cases, while a further 14 percent of the cases had no history of problems but had drunk alcohol before the event (Terroba et al., 1986). In a study conducted in emergency rooms, Borges et al. (1993) found that 44 percent of persons who had attempted suicide had positive alcohol readings in a breath test. This proportion was higher than that observed among a control group which included patients with injuries from other external causes (bites and recreational and work accidents). The odds ratio for self-report use in the six hours previous to the event was 2.01 for abstainers[12] as compared to 31.11 for drinkers.[13] The risk of suicide was also associated with habitual use, though less strongly (odds ratios of 0.67 for abstainers vs. 1.10 for drinkers). Further analysis controlling for confounding variables (sociodemographics, day of the event, use of other drugs) showed an increased risk of suicide with positive alcohol levels or with a history of habitual use of alcohol.

In Mexico, death from liver cirrhosis (30.7 per 100,000 inhabitants) is among the 10 leading causes of death among the country's population and is the first among males between 35 and 54 years of age. The trend in mortality

[12]0.001 to 100 grams of alcohol.
[13]100 grams of alcohol or more.

from liver cirrhosis related to alcohol is increasing, rising from 7.8 per 100,000 in 1970 to 12.0 in 1993 (Narro-Robles et al., 1992).

It has been estimated that alcohol is responsible for 9 percent of the total burden of disease in terms of days of healthy life lost due to premature death or disability, with an especially strong role in cirrhosis (which accounts for 39 percent of the burden), automobile accidents (15 percent), and dependence (18 percent) (Frenk et al., 1994).

Cross-Cultural Comparisons

In the alcohol field, cross-cultural research has proved to be highly effective in providing useful information to explain the high rate of problems observed in Mexico. From different surveys and information systems, it became apparent that the level of problems exceeded the rate that might be expected from the total consumption. While the rate of consumption was five times lower than that observed in the United States, the rate of problems was considerably higher.

One such experience came from a WHO collaborative project, substantially funded by the U.S. National Institute on Alcohol Abuse and Alcoholism (NIAAA) on "Community Response to Alcohol Related Problems." A comparison of local patterns of alcohol use and sociocultural variables in Mexico, Scotland, Zambia (Rootman & Moser, 1984a, 1984b; Rootman, 1988; Roizen et al., 1980) revealed marked variations in drinking habits between the different gender and age groups. These differences were also apparent in the social controls surrounding drinking. The variations found in the countries' data were of such a nature that they permitted the study of the influence of behavioral norms as well as the analysis of the social controls derived from different ways of consuming alcohol.

Strong variations were found across cultures in both drinking and abstention. While in Scotland and the United States almost all the population reported some amount of drinking in the past 12 months, this behavior was observed in less than two-thirds of the Mexican respondents, because of the low frequency of drinking reported by females. Rates for males were similar to those observed in Scotland and the United States.

Events of intoxication were quite frequent in Mexico and Zambia, where the rates of abstention were also high. About one-third of Mexican male respondents reported the same frequency of drinking and drunkenness, while drinkers in the Anglo-Saxon cultures tended to distribute their consumption over more drinking occasions. Mexico was also the country where the highest rate of problems was reported, in spite of the lower frequency of drinking.

Later comparative studies on alcohol-related casualties conducted by Stephens from the Alcohol Research Group at Berkeley and Rosovsky from the Mexican Institute of Psychiatry showed that the proportion of cases with positive blood alcohol levels among emergency room admissions involving trauma was higher in Mexico City than a county in California, while positive blood alcohol levels in nontrauma cases were more frequent in the United States (Stephens & Rosovsky, 1990; Cherpitel et al., 1993).

When norms regarding abstention, drinking, and inebriation were compared as part of the World Health Organization (WHO) community response project, it became apparent that in Mexico, norms governing moderation were weak compared to those observed in the U.S. and Scotland. In Mexico, it was more important to determine who may drink (males) than to control consumption and the amount ingested, both in general and in relation to specific occasions and contexts (Roizen et al., 1980).

From these and other studies, it became evident that the high rate of problems was related chiefly to the way alcohol was being consumed, and, in particular, to acute intoxication and the lack of social controls to limit consumption on occasions and in circumstances of risk. This finding opened an important avenue for research and prevention.

It is of interest to note the relative position of Mexico in Room's continuum (1989), which characterizes the cultural position reflecting patterns of drinking, attitudes and norms, and the culture's policy response to alcohol. The continuum extends from "wet"—the complete integration of alcohol into daily life as a consumer commodity like any other—to "dry," where alcohol is excluded as a harmful commodity, singled out from ordinary commerce for special treatment.

Mexico is a good example of a dry culture where the rate of abstainers is high, the dominant pattern of heavy drinking is rarely very heavy, and binge drinking is common, amid high rates of death from alcohol poisoning, violence, and social disruption associated with heavy drinking. Nonetheless, in contrast to what might be expected, deaths from cirrhosis are also high, pointing to an important avenue for research.

Extended collaboration has proved very helpful in understanding some cultural determinants of alcohol-related problems in Mexico. An important part of the puzzle still needs to be resolved. As we do not share a strong temperance tradition with other so-called dry cultures (on the contrary, the specific form in which the Catholic tradition is imbedded in our culture integrates use—including heavy intake—as part of the rituals and festivities), more research on the cultural position towards alcohol and the responses to it is needed. Although it is integrated in everyday life, alcohol is at the same time seen as dangerous and harmful.

This field of research leads to the study of public policy related to alcohol. Rosovsky (1985; 1994) studied the public health aspects of availability, with a focus on the structure and evolution of the beverage alcohol industry, its role in the country's development, production and marketing mechanisms, the volume of sales over time, as well as the evolution of per capita consumption, control mechanisms, and regulations introduced by the government. Results from these lines of research were included in the draft for the national program against alcohol abuse and alcoholism of 1986.

SOCIAL RESPONSE TO ALCOHOL-RELATED PROBLEMS

Public concern with alcohol-related problems is not new in Mexico. The inclusion in the Constitution of 1917 of an obligation to conduct a program against alcoholism is a reflection of this interest. Since then several efforts and measures have been carried out, though isolated in nature. It was not until the 1980s that the various measures and activities were integrated within a national program.

This program was developed as part of a substantial reform of the health sector. Perhaps the most important advance was the introduction of health protection as a civil right in the Mexican Constitution (Article 4). The Ministry of Health assumed responsibility for determining and coordinating public health policy, enabling the activities of the country's major health bodies to be integrated under a national council.

The national program was developed as an obligation under the 1984 General Health Law, which established the requirement to develop programs to deal with this problem. To meet this obligation, a General Council Against Addictions was instituted. The Council is coordinated by the Ministry of Health and comprises representatives from the government, private, and social sectors, including all the secretaries of state that deal directly or indirectly with the problem. Its first action was the development of programs, which have a general objective, specific objectives, strategies, and lines of action.

The Minister of Health requested the Mexican Institute of Psychiatry to develop a draft of the national program, with the participation of the different departments within the Ministry of Health, which served as a basis for the discussion of policies. More than 100 representatives from the public, social, and private sectors (including producers and distributors), researchers, legislators, and prevention and treatment experts, were invited to discuss the project and develop a program by consensus.

This turned out to be an enriching experience for all participants, as problems had previously been examined from only one side. An important aspect of this project was the participation of the alcohol beverage industry. Its representatives objected to the proposed policy on reduction of availability as the economic crisis had already affected its financial interests and prices had inevitably gone up. But even more important was the danger of illegal production and the increasing use of 96-proof alcohol. Because of a reduction in the volume denaturalized, this was being sold by itself or in combination with other products as beverage alcohol, in recycled bottles from licensed beverages, and even in the same place on the shelves as the latter in supermarkets and retail stores.

Although the discussion was not free from tension, important lessons were learned by both sides and a consensus was reached. Many of the recommendations set out in the draft, mainly those related to price increases and other measures aimed at controlling availability (e.g., through licences) were not accepted or included in the national program of 1985 or in its 1992 update. Among the difficulties encountered, apart from an economic crisis and a devaluation that took care of prices for a short period, lack of sound evidence was an important factor. This underlines the need to conduct basic and applied research on such factors as the effect of price on demand, use patterns, and problems, as well as demonstration projects aimed at assessing the impact of specific policies on rates of abuse and problems.

The resulting program against Alcoholism and Alcohol Abuse had as a main objective: "To reduce ... alcoholism, damages and risks to health, and the psychological, economic, and social problems related to the ... abuse of alcohol." It included among other strategies the need to 1) develop regulatory measures to control the availability of alcohol and enforce their application; 2) modify the existing patterns of alcohol use, with a view to reducing intoxication and abuse; 3) develop preventive programs aimed at the early detection of and interventions with problem drinkers; 4) improve treatment resources for the alcoholic and the family; and 5) conduct research projects on different aspects of the problem and on the evaluation of preventive programs.

An outstanding feature during the process was the political good will and commitment of the Minister of Health. Unfortunately, during his period of office there was not enough time to introduce the new regulations and the spirit of the program in the structure of the government and of the private sector, so that with his departure the Council lost power and its activities were reduced.

The program is now being reviewed anew. In general, it is quite comprehensive, although some adaptations are required. More emphasis needs to be placed on local problems, together with the development of specific subprograms.

CONCLUSIONS

This review highlights a number of distinctive characteristics of Mexican culture and drinking habits that have important implications for policymaking:

- A culture that promotes heavy use among specific sectors of the population and does not limit drinking, as happens in cultures with a temperance tradition. In Mexico the high abstention rate is more related to low levels of consumption among specific sectors of the population, such as women, than to temperance among males.
- A real danger of production and sale of nondrinkable alcohol,[14] the use of 96-proof alcohol, or the consumption of homemade beverages with no health controls during preparation, as a possible result of restrictions on availability. Thus education of the public should precede any measure, and measures should be directed toward the restriction of availability on occasions and in

---

[14] In 1994, there were more than 100 deaths by alcohol poisoning in a community in the state of Morelos caused by *Mezcal* made with a nondrinkable alcohol.

circumstances of high risk such as the sale of alcohol on or near entrances to highways, happy hours, and so on.

- A specific pattern of drinking, i.e., not daily, but with large quantities at one sitting, linked to specific risks, which calls for promotion of moderation and public education on the dangers of consuming large quantities of alcohol in a very short period of time.
- A lack of proper services and low regard among medical doctors, and a sense of uselessness associated with treatment among patients. Persons with alcohol problems have the right to treatment and personnel in health facilities should be made aware of it.
- The need for continuous action oriented towards increasing awareness among policymakers and people from the beverage alcohol industry of the importance of including health concerns when the policy is drafted.
- The value of introducing specific measures directed at people with different levels of risks requiring different modes of intervention.
- An urgent need for research designed to support the national program and answer questions such as: How elastic is the market for beverage alcohol? How would measures aimed at limiting alcohol availability in circumstances of risk be accepted and affect drinking habits? What is the cost-benefit outcome of treatment of alcohol problems in terms of quality of life for patients, reduction of DALYs, and use of services for related problems such as cardiovascular conditions and cirrhosis? How can moderate drinking be defined and communicated to the population?

These characteristics illustrate the important responsibility facing researchers, policymakers, drinkers, educators, treatment providers, human resource developers, alcohol producers, marketers and sellers, advertising companies—in short, all society.

REFERENCES

Berruecos, L. & Velasco, M. L. P. (1977). *Lástima que Mhountia Queria y no Papa: Patrón de Ingeston de Alcohol en una Comunidad Indigena de la Sierra Norte de Puebla.* Mexico City: Centro Mexicano de Salud Mental.

Boltvinik, J. (1994). La magnitud de la pobreza. Prioridades de asignación del gasto publico social (The magnitude of poverty. Priorities for the allocation of public social expenditure). *Demos, Carta demografica sobre Mexico, 7,* 29–30.

Borges, G., et al. (1993). Análisis de casos y controles de los intentos de suicidio en una muestra de servicios de urgencia. *Anales 4. Instituto Mexicano de Psiquiatria,* 198–203.

Bunzel, R. (1940). The role of alcoholism in two Central American cultures. *Psychiatry, 3,* 361–387.

Bustamante, J., Santibañez, J., & Corona, R. (1994). Los flujos migratorios de México a Estados Unidos (Migratory flows from Mexico to the United States). *Demos, Carta demografica sobre Mexico, 7,* 23–24.

Caetano, R. & Medina-Mora, M. E. (1988). Acculturation and drinking among people of Mexican descent in Mexico and the United States. *Journal of Studies on Alcohol, 49,* 462–471.

Calderon, G., Campillo, C., & Suarez, C. (1981). *Respuestas de la comunidad ante los problemas relacionados con el alcohol* (Community responses to alcohol-related problems). Mexico City: Mexican Institute of Psychiatry.

Campillo, C. (1995). *Alcohol Treatment Research in Mexico.* International Workshop on Cooperation in Alcohol and Drug Abuse Research: "Predictors, Consequences, and Intervention." Mexico City.

Cherpitel, C. J. (1993). Alcohol and injuries: A review of international emergency room studies. *Addiction, 88,* 923–937.

Cherpitel, C. J., Pares, A., Rodes, J., & Rosovsky, H. (1993). Drinking in the injury event: A comparison of emergency room populations in the United States, Mexico, and Spain. *International Journal of the Addictions, 28,* 931–943.

Corcuera de Mancera, G. (1991). *El fraile, el Indio y el Pulque: Evangelización y Embriaguez en la Nueva España,* (1523–1548) (The friar, the Indian, and pulque: Evangelism and drunkenness in New Spain (1523–1548)). Mexico: Fondo de Cultura Económica.

Cuevas, S. (1991). *Alcohol y Migración* (Alcohol and Migration). Twelfth National Congress of the Mexican Psychiatric Association, Acapulco.

de la Fuente, J. (1955). *Alcoholismo y Sociedad* (Alcohol and Society). Manuscript. Mexico City.

Dirección General de Epidemiologiá (1993). Secretariá de Salud. *Encuesta Nacional de Adicciones.*

Edwards, G., et al. (1994). *Alcohol Policy and the Public Good.* Oxford: Oxford University Press.

Frenk, J., et al. (1994). *Economia y Salud: Propuesta para el avance del Sistema de salud en Mexico Informe final* (The Economy and health: A proposal for progress in the health system in Mexico. Final Report). Mexico City: Fundación Mexicana para la Salud.

INEGI (Instituto Nacional de Estadística Geografía e Informática (National Institute of Statistics, Geography, and Information). (1990). *Censo General de Población y Vivienda* (General Census of Population and Households). Mexico City: Instituto Nacional de Estadística, Geografíca e Informática.

Kennedy, J. G. (1963). *Tesgüino* complex: The role of beer in *Tarahumara* culture. *American Anthropologist, 65,* 620–640.

Maccoby, M. (1965). El alcoholismo en una comunidad campesina (Alcoholism in a rural community). *Revista de Psicoanálisis, Psiquiatriá, Psicologiá.* Fondo de Cultura Economica 1, 63–64.

Madsen, W. & Madsen, C. (1969). The cultural structure of Mexican drinking behavior. *Quarterly Journal of Studies on Alcohol, 30,* 701–718.

Medina-Mora, M. E. (1993). Diferencias por genéro en las practicas de consumo de alcohol (Gender differences in alcohol consumption practices). Doctoral thesis in social psychology, Universidad Nacional Autónoma de México. Mexico.

Medina-Mora, M. E., et al. (1991). *Patterns of alcohol use in Mexican urban population: Results from a national survey.* Seventeenth Annual Alcohol Epidemiology Symposium, Sigtuna, Sweden.

Medina-Mora, M. E., et al. (1995). Los factores que se relacionan con el inicio, el uso continuado y el abuso de sustancias psicoactivas en adolesentes Mexicanos. *Gaceta Médica de Mexico, 131,* 383–393.

Medina-Mora, M. E., Rascon, M. L., Otero, B. R., & Gutierrez, E. (1988). Patterns of alcohol consumption in Mexico. In J. Gilbert (Ed.), *Alcohol Consumption among Mexicans and Mexican Americans: A Binational Perspective* (27–52). Los Angeles, CA: University of California Press.

Narro-Robles, J., Guttierrez-Avila, J. H., Lopez-Cervantes, M., Bórges, G., & Rosovsky, H. (1992). La mortalidad por cirrosis hepática en México. I. Características epidemiológicas relevantes (Liver cirrhosis mortality in Mexico. I. Relevant epidemiological characteristics). *Salud Publica de México, 34,* 378–387.

Natera, G. (1977). El consumo de alcohol en zonas rurales (Consumption of alcohol in rural areas). *Revista de Estudios sobre la Juventud, 2,* 39–48.

Roizen, R., Brace, S., Cameron, T., & Dixon, C. (1980). Drinking behavior in cross-cultural perspective: Some preliminary findings from the World Health Organization project. In R. Roizen (Ed.), *The World Health Organization Study of Community Responses to Alcohol-Related Problems*. Berkeley, CA: California Pacific Medical Center Research Institute, Alcohol Research Group.

Rojas, E., et al. (1998). *Tendencias del consumo de sustancias psicoactivas en poblacion estudiantil Mexicana de areas urbanas*. Forthcoming.

Rojas, E., Medina-Mora, M. E., Villatoro, J., Juárez, F., Carreño, S., Berenzon, S. (1998). Evolución del consumo de drogas entre estudiantes del Distrito federal. *Salud Mental, 21*, 37–42.

Rojas-Gonzalez, F. (1942). Estudio histórico-etnográfico del alcoholismo entre indios de México (Historical and ethnographic study of alcoholism among Mexican Indians). *Revista Mexicana de Sociología, 4*, 111–125.

Room, R. (1989). *Response to alcohol-related problems in an international perspective: Characterizing and explaining cultural wetness and dryness*. Conference La ricerca Italiana sulle bevande alcoliche nel confronto internazzionale, Santo Stefano Belbo, Italy, September 22–23.

Rootman, I. (1988). WHO Project on community response to alcohol-related problems. In *NIAAA Research Monograph No. 19: Cultural influences and drinking patterns—a focus on Hispanic and Japanese populations* (41–19). Rockville, MD: U.S. Department of Health and Human Services/Public Health Service/Alcohol, Drug Abuse, and Mental Health Administration/National Institute on Alcohol Abuse and Alcoholism.

Rootman, I. & Hawks, D. (1987). Some reflections on the WHO project on Community Response to Alcohol-Related Problems. *British Journal of Addiction, 82*, 727–733.

Rootman, I. & Moser, J. (1984a). *Community Response to Alcohol-Related Problems—A World Health Organization Project Monograph* (DHHS Publication (ADM) 85-1371). Washington, DC: National Institute on Alcohol Abuse and Alcoholism.

Rootman, I. & Moser, J. (1984b). *Guidelines for investigating alcohol problems and developing appropriate responses* (Offset Publication No. 81). Geneva: World Health Organization.

Rosovsky, H. (1985). Public health aspects of the production, marketing, and control of alcoholic beverages in Mexico. *Contemporary Drug Problems, 12*, 659–677.

Rosovsky, H. (1994). Salud pública, disponibilidad y consumo de alcohol: Implicaciónes y controversias (Public health, availability and alcohol consumption: Implications and controversy). In R. Tapia (Ed.), *Las Adicciónes: Dimensión, Impacto y Perspectivas (Addictions: Dimensions, Impact, and Perspectives)* (189–211). Mexico City: Manual Moderno.

Rosovsky, J. (forthcoming). Salud Pública, Disponibilidad y consumo de alcohol. Implicaciones y controversias. In R. Tapia-Conyer (Ed.), *Las Adicciones, dimensión, impacto y perspectivas* (Manual Moderno, 2nd ed.).

Rosovsky, H., Garcia, G., Lopez, J. L., & Narvaez, A. (1988). El papel del consumo de alcohol en las urgencias médicas y traumáticas (The role of alcohol consumption in medical and traumatic emergencies). *An. IV Reunión de Investigación*, 261–267.

Rosovsky, H., Narvaez, A., Borges, G., & Gonzalez, L. (1992). Evolución del consumo *per capita* de alcohol en Mexico. *Salud Mental, 15*, 35–41.

Stephens, C. H. & Rosovsky, H. (1990). Alcohol consumption and casualties: A comparison of U.S. and Mexican emergency room populations. *Journal of Studies on Alcohol, 51*, 319–326.

Taylor, W. B. (1979). *Drinking, Homicide, and Rebellion in Colonial Mexican Villages*. Stanford, CA: Stanford University Press.

Terroba, G., Saltijeral, T., & Del Corral, R. (1986). El consumo de alcohol y su relación con la conducta suicida. *Salud Pública de México, 28*, 489–494.

WHO (1992). *The ICD-10 classification of mental and behavioural disorders: Clinical descriptions and diagnostic guidelines*. Geneva: World Health Organization.

World Drink Trends (1997). Henley-on-Thames: NTC Publications Ltd.

Part Two

Encouraging Better Practice

Beverage Alcohol in Developing Regions: An Anthropological and Epidemiological Perspective on Public Health Issues

Dwight B. Heath

Much that has been written about beverage alcohol during the past half-century has opened with statements about how accelerating consumption around the world is accompanied by the accelerating occurrence of a host of problems, and that this is especially prevalent and dangerous in developing regions. The assertion is treated as if it were self-evident and axiomatic, even though the distinguished pioneer and authority in terms of cross-national studies, Robin Room, admitted that "At least in the alcohol field, there is no country which has an adequate data base on different consequences of drinking" (Room, 1989). In this paper, I will demonstrate how that shortcoming is manifest in many countries, and why it calls for a fresh approach to the assessment of the many roles, both positive and negative, that alcohol appears to play throughout the developing world.

According to the World Health Organization (WHO), alcohol problems rank among the world's major public health problems, constituting a serious obstacle to socioeconomic development in many parts of the world and threatening to overwhelm health services (Resolution WHA32.40 of the 32nd World Health Assembly, May 1979; see WHO, 1985). Among the problems listed by a WHO Expert Committee (1980) were cirrhosis, risk of cancers, alcohol dependence, impaired cognitive functioning, road accidents, violent crime, industrial accidents, inefficiency, absenteeism, and psychotic states.

A few volumes have been published that contain several chapters on alcohol in various developing countries. Most of the quantitative studies were written by local clinicians or administrators (Rutledge & Fulton, 1977; Edwards et al., 1983; Kortteinen, 1989b; Maula et al., 1990), and the qualitative ones by anthropologists (Marshall, 1979; Heath & Cooper, 1981). In a striking display of editorial risk in the interest of transnational responsibility, Edwards dedicated a regular section of *The British Journal of Addiction* (renamed *Addiction* in 1993) to a series of country reports by local authors. They are, however, uneven in quality and uniformly thin in terms of substantive content. Unfortunately, the same is true of most of the articles on specific research projects that originated in developing countries, regardless of where they were published. An early review of drinking in Latin America was published by Horwitz, Marconi, and Adis (1967); progress and problems were summarized by the Institute of Medicine (1982). Caetano (1989) offered an update, and brief responses from a number of colleagues dealt with developments in specific countries. With reference to Oceania as a whole, see Casswell (1985); on Papua New Guinea, see Marshall (1982). The literature on alcohol in Africa was reviewed by Pan (1975) and more recently by Partanen (1991). For India, see Ray and Pickens (1989); on the rest of Asia, there are a few qualitative reports, fewer quantitative ones, and not yet a broad overview.

What follows is a selective review, with some recommendations for bettering the quality of our knowledge and bringing it to bear on the improvement of life for many people. The topics treated are: a brief note on the nature of "developing regions"; a critique of the value of both quantitative and qualitative data that are available; comments on problems (some expected and some unanticipated) and possible benefits that appear to be alcohol-related; and a tentative formulation of some promising implications for action.

THE NATURE OF DEVELOPING REGIONS

Controversy over the classification of societies, whether along a scale between "primitive" and "civilized," or a continuum from "developed" to "developing," "underdeveloped," and "undeveloped," long antedates the current fad for political correctness.

No matter the indices that have been devised to summarize various combinations of such factors as are generally viewed as measures of development, the same countries tend to cluster in the lower half. This is especially true if we count only flags or nation states instead of individuals. (Some comparativists seem to lose sight of the fact that the population of the entire continent of Africa is less than one-half that of India *or* China!) Without considering at length the validity of statistics that are treated *as if* they were real by the United Nations, the World Bank, and others, and without weighing the reasons or justification for such variation, it is altogether possible to assume that this relatively disadvantaged segment of the world constitutes a category worthy of study, while noting occasional specific details that illustrate real and important patterns, or exceptions to patterns. It is in that sense that I feel justified in dealing with beverage alcohol in developing regions, without at first naming and mapping in more detail my areas of concern.[1] In general, those poorer countries are found in Africa, Asia, Latin America (including the Caribbean), and the islands of the Pacific.

THE QUALITY OF THE DATA AVAILABLE

A chapter in a recent book that focuses on alcohol in developing countries opens with the statement:

> Despite common knowledge and concern about heavy consumption of alcohol and the current seriousness of alcohol problems in developing countries, very little research has actually been done in most of these countries to define, with any degree of accuracy, the extent and nature of the problems (Acuda, 1990, p. 15).

Key officials in the WHO made it clear at an early stage that any effort at devising or even recommending cross-national policies about alcohol would run afoul of a serious shortage of data, and of difficulties in comparing what few data were available (Grant, 1985; Moser, 1979; 1985). Far from serving as an indictment of colleagues who work on the subject in developing areas, this criticism should focus our attention on difficulties under which they have operated and obstacles that remain to be overcome. Reasons for the shortcomings of research in developing regions are not hard to ascertain. Not only are many people there less broadly educated and less specifically trained, but they often bring to their jobs very different views about the fundamental importance of information, its collection, interpretation, and dissemination. Often they are working with minimal logistic, economic, and administrative support, under inherently difficult conditions, on a subject that many consider uninteresting, inappropriate, or overly sensitive. They are often hampered by traditions that devalue meticulous documentation, and that esteem privacy or congeniality over accuracy. And, of course,

> Most of the problems that have hindered research on alcohol in developing countries are in fact common problems frequently encountered during any medical or

[1] There is also abundant literature concerning both drinking patterns and related problems among such diverse populations as Native Americans and Alaska Natives ("American Indians"), Yupik and Inuit ("Eskimos"), Canadian Natives, Australian Aborigines, Maoris, and a number of other culturally distinctive minorities who live in the United States, Canada, Australia, New Zealand, and other developed countries. Although their ways of life may mirror those of other populations in developing regions, they are residents (and usually citizens) of some of the most urbanized, modern, industrial nations in the world, so they are not included in this survey.

sociological research conducted in a developing country: namely, shortage of funds, shortage of trained personnel, geographical mobility, the diverse cultural and ethnic differences, and illiteracy. But there are also problems specific to alcohol. These include the nature (content) of the alcoholic drinks and the cultural or traditional patterns of the use of alcohol (Acuda, 1990, p. 15).

Quantitative Approaches

One especially disappointing and disconcerting conclusion that is derived from a thorough review of the literature on alcohol in developing regions is the continuing weakness of substantive epidemiological and other quantitative data, even after decades of interest on the part of scientists and others. It would be unfair, however, to ignore the fairly large and rapidly growing literature that purports to deal with quantitative aspects of "alcohol-related problems" in the developing world simply on grounds that the data are often neither valid nor reliable.

As indicated in the preceding chapters, different countries have different ways of defining a number of alcohol-related variables, assessing the social consequences, and then measuring and reporting them. The reliability and adequacy of each step varies across nations. We must also keep in mind that international scholarly standards in this connection have been rising markedly in recent years, and that many of our colleagues who work in developing areas have only lately been engaging in research, often without the benefit of specialized training in methodologies of data collection and analysis. It is important that we not fall into the temptation of attributing a kind of "misplaced concreteness" to the numbers that are presented in such a context. At the same time, it is altogether probable that such numbers may be symbolically important as indices that are helpful in drawing our attention to trends, themes, or likely areas of change before they become manifestly problematic. It is these insights, rather than the questionable numbers themselves, that should command our attention.

What Singh said about India could well be generalized to virtually all of the developing world:

> It is difficult to generalize the results of most surveys, since many are not often representative of their populations and vary widely in reliability and validity. Further, alcohol consumption varies widely between different sections of populations and also within the same section over a period of time. Finally in relapsing behavior ... the difference between prevalence and incidence becomes rather obscure. [Such data are] of rather limited utility—however, the lay public and administrators tend to accept them as absolute truths and apply them as if they referred to actual people in the real world (Singh, 1989, pp. 4–5).

At the same conference, another speaker warned that "We need to be extremely cautious (because) sometimes the findings of epidemiologists are used for political and social purposes, which go far beyond the data and give the public some sort of misplaced concreteness."

The same problem occurs in the developed world as well. One ambitious effort to muster cross-national evidence about the way in which alcohol problems are supposed to increase in proportion to increases in per capita consumption (Giesbrecht et al., 1983) faltered because, even in the Euro-American countries that were chosen for study, comparable data were difficult to find. With such a shortcoming among wealthy nations that share a long tradition of similar concern for compiling information and for assessing impacts on public health and welfare, there seems to be little hope for success in poorer areas where record-keeping has never been viewed as important in agencies that are ill-equipped to keep up with daily demand for services.

It is evident that such strong criticism is more credible if it comes from the people who are themselves actively involved. For example, one of the most cautious and thorough of recent books on the subject (Kortteinen, 1989a) included the following shortcomings as admitted to by the contributing authors themselves, who were long-term residents in the developing countries about which they wrote. The volume's contributors noted the inaccessibility of data, explaining that data were scattered among many institutions and often partly buried. Data collection and analysis was further hampered by inconsistencies in classification and measurement, unregistered consumption, and an unwillingness of drinkers to participate in research. That the investigators themselves were so frank and explicit, even in brief articles, in acknowledging the weaknesses of their data and in warning readers that the numbers were misleading indicates that our judgment is not hypercritical. The same theme pervades the contributions to several other anthologies on the subject. With such caveats, one wonders about the feasibility of the authors' efforts to compile elaborate tables, calculate percentages, and report data that they know are so fragmentary, unrepresentative, or otherwise misleading. In the current volume, an effort has clearly been made to avoid claims which cannot be substantiated and to be parsimonious in interpreting from fragmentary data. Although such cautious analysis is to be welcomed, this volume—like others before it—can only reflect those data that are indeed available.

An immensely ambitious effort by WHO to respond to international concern about alcohol-related problems grew into a major study, with supposedly comparable data from Mexico, Scotland, and Zambia, plus complementary data from the United States and Canada (Rootman & Moser, 1984a). Dissatisfied with general population surveys, they set out also to compile information on a broad range of issues including production, distribution, and consumption of beverage alcohol, views and data from various agencies (including police as well as health and social services) about different kinds of problems, attitudes among the populace about appropriate and inappropriate manners of drinking and comportment, and responses of individuals and agencies to what they perceived as problems. Unfortunately, although the collaborators were well aware of considerable cultural differences—often within individual nations, as well as among them—the momentum of methodological preoccupations dominated, and much time and money was spent on standardizing and translating a long set of precoded close-ended questions or items on a survey or questionnaire. The authors admit that "In retrospect, it may have been unwise to invest so many of the project resources in this approach" (Rootman & Moser, 1984a, p. 160).

The original expectations that the study would yield significant quantitative outcomes were not met, and it was the qualitative and descriptive information that proved to be the most valuable outcome of that large project.

Even with the best-written survey, pretested and precoded, researchers should still expect to have significant difficulties. In what was intended to be a reassuring set of guidelines, Rootman and Moser admitted:

> Many factors contribute to unreliability and invalidity, including a number already discussed—unrepresentativeness, varying interpretation of instructions, inappropriately applied statistical analyses and errors in punching and coding. In addition, respondents may fail to report the truth because they have not understood the question, do not know the answer, or are unwilling to reveal it (1984b, p. 33).

The illegal production of alcoholic beverages is an especially thorny question in many developing countries because it is economically important but subject to governmental penalties. This would be less significant if it did not account for so great a portion of overall consumption. In Sri Lanka, it is estimated at 30 percent (Hettige, 1990); in Tanzania, at least 80 percent and maybe closer to 90 percent (Maula, 1990), and 50 percent in India (Singh, 1989). One simple but important implication of the fact that illicit production is generally high, even if it is not specifically known in detail, would be the caveat that apparent per capita consumption data that are based upon registered production should be viewed as conservative, and likely to underestimate the real consumption. But confusion on this point is easily compounded in many African countries where 30–60 percent of adults are said to be abstainers, resulting in a J- or U-shaped curve of distribution of consumption, including many heavy drinkers.

In an ambitious joint effort by the National Institute on Alcohol Abuse and Alcoholism, the Pan American Health Organization, and the National Academy of Sciences to provide an up-to-date review of what was known about alcohol throughout Latin America, the workshop speakers—many of them representatives from the countries under discussion—repeatedly and almost unanimously made the point that data were either completely lacking or grossly inadequate (Institute of Medicine, 1982).[2] If it is difficult to compile data in any given

---

[2] In various Latin American countries, there exists a "grey literature" on alcohol, consisting of reports from government agencies, commissions, university or hospital departments, visiting consultants, and others dealing with aspects of alcohol as it relates to public health or social welfare. Such documents are usually issued in small numbers, and tend not to have been accessioned by major libraries, reviewed in professional journals, or otherwise to have come to the attention of outsiders except occasionally when cited in a published dissertation, article, or book. Chile, Costa Rica, Honduras, and Mexico are known to be especially rich in this respect, but presumably a similar "grey literature" exists in most countries. For example, among African nations, Zambia and South

nation, the problems are compounded when one tries to do comparative studies. A variety of ambitious efforts at compiling cross-national studies have consistently been frustrated (Rootman & Moser, 1984a; 1984b). In one instance, Sulkunen (1976) tried to examine trends in alcohol consumption over 20 years in 176 countries, but could find what he called "adequate information" from only 32, all of which were "developed capitalist" or "developed socialist" countries. When Moser (1979) examined drug dependency in 33 countries, using a broad variety of sources and records, only one had data on changing alcohol consumption (and they were all "developed" nations). In another major effort to assess research priorities in relation to mental health and drug use, the usual epidemiological indices were dismissed as not nearly so promising as exploring a variety of often neglected social factors (Institute of Medicine, 1982). Similarly, the faculty of a seminar held in Salzburg, after intensive and extensive discussion among themselves and with representatives from 21 countries, decided that it was important to temper the mechanistic view that many people had about the supposed direct and invariant correlation between alcohol consumption and problems. "Comparisons across countries reveal the central role played by cultural factors not only in the way alcohol is used and regulated around the world, but also in the very definition of the nature, extent, and sources of subsequent problems" (Walsh et al., 1989, p. 49). Similarly, in very different contexts, several researchers have independently implied that drinking patterns are probably more important in relation to alcohol-related problems than is sheer quantity of alcohol consumed (Rehm et al., 1996; Grant & Litvak, 1998).

The difficulty is not that there are no quantitative reports about alcohol use and various alcohol-related problems in developing regions (Roizen, 1989). A number of studies have been made, in various countries, and some have the apparent advantage of dealing with data from different times, affording some insight into the dynamics of change. The difficulty is that the studies have only limited validity and questionable reliability—in the judgment of the authors themselves.

Africa have established research centers on alcohol, and probably many other countries throughout the developing world have turned at least some attention to the subject. The quality of such material is highly uneven, often sharing many of the general problems that have been discussed with respect to the published literature. Nevertheless, it might be a worthwhile project to attempt to compile a thorough listing and central repository of such material, so that it not be "lost," languishing unused on the shelves of offices and unknown to researchers.

In an interesting experiment, alcohol use and outcomes were studied in Honduras (Almendares et al., 1979), using Jellinek's method of group interviews. The method proved to be considerably less expensive and time-consuming than a standard survey would have been, and yielded data that appear strikingly similar to those compiled in nearby countries using other methods. Early and continuing efforts at compiling relevant quantitative data on the epidemiology of alcoholism were justly noted as pioneering, most often in Chile but sometimes throughout Latin America (Horwitz et al., 1967). In a series of topical bibliographies and essays about them, Menendez (1988) and his colleagues did a remarkable job of reviewing the literature on "alcoholization" (a term which, in their usage, includes both drinking patterns and related benefits and problems) throughout Latin America.

Saying this does not for a moment discredit or diminish the potential value of epidemiological concerns and approaches, which have repeatedly proven to be helpful, and promise more as precision and comprehensiveness enhance the validity and reliability of such studies wherever they occur. The Epidemiological Catchment Area study approach (Helzer & Canino, 1992) holds considerable promise, combining clinical concepts with quasi-clinical interviews, but it has heretofore been tried only in highly developed areas of the world. If ethnocentrism is an obstacle (in the sense of being unable to deal with culture-bound illnesses or problems), perhaps a combination of this with the other methods that have been discussed would prove more fruitful for the quantitative portion of research and reporting. The numbers could, in turn, be significantly strengthened by complementary qualitative data (some based on observation, some on directed or undirected interviewing, some inferred from media or performances, and from other sources).

In sum, quantitative research methods have often been uncritically applied, so that extant bodies of data are generally inaccurate in detail. Nevertheless, that lack of precision—as long as we are not misled into viewing the numbers as a close approximation of reality—does not necessarily mean that nothing can be learned from such studies. On the contrary, they can be helpful in providing general bases for valid, if cautious, inferences about at least some of the major public health questions.

Qualitative Approaches

If quantitative studies that are brimming with what appear to be "hard" or "objective" numbers are not to be trusted—as the authors themselves often warn us—what hope is there that we can learn anything substantive from qualitative studies that may have only a few numbers in them? In fact, the two approaches can better be viewed as complementary, not contrasting. In the best of cases, each set of data can illuminate and provide fuller context for the other. It is noteworthy that many authors who, in reporting on alcohol in developing countries, apologize profusely for the weakness of their quantitative data also venture to offer (without calling them such) qualitative data that provide further insights into the local situation.

It is well known, and conceptually important, that different populations have very different ideas and patterns of behavior with respect to beverage alcohol. These differences range from total abstinence, in which alcohol is viewed as an abomination, to savoring it as a special treat and an ideal offering to the gods on festive occasions. Drinking is tolerated for women almost as often as for men. Drunkenness, on the other hand, tends to be condemned for women, whereas it may be viewed as an important way of achieving transcendence for a man. Different beverages have very different values, and some settings are apt whereas others are not. These significant findings are not derived from quantitative studies but from qualitative ones, often even as serendipitous by-products of research that had very different aspects of life as its focus. In other contexts, I have already reviewed the worldwide literature on observational studies of alcohol (Heath, 1975; 1976; 1987) and prepared a brief manual to guide people in developing countries on how to do such research (Heath, 1983).

Such work is often cavalierly dismissed as being "anecdotal," "impressionistic," "journalistic," liable to be "subjective," and yielding "mushy data." But qualitative data are often of unique value, especially if one is concerned in learning about beliefs and practices with which one is not already familiar in detail (Akins & Beschner, 1980; Lambert, 1990). There is no question that it is more difficult to control variables and to replicate experiments when both the observer and the subjects are human beings, with few standardized instruments and few quantifiable measures intervening. But that does not mean that important things cannot be counted, classified, set into a time perspective, assessed in relation to typicality or rarity, and otherwise rendered meaningful, in terms of both the specific situation and comparison with other times, places, or populations (Murphy, 1992).

Most of what we do know from cross-cultural studies on alcohol (Heath, 1984) is derived from qualitative observational reports, and it is gratifying to see how substantive and meaningful most audiences find such data when they are confronted with them. Although there is rarely an attempt to deal with an entire nation-state's relation to alcohol in qualitative terms (Heath, 1986), that may be a strength rather than a weakness inasmuch as the emphasis is more on comprehending systematic meanings, values, combinations of norms, ranges of variation, and such, all within a given sociocultural context (where "environmental" factors tend to be more fully specified). On alcohol, few social surveys approach the richness of detail that can be achieved in a brief interview with respect to who may drink how much of what, where, when, in the company of whom, from what vessels, with what words and gestures, for what purposes, and with what outcomes. And who may not? And who not only may but should? And who not only may not but dare not?

ALCOHOL-RELATED PROBLEMS AND BENEFITS

A danger inherent in the reporting of faulty statistics from developing areas is that the numbers may, by their very appearance in print, take on an inappropriate appearance of reality. Estimated consumption figures, for example, might become the basis for a variety of legal and regulatory efforts to control the availability of alcohol (through heavy taxation, bans on advertising, restrictions on sales, etc.) on the basis of "the availability hypothesis," which has become a popular rationale for such controls. The original cautious conclusion was that "changes in the overall consumption of alcoholic beverages have a bearing on the health of the people in any society. Alcohol control measures can be used to limit consumption: thus control of alcohol availability becomes a public health issue" (Bruun et al., 1975, p. 90). After undergoing a series of recent changes

(Room, 1991), it has emerged in an assertive mode that makes it sound like an invariant scientific law linked with a moral imperative. Many authors use the presumption but few phrase it as baldly and succinctly as Archibald: "It has been found that rates of alcohol consumption hazardous to health are linked to the general level of alcohol consumption. This implies that the *only* feasible approach to the prevention of this problem is to effect a decrease in the average level of consumption within the drinking population as a whole" (Addiction Research Foundation, 1969 (emphasis added)). Internationally, that way of thinking has been firmly established in WHO publications for years, as exemplified by the Director-General's unequivocal assertion that "any reduction in per capita consumption will be attended by a significant decrease in alcohol-related problems" (WHO, 1978, p. 4).

The Social Construction of Problems

We should not be surprised that a thoughtful observer, after having long been engaged in a major international research project on the subject, admitted to the inherent difficulty of even identifying "alcohol-related problems":

> Defining what is a "problem" in general, and a "drinking problem" in particular, is by no means simple, as it involves different values and the differing views of individual observers. What is considered a problem in one society may not necessarily be so considered in another.... Thus reports on alcohol-related problems have to be somewhat arbitrary (Ritson, 1985, p. 15).

It is not merely a conceit of social scientists to hold that the nature and labeling of problems is a matter of social construction. Thus,

> If we take the definition of what counts as a problem as being essentially socially and culturally determined, we may also expect to see profound shifts in the process of definition.... At present, alcohol use is not seen in most countries as a problem in terms of its mere use; it is alcoholism that attracts concern. A movement is under way, however, to define a certain level of alcohol use as a problem for societies (Edwards et al., 1983, p. 271).

This implicitly notes the intrusive quality of a modern temperance movement that spokespersons from a few Scandinavian and North American nations (Levine, 1992) have been promulgating for developing countries as well as the rest of the world.

Problems That Were Anticipated

World Health Organization researchers spelled out early in some detail their own ideas of the broad range of problems that they considered were intimately related with alcohol, whether in a causative or other manner (Moser, 1979). These were subdivided in terms of who bore the major costs. For the drinker, they included the possible consequences of an acute episode of heavy drinking (short-term impairment of functioning and control, aggressiveness, accidents, exposure to climatic conditions, physical disorders, and arrest for drunkenness); the possible consequences of prolonged heavy drinking (liver cirrhosis, aggravation of other physical disorders, malnutrition, prolonged impairment of functioning and control, accidents, impairment of working capacity, alcohol dependence syndrome, and alcoholic psychosis); and possible concomitants (loss of friends, family, health, self-esteem, job, means of support, and liberty). For the drinker's family, they included: family disruption (including marital discord, child and spouse abuse, and loss of esteem for the drinker), mental disorders, fetal damage (from maternal drinking), child neglect, child development problems, dropping out of school, and juvenile drinking, and delinquency. For the general community, they included: effects on public order (obnoxious behavior, violence, and property damage), output losses (on the farm, in the factory, administrative inefficiency, and loss of skilled manpower through premature death), victims of drinker-caused accidents, and manpower and financial costs of services (health, welfare, and law enforcement).

Apart from the obvious fact of differences among cultures, and different social constructions of reality which dominate in a given culture at different times, there are also forces that academics long neglected to mention in connection with the selection of research topics or the compilation of research data. Singer (1986) made the point forcefully that political and economic factors appeared to have been "swept under the rug" in a broad range of alcohol studies and should be recognized as having significantly limited the attention paid to crucial differences in the distribution of power and wealth. Much the same point was made by Morgan (1983) who emphasized that beverage alcohol and the characteristics attributed to it have often been used, both symbolically and instrumentally, to promote and support systems of domination and subordination. Just as belief in the alcohol-disinhibition link can be used to deny or limit the availability of alcohol to subordinate groups, it can also be used to justify supplying it as a way of dissipating potential political problems. And the attribution of a variety of alcohol-related problems to lower-class people can be used to discredit and even oppress them (Levine, 1982).

With prompting from the WHO, many nations, including several in the developing world, have increasingly reported a variety of alcohol-related problems in recent years. As is always the case in such instances, it is difficult to judge whether the incidence and prevalence of such untoward results of drinking are actually increasing, or whether recording and reporting have markedly increased (or both)—for whatever reason that may be. Most of the sources cited in the above section on the quality of available data are replete with what appear to be impressive numbers about cirrhosis mortality, admissions to psychiatric wards, deaths from alcoholism, and crimes supposedly committed under the influence. Hospital statistics and police records, while not necessarily reliable (in the sense of being replicable and objectively accurate) may be quite valid as indicators of problematic areas in which alcohol use has a deleterious impact on the lives of people. Although such data have little scientific value for detailed analysis and comparison, or in providing a baseline for studies of change, they may have real social value in drawing our attention to some of the specific aspects of public health and social welfare where alcohol and its use have a variety of outcomes that can realistically be viewed as problematic, regardless of whether they conform to any Western definition of "problem drinking." The emergence of such destructive patterns can be sufficient to provide impetus for preventive action before problems become endemic or overwhelming. For these reasons, it may be appropriate to use less rigorous criteria than usual for evaluating the utility of measures, as long as it is kept in mind that the numbers are not to be taken as reflecting the real situation in any detail.

In sum, there is general consensus that increasing alcohol consumption, in new ways that are not subject to traditional social controls, often results in a wide range of mental, physical, and social morbidity. We should probably ignore the numbers, which most of the authors themselves admit are inaccurate, and focus more on the cluster of indicators that suggest alcohol abuse is increasing in more than half of the developing countries from which studies are available. Increasing numbers of alcohol-related social problems, including family disruption, are being reported by social welfare workers. Hospital admissions with alcohol-related psychosis, disease, and accidents are said to be rising. The police are making more arrests and prosecutions for illicit brewing, illicit selling, and alcohol-related violence. As indicated above, the numbers involved in such trends are far from accurate, but the direction of change appears to be consistent for many of the nations that report on them. One must wonder about the situation in other nations where, even when alcohol-related problems were looked for, they seem not to have been found.

Few of the many problems listed by Moser (1979) are actually mentioned by subsequent investigators. Among those that she anticipated, only the following have been analyzed at all in developing regions: traffic accidents (in Trinidad and Tobago, because they were well documented there, but elsewhere often ignored because they were known to be few and of minor consequence); liver cirrhosis (relatively well documented, and treated as if it were a key index to overall problems, although nonalcoholic etiology is sometimes stressed); malnutrition (sometimes cited as a by-product of abandonment of healthful traditional home-brews); alcoholic psychosis (rare, but relatively well documented in those few areas that have facilities for treatment); spouse abuse (more often noted in qualitative than in quantitative studies); fetal damage (sometimes mentioned as an expected problem that did not actually occur); and national economic losses (more feared if consumption diminished than if it increased, because of the customs duties, excise taxes, licensing fees, and other profits earned from beverage alcohol). This means that a larger number of the problems that were anticipated could not be found in police or public records, or were presumably of so little consequence that they were not reported by local alcohol researchers.

It would be helpful if we were able to compare drinking patterns and their outcomes, for example, in relation to a variety of other categories that are meaningful in a cross-cultural sense. Unfortunately, there are few such comparisons, and they do not generally coincide with the categories that WHO officials and others concerned with health and welfare have focused upon as prototypical "alcohol-related problems." For example, fetal alcohol syndrome (FAS) and fetal alcohol effects (FAE) are two of the potential outcomes of long-term heavy drinking that one might expect to be of special concern in developing regions, where women have tended to be pregnant earlier and more often than elsewhere. Few of the various reports in all of the volumes cited in this chapter even mention FAS or FAE, and none cite it as a problem.

In what many might consider a salutary reversal of his earlier stance (Room et al., 1984) denouncing the likelihood of "problem deflation" on the part of ethnographers, Room appears to have been challenging the opposite tendency, that of "problem inflation," when he noted,

> There are strong tendencies to overstate alcohol's role in health and social problems, to forget that its causation is usually conditional, to overlook solutions to the problems that are not alcohol-specific. . . . In the U.S. at least, alcohol epidemiologists often feel that the only political interest in their work is as a source of figures on alcohol's role in health and social problems pushed as high as would seem credible ("up to 70 percent of X is due to drinking") to put at the front of official or quasi-official reports (Room, 1990, pp. 1357–1360).

It would be unfortunate if a similar pattern were to become widespread in developing countries as well.

Some Unanticipated Problems

The fact that researchers in developing countries have generally not been able to document, in convincing quantitative detail, the occurrence of those problems that WHO consultants predicted certainly does not mean that the investigators are deliberately practicing "problem deflation." On the contrary, their introductory and concluding statements are, in most instances, in keeping with the alarmed views of outsiders, even when the data they present do not support such a pessimistic view. Neither does it mean that there are no difficulties in their countries that might plausibly be labeled "alcohol-related problems." It is in this context that the qualitative interpretive comments that are added by investigators often have greater value than do the quantitative data for which they are so apologetic.

Few authors make specific mention of specific physiological outcomes of long-term heavy drinking (other than cirrhosis), but those who do, normally dismiss them as being rare. The same is true for delirium tremens (DT) and peripheral neuropathy (Gelfand, 1966). Those authors who do write about cirrhosis rates or mortality rates from cirrhosis, usually couch their data in terms of the early work by Jellinek (subsequently retracted by him and often discredited by others) that used those numbers as direct indices of the rate of alcoholism in the same population. Often there is specific mention of the supposed connection, although growing awareness of the diversity of etiologies of cirrhosis—especially hepatitis B—has led to the abandonment of that avenue of investigation in most of the industrialized nations. One investigator attributes esophageal cancer among some African populations to the large amounts of zinc and nitrosamine-like compounds that turn up in liquors produced from faulty stills (McGlashen, 1969). The attempt to demonstrate the carcinogenic nature of moderate drinking was unsuccessful, first in Africa (Collis et al., 1971) and subsequently on an international scale (IARC, 1988). As police crack down on home-brewing, illegal distillation often ensues, with far greater danger to health because of toxic congeners (Anon., 1958). In the Congo (Maula et al., 1990), the therapeutic, religious, and traditional functions of palm wine were contrasted with the hedonistic and prestige functions of new commercial drinks. However, some unexpected benefits were also discerned, including social and supposed medical and nutritive functions of the new beverages, as well as the significant economic profits they bring to those who are engaged in the trade.

It is noteworthy that some investigators have been sufficiently observant, and faithful to the data, to report problems and benefits that may be distinctive to their situations. For example, Menendez (1988) reviewed the ethnographic literature on Latin American drinking and identified a series of problems that are of concern to the people themselves. One study that paid close attention to ethnic differences in South Africa (Mears, 1942) denigrated the nutritional value of home-brew, suggesting that its use is associated with high rates of pellagra; in another, iron overload was reported to be diminishing as people switched from home-brew (boiled in iron pots) to factory-bottled beer.

The United States' preoccupation with traffic fatalities and work accidents has little relevance in many developing areas (Hettige, 1990). Alcohol dependence (a large part of what used to be called "alcoholism") appears to be incapacitating to a few, but intoxication tends to be compartmentalized so that it seldom interferes with work, school, or other commitments.

In both Micronesia (Marshall & Marshall, 1989) and southern Mexico (Eber, 1993), it is explicitly stated that women and children disproportionately bear the burden of alcohol abuse, because spouse and child abuse and neglect are commonplace. These settings are unusual in that private violence is sometimes an outcome of heavy drinking and some men spend large portions of their limited incomes on alcohol. The same characteristics may be true for other areas, but they are rarely reported. On Truk, Marshall and Marshall (1989) mentioned some unusual negative consequences of drinking such as drunk driving, aggression, and injuries (all rarely mentioned in other developing areas), but also noted some negative consequences of prohibition, such as a damaging loss of state revenues, increasing concentration of wealth, and political cynicism. In a somewhat similar vein, after having devoted an entire book to the proceedings of a conference that brought representatives from more than six countries and 14 of Papua New Guineas's 19 provinces to discuss alcohol, Marshall concluded that "alcohol has not yet become a major social problem in most rural areas of Papua New Guinea" (Marshall, 1982, p. 452).

In the only serious effort I have been able to find to estimate the economic costs and benefits of beverage alcohol in a developing country, Gipey (1982) applied to Papua New Guinea two different sets of assumptions that had been used in North America (and that had been generally discredited there (Heien & Pittman, 1989)), and came up with two contrasting conclusions: one showing a slight benefit, and the other a slight loss. In neither instance were the amounts significant enough to prompt anyone to change the liberal national policy, which is tempered by a patchwork of local options ranging from an unrestrictive regime to absolute prohibition. But it is just such problematic extrapolated use of flawed numbers that should cause us to be concerned about the "misplaced concreteness" that may distort the importance of results from quantitative studies that the authors themselves recognize as faulty or questionable.

In a few jurisdictions of Papua New Guinea, the disinhibiting effect of drink is blamed (without evidentiary support for the presumption) for the revival of intervillage warfare (Marshall, 1982). In others, cases of beer are being generously distributed by leaders and ritually consumed by their followers in ceremonies that promote regional harmony among diverse peoples. An economic loss of which the local people are acutely aware in such a situation is that, while the goods are distributed, the value paid for them has gone out of the community. This stands in marked contrast to the income redistribution effect of such lavish gifting when expenditures had previously been made locally. Much the same problem occurs throughout many parts of Latin America, where bottled drinks are supplanting home-brews, so that a major part of the cost of sponsoring a fiesta goes to outside commercial interests rather than to local brewers. In large parts of Africa, the growing predominance of factory-made beverage alcohol has meant diminishing profits and prospects for disadvantaged women who used to command the market with homemade fermented beers.

Some of the major problems that stem from the proliferation of factory-made beer in areas where home-brews used to dominate are fundamental economic and social dislocations that have nothing to do with drinking on the part of those who are injured. The fact that home-brews were made from local foods meant that they were a product of traditional agriculture, with some value added. Most factory-bottled beers are barley-based, so that large areas of good land have been given over to that new crop, which has no place in the traditional diet. For example, the large-scale shift from millet-based home-brew to barley-based lager in Nigeria had a significant impact upon land tenure and agricultural practices. Such grain-farming on an extensive scale employs machinery in place of human labor, and often uses petrochemical fertilizers, insecticides, and pesticides as well. The heavy use of imported inputs is a drain on the balance of payments, and increases a country's dependence on aspects of the international market over which there is no local control. Environmental damage, pollution, and erosion are common outcomes of the new agriculture. Moreover, when it employs irrigation, water loss quickly becomes serious. The new fields are so large that they dwarf many of the multicrop farms from which they were consolidated. So much land retired from the raising of food crops has forced peasants into a cash market to buy staples, and has even made the country a net importer of food, whereas it used to be not just self-sufficient but a net exporter. Many of the former small-scale farmers have not only been displaced from farmsteads but are unemployed, moving to the fringes of the major cities, where sufficient jobs are still not available and social and health problems become exaggerated (Kortteinen, 1989a). Women who used to make major contributions to supporting their families through profits from brewing have lost that important source of income and have few other marketable skills to offer. Many turn to prostitution, accelerating the spread of HIV/AIDS. Similar instances of how the increasing wealth of an urban few has been linked with decreasing opportunities for the rural peasant majority could be cited elsewhere.

The unusually rapid growth of cities in developing areas, often without expansion of infrastructure or jobs to accommodate the flow of migrants, can result in a variety of problems that differ markedly from those that characterize more slowly growing centers of population. Peer pressure is real and immediate in small communities, where gossip, shunning, and other informal mechanisms have long met the needs for conformity that must be more impersonally enforced (e.g., by police or other authorities) in the city.

Some development economists are well aware of the costs mentioned here, and there have been a few sophisticated quantitative attempts to weigh them against potential benefits (Kortteinen, 1989a, 1989b). Among the benefits are excise taxes, income from licensing or monopoly, and a number of other sources of income based on the alcohol business, all of which have become important in the budgets of many developing nations. Not only does a brewery or distillery symbolize modernity, but it provides jobs, not only in bottling operations but also in transportation and distribution, the manufacture of containers and labels, purchase of agricultural ingredients, and so forth. At worst, officials must consider such an industry to be a mixed blessing.

The Possibility of Benefits

It is not only economists who should weigh costs against benefits, but public health planners as well. There are few in clinical or academic circles these days who would speak in favor of moderate regular use of beverage alcohol, although epidemiological evidence, with apparently valid and reliable quantitative significance, is abundantly available and rapidly increasing concerning the inverse correlation (to a point) between daily consumption and mortality from coronary heart disease, especially arteriosclerosis.

In other contexts (Heath, 1990, 1995), I have already discussed in considerable detail the many and varied benefits, from a social and cultural viewpoint that people derive from drinking. They include its value as a boundary marker between groups, the enhancement of sociability, religious and ceremonial symbolism, prestige, stratification and exchange, among others. In the same volume as the first of those contributions (Cox, 1990), other authors spelled out a vast range of psychic, physical, and other reinforcements that alcohol provides. Among those are relaxation, titrated relief from pain or self-consciousness, regular reduction of stress, conspicuous consumption, and many others. This is not an appropriate place to emphasize the potential benefits—and their likelihood—that should be weighed against potential problems—and their likelihood of occurrence—but it is a valid issue that should be considered in any planning where beverage alcohol is being considered in relation to public health and social welfare.

CONCLUSIONS

Implications For Action

The subject matter of this chapter is so diverse, and the importance of specificity so great, that any summary or conclusion might seem extraneous. However, it is appropriate to signal, as implications for action, a few themes that have not been discussed above and that hold promise of increasing and improving our understanding of beverage alcohol in developing regions, and of decreasing the threat of alcohol-related problems there.

Attending to the mental health and related problems of adjustment among migrant workers and other aspects of industrialization, modernization, and urbanization has heretofore been an area of low priority for most governments in developing regions. The reasons for that shortcoming may, in part, be similar to the reasons given by several investigators from those same countries for shortcomings in their quantitative data: shortage of skilled personnel, scarcity of facilities, inadequate funding, and—in all candor—low priority in relation to other pressing demands on limited resources.

At a different level of concern, the widespread ecological and economic costs of commercial farming to support the new beverage industries may not be so clearly and directly linked in the minds of officials to drinking patterns and alcohol consumption, but should be a major element in the widespread web of significance that surrounds them.

In accordance with Engel's law, as a household's income rises, the proportions spent on food and other necessities decline, and those spent on discretionary items rise. Beverage alcohol in the form of traditional home-brew is sometimes thought to be a necessity, but, with economic development, manufactured beers, wines, and liquors tend to be viewed as attractive luxuries. Serious problems can ensue if they drain a family's resources away from food, shelter, clothing, education, or health care.

Although some observers consider prohibition a simple and sure preventive measure, few who are active in the field of public health at any level today would recommend it. Even in areas where legal prohibition has been in force for some time, it has proven to be neither simple nor sure. Quite apart from the flawed experiment that ended in repeal in every developed country where it was tried, prohibition in developing areas has been accompanied by smuggling, domestic production, illegal sales, considerable drinking, and increased public drunkenness and disturbances (see, for example, Al-Qthami (1978), Marshall (1982), Marshall and Marshall (1989)).

An eloquent demonstration of the extent to which changes in policy affect definitions of problems, as well as estimates of prevalence and social and economic costs of drinking, is provided by Fillmore (1984). She shows strongly how controls are most readily imposed on those who have little power or wealth (Fillmore, 1991), and how our hypotheses about the etiology of alcoholism are often culture-bound. On the basis of a long historical sequence, using data from the relatively well-documented Euro-American nations, Levine demonstrated that "compared to modern economic and political factors, alcohol consumption is not important in determining economic growth and development" (Levine, 1982, p. 46).

At least one specific theory about the relationship between the development process itself and various alcohol-related problems deserves special attention in this context. There is now widespread recognition that modernization, industrialization, urbanization, and other aspects of development occur in many different ways, and the presence of an intricately interrelated world system makes it virtually impossible that any nation might ever replicate conditions that supported such developments in the history of Europe and North America. Nevertheless, a widespread presumption persists that development in itself is a major risk factor for alcohol dependence and alcohol abuse. There is a surprisingly large amount of literature that uses this premise. Although it is rarely phrased in exactly those terms, it is implicit in much that is written about "stress," "anomie," "sociocultural deprivation," "acculturation," and a host of related concepts. The idea briefly is that "sociocultural deprivation" has a harmful effect on self-image and creates feelings of inferiority and a lack of other ego-needs, leading to heavy drinking which in turn results in manifest problems, especially in developing areas. This can occur even among those subpopulations that have had stable family units and adequate male role models (Beaubrun, 1967). The presumption is that individuals find themselves "between two worlds," having abandoned traditional ways of thinking and acting, but not yet being competent (or accepted) to behave and believe in modern ways. There is an almost mechanistic, quasi-inevitable quality to the way many observers seem to think that every change must be stressful for every individual, and that alcohol is the ever-present tension-reducer of choice. In two earlier papers (Heath, 1975; 1988), I have traced the checkered history of this simplistic view of drinking on the part of populations among whom unemployment, various kinds of marginality, pauperism, and other forms of subordination were labeled "anomie," and heavy drinking with manifest problems was assumed to be a direct consequence. The psychosocial dynamics of hegemony are never simple, and frequent exceptions to this posited automatic linkage combine to demand a major rethinking of this approach to alcohol and development.

A salutary recent development in terms of the prevention and ameliora-tion of alcohol-related problems is the increasing attention being paid to the concerns and capabilities of members of the community themselves. In part, this is a reflection of what has long been favored under the rubric of "the sociocultural model" (Heath, 1988), but the addition of political activism and a component of strong guidance from public health personnel has had dual effects. For one thing, it has made the idea of community involvement accept-able in bureaucratic circles (Giesbrecht et al., 1990; Holder & Howard, 1992). At the same time, it appears to be promulgated on the assumption that mem-bers of the community will certainly accede to the plans and programs that "are best for them," as judged by experts in the public health field. However, that latter assumption appears to be highly questionable, in the light of our long experience in other aspects of development, especially in cross-cultural contexts.

A global overview of both the quantitative and qualitative data available on the relation between beverage alcohol and alcohol-related problems in develop-ing regions allows one to recognize the following points that are important from a public health policy perspective:

- As is true in other domains, the sociocultural context (or "environment") in which people live is a powerful factor in shaping whatever problem(s) they may encounter in connection with alcohol in developing regions.
- There is no uniform developmental sequence that applies cross-culturally to the way in which various alcohol-related problems may occur.
- Traditional forms of drinking tend to be deeply imbedded and tightly in-tegrated with other customs and values in the sociocultural context. New patterns of drinking can supplant those, add new dimensions to them, or find strikingly new forms of expression in developing cultures.
- Rates of abstention tend to be high in some developing societies, se-riously distorting supposed per capita consumption figures. The prevalence of heavy drinkers is obscured by such averaging.
- Social relational problems associated with drinking tend to be intrafa-milial, and easily escape the attention of outside observers who are not attuned to qualitative data.

• Economic problems similarly tend to be related to household budget rather than job security, and to accessibility primarily in qualitative terms. The supplanting of women as principal actors in the beverage industry portends serious problems for them, just as proliferation of modern beverages portends monetary profits for the state but losses in agricultural terms.

All in all, it seems crucial to recognize that both quantitative and qualitative approaches can be helpful in identifying the nature and extent of problems, many of which have only been rarely mentioned in the literature on developing areas up to the present.

REFERENCES

Acuda, W. (1990). Alcohol research in developing countries: possibilities and limitations. In J. Maula, M. Lindblad, & C. Tigerstedt (Eds.), *Alcohol in Developing Countries* (15–27). Helsinki: Nordic Council for Alcohol and Drug Research.

Addiction Research Foundation. (1969). *18th Annual Report: 1968.* Toronto: Addiction Research Foundation.

Akins, C. & Beschner, G. (1980). *Ethnography: A Research Tool for Policymakers in the Drug and Alcohol Fields* (DHHS Publication ADM 80-946). Rockville, MD: National Institute on Drug Abuse.

Almendares, B. J., de Almandares, R., & Reconco de Quiroz, M. (1979). *Estudio del uso del alcohol y los problemas del alcoholismo en Honduras, usando el mètodo de E M. Jellinek (Study of alcohol use and problems of alcoholism in Honduras, using E. M. Jellinek's method).* Tegucigalpa: Ministerio de Salud Pública y Asistencia Social.

Al-Qthami, H. (1978). Alcohol and drugs in Saudi Arabia. In *Proc. 29th Annual Meeting* (10–12). Washington, DC: Alcohol and Drug Problems Association of North America.

Anon. (1958). Native liquors in southern Rhodesia. *Central African Journal of Medicine, 4,* 559–559.

Beaubrun, M. H. (1967). Treatment of alcoholism in Trinidad and Tobago. *British Journal of Psychiatry, 113,* 643–658.

Bruun, K., Edwards, G., & Lumio, M. (1975). *Alcohol Control Policies in Public Health Perspective* (Monograph 25). Helsinki: Finnish Foundation for Alcohol Studies.

Caetano, R. (1989). Alcohol research in Latin America: Is the cup half full or half empty? *British Journal of Addiction, 84,* 237–239.

Casswell, S. (1985). *Alcohol in Oceania.* Auckland: University of Auckland Alcohol Research Unit.

Collis, C. H., Cook, P. J., Foreman, J. K., & Palfaram, J. F. (1971). A search for nitrosamines in East African spints samples from areas of varying oesophageal cancer frequency. *Gut, 12,* 1015–1018.

Cox, W. M. (Ed.). (1990). *Why People Drink: Parameters of Alcohol as a Reinforcer.* New York: Gardner.

Eber, C. E. (1993). *Before God's Flowering Face: Women and Drinking in a Tzotzil-Maya Community.* Austin, TX: University of Texas Press.

Edwards, G., Arif, A., & Jaffe, J. (Eds.). (1983). *Drug Use and Misuse: Cultural Perspectives.* London: Croom Helm.

Fillmore, K. M. (1984). Research as a handmaiden of policy: An appraisal of estimates of alcoholism and cost in the workplace. *Journal of Public Health Policy, 5,* 40–64.

Fillmore, K. M. (1991). Risk factors for alcohol problems: Social and ethical considerations. In P. M. Roman (Ed.), *Alcohol: The Development of Sociological Perspectives on Use and Abuse* (289–314). New Brunswick, NJ: Rutgers Center of Alcohol Studies.

Gelfand, M. (1966). Alcoholism in contemporary African society. *Central African Journal of Medicine, 12*, 12–13.

Giesbrecht, N., et al. (1983). *Consequences of Drinking: Trends in Alcohol Problem Statistics in Seven Countries.* Toronto: Addiction Research Foundation.

Giesbrecht, N., et al. (Eds.). (1990). *Research, Action, and the Community. Experiences in the Prevention of Alcohol and other Drug Problems* (Prevention Monograph 4). Rockville, MD: Office of Substance Abuse Prevention.

Gipey, G. (1982). Measuring costs and benefits of alcohol: Methodological difficulties, a suggested method, and some estimates. In M. Marshall (Ed.), *Through a Glass Darkly: Beer and Modernization in Papua New Guinea* (37–47). Boroko: Institute of Applied Social and Economic Research.

Grant, M. (Ed.). (1985). *Alcohol Policies* (Regional Publications, European Series 18). Copenhagen: WHO Regional Office for Europe.

Grant, M. & Litvak, J. (1998). *Drinking Patterns and Their Consequences.* Washington DC: Taylor & Francis.

Heath, D. B. (1975). A critical review of ethnographic studies of alcohol use. In R. J. Gibbins et al. (Eds.), *Research Advances in Alcohol and Drug Problems, Vol.* 2 (1–92). New York: Wiley.

Heath, D. B. (1976). Anthropological perspectives on alcohol: an historical perspective. In M. W. Everett, J. O. Waddell, & D. B. Heath (Eds.), *Cross-Cultural Approaches to the Study of Alcohol—An Interdisciplinary Perspective* (41–101). The Hague: Mouton.

Heath, D. B. (1983). Annex 30: Observational studies into alcohol-related problems. In I. Rootman & J. Moser (Eds.), *Community Response to Alcohol-Related Problems, Phase I,* (A30-1–A30-38). Geneva: World Health Organization.

Heath, D. B. (1984). Cross-cultural studies of alcohol use. In M. Galanter (Ed.), *Recent Developments in Alcoholism, Vol.* 2 (405–415). New York: Plenum.

Heath, D. B. (1986). Concluding remarks. In T. F. Babor (Ed.), *Alcohol and Culture: Comparative Perspectives from Europe and America* (234–238). Annals of the New York Academy of Sciences 472. New York: New York Academy of Sciences.

Heath, D. B. (1987). A decade of development in the anthropological study of alcohol use: 1970–1980. In M. Douglas (Ed.), *Constructive Drinking: Perspectives On Drink from Anthropology* (16–69). Cambridge: Cambridge University Press.

Heath, D. B. (1988). Emerging anthropological theory and models of alcohol use and alcoholism. In C. D. Chaudron & D. A. Wilkinson (Eds.), *Theories on Alcoholism* (353–410). Toronto: Addiction Research Foundation.

Heath, D. B. (1990). Anthropological and sociological perspectives on reinforcement from alcohol. In W. M. Cox (Ed.), *Why People Drink: Parameters of Alcohol as a Reinforcer* (263–290). New York: Gardner.

Heath, D. B. (1995). *International Handbook on Alcohol and Culture.* Westport, CT: Greenwood.

Heath, D. B. & Cooper, A. M. (1981). *Alcohol Use and World Cultures: A Comprehensive Bibliography of Anthropological Sources* (Bibliographic Series 15). Toronto: Addiction Research Foundation.

Heien, D. M. & Pittman, D. J. (1989). The economic cost of alcohol abuse: An assessment of current methods and estimates. *Journal of Studies on Alcohol, 50,* 567–579.

Helzer, J. E. & Canino, G. J. (Eds.). (1992). *Alcoholism in North America, Europe, and Asia.* New York: Oxford University Press.

Hettige, S. T. (1990). Social research on alcohol in Sri Lanka: Background issues and prospects. In J. Maula, M. Lindblad, & C. Tigerstedt (Eds.), *Alcohol in Developing Countries* (206–223). Helsinki: Nordic Council for Alcohol and Drug Research.

Holder, H. D. & Howard, J. M. (Eds.). (1992). *Community Prevention Trials for Alcohol Problems: Methodological Issues.* Westport, CT: Praeger.

Horwitz, J., Marconi, J., & Adis, C. G. (Eds.). (1967). *Bases para una Epidemiología del alcoholismo en América Latina, Acta 1* (Foundation for an epidemiology of alcoholism in Latin America, Vol. 1). Buenos Aires: Fondo para la Salud Mental.

IARC. (1988). *Alcohol Drinking* (Monograph 44). Lyon: International Agency for Research on Cancer.

Institute of Medicine. (1982). *Legislative Approaches to Prevention of Alcohol-Related Problems: An Inter-American Workshop on Mental Illness and Addictive Disorders: Progress and Prospects.* Washington, DC: National Academy Press.

Kortteinen, T. (1989a). *Agricultural Alcohol and Social Change in the Third World* (Monograph 38). Helsinki: Finnish Foundation for Alcohol Studies.

Kortteinen, T. (Ed.). (1989b). *State Monopolies and Alcohol Prevention* (Monograph 181). Helsinki: Social Research Institute of Alcohol Studies.

Lambert, E. Y. (Ed.). (1990). *The Collection and Interpretation of Data from Hidden Populations* (Research Monograph 98). Rockville, MD: National Institute on Drug Abuse.

Levine, H. G. (1982). Industrialization, economic development, and worker drinking: Historical and sociological observations. In *Legislative Approaches to Prevention of Alcohol-Related Problems: An Inter-American Workshop on Mental Illness and Addictive Disorders: Progress and Prospects* (26–46). Institute of Medicine. Washington, DC: National Academy Press.

Levine, H. G. (1992). Temperance cultures: Alcohol as problem in Nordic and English-speaking cultures. In M. Leder & G. Edwards (Eds.), *The Nature of Alcohol and Drug-Related Problems* (16–36). Oxford: Oxford University Press.

Marshall, M. (Ed.). (1979). *Beliefs, Behaviors, and Alcohol: A Cross-Cultural Perspective.* Ann Arbor, MI: University of Michigan Press.

Marshall, M. (Ed.). (1982). *Through a Glass Darkly: Beer and Modernization in Papua New Guinea* (Monograph 18). Boroko: Institute of Applied Social and Economic Research.

Marshall, M. & Marshall, L. B. (1989). *Silent Voices Speak: Women and Prohibition in Truk.* Belmont, CA: Wadsworth.

Maula, J. (1990). Research in production and consumption of alcohol in Tanzania: Background, issues and prospects. In J. Maula, M. Lindblad, & C. Tigerstedt (Eds.), *Alcohol in Developing Countries* (193–205). Helsinki: Nordic Council for Alcohol and Drug Research.

Maula, J., Lindblad, M., & Tigerstedt, C. (Eds.). (1990). *Alcohol in Developing Countries* (Publication 18). Helsinki: Nordic Council for Alcohol and Drug Research.

McGlashen, N. D. (1969). Oesophageal cancer and alcoholic spirits in central Africa. *Gut, 10,* 643–650.

Mears, A. R. R. (1942). Pellagra in Tsolo district. *South African Medical Journal, 16,* 385–387.

Menendez, E. L. (Ed.). (1988). *Aportes Metodológicos y Bibliográficos para la Investigación del Proceso de Alcoholización en América Latina* (Methodological and Bibliographic Elements for the Study of the Alcoholization Process in Latin America). Tlálpan, Mexico: Casa Chata.

Morgan, P. (1983). Alcohol, disinhibition, and domination: A conceptual analysis. In R. Room & G. Collins (Eds.), *Alcohol and Disinhibition: Nature and Meaning of the Link* (Research Monograph 12, pp. 405–420). Rockville, MD: National Institute on Alcohol Abuse and Alcoholism.

Moser, J. (1979). *Prevention of Alcohol-Related Problems: An International Review of Preventive Measures, Policies, and Programmes.* WHO/Programme on Mental Health (MNH)/79.16. Geneva: World Health Organization.

Moser, J. (Ed.). (1985). *Alcohol Policies in National Health and Development Planning* (Offset Publication 89). Geneva: World Health Organization.

Murphy, J. M. (1992). Contributions of anthropology and sociology to alcohol epidemiology. In J. E. Helzer & G. J. Canino (Eds.), *Alcoholism in North America, Europe, and Asia* (21–32). New York: Oxford University Press.

Pan, L. (1975). *Alcohol in Colonial Africa* (Monograph 22). Helsinki: Finnish Foundation for Alcohol Studies.

Partanen, J. (1991). *Sociability and Intoxication: Alcohol and Drinking in Kenya, Africa, and the Modern World* (Monograph 39). Helsinki: Finnish Foundation for Alcohol Studies.

Ray, R. & Pickens, R. W. (Eds.). (1989). *Proc. Indo-U.S. Symposium on Alcohol and Drug Abuse* (Publication 20). Bangalore: National Institute of Mental Health and Neurosciences.

Rehm, J., Ashley, M. J., Room, R., Single, E., Bondy, S., Ferrence, R., & Giesbrecht, N. (1996). On the emerging paradigm of drinking patterns and their social and health consequences. *Addiction, 91*, 1615–1621.

Ritson, E. G. (1985). *Community Responses to Alcohol-Related Problems: Review of an International Study* (Public Health Paper 81). Geneva: World Health Organization.

Roizen, J. (1989). Opportunities and problems in conducting research on alcohol and casualties in developing countries. In N. Giesbrecht et al. (Eds.), *Drinking and Casualties: Accidents, Poisonings, and Violence in an International Perspective* (356–380). New York: Tavistock.

Room, R. (1989). The epidemiology of alcohol problems: Conceptual and methodological issues. In R. Ray & R. W. Pickens (Eds.), *Proc. Indo-U.S. Symposium on Alcohol and Drug Abuse* (Publication 20, pp. 13–34). Bangalore: National Institute on Mental Health and Neurosciences.

Room, R. (1990). Review of D. Anderson, Drinking: To Your Health. *British Journal of Addiction, 85*, 1355–1363.

Room, R. (1991). Social science research and alcohol policy making. In P. M. Roman (Ed.), *Alcohol: The Development of Sociological Perspectives on Use and Abuse* (315–339). New Brunswick, NJ: Rutgers Center of Alcohol Studies.

Room, R., et al. (1984). Alcohol and ethnography: A case of problem deflation? *Current Anthropology, 25*, 169–191.

Rootman, I. & Moser, J. (1984a). *Community Responses to Alcohol-Related Problems* (DHHS Publication ADM 85-1371). Washington, DC: National Institute on Alcohol Abuse and Alcoholism.

Rootman, I. & Moser, J. (1984b). *Guidelines for Investigating Alcohol Problems and Developing Appropriate Responses* (Offset Publication 81). Geneva: World Health Organization.

Rutledge, B. & Fulton, E. K., eds. (1977). *International Collaboration: Problems and Opportunities*. Toronto: Addiction Research Foundation.

Singer, M. (1986). Toward a political-economy of alcoholism: The missing link in the anthropology of drinking. *Social Science and Medicine, 23*, 113–130.

Singh, G. (1989). Epidemiology of alcohol abuse in India. In R. Ray & R. W. Pickens (Eds.), *Proc. Indo-U.S. Symposium on Alcohol and Drug Abuse* (Publication 20, pp. 3–12). Bangalore: National Institute of Mental Health and Neurosciences.

Sulkunen, P. (1976). Drinking patterns and the level of alcohol consumption. In R. J. Gibbins et al. (Eds.), *Research Advances in Alcohol and Drug Problems, Vol.* 3 (223–281). New York: Wiley.

Walsh, D. C., et al. (1989). Cultural dimensions of alcohol policy worldwide. *Health Affairs, 8*, 48–62.

WHO. (1978). *Alcohol Related Problems: The Need to Develop Further the WHO Initiative*. Executive Board at the 63rd session of the WHO. Geneva: World Health Organization.

WHO. (1980). *Problems Related to Alcohol Consumption: Report of a WHO Expert Committee* (Technical Report Series 650). Geneva: World Health Organization.

WHO. (1985). *Handbook of Resolutions and Decisions of the World Health Assembly and the Executive Board, Vol. II: 1973–1984* (103–104). Geneva: World Health Organization.

Chapter 12

Economic Issues and the Emerging Global Alcohol Market

Brendan Walsh

Beverage alcohol has a well-established place in the economies of the developed countries of the world. The production and distribution of beer, wine, and spirits are significant activities, generating considerable employment and providing an important source of tax revenue for many governments. Consumer spending on these items is an important component of total expenditure. At the same time, it is generally acknowledged in these countries that problem drinking imposes serious costs on society. These are due to the excess morbidity, premature mortality, crime, policing, accidents, and other burdens that can be linked to alcohol abuse. The quantification of these costs has been a concern of researchers at least since the first decade of the 20th century, but large unresolved issues concerning their classification and measurement persist. The treatment of the entries in the other side of the balance sheet—the benefits derived from drinking—also poses considerable conceptual problems.

In the developing countries of the world, where incomes are low and most of the population lives at or close to the subsistence level, commercial production and distribution of alcohol tends to be much less significant in the aggregate. In many of the poorest countries of the world, consumption of commercially produced beer, wine, and spirits is a novel phenomenon, confined to small urban elites. Aggregate consumption levels are still very low. Nonetheless, the rapid spread of drinking and its attendant problems have already generated concern among policymakers in many developing countries.

This chapter has two aims. The first is to review the methodology and findings of studies of the economic costs and benefits of alcohol consumption in developed countries. A review of this literature is important to this book because the issues raised by the growth of drinking in poorer countries will ultimately have to be assessed by some variant of the methodologies already established in countries with a tradition of alcohol studies. The second aim of the chapter is to outline the changing patterns of alcohol consumption around the world, providing a global perspective on the spread of drinking and the evolution of drinking patterns in an economic context.

METHODOLOGICAL ISSUES

Should we treat beverage alcohol as similar to other items of consumption, whose benefit to the consumer is accurately measured by the amount he[1] spends on them? Or is there a sense in which these commodities differ from others in this regard? The answer would seem to be "no" to the first and "yes" to the second question, because drinking is widely acknowledged to have implications for the economy and society that differentiate the production, distribution, and consumption of beverage alcohol from that of most "ordinary" commodities. This is primarily because of what economists refer to as the "spillover" or "external" effects of drinking. These effects have given rise to a voluminous literature on the costs and benefits of alcohol consumption—a literature which is without counterpart for most other sectors of the economy. A review of this literature is valuable because it provides a framework for analyzing the likely impact of the growth of drinking on developed countries.

Despite the long tradition of alcohol studies in developed countries, there is still a considerable lack of agreement on how to measure the social costs and benefits of drinking. As has been remarked in the context of the attempts to estimate the social costs of tobacco smoking, which raise methodological issues some of which are similar to those encountered in the assessment of the costs and benefits of drinking, "authors frequently secure estimates without asking what it is they are measuring, and certainly without reference to any stated methodology" (Markandya & Pearce, 1989, p. 1149).

Benefits

The benefit consumers derive from drinking is measured in the first place by the price drinkers pay for alcohol. If drinkers are informed and free in their consumption decisions, this outlay represents a minimum estimate of their valuation of the benefits they derive from drinking.[2] However, beverage alcohol is

---

[1]For stylistic convenience, our representative drinker is subsequently referred to as "he."

[2]Minimum because economic theory assumes that the rational consumer equates the utility of the last unit consumed with the price paid. Because the marginal utility of additional consumption

often regarded as addictive, and this may alter the way in which we treat consumer expenditure in a benefit-cost study. *Addictive goods* have been defined by economists as those for which the utility derived from future consumption depends on the present and past levels of consumption. A good is "harmfully addictive" if increased present consumption reduces the utility derived from a given level of consumption in the future (Becker, 1996).[3] In the limiting case of harmful addiction, present consumption simply satisfies a craving derived from past consumption and bestows no new satisfaction. While the addict's expenditure should be regarded as an overestimation of its value or benefit to him (Atkinson & Meade, 1974), actual outlays on drink may be taken as the best available measure of the overall benefit derived from drinking.

If moderate drinking bestows health advantages that are not part of the drinker's motivation for drinking, this is an additional benefit that should be included in a social evaluation of drinking. Any resultant reduction in health charges should also be taken into account. The magnitude of the beneficial effects of moderate drinking is still uncertain but their existence is increasingly accepted (Ashley et al., 1994). The most significant beneficial side effect is some reduction in the risk of coronary heart disease. This is a much more important cause of premature death in developed than in developing countries, which would reduce its relevance to poorer countries. None of the existing studies of the costs and benefits of drinking takes this consideration into account.

Beverage alcohol is a convenient source of tax revenue, especially in countries with weak administrative infrastructures. Special taxes on beer, wine, and spirits were important sources of revenue in many developed countries in the past, and they continue to be important in some northern European countries, states in the U.S., and Canada. By paying these taxes, drinkers not only cover the costs of producing and distributing beverage alcohol but they also make money available to government which could be used to cover the social costs of drinking.[4] While these taxes are included in the expenditure on alcohol, some or all of these taxes could be deducted from any social costs imposed by drinkers to arrive at net social cost.

We noted that the outlay on beverage alcohol by consumers may be taken as the best available measure of the benefit derived from drinking. To treat employment in the drinks industry, the value of the raw materials purchased and other costs of production also as benefits would involve double counting. While these costs are relevant to an assessment of the economic significance of

declines, earlier units bestow higher utility than later units. The difference between the valuation placed by the consumer on *all* the units consumed and the total actually paid for the good is referred to as *consumer's surplus*, a concept that occupies a pivotal role in benefit-cost analysis.

[3]"Beneficial addiction" refers to goods the more of which are consumed, the greater the future enjoyment, associated with a given level of their consumption; listening to classical music or watching football are possible examples.

[4]These taxes may not, in fact, have been imposed with this in mind or used for this purpose. As a rule special taxes on alcohol are simply a convenient way of raising revenue by targeting products whose demand is price-inelastic.

the industry to a country or region, to regard them as a benefit over and above the value of drinking to drinkers is to assume that the resources used in the industry would otherwise be unemployed. This is implausible, especially in the context of developing countries, where scarce resources such as water and skilled management have to be diverted from other potential uses to the production of beverage alcohol. Only the income of the factors of production specific to the industry, whose opportunity cost is zero, should be treated as a benefit additional to the existence or creation of the industry. An example might be the rental income of land employed for the cultivation of grapes if this land has no value in alternative applications. But, in general, very little of the income generated in an industry falls into this category. Even in the countries characterized by high rates of unemployment, it is misleading to claim as a benefit of the beverage alcohol industries that they provide "work for the otherwise unemployed" (Lehto, 1995). In this context what matters is the *additional* income earned by employment in the drinks industry over and above what workers would earn if deployed in their next most productive occupation. Finally, account should be taken of the longer-run implications of reallocating the money spent on drink to other items. A *general equilibrium* framework of this type is the most appropriate for an evaluation of the economic benefits of the drinks industry.[5] This is analogous to consumers' surplus.[6]

Costs

Much more attention has been devoted to the assessment of the social costs of drinking than to discussion of its benefits. The key distinction is between that of *private* and *social* costs. The *private* costs of drinking are borne by the drinkers themselves. They include payments for the scarce resources (labor, raw materials, etc.) used to produce and distribute beverage alcohol, as well as the taxes imposed on it. Private costs are generally irrelevant from a policy perspective. A rational consumer knowingly incurs these costs. In the case of alcohol, the consumer implicitly calculates that at the margin the benefit derived from the consumption of alcohol equals the price paid. This logic may also be extended to cover the nonmonetary costs of drinking borne by the drinker, such as damage to health, reduced earnings, and premature death, to the extent that these are knowingly incurred.

However, not all of the private costs of drinking are knowingly incurred. Although economists adopt the rational consumer model as the norm, they also accept the possibility that consumers may be myopic in the sense of attaching

---

[5] Another way of looking at this issue is to recall that in benefit-cost analysis the appropriate measure of cost is *opportunity cost*. In the case of the drinks industry, this is the output of other goods and services foregone by devoting resources to the production of beverage alcohol. The excess of the wages, salaries, and profits earned by the labor and capital employed in an industry over and above what they would earn if employed elsewhere is *economic rent*, which is not part of the economic concept of cost.

[6] For a discussion of these concepts, see Zerbe and Dively (1994).

a very low importance in their present calculations to costs that will only materialize in the future. Drinkers cannot be aware of all of the long-term effects of drinking on health. In fact, these effects are still being debated among scientists, who have only recently established an association between moderate drinking and reduced risks of certain conditions such as coronary heart disease, while the link between heavy drinking and conditions such as liver cirrhosis and various cancers is still a subject of research (Anderson, 1995). Studies of young drinkers generally confirm their awareness of adverse short-term consequences such as hangovers, stomach upsets, and financial problems, but show that they are less aware of more serious, longer-term problems (Plant & Plant, 1992). However, it has been found that regular teenage drinkers have lower estimates of the risks of adverse repercussions of drinking than have nondrinkers (Morgan & Grube, 1994). Thus even in developed countries where drinking is long-established and the evidence of its effects is reasonably well known, it is normal to treat many of the adverse effects of drinking as *unanticipated private costs* and to include them as a debit in benefit-cost studies. The commercialization of the production and distribution of beverage alcohol is likely to extend drinking to groups previously unaffected by drinking, leading to higher levels of drinking-related harm. Ignorance of longer-term consequences and myopia regarding those that are known provide a justification for attaching policy significance to some of the private costs of drinking.

The following are some private costs of drinking that may be to a greater or lesser extent unanticipated by consumers.

If a drinker anticipates a loss of income due to alcohol-related illness and absenteeism, this is a cost that has been counted as part of the private cost of drinking and should not be included in a social cost calculation. However, to the degree that such loss is not internalized it constitutes a social cost that should be debited against drinking. When this is done, any income maintenance payments received while absent from work should be regarded as compensation for this cost and not counted as an additional social cost. This consideration is generally not very relevant in developing countries, where such payments are not usually made by the state and the burden of looking after the ill and unemployed falls more heavily on the extended family.

To the extent that they are not factored in by the drinker as part of the price to pay for his behavior, the discomfort, pain, and suffering caused by heavy drinking constitute a social cost. Identifying and putting a valuation on these costs is fraught with problems and they are generally ignored in studies of the costs of drinking.

If drinkers underestimate the risks to their health and life caused by drinking, a valuation should be placed on this factor and it should be entered on the debit side of the cost-benefit evaluation.[7] An estimate of the economic value

---

[7]Note that this magnitude differs from the value of the output that would have been produced over the years of life lost due to premature mortality, which is often used in estimates of the cost of drinking.

attached to life is provided by society's willingness to pay for reductions in life-threatening risk. Economists have shown that individuals differ greatly in how much they are willing to pay to reduce risk (Viscusi, 1990). Poor people appear to attach lower value to health and safety than the rich, and this implies that the loss of welfare associated with drinking-related hazards would be smaller in developing than in developed countries.

The *social costs* of an activity include private costs *plus* those that are external to the consumer. The *external costs* of drinking are not borne by the drinker but are imposed on others or on society at large. Even if foreseen, they are not taken into account by the individual drinker. A divergence between private and social cost in any sphere of activity can result in resource misallocation.

The list of the external costs associated with drinking is familiar, but it is important to explain the rationale for each element in it.

The cost of medical treatment attributable to illness arising from drinking is an external cost *to the extent that it results in higher taxation or insurance premiums* and is not paid for by the drinker himself. Ideally this cost should be evaluated as the present value of the health costs imposed on the state by a drinker over his lifetime compared with the present value of the costs imposed by a similar individual who does not drink.[8] The emphasis on a lifetime approach is important. The savings in health expenditure and care of the elderly arising from alcohol-related premature deaths should be offset against the burden drinkers place on the health services (Atkinson & Meade, 1974; Cook, 1984; Markandya & Pearce, 1989). While there is general agreement among economists that this is the appropriate methodology, in fact it is rarely implemented.

To the extent that the loss of earnings due to alcohol-related absenteeism is an outcome anticipated by the drinker, payment of sickness benefit lowers the private costs of drinking. These payments may be financed out of general taxation or by special social security taxes. Either way they are shifted from the drinker to others. This consideration is likely to have greater weight in developed countries, with their elaborate social security systems, than in developing countries.

While there is some dispute about the causal role of drinking, there is strong evidence that alcohol is associated with numerous forms of violence (homicide, suicide, assaults, riotous behavior, etc.) in developed countries (Romelsjö, 1995). Recent research attributes a considerable volume of urban crime in the United States to the externalities associated with the concentration of liquor outlets in inner-city neighborhoods (DiIulio, 1995). There is some evidence of a rising incidence of social problems being linked to the spread of drinking in developing countries (Medina-Mora & Gonzáles, 1989). The costs that should be taken into account under this heading include the value of the loss of life and the pain and

---

[8]The comparison should be between the health outcomes of drinkers as a class and those of nondrinkers. This would take account of any beneficial effects of moderate drinking as well as of the deleterious effects of excessive drinking.

suffering of the victims of drink-related crimes, as well as the costs of policing drunks and enforcing laws related to drinking.

Drinking is implicated in a large proportion of many types of accidents, road traffic accidents in particular. While most developed countries have gradually put in place elaborate control policies to limit the risk of alcohol-related accidents, in developing countries this adverse consequence of drinking problems is likely to spread before any control policies are put in place. The proportion of all accidental deaths attributable to alcohol may, therefore, be larger in poor countries (World Bank, 1993, p. 88). The costs due to these accidents are properly included in the social costs of drinking. Their valuation involves calculating the value of loss of life, pain and suffering, medical costs, and material damages.

Premature death reduces the taxes that are paid by drinkers over their lifetime and also reduces the benefits which they claim from the state. The difference between these two streams, discounted to their present values, represents a social cost or benefit, depending on whether it is positive or negative, of drinking. In developing countries this is not likely to be a major cost element.

Many other, relatively minor, costs are also imposed on society by alcohol abuse. These include the social response to alcoholism—for example, publicly financed educational and rehabilitation programs, and the cost of social workers dealing with alcoholics and their families. These, too, are more likely to be significant in richer countries than in the developing world.

The Uses of Cost Estimates

The earliest studies of the costs of alcohol abuse were motivated by a desire to justify prohibition (Österberg, 1983).[9] Proponents of drinking, on the other hand, have appealed to benefits such as employment and income generated, taxes paid, or contributions to local economies to defend the industry against the attacks of prohibitionists or the temperance movement. Global estimates of the costs of drinking can be expected to result in large cash figures, but these can be counterbalanced by perhaps equally large figures purporting to measure the benefits that accrue to society from the availability of beverage alcohol or the economic importance of the drinks industry. A debate conducted on these terms is unlikely to result in better public policies.

The most valuable application of benefit-cost analysis in this area is to weigh the possible benefits of marginal changes in the level of consumption or in the pattern of drinking against the costs of bringing them about. In general, economists would prefer to see cost estimates "applied in the context of evaluating a specific, well-defined government action or program, rather than as

---

[9]This literature was first developed in Scandinavia before the First World War. The most notorious estimate of the effects of prohibition was Irving Fisher's claim that it had boosted the United States' GNP by between 5 and 10 percent (Fisher, 1927). Österberg notes that "the temperance movement has been disappointed. It has proved almost impossible to demonstrate that alcohol costs are greater than alcohol benefits" (p. 96).

a device for indicating the overall impact of alcohol abuse on society" (Cook, 1984, p. 65).

THE DEVELOPMENT CONTEXT

The study of the costs and benefits associated with drinking has evolved almost exclusively in the developed countries of the world. While the general methodology developed in this literature is valid in low-income countries, some special considerations are also relevant.

Not all of the growth in the commercial production of beverage alcohol in low-income countries represents a net increase in consumption. There can be considerable displacement of traditionally distilled and brewed beverages, whose production and consumption have never been accurately recorded. In many African countries, for example, the tradition of local millet beer production by a family group or by a village is well established. Such beers, which have a short shelf life, are frequently of high nutritional value, supplying many of the vitamin and energy requirements of the population. In general, though, it is important to bear in mind that, in countries where there is a shortage of cereals, they are likely to be of greater nutritional value when consumed in solid than in liquid form. However, there is not much evidence that such beverages, which include, for example, traditional palm wine as well as family beers, are toxic to any significant extent. For commercially produced beers, the question of toxicity is unlikely to arise, but they tend to have lower nutritional values than the traditional beverages they replace.

The opposite may well be true of distilled beverages. Uncontrolled home production of distilled spirits is certainly more hazardous, carrying with it the possibility of quite high levels of toxicity but offering few nutritional benefits to the drinker. Here, the quality-control mechanisms of commercial production probably work to the benefit of the drinker, since there is a greatly decreased risk of accidental poisoning.

Another concern in the development context is the importance attached to developing industrial employment opportunities for the surplus labor employed in the rural areas and the informal urban sector. Brewing, and to a lesser extent distilling, are examples of industries that have been successful at a relatively early stage in the development process. Rapidly growing urban populations provide an easily reached market for local breweries, which can compete successfully with imported products because of the high transport costs associated with beer. The technology required for modern brewing can be acquired under license or through joint ventures with companies in the developed world.

All of the costs discussed in the previous section would tend to be much lower in developing than in developed countries. So too would the relevant denominator, such as GDP per person. But of greater significance is the fact that the health services in developing countries tend to be very poorly resourced. The additional burden imposed on publicly funded hospitals and clinics by the growth of alcohol-related problems may divert the limited available resources from achieving reductions in maternal and infant mortality and in the incidence of curable and preventable diseases. These opportunity costs may be greater than those incurred in countries with high levels of public health care where life expectancy is already quite high.

Estimates of the Costs of Drinking

Table 12.1 sets out in summary form the headings that have been used in some recent studies of the costs of drinking in some developed countries and the amounts estimated under each heading. In order to achieve comparability across studies, all money estimates have been converted to percentages of the relevant GDP.

It may be seen that there is reasonable conformity among the studies regarding what should be included as a social cost of drinking.[10] All include some estimate of the costs imposed on the health services, and all but one include a figure for "lost production." There is some variation between the studies in the treatment of items such as criminal damage, accidents, and social responses, but this is not very significant. However, only two studies include estimates of the value of loss of life.

The difficulty of establishing the grounds on which some items have been included as costs is more worrying than the inconsistencies between studies in the coverage of costs. For example, the rationale for including "lost production" is not always clear. The discussion above stressed that loss of earnings is a cost only to the extent that it is unanticipated or ignored by drinkers in their calculations of the costs and benefits of drinking. The authors of studies summarized here do not make clear whether they believe that all or only some of the value of the loss of productivity or earnings due to drinking should be treated in this way. Furthermore, some of them appear to treat as a cost to society the output that a drinker would have produced had he lived longer. We have argued above that this is erroneous. The importance of clarity on these issues can be gauged from the fact that "lost production" accounts for up to two-thirds of the total estimated costs of alcohol in the studies reviewed. Failure to consider the rationale for including this element as a cost of drinking is very likely to result in an overestimation of the relevant magnitude.

The treatment of the costs imposed on the health services by drinking also calls for comment. All of the studies reviewed take account only of the extra burden imposed on the health services due to the excess morbidity of drinkers *over their lifetime.* No allowance is made for the effect of the premature mortality experienced by drinkers on the demand for health care. If drink-related deaths were eliminated, the result would be an increase in longevity, which

[10]This is partly due to the reclassification of certain items and an interpretation of some of the headings used in the original studies.

TABLE 12.1   Estimates of the costs of drinking.

Study	Country and year	Cost category	Amount (%GDP)
Berry (1976)	United States, 1971	Lost production	1.3
		Health care costs	0.8
		Motor vehicle damage	0.4
		Fire losses	0.02
		Violent crime	0.1
		Social response	0.2
		Total	2.9
Schifrin (1983)	United States, 1979	Lost production	3.1
		Health care costs	0.8
		Motor vehicle damage	0.3
		Fire losses	0.03
		Violent crime	0.2
		Social response	0.1
		Total	4.6
Rice (1993)	United States, 1990	Health care costs	0.7
		Loss of life	0.6
		Crime	0.1
		Motor vehicle damage	0.1
		Fire losses	0.01
		Social response (including jail)	0.1
		Total	1.9
Single et al. (1996)	Canada, 1992	Lost production	0.6
		Health care costs	0.2
		Law enforcement	0.2
		Other	0.1
		Total	1.1
		(range)	(0.9–1.3)
Salomaa (1993)	Finland, 1990	Lost production	0.7
		Health care costs	0.2
		Social response	0.2
		Value of loss of life	1.7
		Other	0.3
		Total	3.1
Maynard et al.	England & Wales, 1985	Lost production	0.3
		Health costs	0.04
		Material damage, crashes, criminal activities, and social response	0.04
		Unemployment and loss of life	0.3
		Total	0.7

would impose additional burdens on the health services. Calculations of this offset in a recent study of the costs of smoking in Canada concluded that the net costs imposed on the health services were only 31 percent of the gross costs (Raynauld & Vidal, 1992). The importance of accidents and suicides among alcohol-related deaths suggests that this offset to the gross health costs of drinking would be proportionately even greater. This is implied by the estimate, contained in Single and colleagues (1983), that on average an alcohol-related death in Canada represents 27.8 years lost years of life. Failure to take an account of how the health services would be affected by these extra years of life is potentially a serious shortcoming in a study of the cost implications of drinking.

Wide variation is apparent in the reported cost estimates. Owing to the inclusion of a large figure for "lost production," Schifrin (1983) estimates that the total cost of alcohol abuse in the United States equals 4.6 percent of GDP. At the other end of the spectrum, Maynard and colleagues (1987) put the total cost of alcohol abuse in England and Wales at only 0.7 percent of GDP. This contrast cannot be due to differences in levels or patterns of alcohol consumption; in 1990 per capita alcohol consumption in Britain, Canada, and the United States was almost identical at 7.5 liters of ethanol equivalent per capita (Edwards et al., 1994). It reflects differences in methodology and estimation procedures rather than genuine differences in cost. This is also suggested by the range of estimates published for the same country. The estimates for the United States vary from 1.9 to 4.6 percent of GDP, while the more recent estimate for Canada is less than one-half that reported by Adrian (1988) for 1984.

The estimates of alcohol-related health care costs in the United States are relatively consistent at 0.7 or 0.8 percent of GDP, although none allows for any offset arising from the increased burden on the system that would occur as a result of people's increased longevity following the elimination of drink-related health problems. Much lower health costs have been estimated for Canada, Finland, England, and Wales. While the cost of health care in the United States is relatively high, this could not account for a fourfold discrepancy in the estimates of alcohol-related health costs between that country and Canada. It is also surprising that the estimates of health care costs imposed on society by drinkers should be so much lower in the three countries that have largely socialized medical care systems.

The wide variation in the estimated health costs of drinking underlines the tentative nature of our knowledge of how alcohol affects health, even in countries with a long tradition of making such estimates. This has been emphasized by Maynard et al. (1987), who make clear that their estimate is a minimum bound to the range of plausible estimates. They note that published studies of the annual number of alcohol-related deaths in Britain in the 1980s contain estimates ranging from 4,000 to 40,000. In the light of the large degree of uncertainty surrounding this variable, it is inevitable that cost estimates based on it are very uncertain.

The estimates of the smaller components of the total costs of drinking, such as material damage due to accidents and crime, are similar across the studies surveyed, at about one-half of 1 percent of GDP.

It should finally be noted that the cost estimates for England and Wales prepared by Maynard and colleagues are presented inclusive and exclusive of the cost of unemployment and loss of life. The authors acknowledge that there is no consensus as to how such losses are altered by the existence of the high levels of unemployment and underemployment that characterize developing countries.

A recent econometric study concluded that problem drinking tended to reduce employment and raise unemployment (Mullahy & Sindelar, 1995). No estimate of the impact of these effects on the labor force nor of their social cost implications is provided, but the study does address the question of the direction of causation and tries to show the extent to which problem drinking is a cause of poor labor market outcomes, rather than vice versa.

As we noted in the previous section, the ultimate purpose of studies of the costs and benefits of alcohol consumption is to inform policy and to suggest appropriate interventions. In view of the wide spread of variables revealed by a survey of the costs of alcohol abuse, it is hardly surprising to record that there is also disagreement regarding the balance between the special taxes paid by drinkers and the additional costs to the health services imposed by alcohol abuse in the United States. While most of the economists who have studied the issue conclude that the optimal tax on beverage alcohol is higher than the present level (Grossman et al., 1993), this claim has been contested by Heien (1995), who believes that "alcohol taxes may already be too high and are surely ill-distributed between abusers and moderate drinkers."

The Economic Significance of Alcohol

The picture regarding other indicators of the economic significance of alcohol, such as the employment associated with the drinks industries, or the proportion of total tax revenue collected through excise taxes on alcohol, is quickly assessed through a summary of Lehto's (1995) study:

Direct employment in the production of beverage alcohol is a very small proportion of total employment in developed countries—less than one-half of one per cent even in countries such as Ireland and the United Kingdom with significant exports of beverage alcohol. Moreover, this proportion has been falling due to the introduction of labor-saving technologies in distilling and brewing. There are, of course, regions and communities within countries where brewing, distilling, or wine making is the mainstay of the local economy.

Indirect employment in the distribution and sale of beverages is more significant, but this employment is increasingly intertwined with the provision of other services, such as the sale of food and provision of entertainment and not exclusively attributable to the distribution of drink.

Tax revenue from special taxes on alcohol are relatively unimportant in most countries. Dependence on alcohol excise taxes is highest in Ireland, Britain, and the Scandinavian countries, but it has declined sharply over the years. For example, in Ireland alcohol excise taxes now contribute less than 5 percent of total tax receipts, compared with more than 12 percent in 1971. In most other OECD countries the contribution of special alcohol taxes to the public finances is minor (Lehto, 1995).

While of some general interest, these figures from Europe have no direct policy relevance. For instance, it would be wrong to take the estimate of alcohol-related costs for the United Kingdom (0.7 percent of GDP) and relate it to the 6 percent of personal consumer expenditure on alcohol in Britain or the 1.5 percent of GDP paid in excise taxes on alcohol. To compare the taxes paid by drinkers with estimates of the costs they impose on the economy is implicitly to compare the present situation with a hypothetical situation from which alcohol has been excluded. From a policy perspective it is more relevant to consider the responsiveness of drinkers to changes in policy instruments such as prices and taxes. Of greatest interest is to explore how changes in these instruments affect the level of alcohol-related problems. Some studies that address this topic were summarized in the previous section.

The Growth of Alcohol Consumption Around the World

It is possible to document the growth of alcohol consumption around the world using data from a variety of sources (Walsh & Grant, 1985). Considering a data series ranked by per capita consumption in 1990, it is immediately obvious that the high-ranking countries in terms of consumption of beer, wine, spirits, and total alcohol are all relatively rich. None of the countries classified by the World Bank as "low income" (a per capita GDP of less than US $1,000 a year) would appear. It is also striking that there was a decline in alcohol consumption between 1965 and 1990 in the countries where the highest levels were recorded in 1965, notably France, Spain, Portugal, Italy, and Argentina. In all cases this decline was due to a sharp fall in wine consumption. In all these countries, except France, there was a pronounced increase in beer consumption over the same period, but this was not sufficient to offset the reduced wine consumption, and total alcohol intake declined.

In the majority of countries, however, total alcohol consumption increased over the period, with high rates of growth recorded up to 1980 or 1985 and slower growth or decline thereafter. The countries recording the highest proportional increases were Brazil, Paraguay, Finland, Cuba, the former German Democratic Republic, Mexico, Cyprus, and Venezuela, in all of which alcohol intake per person more than doubled. Some of these, however, started from a very low base and even in 1990 total consumption remained relatively modest. The pattern of growth revealed in these countries indicates that high levels of per capita consumption can be attained over a relatively short period. It is clear that a continuation of these trends would bring many additional countries to the level of alcohol consumption now recorded in the countries where concern about the social costs of drinking is high.

A study of the trends in consumption between and within beverage types shows a strong movement towards convergence in levels and patterns of alcohol consumption between countries. For each beverage type, and for total alcohol consumption, there has been a pronounced tendency for those countries where consumption was high at the start of the period to record the smallest percentage increase over the period. Omitting four countries in which Islamic influences are very important (Turkey, Tunisia, Algeria, and Morocco), the ratio of per capita consumption in the highest and lowest countries (France and Paraguay) was 43:1 in 1965, but this had fallen to 11:1 by 1990, because of the rise in consumption in the latter and the decline in the former. Similar compressions of the ranges are evident for beer, wine, and spirits. As a consequence, the rankings of countries by total alcohol consumption changed significantly over the period. While France remained in first place in both years, Portugal, Italy, and Argentina moved down from their previous places among the 10 highest consumers. Significant declines also occurred in the rankings of Yugoslavia, Chile, Greece, and the former USSR. On the other hand, Luxembourg and the former German Democratic Republic moved up into the top 10 countries, and Denmark, the Netherlands, Cyprus, and Finland also moved rapidly up the league table.

To account for the observed pattern of growth in consumption, economists would normally explore the relationship between consumption of alcohol—the dependent variable—and income, price, and a variety of demographic and social influences as explanatory variables. Certain features of the data, however, restrict the extent to which we can adopt a conventional econometric approach in analyzing them. In the first place, there are no suitable internationally comparable price data for beverage alcohol. Except for a limited range of countries, typically the members of the European Community, comparisons of the price of various beverage alcohol have not been published. Second, in the present study alcohol consumption has been measured in terms of the quantities of beer, wine, and spirits, or their alcohol content. Expenditure data, which are usually used in econometric studies, have not been used. A variable (*ISLAM*) indicating whether the country is predominantly Islamic in religion was also included to take into account one possibly important noneconomic influence on the level of alcohol consumption.

From Table 12.2 it may be seen that the level of alcohol consumption in both 1965 and 1990 was positively related to the level of per capita income. However, the coefficient of the income variable declined over the period. The income elasticity of demand for alcohol, that is, the percentage growth in consumption with respect to the percentage growth in income, is quite low on the basis of the cross section; moreover, it declined from 0.63 in 1965 to 0.52 in 1990. It is likely that if expenditure, rather than quantity, data had been used the estimated

TABLE 12.2   Regression results for total alcohol consumption, 1965 and 1990.

	Dependent variable: alcohol consumption per person	
	1965	**1990**
Intercept	−3.95	−2.98
	(2.26)	(2.67)
GDP per capita	0.6296	0.5222
	(3.14)	(4.32)
ISLAM	−1.852	−2.369
	(4.34)	(9.37)
R^2	0.536	0.800
No. of countries	38	38

Notes: Total alcohol consumption calculated from consumption of beer, wine, and spirits reduced to their equivalent in 100% alcohol. Consumption and income in logarithms. Absolute t-ratios in parentheses.

elasticities would have been higher. The highly significant, negative coefficient of *ISLAM* in both equations indicates that, as expected, when the influence of income is controlled, alcohol consumption per capita is lower in predominantly Islamic countries, where people consume less alcohol than in other countries.

Even though the level of per capita alcohol consumption was fairly closely related to the level of income in both 1965 and 1990, it is apparent from the result reported in Table 12.3 that the rate of growth of income does not, of itself, provide a satisfactory explanation of the rate of growth of consumption. The changing income elasticity of demand for alcohol over the period would tend to weaken the association between the growth in income and the growth in alcohol consumption.

Among the variables omitted from this simple model, price is clearly the most important. However, it is doubtful whether over the period 1965–1990 international variations in the price of alcohol could account for much of the observed variation in the growth of alcohol consumption. Differences between countries in the price of beverage alcohol relative to other goods and services arise mainly from national differences in taxation policies. The heavy excise taxes levied on beer and spirits in northern European countries (Scandinavia, the United Kingdom, and Ireland) make alcohol relatively expensive in these countries. However, these taxes have been fairly stable in real terms over the period studied. Similarly, other relevant factors, such as the age structure of the population, change fairly slowly over time and are not likely to have been

TABLE 12.3   Regression results for growth of total alcohol consumption, 1965–1990.

	Dependent variable: change in per capita total alcohol consumption, 1965–1990	
Intercept	0.9940	0.8107
	(10.55)	(5.95)
Per capita alcohol	−0.4285	−0.4188
consumption 1965	(7.79)	(7.67)
GDP growth rate	–	0.0634
	–	(1.59)
ISLAM	−1.4220	−1.3922
	(7.18)	(7.26)
R²	0.6083	0.6815
No. of countries	47	38

Note: Consumption variables in logarithms. Absolute t-ratios in parentheses.

TABLE 12.4   Regression results for growth of beer consumption, 1965–1990.

	Dependent variable: change in per capita beer consumption, 1965–1990	
Intercept	2.3850	2.1338
	(10.46)	(7.30)
Per capita beer	−0.5043	−0.5085
consumption 1965	(7.79)	(7.49)
GDP growth rate	–	0.1158
	–	(1.99)
ISLAM	−1.5106	−1.5514
	(5.52)	(7.26)
R²	0.5828	0.6675
No. of countries	47	38

Note: Consumption variables in logarithms. Absolute t-ratios in parentheses.

major influences on the changing pattern of alcohol consumption over the period 1965–1990.

The initial level of consumption as well as the growth rate of income was included in the equations. The results for growth rates in total alcohol consumption, and for beer, wine, and spirits separately, are reported in Tables 12.3, 12.4, 12.5, and 12.6. They provide striking confirmation of the hypothesis that there was a pronounced tendency for countries with low initial levels of con-

TABLE 12.5   Regression results for growth of wine consumption, 1960–1995.

Dependent variable: change in per capita wine consumption, 1965–90		
Intercept	1.0435	1.0536
	(6.66)	(3.20)
Per capita wine	−0.2982	−0.2826
consumption 1965	(5.07)	(4.23)
GDP growth rate	−	0.0074
	−	(0.07)
ISLAM	−1.3610	−1.3629
	(4.27)	(3.97)
R^2	0.4591	0.4623
No. of countries	44	36

Notes: Consumption variables in logarithms. Absolute t-ratios in parentheses.

TABLE 12.6   Regression results for growth of spirits consumption, 1965–1990.

Dependent variable: change in per capita spirits consumption, 1965–90		
Intercept	0.4389	0.1829
	(3.93)	(0.75)
Per capita spirits	−0.5032	−0.5072
consumption 1965	(2.19)	(3.30)
GDP growth rate	−	0.0462
	−	(0.52)
ISLAM	−1.2487	−1.1194
	(2.19)	(2.51)
R^2	0.2059	0.4623
No. of countries	33	25

Note: Consumption variables in logarithms. Absolute t-ratios in parentheses.

sumption to experience high rates of increase in consumption over the period and, conversely, that countries with high initial levels of consumption recorded relatively low growth rates. This is shown by the *negative* coefficients of the initial level of consumption, which in all equations are highly significant statistically. Because the growth rate of consumption is inversely related to the initial level of consumption, the *convergence* of consumption levels is implied and the low-consumption countries have tended to catch up with the countries that had high levels of consumption in 1965. If the relationship observed for the period 1965–1990 were to continue to hold, then countries would eventually converge on a common level of alcohol consumption, conditional on the level of income per person and whether they are Islamic in culture.

It is striking that when allowance is made for the initial level of consumption, the influence of the growth of income per capita on the growth of consumption is relatively slight. Although in all cases the association between the growth of income and consumption is positive as expected, only in the case of beer is the coefficient statistically significant. It is possible to conclude that over the past 25 years the tendency for alcohol consumption patterns to converge has dominated over the influence of the growth in real income on consumption.

Implications of Growth in Consumption

Most studies of the effects of drinking on the risk of illness and accidents are based on individuals' response to different levels of intake (for surveys see Andersen (1995) and Romelsjö (1995)). A general conclusion of these studies is that the association between alcohol consumption and risk is nonlinear. While low levels of drinking may be associated with little or no risk (or even, in the case of some conditions such as coronary heart disease, a reduction in risk compared with the abstinent population), high levels of consumption are generally associated with sharply increased risks of adverse consequences. A similar finding has been reported with regard to labor market outcomes. A recent study concluded that "consumption *per se* is not detrimental, but rather it is problem drinking that has adverse effects on employment" (Mullahy & Sindelar, 1995, p. 36).[11]

In many poor countries, although the level of alcohol consumed per person is very low, heavy drinking occurs in certain groups and at certain times of the year. Widespread abstinence over time and across population groups has the effect of making the aggregate consumption data an unreliable guide to the level of drinking and, in particular, to the incidence of heavy drinking in certain subpopulations.

These considerations highlight the difficulty of extrapolating from the level of per capita ethanol consumption to the overall level of alcohol-related damage. Moreover, because most of the adverse repercussions of drinking—and especially the social consequences such as accidents, violence, and crime—are directly related to intoxication, it is likely that for a given level of national consumption per capita the economic costs will be higher the more consumption is concentrated, both in time and in demographic groups. We would therefore expect that for a given level of per capita consumption, a country with a high

[11] This conclusion is based on results that show that a variable measuring alcohol abuse is related to employment outcomes, but total consumption of ethanol is not. Both variables were constructed from questionnaire data.

level of abstinence and a high average intake among drinkers would record more alcohol-related problems than one where the same average level of consumption was spread more evenly across the population. Presumably, too, the more a given level of drinking is concentrated in heavy drinking bouts, the greater the resultant damage.

These aspects of drinking patterns also seem to be converging internationally. For example, although reliable information on abstinence rates is scarce, a study of the evidence for developed countries led to the conclusion that

> It is difficult to detect any remarkable systematic differences in abstinence rates, either by national beverage preference or by average level of consumption. On the contrary, it is perhaps surprising that countries at very different consumption levels have such similar abstinence rates (Simpura, 1995, p. 23).

The very limited data available on frequency of drinking occasions suggest, predictably, that daily consumption is much more frequent in traditionally wine-consuming countries such as Italy, France, and Portugal than in northern European countries. Because relatively few studies of the adverse consequences of drinking have been conducted in the former group, it is difficult to know whether their high but more evenly spaced intake of alcohol is associated with fewer alcohol-related problems. There is little or no evidence on this issue for the developing countries.

Even such apparently straightforward indices as liver cirrhosis mortality vary enormously across countries with similar levels and patterns of alcohol consumption. For example, the Italian death rate is more than 50 percent above the French rate. The rates in the former German Democratic Republic, Romania, and Hungary are all more than 10 times higher than the Irish rate. It is clear that many factors, in addition to the level and pattern of drinking, influence the incidence of this condition. The same is *a fortiori* true of other indices of alcohol-related damage, whose link with drinking is more tenuous.

Some evidence is available, however, linking variations over time in the level of alcohol-related problems with variations in the level of per capita alcohol consumption. Walsh (1987) showed that the death rates from liver cirrhosis and road accidents were positively correlated with the level of per capita alcohol consumption in Ireland. A recent study in the United States found that liquor consumption and alcohol-related road accidents both vary procyclically, increasing in times of economic boom and falling during recessions (Ruhm, 1994). However, it is suggested that consumers are likely to shift to cheaper sources of alcohol—from spirits to beer, for example—and from drinking in bars and restaurants to home consumption during downturns, which could dampen the effects of changes in aggregate consumption on the level of alcohol-related problems.

A number of economists have directly addressed the question of how public policy could minimize the number of alcohol-related problems. The main focus of this research in the United States has been on the behavior of young drinkers. It has been shown that increases in beverage alcohol prices and in the minimum legal drinking age reduce the frequency of heavy drinking and alcohol-related accidents among youths (Coate & Grossman, 1988; Laixuthai & Chaloupka, 1993). This literature emphasizes the finding that the impact of these policy instruments is not confined to light or nonproblem drinkers but also extends to the behavior of heavy and problem drinkers.

CONCLUSIONS

This chapter surveys the literature on measuring the costs and benefits of alcohol consumption. Research on this topic has up to now been confined to a handful of countries, all of them at high income levels and with relatively high levels of per capita alcohol consumption. The methodology that has been developed is relevant to a study of the effects of the growth of alcohol consumption on developing countries, in which until recently the level of consumption of commercially produced alcohol was insignificant. However, it is clear from the present survey that many important methodological issues remain unresolved in this context. There is no ready-made cost-benefit template that can be applied to assessing the effects of the growth of alcohol consumption on a low-income society.

The pattern of growth of alcohol consumption over the period 1965–1990 has also been studied in this chapter. A strong tendency toward convergence in the levels of drinking and the distribution of consumption among beverage types was documented. Although higher levels of per capita alcohol consumption are still found only in relatively high-income countries, it is striking that the growth of drinking has not been closely related to the rate of growth of real income. Other factors have been dominant, such as the diffusion of a global pattern of drinking (outside countries where Islamic influences are important). The fact that rapid rates of growth of alcohol consumption have been recorded in countries where overall economic progress has been modest points to the timeliness of addressing in these countries the issues that the experience of the developed world teaches us will be increasingly important as the consumption of alcohol rises. Policymakers must anticipate these issues so that the legitimate benefits associated with drinking can be enjoyed while the problems attendant on alcohol abuse can be minimized.

REFERENCES

Adrian, M. (1988). Social costs of alcohol. *Canadian Journal of Public Health, 79,* 316–322.
Anderson, P. (1995). Alcohol and risk of physical harm. In H. C. Holder & G. Edwards (Eds.), *Alcohol and Public Policy: Evidence and Issues.* Oxford: Oxford University Press.
Ashley, M. J., Ferrence, R., Room, R., Rankin, J., & Single, E. (1994). Moderate drinking and health: Report of an international symposium. *Canadian Medical Association Journal, 151,* 809–828.

Atkinson, A. B. & Meade, T. W. (1974). Methods and preliminary findings in assessing the economic and health services consequences of smoking, with particular reference to lung cancer. *Journal of the Royal Statistical Society* (Serial A), *137*, 297–312.

Becker, G. S. (1996). *Accounting for Tastes.* Cambridge, MA: Harvard University Press.

Berry, R. E., Jr. (1976). Estimating the economic costs of alcohol abuse. *New England Journal of Medicine, 295,* 620–621.

Coate, D. & Grossman, M. (1988). The effect of alcoholic beverage prices and legal drinking ages on youth alcohol use. *Journal of Law and Economics, 31,* 145–171.

Cook, P. J. (1984). The economics of alcohol consumption and abuse. In L. J. West (Ed.), *Alcoholism and Related Problems: Issues for the American Public.* Englewood Cliffs, NJ: Prentice–Hall.

DiIulio, J. J., Jr. (1995). *Broken Bottles: Liquor, Disorder, and Crime in Wisconsin.* Milwaukee, WI: Wisconsin Policy Research Institute.

Edwards, G., et al. (1994). *Alcohol Policy and the Public Good.* Oxford: Oxford University Press.

Fisher, I. (1927). *Prohibition at Its Worst.* New York: Macmillan.

Grossman, M., Sindelar, J. L., Mullahy, J., & Anderson, R. (1993). Policy watch: Alcohol and cigarette taxes. *Journal of Economic Perspectives, 7,* 211–222.

Heien, D. (1995). The economic case against higher alcohol taxes. *Journal of Economic Perspectives, 9,* 207–209.

Laixuthai, A. & Chaloupka, F. J. (1993). *Youth Alcohol Use and Public Policy* (Working Paper 4278). Cambridge, MA: National Bureau of Economic Research.

Lehto, J. (1995). *The Economics of Alcohol Policy* (Europe Series 61). Copenhagen: WHO Regional Publications.

Markandya, A. & Pearce, D. W. (1989). The social costs of tobacco smoking. *British Journal of Addiction, 84,* 1139–1150.

Maynard, A., Hardman, G., & Whelan, A. (1987). Measuring the social costs of addictive substances. *British Journal of Addiction, 82,* 701–706.

Medina-Mora, M. & Gonzáles, L. (1989). Alcohol-related casualties in Latin America: A review of the literature. In N. Giesbrecht et al. (Eds.), *Drinking and Casualties: Accidents, Poisonings, and Violence in an International Perspective.* London: Tavistock Institute.

Morgan, M. & Grube, J. W. (1994). *Drinking among Post-Primary School Pupils.* Dublin: Economic and Social Research Institute.

Mullahy, J. & Sindelar, J. L. (1995). *Employment, Unemployment, and Drinking* (Working Paper 5123). Cambridge, MA: National Bureau of Economic Research.

Österberg, E. (1983). Calculating the costs of alcohol: The Scandinavian experience. In M. Grant, M. Plant, & A. Williams (Eds.), *Economics and Alcohol.* Beckenham, England: Croom Helm.

Plant, M. & Plant, M. (1992). *Risk-Takers: Alcohol, Drugs, Sex and Youth.* London: Tavistock/Routledge.

Raynauld, A. & Vidal, J. P. (1992). Smokers' burden on society: Myth and reality in Canada. *Canadian Public Policy—Analyse de Politiques, 18,* 300–317.

Romelsjö, A. (1995). Alcohol consumption and unintentional injury, suicide, violence, work performance, and inter-generational effects. In H. C. Holder & G. Edwards (Eds.), *Alcohol and Public Policy: Evidence and Issues.* Oxford: Oxford University Press.

Ruhm, C. J. (1994). *Economic Conditions and Alcohol Problems* (Working Paper 4914). Cambridge, MA: National Bureau of Economic Research.

Salomaa, J. (1993). *The Costs of Harm Due to Alcohol Use and the Level of Taxation in Finland.* Helsinki: Alko.

Schifrin, L. (1983). Societal costs of alcohol abuse. In M. Grant, M. Plant, & A. Williams (Eds.), *Economics and Alcohol.* Beckenham, England: Croom Helm.

Simpura, J. (1995). Trends in alcohol consumption and drinking patterns: Lessons from world-wide development. In H. C. Holder & G. Edwards (Eds.), *Alcohol and Public Policy: Evidence and Issues.* Oxford: Oxford University Press.

Single, E. (1983). The costs and benefits of alcohol in Ontario: A critical review of the evidence. In M. Grant, M. Plant, & A. Williams (Eds.), *Economics and Alcohol*. Beckenham, England: Croom Helm.

Viscusi, W. K. (1990). Do smokers underestimate risk? *Journal of Political Economy, 98*, 1253–1269.

Walsh, B. M. (1987). Do excise taxes save lives? The Irish experience with alcohol taxation. *Accident Analysis and Prevention, 19*, 433–448.

Walsh, B. & Grant, M. (1985). *Public Health Implications of Alcohol Production and Trade* (Offset Publication 88). Geneva: World Health Organization.

World Bank (1993). *World Development Report 1993: Investing in Health*. New York: Oxford University Press.

Zerbe, R. O., Jr. & Dively, D. D. (1994). *Benefit-Cost Analysis in Theory and Practice*. New York: Harper Collins.

Chapter 13

Alcohol in Emerging Markets: Identifying the Most Appropriate Role for the Alcohol Beverage Industry[1]

Gaye Pedlow

When the International Center for Alcohol Policies (ICAP) was first established, its sponsors agreed on a number of basic principles.[2] One of those principles was that "alcohol policies need to be based upon an objective understanding of available research on alcohol use and misuse, and should aim to create a reasonable balance of government regulation, industry self-regulation, and individual responsibility."

In practice, this is only achievable if the available research is comprehensive and reliable enough to use as a basis for developing alcohol policies. This may not be the case for many countries, especially in the developing world, which makes it difficult for policymakers to address local needs effectively.

This book represents the first attempt by ICAP to assemble available research data on drinking patterns in Africa, Asia, Latin America, and Central and Eastern Europe. The objective is to provide a benchmark for future research and, ultimately, to assist in the search for effective and relevant alcohol policies.

---

[1]This chapter was written before the merger between Grand Metropolitan and Guinness Plc came into effect in December of 1997. As such, any references to Guinness, IDV, or UD refer to companies that are now part of the Diageo group.

[2]ICAP sponsors include Allied Domecq Spirits and Wine, Bacardi-Martini, Brown-Forman, Coors Brewing Company, Foster's Brewing Group Limited, Guinness PLC, Heineken NV, International Distillers and Vintners, Miller Brewing Company, Joseph E. Seagram & Sons, and South African Breweries.

The countries surveyed include economies at differing stages of development, from the recently turbulent tiger economies of Southeast Asia to the more impoverished economies in remote parts of sub-Saharan Africa. In addition, whatever their economic status, all have distinctively different cultural traditions. Common sense, therefore, suggests that projects led by the companies sponsoring ICAP in New York or Paris may not transfer well to rural India or to urban centers such as Bangkok.

This chapter aims to explore whether the experience gained by ICAP sponsors in dealing with alcohol issues in parts of Europe, Australasia, and North America may also be relevant elsewhere. This is, in effect, the first step in the process of identifying the most appropriate role for the alcohol beverage industry in dealing with alcohol issues in the differing cultural environments of Asia, Africa, Latin America, and Central and Eastern Europe. The chapter concludes with some simple guidelines—a "framework for responsibility"—which ICAP sponsors hope will be helpful to all parties involved in taking this debate forward. This framework is offered on behalf of ICAP sponsors, and reflects their contribution to the construction and implementation of responsible business, social, and policy norms surrounding alcohol in the developing world.

EXPERIENCE IN THE "DEVELOPED" WORLD

In terms of drink industry involvement in alcohol issues, the past decade has seen great changes.

About 10 years ago, a number of the major international drink companies began to take a more strategic look at the way in which the industry responded to alcohol issues—in other words, to health-related aspects of alcohol consumption and to social issues such as underage drinking or drinking and driving. They thought it ought to be possible to demonstrate real success in tackling problems related to alcohol misuse, while at the same time not penalizing the majority of sensible drinkers. The key to this approach was the idea of "partnership." A number of organizations were set up, funded by the alcohol beverage companies, which had as their twin aims the promotion of responsible drinking and the reduction of alcohol misuse. They were known as social aspects organizations (SAOs) and they began to work in partnership with a wide range of other interest groups representing central government, local authorities, police forces, teachers and youth groups, licensing authorities, and many others.

Since the late 1980s, we have seen emerging a steadily expanding network of such organizations. By the beginning of 1998 there were close to 30 such bodies, mostly scattered across Europe and North America, but also including the Industry Association for Responsible Alcohol Use in South Africa and the Drinks Industry Action Group in Mauritius. A pan-European organization, called The Amsterdam Group, was established in 1990 to coordinate activities by the industry on a regional basis and to encourage initiatives in countries where SAOs did not yet exist. A similar coordinating body has now been established for the Asia-Pacific region, known as the Asia-Pacific Alcohol Policy Forum (APAPF).

It is unlikely that anyone in the industry 10 years ago anticipated the rapid expansion of the "partnership" process, or the amount of common ground that could be identified with such a wide range of different interest groups. There was not, nor will there ever be, complete agreement on all aspects of alcohol policy, but the benefits of this cooperative approach soon became clear to all of those involved. Without the lessons learned during this period, it would never have been possible to establish an organization such as ICAP, which aims to encourage worldwide communication and cooperation between the alcohol beverage industry and the public health community. With this step, the theme of partnership entered a new and increasingly international phase.

The question now is, how much of that knowledge and experience is relevant, or can be made relevant, to the rest of the world?

EXPERIENCE IN THE "DEVELOPING" WORLD AND EMERGING OR GROWTH MARKETS

There are some—but not many—examples of individual companies undertaking initiatives to promote responsible drinking or to prevent alcohol misuse outside Europe, North America, and Australia. These include initiatives supported by Bacardi-Martini in Puerto Rico, United Distillers in Hong Kong, Asia-Pacific Breweries in Singapore, and Seagram in India. Japan, however, is an exceptional case, as the major local beer and spirit companies, including Suntory,[3] Kirin, and Sapporo, have run a number of moderation and alcohol education initiatives for many years. Since 1994 they have had annual campaigns which warn of the dangers of "ikki drinking"—a form of drinking competition, popular with students, in which large quantities of alcohol are consumed all at once.[4]

There are even fewer examples of companies working together, or in partnership with third parties, on such issues. This is not altogether surprising, as the whole concept of "partnership" is a relatively new one. However, ICAP sponsors believe, on the basis of their experience so far, that two important factors will influence the approach taken by the drinks industry to alcohol issues in the developing world and emerging economies.

The first of these is the clear need to both understand and respect the culture and values of every country, in particular attitudes towards and historical experience of alcohol beverages. Of course, this is important elsewhere too. A drink-driving campaign that works well in France may not be at all suitable for

---

[3]Highlights from Suntory's responsible drinking campaigns (dating back to 1986) can be found in its publication *The Moderation Book* (1994).

[4]In 1994 the Japanese Brewers Association and Sake Manufacturers joined forces to run an information campaign on "ikki drinking" at 530 universities in Japan, at a cost of just under Y3 million.

Sweden. But respect for cultural values will be essential for the industry as it responds to alcohol issues in Africa, Asia, Latin America, and Central and Eastern Europe.

The second factor is the size and structure of the alcohol beverage industry itself, which will vary from country to country. Both of these factors deserve some attention. However, it is worth looking first at some examples of what has been done up to the present.

Case Study 1: Establishing a Social Aspects Organization in South Africa

The members of the Industry Association for Responsible Alcohol Use (ARA) include all the major manufacturers and wholesalers of alcohol beverages in South Africa.

Its origins go back to 1981, when some industry leaders set up a loosely constituted forum to look at aspects of alcohol consumption and misuse in South Africa. In 1986 this forum evolved into the Social Aspects of Alcohol Committee of the South African Liquor Industry (SAAC). In 1989, its first ever full-time director was appointed and in March 1996 the organization adopted its current name.

Its objectives are:

- To encourage and support research;
- To promote responsible drinking;
- To ensure responsible advertising of alcohol beverages;
- To support and participate in programs aimed at preventing misuse of alcohol beverages;
- To promote dialogue with other interested parties, including the public health community, in order to encourage objective debate about alcohol issues and to identify opportunities for working together on issues where there is common ground;
- To encourage and promote research into alcohol-related issues, through support for the Foundation for Alcohol Related Research at the University of Cape Town.

Since 1989, ARA has sponsored a campaign on university campuses around the country. The campaign, called BUDDY, aims to heighten awareness of the dangers of irresponsible alcohol consumption and of drunk driving. It has the full support of the Department of Transport Safety within the Ministry of Transport.

ARA also has a strong track record in life skills education, having sponsored such programs in some 1,000 schools for children between 12 and 18 years old. In 1995, ARA became a founding funder of the Institute for Health Training and Development, which gives training for teachers on life skills education.

ARA regularly reviews the industry's code of advertising practice to ensure that it is appropriate. Since early 1996, ARA members have included the message "Not for sale to persons under the age of 18" on advertisements.

The most striking feature of ARA is that the organization was established many years before most comparable organizations in Europe or North America. Promoting cooperation between the beer, wine, and spirits sectors of the South African industry was difficult in the early days, but has proved to be not only possible, but also very effective.

Case Study 2: The Formation of a Regional Partnership — The Asia-Pacific Alcohol Policy Forum (APAPF)

The structure of the drinks industry in Asia is such that major international players, such as the sponsors of ICAP, may have very small market shares by comparison with major, long-established Asian companies such as Suntory in Japan, Jinro in the Republic of Korea, Boonrawd (Singha beer) in Thailand, the UB Group in India, and numerous others. The products produced by these companies may differ from Western forms of beer, wine, or spirits—for example, sake, *soju*, and rice wine. To put this into perspective, Jinro *soju* is the second biggest distilled spirit brand in the world, in terms of volume sold, behind the Stolichnaya vodka brand (Flemming, 1998).

There are no social aspects organizations in Asia and, with the exception of Japan, few examples of individual companies taking initiatives which promote responsible drinking or aim to reduce alcohol misuse. However, a number of leading international drink companies began meeting on an informal basis to discuss alcohol issues in the Asia-Pacific region in 1995. They believed that the time was right to begin introducing responsible drinking initiatives similar to those running successfully elsewhere in the world. Without an existing network of national industry associations to work through, they decided that the best approach was to form a regional body, the APAPF, which would act as a catalyst to encourage activities at country level. APAPF was established in 1996, with the intention of promoting partnerships with governments, the public health community, and other decision-makers in the Asia-Pacific region on issues of common interest.

Members of APAPF include Allied Domecq, Anheuser-Busch, Bacardi-Martini, Brown-Forman, Coors, Guinness, Heineken, IDV, Moët Hennessy, and Seagram. A case study of the first APAPF initiative appears later in this chapter.

HISTORICAL EXPERIENCE OF ALCOHOL

It is commonly, if wrongly, believed that in many cultures alcohol beverages have only been introduced fairly recently—or have never been introduced at all. However, as all the authors in this book make clear, alcohol beverages have been enjoyed as part of local culture, as part of family and village life, or as part of the religious and spiritual life of most societies, since before written history.

Both Shen and Wang, writing about China (Chapter 5), and Madrigal, writing about Latin America (Chapter 9), make this point, while Haworth and Acuda describe alcohol beverages as "an integral and indispensable part of the traditional African village life ... abundance of beer was the villagers' glory and a sign of good times. Without it tribal councils could not be held, and marriages and initiation ceremonies could not take place" (Chapter 2).

In India, research quoted by Isaac (Chapter 6) tells us that there is "no cultural tradition ... which could be described as being clearly and unequivocally against the use of alcohol in any form and under all circumstances." Among the early Hindus, it was only the priestly class of Brahmins who were forbidden from drinking.

The folklore associated with drinking also refers to the consequences of alcohol misuse. Just as the Bible tells the story of Noah's drunkenness, so other cultures tell stories of the dangers of excessive consumption. Medina-Mora (Chapter 10) tells us of Mexican societies where drinking without restraint was only permitted for the over-60s, while Shen and Wang recount the story of Yi Di in China, exiled because her emperor believed that the sweet-tasting drink she had discovered would lead to his sons becoming drunkards.

Just as interesting is the fact that many ancient societies believed in the health benefits of alcohol consumption long before there was any scientific basis for such beliefs. This has been the traditional belief in Mexico, Nigeria, China, Japan, and Korea, to give but a few examples (Heath, 1995, p. 342).

It is not necessary to dwell here on the history of drinking, but it is important to recognize that even very early societies acknowledged both the pleasures and the problems associated with alcohol beverages. The fact that such a distinction already exists is helpful when it comes to promoting responsible drinking in the 1990s.

ALCOHOL BEVERAGES AND THE CULTURE OF TODAY

When establishing a network of social aspects organizations throughout Europe and North America in the late 1980s, the major alcohol beverage companies could make certain assumptions. They knew that, by and large, their companies were seen as respectable, law-abiding corporations which paid their taxes on time, treated their employees fairly, and were active in their local communities, as good corporate citizens should be. There was a tradition, even sometimes an expectation, of business getting involved in community relations projects or tackling broader social issues. Industry involvement in alcohol issues, broadly speaking, kept pace with both government regulation and public opinion. This means that the initiatives undertaken by the SAOs were largely noncontroversial and reflected the values and standards that were considered acceptable by society.

In other parts of the world, the values and standards which society considers acceptable or appropriate in the drinks industry are not so clear. The general reputation of the local drinks industry may leave something to be desired— particularly in countries where uncontrolled or illicit production of alcohol beverages is common. There may be no track record of business involvement in social or health-related issues, which may be seen as the remit solely of government or the public health community. Initiatives by the drinks industry in such circumstances may be regarded with suspicion or be wholly misunderstood.

In addition, as many local managers of ICAP companies would fear, it may not be advisable to make responsible drinking initiatives appear to be sponsored only by "foreign" companies or international brands, as this has the potential to backfire. The interpretation may be that "only foreign liquor causes problems" or even that "these foreign companies are so arrogant that they tell our people how to behave."

Finally, in some parts of the world, alcohol misuse is related to much bigger issues such as poverty, unemployment, urban drift, and economic readjustment policies. This theme comes through strongly in Iontchev's chapter (Chapter 7) dealing with Central and Eastern Europe. In Vroublevsky and Harwin's chapter on Russia (Chapter 8) this theme is even more evident. They illustrate that the problems associated with the collapse of the Communist regime in Russia have undoubtedly contributed to the overall levels of misuse.

The ability of companies to make an impact on such problems is extremely limited. Yet at the same time, initiatives to promote responsible drinking may not be successful unless they also address these other social issues in some way.

This may sound like an impossible situation, but in reality it may simply influence the selection of individual projects. For example, it might be possible to run an alcohol education project, industry funded, alongside a job creation or training project funded by another agency, in a particular local community. Common sense tells us that people are more likely to listen to messages about sensible drinking if they have some self-esteem and a certain degree of hope for the future.

One specific area in which ICAP sponsors have much experience, is on the issue of drinking and driving. Across Europe, Australasia, and North America, ICAP companies have been involved in initiatives dealing with this issue for at least 10 years or more. Most of these projects are run in partnership with local police forces, road safety authorities, or ministries of transport.

In general, the countries in which these initiatives have been run so far share the following characteristics:

- A properly defined and well-understood legal framework for dealing with drink-driving issues, including established legal blood alcohol levels;
- Adequate training standards for driving students and the requirement of a driving test before obtaining a driver's licence;
- Proper testing to ensure that the majority of vehicles are roadworthy;

- Specific training standards for commercial and public transport drivers;
- Major roads in relatively good condition with street lighting in urban areas;
- Reliable public transport or taxi services in major urban areas.

As readers acquainted with driving conditions in some developing countries will know, these characteristics are not yet found everywhere in the world.

What this means is that any drink-driving initiative has to start from a good understanding of local road safety problems. For example, private car drivers have been the focus of many campaigns elsewhere. In the developing world, however, the greatest number of accidents may involve motorcycles (Swaddi-wudhipong, 1994) and the greatest number of deaths may be caused by accidents involving commercial drivers who have little, if any, safety training. Therefore, although the overall message may be the same, the target audiences may well be different.

Case Study 3: APAPF Drinking-Driving Initiative in Thailand

The number of road traffic injuries and deaths has been rising in Thailand in recent years, as is the case in many developing countries as traffic has increased (Division of Health Statistics, 1992, pp. 7–13). In November 1995, APAPF member companies met in Bangkok (see Case Study 2 for a list of APAPF members). They invited Dr Tairjing Siriphanich, Director of the Medical Institute of Accidents and Disasters and a member of the Thai National Safety Council Committee, to join the meeting for a discussion on road safety issues. Dr. Siriphanich said that fast or careless driving, and driving while drunk, were becoming a particular problem. Although there is a legal blood alcohol limit of 50 milligrams per 100 milliliters of blood in Thailand, little had been done to educate people, especially young people, about the dangers of driving after excessive alcohol consumption. He indicated that he would welcome the opportunity to work with the forum in developing a suitable education campaign for young people in Thailand.

Forum members believed that a program which had been successfully introduced in Germany, Ireland, Belgium, and Denmark, with support from the Amsterdam Group and the European Commission, could be just as appropriate for Thailand. The program, based on a video filmed in Thailand (in the Thai language), puts a number of young volunteers through a series of driving tests, both before and after they have a few drinks, in order to demonstrate the effect that alcohol has on driving ability. Launched in April 1997 and backed up by an explanatory booklet, the video package is now being distributed by the Ministry of Public Health, the Thai Royal Police, the Land Transports Department, and the Ministry of Education.

This initiative is a good illustration of how one project concept can be made relevant to a number of different cultures. APAPF will be looking for other initiatives which allow examples of best practice elsewhere in the world to be adapted for use in countries in the Asia-Pacific region.

THE ROLE OF "LOCAL" ALCOHOLS

There is one issue that could be said to relate to both "local culture" and "the structure of the industry"—that is, the need to take into account consumption of local alcohols.

The phrase "local alcohols," is used to refer to alcohol beverages that, even if they are produced in commercial quantities, fall outside the usual health and safety or regulatory frameworks. Examples would include arrack in India, *chang'aa* (illicit gin) in Kenya, and many sorts of palm wine. Local alcohols may be fermented or distilled, depending on what sort of raw materials are available. For example, Uganda grows more varieties of banana than any other country in the world. It is hardly surprising, then, that in addition to the use of banana plants as roofing thatch, animal feed, a staple food (eaten like mashed potatoes), for fruit juice, and in basketry, banana wine is a traditional drink, banana beer is very popular, and bananas are also distilled into a white spirit.

Even within the international drinks industry, there are few people who would claim to have an accurate picture of the true status of local alcohols, particularly in developing countries (Cavanagh & Clairmonte, 1985). For this reason, it is good to see that all the authors in this book emphasize the role played by local alcohols in most societies.

Obtaining accurate information about patterns and levels of consumption of local alcohols is often difficult, for the following reasons:

- Many types of local alcohol are produced illegally. In Chapter 11, Heath quotes research which suggests that some 30 percent of consumption in Sri Lanka, 50 percent in India, and 80 percent or more of consumption in Tanzania is of illegal products. Getting people to talk honestly about their consumption of such products is difficult—particularly if they are confronted by a market researcher holding a pen and a clipboard.
- Even if they are legal, the status associated with local alcohols is often very low. If asked, people prefer to talk about and may sometimes exaggerate their consumption of branded products, even if they cannot afford to drink them regularly.
- Local alcohol is frequently used by counterfeiters who convince consumers they are buying mainstream brands.

The factors that drive people to consume local alcohols are likely to relate to availability, particularly in rural areas, and price. High taxes of "official" alcohol beverages, which make the price unaffordable to many people, do not necessarily lead to reductions in alcohol consumption; they simply encourage the establishment of "unofficial" channels for alcohol production and sale (Cavanagh & Clairmonte, 1985, p. 28).[5]

The best documented example of this comes from Western Europe, where illicit production of alcohol is confined almost exclusively to Scandinavia, because low tax rates in southern Europe mean that there is no incentive for people to manufacture their own alcohol beverages (Kolk, 1992).[6]

People who purchase counterfeit alcohol, masquerading as a mainstream brand, may be convinced by the seller that the product is genuine. Or they may simply prefer, for reasons of status, to drink and to offer to their friends a product that they suspect may be dubious, but which comes with the right brand image.

People who produce local alcohols may simply wish to provide their family and friends with a fairly regular source of "home-brew," or may wish to build a business. Some producers continue their output on a relatively small scale, while others become very large operators indeed. Haworth and Acuda point out (Chapter 2) that commercial production of sorghum beer dates back to 1910 in parts of southern Africa. They also note that in Botswana in the early 1980s roughly 30 percent of all households earned regular income from sorghum beer production, making it the largest nonfarm source of employment in the country.

Government attitudes towards unofficial or illicit production of alcohol beverages vary widely. When their production reaches a commercial scale, some choose to legalize and regulate them properly, as they would mainstream alcohol beverages. This means that proper standards of hygiene and workplace safety can be applied, and the government benefits from additional tax revenues.

In other cases, however, the whole business of trying to regulate and control such an industry seems too complicated, and even large-scale commercial production of illicit alcohol is ignored. This can lead to serious problems, not just because the production and consumption of these products is uncontrolled, but also because local alcohols are sometimes adulterated with methanol or other poisons. In one Mexican community in 1994, Medina-Mora tells us (Chapter 10) that over 100 people died from drinking contaminated *Mezcal*.

This is also a problem in India, where, as Isaac says (Chapter 6), there are at least 200 reported deaths from adulterated arrack every year, and no doubt many more that go unreported. In 1981, one single batch of bad "hooch" in Bangalore led to over 300 deaths (Manor, 1993). Jayasuriya and Jayasuriya quote 1993 estimates suggesting that 60 percent of the alcohol masquerading as international spirits brands in India consisted of local counterfeits, at least until a few years ago (Chapter 3).

---

[5]Cavanagh and Clairmonte comment, "In many cases, tax structures and rigorous government control over distribution circuits provide the motive force for the internationalization of illicit trafficking" (p. 28).

[6]See also the website of the Swedish Brewers Association at http://www.swedbrewers.se/english/alcohol/unrecalc.html.

China too has problems with illicit production. On 25 January 1997, the Xinhua News Agency in Beijing reported that five farmers found guilty of producing and selling counterfeit spirit had been executed in Yunnan Province. The spirit contained ethyl alcohol and had led to 36 deaths, with over 100 people ill from poisoning.

Russia, perhaps not surprisingly, reports many cases of alcoholic poisoning from counterfeit or contaminated alcohol. Vroublevsky and Harwin (Chapter 8) refer specifically to Petrov, a "cheap and highly toxic vodka" which came to be known as the black death.

Medina-Mora tells us that there is evidence that consumption of local or illegal alcohols is on the increase in Mexico. The same appears to be true for parts of Africa. In both Ghana and the Seychelles according to industry data (Guinness, unpublished), local alcohols account for over 50 percent of the total volume of alcohol consumed. Regular increases in the excise duty on beer mean that local Seychellois have been priced out of the "official" market for alcohol beverages. The main island of Mahé, with an area of 58 square miles, has an estimated 1,100 producers of local alcohols, of which only 31 are licensed. As a government task force concluded in 1995: "Unhygienic preparation and storage of home-brews for personal consumption and illegal sale often lead to death caused by leptospirosis or toxic effects due to additives" (Task Force on Drug and Alcohol Abuse, 1995, p. 29).

For those who produce home-brews mainly for themselves and their family, education about basic hygiene is clearly a priority. It is equally clear that large-scale commercial production of such products needs to be subject to proper regulation and quality controls and that action needs to be taken in some countries to eliminate the counterfeit business. One area where there may be potential for cooperation between ICAP sponsors and the public health community is in gathering more reliable data on patterns and levels of consumption of local alcohols.

INDUSTRY STRUCTURE

Apart from South Africa, where South African Breweries has been a major industry player since 1895, ICAP sponsors have their headquarters and their "home markets" in Europe, the United States, and Australia. The structure of their operations is very often quite different in the developing world and this will inevitably have an impact on the way these companies, individually or collectively, respond to and deal with alcohol issues.

There are some countries in which ICAP sponsors have local production facilities—bottling plants or distilleries for spirits and/or breweries for beer. Some of these facilities have been established for so long that the local population does not consider these brands to be "foreign" but as part of their own local culture, for example, Guinness in West Africa and parts of the Caribbean.

In these instances, the company concerned has a physical and visible presence in the country, in terms of assets and numbers of people employed.

For many companies, however, business in the developing world is a matter of exporting brands from the home country or from another center in the region. This leads to a very different operational structure, with far fewer personnel on the ground. The emphasis is not on production, but on distribution and sales, which may even be handled by a third party. There will not be a large management team, and there is unlikely to be a "public affairs" manager or an equivalent with any experience of dealing with policy issues.

Joint venture operations with local partners are common, but this limits the control the "outside" company has over local decision-making. Some joint venture partners may initially find the idea of getting involved in alcohol issues alarming, because there is no track record of such activities locally.

While ICAP sponsors compete fiercely with each other for market share, they do work together on noncompetitive issues. Again, the whole idea of working together in this way may be difficult for local industry players to accept, particularly if it involves the beer, wine, and spirits sectors and includes both local producers and importers. Anyone associated with the social aspects organizations in Europe and the United States will know how difficult—and time-consuming—it is to build relationships across the different sectors of the industry and to find a common agenda, even though to the outside world one type of alcohol is more or less the same as another. This process is likely to be just as difficult in the rest of the world, where even basic trade associations, not to mention relatively complex organizations like SAOs, are thin on the ground.

Finally, emerging markets may not generate profit for ICAP sponsors until many years after they first begin to sell their brands there. In Europe and North America, it would be standard practice to fund responsible drinking initiatives out of the company's local profits. With new markets, such activities will have to be funded out of the business development budget, even when the local company is operating at a loss, or else funded from the company's regional or central headquarters.

This is not an argument to do nothing. It does mean, however, that a balance will have to be struck, when setting priorities, between an assessment of local needs and the industry's capability to deliver effective programs in any particular market.

THE WAY FORWARD

From a review of the individual chapters, it is striking that only two chapters—those on Mexico and sub-Saharan Africa—make any reference to the involvement of the drinks industry. Medina-Mora comments on discussions held in 1984 under the auspices of the Mexican Ministry of Health, which for the first time included legislators, researchers, social scientists, prevention and treatment experts, and representatives from the drinks industry. "This turned out to be an enriching experience for all participants, as problems had previously been examined only from one side. An important aspect was the participation of the industry" (Chapter 10). Medina-Mora goes on to say that, despite some tension in the discussions, a consensus was reached.

As Medina-Mora implies, it is not essential for those representing different aspects of the alcohol issues field to agree with each other on every issue. The motivations and expectations of the parties involved may be different. It *is* essential, however, for them to be prepared to listen to each other and to identify common goals.

The companies sponsoring ICAP believe that there are three key areas in which they can cooperate with the public health community and other partners, to the benefit of all concerned: data collection and analysis regarding patterns and levels of consumption; responsible promotional and advertising practice; and alcohol education and initiatives that promote responsible drinking.

Improving the Data on Patterns and Levels of Consumption

It is all too clear from reading the individual chapters on emerging markets that the available data are incomplete and far from reliable. All the authors acknowledge this weakness.

Making comparisons between the countries or regions is all the more difficult because there are so few agreed upon definitions. Take the term "heavy drinking," for example. There is, for instance, a drinking culture in South Korea which considers regular drunkenness to be socially acceptable. In another culture, in Ghana, one ICAP sponsor reports that, even for its own in-house market research, the definition of a heavy drinker is someone who consumes alcohol beverages, even in very small quantities, "at least once a week."

In the long run, the lack of reliable data is in no one's best interests. Heath is right to point out that "A danger inherent in the reporting of faulty statistics from developing areas is that the numbers may, by their very appearance in print, take on an inappropriate appearance of reality" (Chapter 11).

From a public health perspective, if faulty statistics *understate* the extent of alcohol misuse, then the public policy response will be inadequate and problems will continue to get worse. From an industry perspective, any *overstatement* of alcohol misuse is likely to lead to a variety of excessive and unjustified restrictions on alcohol availability or marketing practices. Similarly, a lack of understanding of the role played by local or illicit alcohols will only serve to confuse the issue. Both parties have an interest in ensuring that the data are accurate, but with different motivations.

For these reasons, improving both the quality and the quantity of the data available is a possible area for cooperation between ICAP sponsors and the public health community, and is thus the first item to be addressed in the framework suggested by the ICAP sponsors in the last pages of this chapter.

Responsible Promotional and Advertising Practices

There are a number of references to marketing practices, especially advertising, scattered among the chapters in this book. Most of the authors of the country and regional reviews seem to start from the assumption that advertising is automatically linked to higher levels of consumption and misuse, although the majority of research studies do not support that view (Fisher, 1993, p. 150). Advertising simply aims to persuade consumers to buy one brand in preference to another (Pittman, 1996).

There is also a common misconception that advertising for alcohol beverages is wholly unrestricted in the developing world and very severely restricted everywhere else. But there is barely any country worldwide which does not regulate alcohol advertising in some way, and many developing countries have controls that are more stringent, not less, than the controls in, say, parts of Europe. A 1996 drinks industry survey of over 75 countries in Latin America, Africa, the Middle East, and Asia found that fewer than 20 countries (about 25 percent of the total) reported "no controls" on advertising for alcohol beverages. The rest had a range of voluntary or statutory restrictions—or in some cases complete bans—on alcohol advertising. Similarly, data obtained from the Centre for Information on Beverage Alcohol suggest that of 27 countries within Europe, six reported "no controls"—about 22 percent of the total.

It may seem against the industry's interests to support initiatives that emphasize the need for responsible marketing practices. However, this is not so. The ICAP sponsors believe that the right to advertise their brands is an important commercial freedom, but recognize also that they have to safeguard that freedom by marketing their brands in a responsible manner. If the public or government perception is that the industry is abusing its freedom to advertise, then that will lead to calls for restrictions on all forms of marketing communications.

For these reasons, the need to encourage responsible marketing practices is the second item addressed in the suggested framework that follows.

Alcohol Education and Initiatives Which Promote Responsible Drinking

The third item in the suggested framework relates to the researching and piloting of specific initiatives similar to those undertaken by social aspects organizations elsewhere in the world. ICAP sponsors recognize that many of these initiatives will have to be adapted to make them relevant to the differing cultural environments of Africa, Asia, Latin America, and Central and Eastern Europe.

Ideally, this would best be achieved by the establishment of SAOs at individual country levels. This is beginning to happen in Central and Eastern Europe, where an SAO was due to be launched in Hungary in 1997 and preparatory work is being undertaken in a number of other countries. And although this is being done, making progress in places where the need is perhaps greatest, such as Russia, will inevitably be more of a challenge and more time-consuming.

In Asia the regional organization, APAPF, aims to facilitate dialogue and promote the concept of partnership, both within the regional drinks industry and with governments, the public health community, and other decision-makers. APAPF will act as a catalyst to encourage initiatives at country level throughout the region, as it did with the drinking-driving project in Thailand, and will also encourage the establishment and enforcement of self-regulatory codes of advertising practice.

Within Africa, there is much that can be learned from the experience of South African Breweries and the Industry Association for Responsible Alcohol Use in South Africa.

Within Latin America, there have been a number of encouraging developments. An SAO was established in Peru during the second half of 1996 and efforts are being made to repeat the process in other countries in the region.

As mentioned at the start, this book represents the first attempt by ICAP to assemble the available research data on drinking patterns in Africa, Asia, Latin America, and Central and Eastern Europe. It is also the first step in the process of identifying the most appropriate role for the alcohol beverage industry in dealing with such issues in these societies. There is clearly still a long way to go in terms of defining that role. But at the very least, the ICAP sponsors hope that this work will serve as a benchmark for future research and encourage dialogue between the industry and those involved in the development of alcohol policy.

The ICAP sponsors believe that the alcohol beverage industry has a legitimate and positive role to play in developing those policies, in promoting responsible drinking, and in helping to combat misuse. This is not a short-term initiative, but a long-term objective. The ICAP sponsors are, therefore, committed to revisiting this research, with a view to reporting on how the issues have changed and how the role of the industry has evolved, five years from now. It is hoped that the framework which follows will provide a useful basis for dialogue, and help to identify areas of possible common ground between the alcohol beverage industry, the public health community, and others with an interest in alcohol policies.

A SUGGESTED FRAMEWORK FOR RESPONSIBILITY

Understanding Perceptions of Alcohol and Patterns of Consumption

Levels and patterns of alcohol consumption vary significantly from one country to another, as do social, cultural, and religious attitudes to alcohol beverages. The ICAP sponsors recognize that understanding and respecting those differences is a key requirement for carrying out their business responsibly, particularly in developing countries and emerging economies.

For this reason, ICAP sponsors will encourage where possible:

- Efforts to collect data on patterns of alcohol consumption and any associated problems in developing countries and emerging markets.
- Research projects that will provide or supplement such data in situations where they do not exist or are incomplete.

Responsible Promotional and Advertising Practices

The ICAP sponsors believe that the right to advertise their brands is a most important commercial freedom, but recognize that they must safeguard this freedom by advertising in a responsible manner. They believe that industry self-regulation through voluntary codes of practice is the most efficient means of regulating drinks advertising and promotional activities, while at the same time protecting the rights of individual companies to communicate with their consumers and to compete for market share. For this reason, ICAP sponsors will encourage:

- Strict industry compliance with all existing legislation or self-regulatory codes of practice relating to the advertising and promotion of alcohol beverages.
- Initiatives aimed at establishing self-regulatory codes in countries where they do not already exist.
- Efforts to ensure that such codes of practice adequately reflect local culture and values.
- The development of appropriate enforcement mechanisms to ensure that such codes are adhered to.

Alcohol Education and Initiatives Which Promote Sensible Drinking

Levels of knowledge about the nature and effects of alcohol, and any particular problems associated with alcohol misuse, may vary from one country to another. Initiatives designed to provide information about drinking, or to tackle particular aspects of alcohol misuse, must, therefore, be adapted to suit local situations. Whilst the alcohol beverage industry has been a strong supporter of such programs elsewhere, there are few current examples of similar initiatives in developing countries and emerging economies. The ICAP sponsors will, therefore, encourage:

- The researching and piloting of such initiatives in a selected number of developing countries and emerging markets.

- The sharing of "good practice" through identifying initiatives that have been successful elsewhere.
- Dialogue with government, public health professionals, and other parties to explore possibilities for cooperation and partnership on specific issues or projects.

A CHECKLIST OF RELATED ACTIVITIES

The checklist that follows highlights ways in which the three key principles might be put into practice. Approaches will vary from country to country depending on the structure of the drinks industry—for example, the absence or presence of a local trade association, which at the very least provides a forum where the key producers get together to discuss common issues. They will also vary from company to company depending on the nature of their investment in a particular country.

It is worth illustrating such distinctions by reference to a hypothetical country, Begovia. Companies A, B, and C are all sponsors of ICAP. Company A distributes small volumes of one of its brands via an independent local distributor and has no employees based in Begovia. Company B sees Begovia as an important and growing export market, but has limited resources in-market, with a general manager and a local sales force. Company C has a local production facility and a full management team in-market. It would be unrealistic to expect company A to have much influence on how alcohol issues are addressed in Begovia. Company B would support initiatives if managed through an industry body or sponsored via ICAP, but does not have the resources in place locally to lead the industry's efforts. Company C has significant business interests to protect and the resources to lead an industry initiative or to set the standards for others to follow.

The opening items under each of the following headings reflect the activities likely to be undertaken by companies with little investment or resources in any given country; the later items are clearly more applicable to companies with significant levels of investment, or to initiatives undertaken by industry associations. The checklist, therefore, illustrates a continuum of responsibility that grows with the scale of the company's business in a given country.

1. Perceptions of Alcohol and Patterns of Consumption

- Monitor any major social or political developments that might have an impact on levels or patterns of alcohol consumption in a given country.
- Require a local agency, manager, or distributor to monitor and report (to the parent company) on health and social issues related to alcohol consumption.
- Include questions relating to social issues, perceptions of alcohol-related problems, and so on in market research studies.

- Monitor consumption levels of local alcohols and associated problems as part of company/industry market research.
- Commission research to provide or supplement data on consumption levels/misuse.
- Share research results with the local public health community. Arrange for publication as appropriate.

2. Responsible Promotional and Advertising Practices

- Ensure company compliance with all existing codes of practice/advertising regulations, whether self-regulatory or part of government legislation.
- Where no code/regulation exists, ensure that the parent company gives guidance regarding minimum standards.
- Pay particular attention to developing advertising/promotional activities which are in keeping with local culture, religion, and traditions.
- Establish processes to ensure that joint venture partners, advertising agencies, and other local partners know of the parent company's commitment to responsible marketing practices.
- Respond promptly to criticisms of company advertising/promotional activities, making changes where necessary.
- Work with international and local companies to establish industry trade associations with responsibility for enforcing self-regulation of advertising and marketing practices.
- Improve the effectiveness of such codes through regular reviews, updating, and amendment as necessary.
- Involve nonindustry organizations (broadcasting authorities, media owners, advertising standards authorities, consumer organizations, etc.) in self-regulatory bodies where this is appropriate/practical.
- Publish the findings of self-regulatory review bodies if appropriate.

3. Alcohol Education and Initiatives that Promote Sensible Drinking

- Recognize that the company/industry has a role to play in encouraging responsible use of its products.
- Take steps to establish a company-wide alcohol policy, which aims to educate employees about responsible drinking.
- Ensure that country managers in developing countries and emerging markets know of their parent company's views on responsible drinking and related issues such as drinking-driving.
- Identify priority issues for a given country. Such issues might include the education of young people about moderate drinking or drinking-driving, and similar initiatives.
- Identify possible partners for initiatives (other industry players and trade associations, public health professionals, academics, nongovernmental organizations, etc.).

• Research and pilot responsible drinking initiatives in such markets with appropriate local partners.

• Ensure that examples of successful initiatives are shared through ICAP across the industry for possible application elsewhere.

REFERENCES

Cavanagh, J. & Clairmonte, F. F. (1985). *Alcoholic Beverages: Dimensions of Corporate Power.* New York: St. Martin's Press.

Division of Health Statistics, Thailand Ministry of Public Health. (1992). *Annual Summary of Morbidity and Mortality Data from Health Care Centers, 1990.* Bangkok: Ministry of Public Health.

Fisher, J. C. (1993). *Advertising, Alcohol Consumption, and Abuse: A Worldwide Survey.* Westport, CT: Greenwood.

Flemming, D. (1998). The world's top spirits brands: A look at the challenges ahead. *Impact International, 13,* 1–20.

Heath, D. B. (1995). An anthropological view of alcohol and culture in international perspective. In D. B. Heath (Ed.), *International Handbook on Alcohol and Culture* (328–347). Westport, CT: Greenwood.

Kolk, T. (1992). *Analysis and Calculation of the So-Called Dark Figures.* Stockholm: Swedish Brewers Association.

Manor, J. (1993). *Power, Poverty and Poison: Disaster and Response in an Indian City.* New Delhi: Sage Publications.

Pittman, D. J. (1996). *The effects of alcohol beverage advertising practices and messages on alcohol consumption and alcohol problems: A review of the research since the landmark 1976 Congressional Hearings.* International Council on Alcohol and Addictions (ICAA) Conference, Amsterdam.

Swaddiwudhipong, W. (1994). Epidemiologic characteristics of drivers, vehicles, pedestrians, and road environments involved in road traffic injuries in rural Thailand. *Southeast Asian Journal of Tropical Medicine and Public Health, 25,* 37–44.

Task Force on Drug and Alcohol Abuse. (1995). Government of Seychelles (unpublished report).

Chapter 14

Afterword

Marcus Grant

Some consider the scholarly exchange of views on substance abuse and addictions well served. With almost fifty journals and a steady stream of academic publications, there seems to be ample opportunity for new data, diverse opinion, and fresh approaches to a perennial problem. There is, however, one major flaw in this picture. Seldom—very seldom—do these journals and weighty tomes find space to report on drug and alcohol problems in the developing world. When they do, the contributions are most frequently by respected scientists from the industrialized north who have generously turned their attention to the plight of their less fortunate neighbors and who insist on using the same analytic lens for reading vastly different conditions.

Therefore, I have welcomed the opportunity to work on this volume. It aims to provide an up-to-date account from local experts on drinking patterns, alcohol problems, and current responses in the developing world. There is an array of country and regional reports which covers much of the non-industrialized world. In keeping with the status of beverage alcohol as a legal product in virtually every country, we have chosen to characterize the geographical coverage of this book as "emerging markets," since it is clear that drinking patterns (and therefore probably problems and responses) are changing quite rapidly around the world as part of a general globalization of human behavior. In an effort to address the implications of this trend, the book concludes with chapters which consider the future from a variety of perspectives, including that of the industry which produces beverage alcohol.

Even during the decade I spent at the World Health Organization's headquarters in Geneva, where I was responsible for global activities on the prevention of substance abuse, I rarely had the good fortune of being able to focus exclu-

sively on alcohol and alcohol policies in the developing world. There were—and
still are, no doubt—political pressures which subtly influenced the science of
intergovernmental organizations. In a sense, this is the book which I would have
liked to have issued as a WHO report. It is intended to contrast with other publications which address alcohol problems in the developing world from particular
ideological perspectives.

As I worked with the chapter authors who have contributed to this book,
I came to have the greatest respect for their integrity, commitment, and schol-
arship, as well as their intense concern about the social and health burden of
alcohol abuse. Not only does the book address the all-important questions of
drinking patterns, alcohol-related problems, and current responses in the countries of the developing world, but all the country and regional chapters have been
written by scientists who live and work in those parts of the world. The book
has an authenticity and connectedness with the real world which should make it
the envy of many more conventional publications that attempt to address global
alcohol problems.

Beyond the richness of the individual chapters and the impressive array of
information gathered together between these covers, there are important common
themes. Some of these are quite obvious—for example, that drinking patterns
vary enormously around the world and therefore require a variety of responses.
Others are more controversial—for example, that the beverage alcohol industry
has a legitimate role to play in helping prevent or alleviate problems rather than
just being blamed for having caused them. But these are the themes the book
deals with as a whole and I will not comment upon them here.

What I want to focus on is another persistent theme—the inadequacy of
data. In Chapter 11, Dwight Heath explores this issue from a technical point of
view and makes some suggestions for how it might be improved. My concern
is a broader one: without sound data, it is difficult to negotiate sound policy.
Without sound data, there may be a tendency to rely upon policy approaches
which have been formulated in the industrialized north, which have an indifferent
record of success of and which are certainly far removed from the real needs of
other countries.

Despite the richness of this book, there is a complaint made by every single author of a country or regional chapter. The complaint is that both the
quality and the quantity of the available data are inadequate. As editor of the
book and as somebody who has worked in the substance abuse program of an
inter-governmental agency which gives priority to the health problems of the developing world, I can only echo and amplify this complaint. Around the world,
many people—perhaps most adults—drink beverage alcohol. Most of them do
so responsibly and without negative consequences, but some of them experience
health and social problems associated with their drinking. Unfortunately, unless
these people happen to live in North America, Western Europe, or Australia, we
know very little about their experience, positive or negative.

As an attempt to redress that unacceptable imbalance, this book is at least an honest first step. Indeed, as I worked on it, I got the sense of a new way of looking at drinking patterns and alcohol problems. There seemed to be a groundswell of scientific energy that acknowledged all the excellent research traditions of the past, but wanted to find a quite distinct approach to alcohol research that better fits the real needs and priorities of the developing world. What emerges is an impatience with the weary preoccupation with per capita consumption figures that often obscure more than they reveal. In place of that preoccupation is an eagerness to be able to describe much more comprehensively *how* people drink, not just how much they drink.

A patterns approach to alcohol epidemiology is already gaining ground among scientists from research centers in the industrialized north, but it is still being applied rather unevenly. I sense that the chapter authors in this book want to go beyond what their northern colleagues are willing to accept. They position drinking as an integral expression and manifestation of culture, rather than as a separate phenomenon best described in terms of the quantity and frequency of ethanol ingestion. To understand drinking patterns, these authors are saying, you must understand the culture that has shaped these patterns. Although the data are not always available, that understanding remains a vivid objective for those who want to distinguish between appropriate and inappropriate drinking behavior. In this book, we may be witnessing the first steps toward an approach to describing drinking patterns and alcohol problems that is actually relevant to three quarters of the world's population.

I am particularly pleased to have been able to include a chapter that gives us the industry's own view on what they can and should be doing. Although I suspect that many readers will think it does not go far enough, it is unquestionably a move in the right direction. Here is an industry prepared to make some genuine and specific proposals for what they are actually prepared to do as responsible corporate citizens. It is up to the international community now to see if these sorts of industry proposals make sense, and to engage them in further cooperative efforts in helping to minimize the global burden of alcohol problems.

If we are to create a world environment in which all can work together more productively toward a reduction in alcohol problems, then we certainly need to know more about the nature and extent of current problems and about their relationship to non-problematic, benign drinking patterns. What is needed now is a mechanism for the continuing exchange of experience between the scientists and scholars of the developing world. It is my hope that the publication of this book will stimulate efforts to establish such a mechanism for communication. Until it exists, they cannot be heard. And if they are not heard, there will be no progress.

Index